40 DAYS IN...

40 Days In...

KENNETH
STUCZYNSKI

APG

As I have many times picked up a book and felt connected with a writer, I write this in the hopes that, many years from now perhaps, someone will read my words and appreciate my efforts, however flawed, and find them useful and worthy of their attention. Therefore, I dedicate this book to future historians, researchers, students, and anyone else who seeks knowledge of life as it was experienced in my own time.

First Printing, 2025

AMORPHOUS PUBLISHING GUILD
Buffalo, New York, USA

www. Amorphous.Press

CONTENTS

PRELUDE

Please indulge me with a somewhat biased preamble. This book is primarily a reference for any serious follower of events or students of the past, no matter what their political inclination. But here I must add my own "document" of sorts to prove one man's context of what seems to be the origins of what followed after a four-years intermission.

After all, a story never starts with the person telling it. It has a history, as each circumstance arises out of the last. Roots of where we are stretch way back in different directions, but in my view, the Second Trump Presidency first came together in 2020, at the end of his first term. It was over those months that a framework was laid out to handle, and to some extent prevent, a loss of the election. While election challenges and investigations took place, plans were made and those in various government posts were swapped with Trump loyalists, including the military. Millions were too busy drinking the QAnon kool-aid to look the other direction and connect the dots in any concerning way.

Others lost their minds ("Trump Derangement Syndrome"?) when he was first elected. But then I've seen people take on a panic in previous elections and it all seemed crying wolf to me. By 2020, I had many apologies to make for accusing friends and acquaintances for overreacting. I was busy with other things, very apolitical things, and so I didn't feel the weight until it was running full steam ahead.

Below is something I wrote months after the pattern of autocracy became visible on my radar. Rhetoric no longer seemed to lack the impact of sticks and stones. As in 2015, hate crime statistics soared with the scapegoat *de jour*, at that time being mostly Muslims. In this case Hispanics, due to immigration, and Chinese, due to what the

President (and followers, including people I know) called the "China Virus". And by the end of Summer, QAnon had crept into the mainstream, and the Liberal half of America was to be purged by the coming "Storm", heralded in by a "strong leader" and savior, Trump. Though he knew little about QAnon, he played the role as he had historically been useful to, or at least tolerant of, extremists of various colors.

What we witnessed was a confluence of White Supremacy, Christian Nationalism, and ideology so far Right that there are only words that sound insulting or alarmist to describe it. This was before the GOP became what it now is, since having shut out reasonable Conservatives, or rather anyone not in the ex-President's favor, as RINOs. Even if the reader rejects this view, I here speak for myself and say I should have pulled the fire alarm when I had the chance,

Pulling the Fire Alarm in America

{Article published on blog "ConsiderReconsider.Com", 10 August 2020}

I have studied the psychosocial phenomenon of brainwashing for many years, and it is a blood cousin to something I also research and write about — ideological fanaticism. It took a while to see the pattern before me in our own nation, but now that I do, it's terrifying. The tip-off was the mechanisms for maintaining control spelled out in top-level rhetoric reflected onto widespread public sentiment. Let me explain.

Indoctrination is something we all are subjected to in various ways. We pick up opinions and beliefs, and we may feel strongly about them. That's actually not harmful and often a virtue. The danger comes from when these beliefs become intolerant absolutes and we wage war on challenges to those beliefs.

The way to seal someone's mind and keep them stuck in their narrative is to create mistrust above all else. Not just mistrust of family and friends, but mistrust of education, experts, news, and any and all opposing views. The only trusted source or sources, no matter how incredible, are those that reinforce already embedded beliefs.

To bar the door to freedom further, this is coupled with a belief the rest of the world (country?) outside your view is actively oppressing your beliefs, your rights, and are just plain out to get you. There are always people pushing and pulling these things in a free society, but they become amplified in one direction beyond reason. The typical fanatic diet is constant exposure to anecdotal incidents that reinforce our beliefs. This diet plays out as one of the flaws of human nature — superimposing intentions and agendas onto large, amorphous groups of people. Armies of straw men and scapegoats are easy to fear and valiant to oppose.

If you can instill this fear well enough and direct it outward, you get the Charles Manson murders. Do it on a large enough scale, and you see publicly-supported mass incarceration, violent ideological purges, and even genocide.

People have mistaken such crimes and atrocities as acts of hate. But hate is only the adrenaline, not the engine driving them. The real motivation is fear, making a person's or people's conscience feel blameless, as it's the other person or people who are an existential threat. It's as if those committing these acts have no choice. And the ends always seem to justify the means, especially if the perpetrators are the victors and write the history textbooks for the generations after them.

Let me bring this point home: Ethnic and social and political prejudices didn't cause and allow the Holocaust. That was all just kindling. The sparks and then fire was fear — fear of losing national identity, fear of conspiracies to influence and overthrow the government from within, fear of anarchy, fear of moral perversion, fear of our children being subjected to a way of life we don't approve. And at some point, it feels justified to the bone in thought and heart to take or support actions that otherwise would be unimaginably heinous.

People susceptible to cults or radical conspiracies aren't different from everyday people. The citizens of 1930s Germany weren't some other species of a lower moral or intellectual breed. We assume insanity in cult followers; we ridicule conspiracists (even the reasonable ones); we think Hitler wasn't human and everyone else was just following orders because they had to. And we do this to dissociate ourselves from such people — to allay our fears we might become or do the same things ourselves. And once we can insist it isn't possible, it becomes possible.

But it's problematic and messy. When you see this happening, how do you pull the fire alarm without looking like you're doing the same thing, playing into an opposing, equally invalid fear? It can become a game of he-said-she-said. We already live in a false egalitarianism of opinions because of the Internet, where everyone's view is equally acceptable simply because we share the same access to information and audience. Worst of all, the common man's seeming inability to discern or critically think makes pulling the fire alarm too early a risk of starting the fire itself.

It's also hard to call out the man behind the curtain. Love of their beliefs — often confused as "love of country" or "love" of their God (via dogmatic proxies) — prevents them from turning around to see who is holding the flashlight and making the shadows they are being told to arm themselves against. If we are afraid enough, we are grateful rather than hateful of those who, if we look closely, have agendas of power and control everyone but us is willing to see. After all, they are our protectors, and it would break our hearts to recognize them as the abuser. And we don't want to risk losing a rose-colored promised land on the other side of an ideological battleground.

We've covered the weapon, the opportunity, and the motive to capture minds and hearts, but of what use? Once confronted, can we have that "Aha!" moment and snap out of it? Or will embarrassment of being duped make us double down on a lost bet, digging our heels in further, as is human nature? It is hard enough to "deprogram" people in a cult, or de-radicalize fanatics.

Faith in education, experts, the press, even free speech and assembly, have been increasingly eroded over recent years. Today, mistrust is the coin of the realm, bought and sold in daily, 280-character increments. These barriers to allowing minds to change and eyes to open have been built like a concrete wall on the borders of our very souls, separating us even from our own families. How do we get through to voting and fear-prepping citizens before sentiments and Facebook rants manifest as a historic tragedy?

I wish I knew. But I do know the right answer to this question may make or break our nation right here, right now.

INTRODUCTION

This book was born from the need to give witness to a historical time as it unfolds before us. One may never know what textbooks will say in twenty or a hundred years, or what facts and words are preserved and what will be lost, censored, or buried in a mountain of pulp and algorithms.

Every generation has one or more moments in which they believe they are living in pivotal times. And maybe they are. But I would argue that the sweeping changes in governance and policy we are seeing RIGHT NOW, at the beginning of the term of the 47th President of the United States, may be more important than most. There are so many possibilities what the future may hold, and depending on one's beliefs, we are bracing for either a "Golden Age of America" or a dystopian regime to be resisted. It is not inconceivable that there may be civil unrest or even open war at some point. But we can all agree that what is happening in these first several weeks of a new administration is setting the stage.

As for the title of this book, "40 Days In..." does not strictly bookend these events and texts (the 20th of January to the 1st of March). A few were precursors to other content within that time, and a few followed very shortly thereafter and concluded or continued things already covered. In Hebrew connotation, '40 days' simply means a good while -- not a particularity long time but certainly not overnight, although it may feel the history in this book happened that suddenly.

Will we look back and say there were no signs of what was to come? Will we be pleasantly surprised or live to regret our choices? The question we may have -- and our children certainly will -- is what really was happening in government, media, and society in this slice of American history. What can we rely on as fact versus propaganda? Most concerning of all, is history being rewritten in real time, right before our eyes?

This book will not answer that question for the reader. But it does provide a showcase of documents, speeches, letters, headlines, and interviews that provide context that cannot be ignored no matter what interpretations and conclusions the reader may choose. At the very least, regardless of your ideological inclinations, I hope you find this a useful reference for those things that are meaningful to you.

I cannot say there will be no bias. I have even included a few of my own editorials here, and commentary borrowed from my research in writing "Some White Guy's Book" in 2020. But much effort was given -- as much as could be expected in the three weeks I compiled all this -- to focus on one purpose. That purpose is to provide important primary source materials with as little editing as possible and in their full textual form. Some of the information may be incorrect. Some of it is downright lies, but truthful in that such lies were documented as having been told.

It may seem that some topics were underrepresented or even omitted. Economics have always been hard to untangle given disparate views on even basic premises, though the negative effect of tariffs seems to be a majority opinion. Then there are more technical concepts, talked about more by Wall Street than Main Street, such as the 'Mar-a-Lago Accord', an agenda to restructure the international financial system in America's favor by weakening the US Dollar to boost export competitiveness. The abortion issue is raging, but the Supreme Court had recently thrown the power to regulate it back to the states. Cuts to Social Security, Medicaid, and other such programs are a Congressional budget issue, though presidential promises seem to differ greatly not just from the proposed budget but Elon Musk calling Social Security a Ponzi scheme. These are all important issues of the time, but here I choose to focus on what hits the headlines the most. I have omitted many details that did not pass a fact-check. And I tend to give greater consideration to those media outlets high and middle on "Media Bias Curve" charts. My goal is for those in the future to go back in time and see what we see, not merely what I see.

Due to time constraints, there are no detailed citations as to where each document or transcript was found. Anyone is welcome to dig and fact check such things, and I welcome corrective criticism if discrepancies are discovered.

Back to my own bias, I consider what is happening now as rhyming with events from 2020. It seemed like every day something (or many things) happened, something was said, or something was done to bring us closer to a breakdown in society. Perhaps my readers sensed this in "Some White Guy's Book", the bulk of which I finished writing around election time of that year. Many of the issues I discussed there are playing out here, and it naturally colors the way I present context to current events.

And, as I suspect with many an author, I write this to exercise my demons. In this case, I am giving these extraordinary events attention without either burying them in frustration or letting it spill into every conversation with my wife and friends. I can go to sleep knowing I did something, even if just memorializing details that may otherwise be denied or twisted into doublespeak down the road.

But this doesn't mean my concerns for our country and the world will end with the publishing of this book. I may write further on these subjects. But no matter what side of history I'm on, I rest assured that although TEXTBOOKS may be written by the victor, REAL history is often written by the outlier who dares to wield a pen in spite of the public opinion of their time. I so dare, and challenge you to read and, if inclined, to do the same.

K. Stucynski
1 March 2025

| 1 |

Inauguration

Inauguration took place at noon of 20 January 2025. A proclamation order was made by Trump before inauguration, "Flying The Flag of The United States at Full-Staff On Inauguration Day". This superseded it being at half-mast for 30 days after the Death of President Jimmy Carter, and broke with tradition of past inaugurations in which this was also the case.

The ceremony and speeches were held indoors, citing the weather, which was similar in temperature to Obama's inauguration, held outdoors. Critics claimed it was to save the embarrassment of lacking a large crowd size, given that the White House had falsely claimed (as an "alternate fact") that his first inauguration had a larger crowd than Obama. Notable is that there was a significant crowd outside, both in support and in protest of his inauguration.

The Address

Thank you. Thank you very much, everybody. Wow. Thank you very, very much.

Vice President Vance, Speaker Johnson, Senator Thune, Chief Justice Roberts, justices of the Supreme Court of the United States, President Clinton, President Bush, President Obama, President Biden, Vice President Harris, and my fellow citizens, the golden age of America begins right now.

From this day forward, our country will flourish and be respected again all over the world. We will be the envy of every nation, and we will not allow ourselves to be taken advantage of any longer. During every single day of the Trump administration, I will, very simply, put America first.

Our sovereignty will be reclaimed. Our safety will be restored. The scales of justice will be rebalanced. The vicious, violent, and unfair weaponization of the Justice Department and our government will end.

And our top priority will be to create a nation that is proud, prosperous, and free.

America will soon be greater, stronger, and far more exceptional than ever before.

I return to the presidency confident and optimistic that we are at the start of a thrilling new era of national success. A tide of change is sweeping the country, sunlight is pouring over the entire world, and America has the chance to seize this opportunity like never before.

But first, we must be honest about the challenges we face. While they are plentiful, they will be annihilated by this great momentum that the world is now witnessing in the United States of America.

As we gather today, our government confronts a crisis of trust. For many years, a radical and corrupt establishment has extracted power and wealth from our citizens while the pillars of our society lay broken and seemingly in complete disrepair.

We now have a government that cannot manage even a simple crisis at home while, at the same time, stumbling into a continuing catalogue of catastrophic events abroad.

It fails to protect our magnificent, law-abiding American citizens but provides sanctuary and protection for dangerous criminals, many from prisons and mental institutions, that have illegally entered our country from all over the world.

We have a government that has given unlimited funding to the defense of foreign borders but refuses to defend American borders or, more importantly, its own people.

Our country can no longer deliver basic services in times of emergency, as recently shown by the wonderful people of North Carolina – who have been treated so badly –and other states who are still suffering from a hurricane that took place many months ago or, more recently, Los Angeles, where we are watching fires still tragically burn from weeks ago without even a token of defense. They're raging through the houses and communities, even affecting some of the wealthiest and most powerful individuals in our country — some of whom are sitting here right now. They don't have a home any longer. That's interesting. But we can't let this happen. Everyone is unable to do anything about it. That's going to change.

We have a public health system that does not deliver in times of disaster, yet more money is spent on it than any country anywhere in the world.

And we have an education system that teaches our children to be ashamed of themselves — in many cases, to hate our country despite the love that we try so desperately to provide to them. All of this will change starting today, and it will change very quickly.

My recent election is a mandate to completely and totally reverse a horrible betrayal and all of these many betrayals that have taken place and to give the people back their faith, their wealth, their democracy, and, indeed, their freedom. From this moment on, America's decline is over.

Our liberties and our nation's glorious destiny will no longer be denied. And we will immediately restore the integrity, competency, and loyalty of America's government.

Over the past eight years, I have been tested and challenged more than any president in our 250-year history, and I've learned a lot along the way.

The journey to reclaim our republic has not been an easy one — that, I can tell you. Those who wish to stop our cause have tried to take my freedom and, indeed, to take my life.

Just a few months ago, in a beautiful Pennsylvania field, an assassin's bullet ripped through my ear. But I felt then and believe even more so now that my life was saved for a reason. I was saved by God to make America great again.

Thank you. Thank you.

Thank you very much.

That is why each day under our administration of American patriots, we will be working to meet every crisis with dignity and power and strength. We will move with purpose and speed to bring back hope, prosperity, safety, and peace for citizens of every race, religion, color, and creed.

For American citizens, January 20th, 2025, is Liberation Day. It is my hope that our recent presidential election will be remembered as the greatest and most consequential election in the history of our country.

As our victory showed, the entire nation is rapidly unifying behind our agenda with dramatic increases in support from virtually every element of our society: young and old, men and women, African Americans, Hispanic Americans, Asian Americans, urban, suburban, rural. And very importantly, we had a powerful win in all seven swing states ... and the popular vote, we won by millions of people.

To the Black and Hispanic communities, I want to thank you for the tremendous outpouring of love and trust that you have shown me with your vote. We set records, and I will not forget it. I've heard your voices in the campaign, and I look forward to working with you in the years to come.

Today is Martin Luther King Day. And his honor — this will be a great honor. But in his honor, we will strive together to make his dream a reality. We will make his dream come true.

Thank you. Thank you. Thank you.

National unity is now returning to America, and confidence and pride is soaring like never before. In everything we do, my administration will be inspired by a strong pursuit of excellence and unrelenting success. We will not forget our country, we will not forget our Constitution, and we will not forget our God. Can't do that.

Today, I will sign a series of historic executive orders. With these actions, we will begin the complete restoration of America and the revolution of common sense. It's all about common sense.

First, I will declare a national emergency at our southern border.

All illegal entry will immediately be halted, and we will begin the process of returning millions and millions of criminal aliens back to the places from which they came. We will reinstate my Remain in Mexico policy.

I will end the practice of catch and release.

And I will send troops to the southern border to repel the disastrous invasion of our country.

Under the orders I sign today, we will also be designating the cartels as foreign terrorist organizations.

And by invoking the Alien Enemies Act of 1798, I will direct our government to use the full and immense power of federal and state law enforcement to eliminate the presence of all foreign gangs and criminal networks bringing devastating crime to U.S. soil, including our cities and inner cities.

As commander in chief, I have no higher responsibility than to defend our country from threats and invasions, and that is exactly what I am going to do. We will do it at a level that nobody has ever seen before.

Next, I will direct all members of my cabinet to marshal the vast powers at their disposal to defeat what was record inflation and rapidly bring down costs and prices.

The inflation crisis was caused by massive overspending and escalating energy prices, and that is why today I will also declare a national energy emergency. We will drill, baby, drill.

America will be a manufacturing nation once again, and we have something that no other manufacturing nation will ever have — the largest amount of oil and gas of any country on earth — and we are going to use it. We'll use it.

We will bring prices down, fill our strategic reserves up again right to the top, and export American energy all over the world.

We will be a rich nation again, and it is that liquid gold under our feet that will help to do it.

With my actions today, we will end the Green New Deal, and we will revoke the electric vehicle mandate, saving our auto industry and keeping my sacred pledge to our great American autoworkers.

In other words, you'll be able to buy the car of your choice.

We will build automobiles in America again at a rate that nobody could have dreampt possible just a few years ago. And thank you to the autoworkers of our nation for your inspiring vote of confidence. We did tremendously with their vote.

I will immediately begin the overhaul of our trade system to protect American workers and families. Instead of taxing our citizens to enrich other countries, we will tariff and tax foreign countries to enrich our citizens.

For this purpose, we are establishing the External Revenue Service to collect all tariffs, duties, and revenues. It will be massive amounts of money pouring into our Treasury, coming from foreign sources.

The American dream will soon be back and thriving like never before.

To restore competence and effectiveness to our federal government, my administration will establish the brand-new Department of Government Efficiency.

After years and years of illegal and unconstitutional federal efforts to restrict free expression, I also will sign an executive order to immediately stop all government censorship and bring back free speech to America.

Never again will the immense power of the state be weaponized to persecute political opponents — something I know something about. [Laughter.] We will not allow that to happen. It will not happen again.

Under my leadership, we will restore fair, equal, and impartial justice under the constitutional rule of law.

And we are going to bring law and order back to our cities.

This week, I will also end the government policy of trying to socially engineer race and gender into every aspect of public and private life. [Applause.] We will forge a society that is colorblind and merit-based.

As of today, it will henceforth be the official policy of the United States government that there are only two genders: male and female.

This week, I will reinstate any service members who were unjustly expelled from our military for objecting to the COVID vaccine mandate with full back pay.

And I will sign an order to stop our warriors from being subjected to radical political theories and social experiments while on duty. It's going to end immediately. Our armed forces will be freed to focus on their sole mission: defeating America's enemies.

Like in 2017, we will again build the strongest military the world has ever seen. We will measure our success not only by the battles we win but also by the wars that we end — and perhaps most importantly, the wars we never get into.

My proudest legacy will be that of a peacemaker and unifier. That's what I want to be: a peacemaker and a unifier.

I'm pleased to say that as of yesterday, one day before I assumed office, the hostages in the Middle East are coming back home to their families.

Thank you.

America will reclaim its rightful place as the greatest, most powerful, most respected nation on earth, inspiring the awe and admiration of the entire world.

A short time from now, we are going to be changing the name of the Gulf of Mexico to the Gulf of America and we will restore the name of a great president, William McKinley, to Mount McKinley, where it should be and where it belongs.

President McKinley made our country very rich through tariffs and through talent -- he was a natural businessman -- and gave Teddy Roosevelt the money for many of the great things he did, including the Panama Canal, which has foolishly been given to the country of

Panama after the United Spates -- the United States -- I mean, think of this -- spent more money than ever spent on a project before and lost 38,000 lives in the building of the Panama Canal.

We have been treated very badly from this foolish gift that should have never been made, and Panama's promise to us has been broken.

The purpose of our deal and the spirit of our treaty has been totally violated. American ships are being severely overcharged and not treated fairly in any way, shape, or form. And that includes the United States Navy.

And above all, China is operating the Panama Canal. And we didn't give it to China. We gave it to Panama, and we're taking it back.

Above all, my message to Americans today is that it is time for us to once again act with courage, vigor, and the vitality of history's greatest civilization.

So, as we liberate our nation, we will lead it to new heights of victory and success. We will not be deterred. Together, we will end the chronic disease epidemic and keep our children safe, healthy, and disease-free.

The United States will once again consider itself a growing nation — one that increases our wealth, expands our territory, builds our cities, raises our expectations, and carries our flag into new and beautiful horizons.

And we will pursue our manifest destiny into the stars, launching American astronauts to plant the Stars and Stripes on the planet Mars.

Ambition is the lifeblood of a great nation, and, right now, our nation is more ambitious than any other. There's no nation like our nation.

Americans are explorers, builders, innovators, entrepreneurs, and pioneers. The spirit of the frontier is written into our hearts. The call of the next great adventure resounds from within our souls.

Our American ancestors turned a small group of colonies on the edge of a vast continent into a mighty republic of the most extraordinary citizens on Earth. No one comes close.

Americans pushed thousands of miles through a rugged land of untamed wilderness. They crossed deserts, scaled mountains, braved untold dangers, won the Wild West, ended slavery, rescued millions from tyranny, lifted billions from poverty, harnessed electricity, split the atom, launched mankind into the heavens, and put the universe of human knowledge into the palm of the human hand. If we work together, there is nothing we cannot do and no dream we cannot achieve.

Many people thought it was impossible for me to stage such a historic political comeback. But as you see today, here I am. The American people have spoken.

I stand before you now as proof that you should never believe that something is impossible to do. In America, the impossible is what we do best.

From New York to Los Angeles, from Philadelphia to Phoenix, from Chicago to Miami, from Houston to right here in Washington, D.C., our country was forged and built by the generations of patriots who gave everything they had for our rights and for our freedom.

They were farmers and soldiers, cowboys and factory workers, steelworkers and coal miners, police officers and pioneers who pushed onward, marched forward, and let no obstacle defeat their spirit or their pride.

Together, they laid down the railroads, raised up the skyscrapers, built great highways, won two world wars, defeated fascism and communism, and triumphed over every single challenge that they faced.

After all we have been through together, we stand on the verge of the four greatest years in American history. With your help, we will restore America promise and we will rebuild the nation that we love — and we love it so much.

We are one people, one family, and one glorious nation under God. So, to every parent who dreams for their child and every child who dreams for their future, I am with you, I will fight for you, and I will win for you. We're going to win like never before.

Thank you. Thank you.

Thank you. Thank you.

In recent years, our nation has suffered greatly. But we are going to bring it back and make it great again, greater than ever before.

We will be a nation like no other, full of compassion, courage, and exceptionalism. Our power will stop all wars and bring a new spirit of unity to a world that has been angry, violent, and totally unpredictable.

America will be respected again and admired again, including by people of religion, faith, and goodwill. We will be prosperous, we will be proud, we will be strong, and we will win like never before.

We will not be conquered, we will not be intimidated, we will not be broken, and we will not fail. From this day on, the United States of America will be a free, sovereign, and independent nation.

We will stand bravely, we will live proudly, we will dream boldly, and nothing will stand in our way because we are Americans. The future is ours, and our golden age has just begun.

Thank you. God bless America. Thank you all. Thank you. Thank you very much. Thank you very much. Thank you. Thank you.

Post-Inauguration Celebration

{Speech from Elon Musk at the Capital One Arena}

Yes. This is what victory feels like. Yeah. This was no ordinary victory. This was a fork in the road of human civilization. Okay? There are elections that come and go. Some elections are important, some are not. But this one really mattered. I just want to say thank you for making it happen. Thank you.

["Roman" salute to crowd in front and then behind him]

My heart goes out to you. It is thanks to you that the future of civilization is assured. Thanks to you. We're going to have safe cities, finally. Safe cities, secure borders, sensible spending, basic stuff. We're going to take Doge to Mars. Can you imagine how awesome it will be to have American astronauts plant the flag on another planet for the first time? Bam. Bam. Yeah. How inspiring would that be?

There's always problems in life. There's this problem, solve that problem, solve that problem. But there need to be things that inspire you. There need to be things that make you glad to wake up in the morning and say, I'm looking forward to the future. I love you guys. Let me tell you, I'm going to work my ass off for you guys. I really will. I really will. Yeah. But I'm super fired up for the future. It's going to be very exciting. As the president said, we're going to have a golden age. It's going to be fantastic. One of the fundamental things, one of the most American values that I love is optimism. This feeling like we're going to make the future good. We're going to make it good. So, man, I can't wait. This is going to be fantastic. So thank you. Thank you again. Yeah, I'm just so excited about the future. Thank you guys. Thank you.

The Salute

The gesture of a "Roman salute" was never used historically by the Romans, but by fascists in Italy, which was later adopted by the Nazis. Musk denied his salute was intended as such, and was a spontaneous gesture of his heart going out to others. Most Jews and Jewish groups that weighed in (exceptions being the Anti-Defamation league and Israeli President Benjamin Netanyahu) condemned his act and various European political parties demanded that he be banned from visiting their countries, while White Supremacists and Neo-Nazi groups applauded the gesture. The Lemkin Institute for Genocide Prevention responded by issuing a "red flag alert" for genocide in the United States.

A series of apparent copycat gestures occurred, resulting in resignations, firings, and even the defrocking of an Anglican priest. In February, Steve Bannon gave a blatant "Roman" salute at CPAC, which was met by applause. He claimed it was just "a wave to the crowd". (See chapter on CPAC later in book)

| 2 |

The National Cathedral

The National Cathedral in Washington, D.C. is a national shrine under the auspices of the Episcopal Church. A number of funerals and memorial services for American presidents have been held there, the first being in 1913. Presidential prayer services have been held the day after every presidential inauguration since 2001. Although used for events related to public figures over the years, it is independent of any government body or program.

The Homily

{Given by The Rt. Rev. Mariann Edgar Budde, Bishop of Washington, delivered 21 January 2025}

O God, you made us in your own image and redeemed us through Jesus your Son: Look with compassion on the whole human family; take away the arrogance and hatred which infect our hearts; break down the walls that separate us; unite us in bonds of love; and work through our struggle and confusion to accomplish your purposes on earth; that, in your good time, all nations and races may serve you in harmony around your heavenly throne; through Jesus Christ our Lord. Amen.

Jesus said, "Everyone then who hears these words of mine and acts on them will be like a wise man who built his house on rock. The rain fell, the floods came, and the winds blew and beat on that house, but it did not fall, because it had been founded on rock. And everyone who hears these words of mine and does not act on them will be like a foolish man who built his house on sand. The rain fell, and the floods came, and the winds blew and beat against that house, and it fell—and great was its fall!" Now when Jesus had finished saying these things, the crowds were astounded at his teaching, for he taught them as one having authority, and not as their scribes. — Matthew 7:24-29

Joined by many across the country, we have gathered this morning to pray for unity as a nation — not for agreement, political or otherwise, but for the kind of unity that fosters community across diversity and division, a unity that serves the common good.

Unity, in this sense, is the threshold requirement for people to live together in a free society, it is the solid rock, as Jesus said, in this case upon which to build a nation. It is not conformity. It is not a victory of one over another. It is not weary politeness nor passivity born of exhaustion. Unity is not partisan.

Rather, unity is a way of being with one another that encompasses and respects differences, that teaches us to hold multiple perspectives and life experiences as valid and worthy of respect; that enables us, in our communities and in the halls of power, to genuinely care for one another even when we disagree. Those across our country who dedicate their lives, or who volunteer, to help others in times of natural disaster, often at great risk to themselves, never ask those they are helping for whom they voted in the past election or what positions they hold on a particular issue. We are at our best when we follow their example.

Unity at times, is sacrificial, in the way that love is sacrificial, a giving of ourselves for the sake of another. Jesus of Nazareth, in his Sermon on the Mount, exhorts us to love not only our neighbors, but to love our enemies, and to pray for those who persecute us; to be merciful, as our God is merciful, and to forgive others, as God forgives us. Jesus went out of his way to welcome those whom his society deemed as outcasts.

Now I grant you that unity, in this broad, expansive sense, is aspirational, and it's a lot to pray for–a big ask of our God, worthy of the best of who we are and can be. But there isn't much to be gained by our prayers if we act in ways that further deepen and exploit the divisions among us. Our Scriptures are quite clear that God is never impressed with prayers when actions are not informed by them. Nor does God spare us from the consequences of our deeds, which, in the end, matter more than the words we pray.

Those of us gathered here in this Cathedral are not naive about the realities of politics. When power, wealth and competing interests are at stake; when views of what America should be are in conflict; when there are strong opinions across a spectrum of possibilities and starkly different understandings of what the right course of action is, there will be winners and losers when votes are cast or decisions made that set the course of public policy and the prioritization of resources. It goes without saying that in a democracy, not everyone's particular hopes and dreams will be realized in a given legislative session or a presidential term or even a generation. Not everyone's specific prayers -- for those of us who are people of prayer -- will be answered as we would like. But for some, the loss of their hopes and dreams will be far more than political defeat, but instead a loss of equality, dignity, and livelihood.

Given this, is true unity among us even possible? And why should we care about it?

Well, I hope that we care, because the culture of contempt that has become normalized in our country threatens to destroy us. We are all bombarded daily with messages from what sociologists now call "the outrage industrial complex," some of it driven by external forces whose interests are furthered by a polarized America. Contempt fuels our political campaigns and social media, and many profit from it. But it's a dangerous way to lead a country.

I am a person of faith, and with God's help I believe that unity in this country is possible -- not perfectly, for we are imperfect people and an imperfect union -- but sufficient enough to keep us believing in and working to realize the ideals of the United States of America, ideals expressed in the Declaration of Independence, with its assertion of innate human equality and dignity.

And we are right to pray for God's help as we seek unity, for we need God's help, but only if we ourselves are willing to tend to the foundations upon which unity depends. Like Jesus' analogy of building a house of faith on the rock of his teachings, as opposed to building a house on sand, the foundations we need for unity must be sturdy enough to withstand the many storms that threaten it.

What are the foundations of unity? Drawing from our sacred traditions and texts, let me suggest that there are at least three.

The first foundation for unity is honoring the inherent dignity of every human being, which is, as all faiths represented here affirm, the birthright of all people as children of the One God. In public discourse, honoring each other's dignity means refusing to mock, discount, or demonize those with whom we differ, choosing instead to respectfully debate across our differences, and whenever possible, to seek common ground. If common ground is not possible, dignity demands that we remain true to our convictions without contempt for those who hold convictions of their own.

A second foundation for unity is honesty in both private conversation and public discourse. If we aren't willing to be honest, there is no use in praying for unity, because our actions work against the prayers themselves. We might, for a time, experience a false sense of unity among some, but not the sturdier, broader unity that we need to address the challenges we face.

Now to be fair, we don't always know where the truth lies, and there is a lot working against the truth now, staggeringly so. But when we do know what is true, it's incumbent upon us to speak the truth, even when–and especially when–it costs us.

A third foundation for unity is humility, which we all need, because we are all fallible human beings. We make mistakes. We say and do things that we regret. We have our blind spots and biases, and we are perhaps the most dangerous to ourselves and others when we are persuaded, without a doubt, that we are absolutely right and someone else is absolutely wrong. Because then we are just a few steps away from labeling ourselves as the good people, versus the bad people.

The truth is that we are all people, capable of both good and bad. Aleksandr Solzhenitsyn astuely observed that "The line separating good and evil passes not through states, nor between classes, nor between political parties , but right through every human heart and through all human hearts." The more we realize this, the more room we have within ourselves for humility, and openness to one another across our differences, because in fact, we are more like one another than we realize, and we need each other.

Unity is relatively easy to pray for on occasions of solemnity. It's a lot harder to realize when we're dealing with real differences in the public arena. But without unity, we are building our nation's house on sand.

With a commitment to unity that incorporates diversity and transcends disagreement, and the solid foundations of dignity, honesty, and humility that such unity requires, we can do our part, in our time, to help realize the ideals and the dream of America.

Let me make one final plea, Mr. President. Millions have put their trust in you. As you told the nation yesterday, you have felt the providential hand of a loving God. In the name of our God, I ask you to have mercy upon the people in our country who are scared now. There are transgender children in both Republican and Democratic families who fear for their lives.

And the people who pick our crops and clean our office buildings; who labor in our poultry farms and meat-packing plants; who wash the dishes after we eat in restaurants and work the night shift in hospitals — they may not be citizens or have the proper documentation, but the vast majority of immigrants are not criminals. They pay taxes, and are good neighbors. They are faithful members of our churches, mosques and synagogues, gurdwara, and temples.

Have mercy, Mr. President, on those in our communities whose children fear that their parents will be taken away. Help those who are fleeing war zones and persecution in their own lands to find compassion and welcome here. Our God teaches us that we are to be merciful to the stranger, for we were once strangers in this land.

May God grant us all the strength and courage to honor the dignity of every human being, speak the truth in love, and walk humbly with one another and our God, for the good of all the people of this nation and the world.

Social Media Responses

> She brought her church into the World of politics in a very ungracious way She was nasty in tone, and not compelling or smart. She failed to mention the large number of illegal migrants that came into our Country and killed people. Many were deposited from jails and mental institutions. It is a giant crime wave that is taking place in the USA. Apart from her inappropriate statements, the service was a very boring and uninspiring one. She is not very good at her job! She and her church owe the public an apology!
> -- President Donald Trump

As an American leader, but also just as an American citizen, your compassion belongs first to your fellow citizens. It doesn't mean you hate people from outside of your own borders, but there's this old school and I think it's a very Christian concept, by the way, that you love your family and then you love your neighbour and then you love your community and then you love your fellow citizens in your own country, and then after that you can focus and prioritise the rest of the world. A lot of the far left has completely inverted that. They seem to hate the citizens of their own country. Country and care more about people outside their own borders. That is no way to run a society. -- Vice-President J. D. Vance

Do not commit the sin of empathy. This snake is God's enemy and yours too. She hates God and His people. You need to properly hate in response. She is not merely deceived but is a deceiver. Your eye shall not pity. -- Ben Garrett, Church leader in Ogden, Utah

Papal Response

Dear Brothers in the Episcopate,

I am writing today to address a few words to you in these delicate moments that you are living as Pastors of the People of God who walk together in the United States of America.

1. The journey from slavery to freedom that the People of Israel traveled, as narrated in the Book of Exodus,

invites us to look at the reality of our time, so clearly marked by the phenomenon of migration, as a decisive moment in history to reaffirm not only our faith in a God who is always close, incarnate, migrant and refugee, but also the infinite and transcendent dignity of every human person.

2. These words with which I begin are not an artificial construct. Even a cursory examination of the Church's social doctrine emphatically shows that Jesus Christ is the true Emmanuel (cf.Mt1:23); he did not live apart from the difficult experience of being expelled from his own land because of an imminent risk to his life, and from the experience of having to take refuge in a society and a culture foreign to his own. The Son of God, in becoming man, also chose to live the drama of immigration. I like to recall, among other things, the words with which Pope Pius XII began his Apostolic Constitution on the Care of Migrants, which is considered the "Magna Carta" of the Church's thinking on migration:

"The family of Nazareth in exile, Jesus, Mary and Joseph, emigrants in Egypt and refugees there to escape the wrath of an ungodly king, are the model, the example and the consolation of emigrants and pilgrims of every age and country, of all refugees of every condition who, beset by persecution or necessity, are forced to leave their homeland, beloved family and dear friends for foreign lands."

3. Likewise, Jesus Christ, loving everyone with a universal love, educates us in the permanent recognition of the dignity of every human being, without exception. In fact, when we speak of "infinite and transcendent dignity", we wish to emphasize that the most decisive value possessed by the human person surpasses and sustains every other juridical consideration that can be made to regulate life in society. Thus, all the Christian faithful and people of good will are called upon to consider the legitimacy of norms and public policies in the light of the dignity of the person and his or her fundamental rights, not vice versa.

4. I have followed closely the major crisis that is taking place in the United States with the initiation of a program of mass deportations. The rightly formed conscience cannot fail to make a critical judgment and express its disagreement with any measure that tacitly or explicitly identifies the illegal status of some migrants with crimi-

nality. At the same time, one must recognize the right of a nation to defend itself and keep communities safe from those who have committed violent or serious crimes while in the country or prior to arrival. That said, the act of deporting people who in many cases have left their own land for reasons of extreme poverty, insecurity, exploitation, persecution or serious deterioration of the environment, damages the dignity of many men and women, and of entire families, and places them in a state of particular vulnerability and defenselessness.

5. This is not a minor issue: an authentic rule of law is verified precisely in the dignified treatment that all people deserve, especially the poorest and most marginalized. The true common good is promoted when society and government, with creativity and strict respect for the rights of all -- as I have affirmed on numerous occasions -- welcomes, protects, promotes and integrates the most fragile, unprotected and vulnerable. This does not impede the development of a policy that regulates orderly and legal migration. However, this development cannot come about through the privilege of some and the sacrifice of others. What is built on the basis of force, and not on the truth about the equal dignity of every human being, begins badly and will end badly.

6. Christians know very well that it is only by affirming the infinite dignity of all that our own identity as persons and as communities reaches its maturity. Christian love is not a concentric expansion of interests that little by little extend to other persons and groups. In other words: the human person is not a mere individual, relatively expansive, with some philanthropic feelings! The human person is a subject with dignity who, through the constitutive relationship with all, especially with the poorest, can gradually mature in his identity and vocation. The true ordo amoris that must be promoted is that which we discover by meditating constantly on the parable of the "Good Samaritan" (cf.Lk10:25-37), that is, by meditating on the love that builds a fraternity open to all, without exception.

7. But worrying about personal, community or national identity, apart from these considerations, easily
introduces an ideological criterion that distorts social life and imposes the will of the strongest as the criterion of truth.

8. I recognize your valuable efforts, dear brother bishops of the United States, as you work closely with migrants and refugees, proclaiming Jesus Christ and promoting fundamental human rights. God will richly reward all that you do for the protection and defense of those who are considered less valuable, less important or less human!

9. I exhort all the faithful of the Catholic Church, and all men and women of good will, not to give in to narratives that discriminate against and cause unnecessary suffering to our migrant and refugee brothers and sisters. With charity and clarity we are all called to live in solidarity and fraternity, to build bridges that bring us ever closer together, to avoid walls of ignominy and to learn to give our lives as Jesus Christ gave his for the salvation of all.

10. Let us ask Our Lady of Guadalupe to protect individuals and families who live in fear or pain due to migration and/or deportation. May the "Virgen morena", who knew how to reconcile peoples when they were at enmity, grant us all to meet again as brothers and sisters, within her embrace, and thus take a step forward in the construction of a society that is more fraternal, inclusive and respectful of the dignity of all.

Fraternally,

Francis

From the Vatican, 10 February 2025

| 3 |

The Golden Age

I s the beginning of this administration ushering in a Golden Age of America? The White House thinks so, and offered lists of what it considers achievements, with quotes of praise to boot. Many claims are vague assertions posited as absolutes. Others reflect extreme bias, attacking so many policies and programs as "radical", dangerous, and with heaps of blame laid at the feet of now ex-President Joe Biden.

Below are the salient entries from the White House website. Please be aware that individual assertions are not fact-checked here and nothing should be assumed true given the track record of statements made by the President and the administration's spokespeople. In fact, many of these have been proven false or misleading from the start, but it is beyond the efforts of writing this book to address them all. Also note that entries on the website have links not shown here that may provide additional information.

The First 100 Hours: Historic Action to Kick Off America's Golden Age

(24 January}

President Donald Trump's second term is off to an historic start.

The President is wasting no time delivering on the promises he made to the American people. The President signed more executive orders on his first day in office than any other president in history.

Within the first 100 hours of his second administration, President Trump taken hundreds of executive actions to secure the border, deport criminal illegal immigrants, unleash American prosperity, lower costs, increase government transparency, and reinstitute merit-based hiring in the federal government.

The President has already secured over $1 trillion in historic new investments.

We're witnessing the Trump Effect:

- President Trump is securing historic investments just days after being sworn in.
  - President Trump secured $500 billion in private sector investment for the largest AI infrastructure project in history, with Softbank CEO Masayoshi Son, Oracle co-founder Larry Ellison and OpenAI CEO Sam Altman all stating that it would not have been possible if not for President Trump's election victory and leadership.
  - Saudi Arabia "wants to invest $600 billion in the United States over the next four years."
  - Stellantis announced it will restart an assembly plant in Illinois and build the new Dodge Durango in Detroit.
    - The Detroit Free Press: "The news, announced in a letter Wednesday to employees from North America Chief Operating Officer Antonio Filosa, also provided some good news to workers in Toledo, Ohio, and Kokomo, Indiana, where investments are planned. The Belvidere plant will start production of a new midsize truck in the next two years. The letter said company Chairman John Elkann had met last week with President Donald Trump

before his inauguration on Monday. Elkann shared 'our enthusiasm for his strong commitment to the United States auto industry and all that this means for American jobs and the broader economy.'"

- President Trump is already securing the border and arresting criminal illegal immigrants.
- The Border Patrol is reporting a significant drop already in attempted illegal crossings.
- Fox News: "The U.S. southern border has seen a sharp drop in illegal immigrant encounters in the first days of the Trump administration, compared to the final few days of the Biden administration."
  - ICE is at work rounding up criminal aliens.
    - Fox News: "Information obtained by Fox News Digital, shows that between midnight Jan. 21 and 9 a.m. Jan 22, a 33-hour period, ICE Enforcement and Removal Operations (ERO) arrested more than 460 illegal immigrants that include criminal histories of sexual assault, robbery, burglary, aggravated assault, drugs and weapons offenses, resisting arrest and domestic violence."
    - Breitbart News: "President Donald Trump's administration arrested 538 illegal aliens on Thursday, ranging from child predators to gang members and a suspected terrorist."
  - The Trump Administration immediately shut down the CBP One app, which "paroled" over 1 million illegal immigrants.
  - Deportation flights have already started and the military is assisting with the effort.
  - The Department of Homeland Security reinstated official use of the term "illegal alien" over "undocumented noncitizen," and the DOJ announced it would be taking action against lawless sanctuary city policies.

- President Donald Trump signed an executive order to designate the cartels as terrorist organizations.
- Common sense has been restored to the government.
  - President Trump signed a series of executive orders ensuring the elimination of discriminatory DEI practices and ensuring merit-based hiring.
  - DEI staff are being placed on leave.
  - The Federal Aviation Administration must now return to merit-based hiring.
  - President Trump ended an affirmative action mandate in federal government hiring.
  - President Trump signed an executive order affirming the reality that there are only two sexes.
  - The State Department issued guidance that embassies should only be flying the American flag, and not any activist flags.
  - President Donald Trump signed an executive order telling agencies to stop remote work practices and directing workers to return to the office.
  - The State Department subsequently ordered workers to return to working in the office.
  - President Donald Trump is unleashing American energy.
  - President Trump declared a National Energy Emergency to unlock America's full energy potential and bring down costs for American families.
  - President Trump rescinded every one of Joe Biden's industry-killing, pro-China, and anti-American energy regulations, empowering consumer choice in vehicles, showerheads, toilets, washing machines, lightbulbs, and dishwashers.
  - President Trump withdrew the United States from the disastrous Paris Climate Agreement that unfairly ripped off our country.

- President Trump paused all new federal leasing and permitting for massive wind farms that degrade our natural landscapes and fail to serve American energy consumers.
- President Trump reversed the burdensome regulations that impeded Alaska's ability to develop its vast natural resources.
- President Trump terminated Biden's harmful electric vehicle mandate.

These opening few days can be summarized as Promises Made, Promises Kept:

- President Donald Trump said he would declassify the JFK Files. He did.
- President Donald Trump said he would end the EV mandate. He did.
- President Donald Trump said he would have the backs of the brave men and women in law enforcement. He did just that by pardoning two Washington D.C. Police officers that were unjustly prosecuted. The Metropolitan Police Department thanked President Trump for the pardon.
- President Donald Trump said he would use the military to secure the border. The Pentagon is deploying troops to the border and the Coast Guard is surging assets to the Gulf of America.
- President Trump said we would drill, baby, drill. The President signed executive orders to open up offshore drilling and allow more energy exploration in Alaska.
- President Donald Trump said he would end the weaponization of government. He signed an executive order doing just that.
- President Donald Trump said he would pardon the J6 Hostages. He did.
- President Donald Trump said he would end government censorship. On his first day in office, he signed an executive or-

der restoring freedom of speech and ending government censorship.

President Trump is being praised for his historic leadership:

The Steel Manufacturers Association: "President Trump has repeatedly demonstrated his strong support for American steel workers. He reiterated that support on day one by directing his agencies to investigate unfair trade and its impact on domestic manufacturing."

American Fuel & Petrochemical Manufacturers President and CEO Chet Thompson: "President Trump promised to end gas car bans and vehicle mandates on Day 1 of his new administration, and we are pleased to see that work already underway. Thank you, President Trump."

American Petroleum Institute President and CEO Mike Sommers: "Americans sent a clear message at the ballot box, and President Trump is answering the call on Day 1. U.S. energy dominance will drive our nation's economic and security agenda. This is a new day for American energy, and we applaud President Trump for moving swiftly to chart a new path where U.S. oil and natural gas are embraced, not restricted."

Job Creators Network CEO Alfredo Ortiz: "Trump's two-fold approach of boosting oil and gas production and repealing the Biden administration's green energy mandates will make American energy cheaper, reliable and more efficient."

Mortgage Bankers Association President and CEO Bob Broeksmit: "President Trump campaigned on lowering costs for Americans, and we appreciate housing supply and affordability being included in an executive order on this issue. We support efforts to cut unnecessary regulatory red tape and to pursue federal housing program enhancements that make renting and homeownership more attainable and sustainable."

Professional Trucking Association Group: "President Trump's decision to freeze regulations and curtail bureaucratic overreach is commendable. This is precisely what America needs: reduced government interference and increased freedom for small trucking businesses and entrepreneurs to flourish."

NetChoice CEO Steve DelBianco: "Upon returning to office, President Trump showed that America is ready to lead in tech and innovation again. By repealing Biden's restrictive rules on energy production and AI development, the president is steering America to remain dominant in creating the best technology in the world."

United Against Nuclear Iran Chairman Governor Jeb Bush and CEO Ambassador Mark Wallace: "We applaud President Trump for his decision today to redesignate the Houthis as an FTO. UANI in its recommended action plan for the Trump administration's first 100 days suggested that the president redesignate the Houthis as an FTO. This will now provide the U.S. government additional authorities to hold the Houthis accountable for their threats to international commerce and U.S. allies and partners."

Wins Come All Day Under President Donald J. Trump

{14 February}

It was another week filled with endless wins for the American people under President Donald J. Trump.

Here are only a few of the many victories from the past week:

- President Trump brought home an American citizen wrongfully detained in Russia and another American detained in Belarus — the tenth and eleventh hostages freed since he took office.
  - Michael McFaul, U.S. Ambassador to Russia under President Obama, reacted to Marc Fogel's release and said: "Hallelujah! Fantastic news! Praise be to President Donald Trump ... This is just fantastic news for anybody who cares about patriotic Americans."
- President Trump restored a 25% tariff on steel imports and elevated the tariff to 25% on aluminum imports to protect these critical American industries from unfair foreign competition.
  - The Steel Manufacturers Association released a statement applauding "President Trump for putting the American steel industry and its workers first by imposing a 25 percent tariff on all steel imports. President Trump understands that America's steel industry is the backbone of our economy. A thriving domestic steel industry is critical to U.S. national, energy and economic security."
  - The president of the Aluminum Association said: "We appreciate President Trump's continued focus on strong trade actions to support the aluminum industry in the United States."
  - Colorado Springs-based, family-owned Western Steel, Inc., praised the move: "What we hope that the tariffs will bring is some sort of stability to U.S. pricing. It allows a little bit more money to be made ... on the intermediate level like us."
- President Trump unveiled a plan for fair and reciprocal trade, making clear to the world that the United States will no longer tolerate being ripped off.
  - The Renewable Fuels Association said: "The Brazilian tariff on U.S. ethanol now stands at 18 percent and has virtually eliminated all market access for U.S. ethanol

producers. We thank President Trump for taking this action and hope this reciprocal tariff will help encourage a return to free and fair ethanol trade relationship with Brazil."

- President Trump spoke with Russian President Vladimir Putin and Ukrainian President Volodymyr Zelenskyy in pursuit of finally securing peace.
- President Trump hosted Jordan's King Abdullah II, who announced the Kingdom will accept 2,000 sick children from Gaza "as quickly as possible."
- President Trump joined Indian Prime Minister Narendra Modi to announce new deals between the two countries on immigration, trade, energy, and artificial intelligence.
- The Department of Energy approved the first liquefied natural gas project since the prior administration banned LNG exports last year.
- President Trump declared all foreign policy must be conducted under the President's direction, ensuring career diplomats reflect the foreign policy of the United States at all times.
- President Trump paused enforcement of the overregulation of American business practices abroad, which negatively impacted national security.
- Hamas agreed to free additional Israeli hostages after President Trump declared "all hell is going to break out" if the terrorist group delayed.
- Taiwan pledged to boost its investment in the United States amid President Trump's tariffs.
- President Trump received his highest ever approval rating in a CBS News poll — with 70% of Americans agreeing he is keeping his promises.
- President Trump attended Super Bowl LIX in New Orleans, becoming first sitting President to do so and bringing back tradition of pre-Super Bowl interviews.
- Illegal border crossings have hit lows not seen in decades.

- Hundreds of illegal aliens from Venezuela were repatriated back to their own country on Venezuelan-owned planes.
- Illegal aliens have started turning around in droves amid the Trump Administration's crackdown on dangerous illegal immigration.
- The Department of Homeland Security "clawed back" tens of millions of dollars in funds paid by rogue FEMA officials to house illegal aliens in luxury New York City hotels.
- President Trump instructed the Secretary of the Treasury to stop production of the penny, which costs 3.69 cents to make.
- Director of National Intelligence Tulsi Gabbard, Secretary of Health and Human Services Robert F. Kennedy, Jr., and Secretary of Agriculture Brooke Rollins were confirmed by the Senate — continuing the Trump Administration's rapid pace of confirmations.
- President Trump signed an executive order barring COVID-19 vaccine mandates in schools that receive federal funding.
- President Trump established the National Energy Dominance Council to advise on achieving energy dominance.
- President Trump established the Make America Healthy Again Commission, which redirects the national focus to promoting health rather than simply managing disease.
- President Trump signed an executive to end the use of paper straws.
- President Trump shut down the Biden-era "Climate Corps" work program.
- President Trump secured the resignations of 75,000+ federal workers, or approximately 3.75% of the federal workforce, in an effort to eliminate inefficiency at taxpayer expense.
- President Trump commenced his plan to downsize the federal bureaucracy and eliminate waste, bloat, and insularity — including an order that agencies hire no more than one employee for every four employees who leave.

- The Trump Administration ordered the Consumer Financial Protection Bureau — the brainchild of Elizabeth Warren, which funneled cash to left-wing advocacy groups — to halt operations.
- President Trump ended the wasteful Federal Executive Institute, which had become a training ground for bureaucrats.
- President Trump ordered the immediate dismissal of the Board of Visitors for the Army, Air Force, Navy, and Coast Guard following years of woke ideologies infiltrating U.S. service academies.
- Secretary of Defense Pete Hegseth restored Fort Liberty, North Carolina, to "Fort Bragg," in honor of a World War II hero.
- President Trump instructed EPA Administrator Lee Zeldin to terminate Biden-era regulations restricting water flow and mandating inadequate lightbulb standards.
- President Trump proclaimed "Gulf of America Day" after the Department of the Interior officially changed the name on its mapping databases.
  - Google Maps and Apple Maps both updated their apps to reflect the new name.
- The Department of Justice filed suit against the State of New York and its elected officials over their willful failure to follow federal immigration law.
- The Environmental Protection Agency canceled tens of millions of dollars in contracts to left-wing advocacy groups and announced an investigation into a scheme by Biden EPA staffers to shield billions of dollars from oversight and accountability.
- The Department of Education announced an investigation into the Minnesota State High School League and California Interscholastic Federation for violation of federal anti-discrimination law by allowing men to compete in women's sports.
- The Federal Bureau of Investigation discovered 2,400 additional records on the assassination of President John F.

Kennedy, which were never provided to the board tasked with reviewing and disclosing the documents. The discovery happened due to President Trump's executive order calling for the declassification of JFK assassination documents.

- The Department of Veterans Affairs implemented a new flag policy to promote the prominence of the American flag and ensure consistency among its facilities.
- President Trump was unanimously elected as Chairman of The Kennedy Center Board of Trustees and fired a slew of the Center's board members over their obsession with perpetuating radical ideologies.
- U.S. crude oil stockpiles continued to rise, which they have done every week since President Trump took office.
- Chicago Lurie Children's Hospital paused sex change surgeries for minors in response to President Trump's executive order ending the radical practice.
- Taxpayer-funded PBS closed its DEI office and Disney dropped two of its DEI programs after President Trump's executive order reining in such discriminatory practices.

Trump Effect Shows No Slowdown

{17 February}

In his first month back in office, President Donald J. Trump has taken extraordinary action to usher in a new Golden Age of America – through border security, deregulation, government accountability, and leveling the playing field for American workers, to name a few.

The positive effects of President Trump's policies continue to be felt across the country.

Here are some headlines you may have missed this weekend:

- Top automaker could move some production out of Mexico amid Trump tariff talks, CEO says
- Trump tariffs spark 'exciting time' for Ohio steel plant as CEO eyes adding jobs, boosting productivity
- San Diego migrant shelter closes after no new arrivals since Trump took office; over 100 employees laid off
- DOGE Discovers $1.9 Billion HUD Money 'Misplaced' By Biden Administration
- USDA Axes Millions in Contracts, Including $230K for 'Brazilian Forest and Gender Consultant'
- Border Czar Tom Homan: "In the last 24 hours the US Border Patrol has encountered a total of 229 aliens across the entire southwest border. That is down from a high of over 11,000 a day under Biden. I started as a Border Patrol Agent in 1984 and I don't remember the numbers ever being that low. President Trump promised a secure border and he is delivering."

America Is Back — and President Trump Is Just Getting Started

{20 February}

President Donald J. Trump took office just one month ago, but has already accomplished more than most presidents do in their entire term as he makes good on his promise to usher in the New Golden Age of America.

Here is a non-comprehensive list of President Trump's wins after just one month:
SECURING OUR HOMELAND:

- President Trump declared a national emergency at the border and deployed the military, including the 10th Mountain Division, to secure our nation.

- Illegal border crossings have hit lows not seen in decades as U.S. Border Patrol is re-empowered to once again enforce the law.
  - ABC News: "From Jan. 21 through Jan. 31, the number of U.S. Border Patrol apprehensions along the southwest border dropped 85% from the same period in 2024, according to data obtained by ABC News. In the 11 days after Jan. 20, migrants apprehended at ports of entry declined by 93%."
- Illegal aliens have started turning around in droves amid the crackdown.
- The Department of Homeland Security announced that arrests of criminal illegal immigrants have doubled under President Trump.
- President Trump signed the Laken Riley Act into law, which requires illegal immigrants arrested or charged with theft or violence to be detained — honoring the legacy of Laken Riley, a Georgia college student brutally murdered by an illegal alien released into the country.
- President Trump ended "catch-and-release," reversing the dangerous Biden-era policy that released dangerous illegal aliens back into our communities.
- President Trump shut down the "CBP One" app, which "paroled" more than one million illegal immigrants into the country.
  - A migrant shelter in San Diego announced it will shut down after it has received no new arrivals since President Trump took office.
- President Trump terminated all taxpayer-funded public benefits for illegal aliens.
- President Trump ramped up deportation flights of criminal illegal aliens.
  - After President Trump announced "urgent and decisive retaliatory measures" against Colombia over its refusal

to accept deportation flights from the U.S., the country's president quickly backtracked — even offering the use of his personal plane for the deportations.

- El Salvadorian President Nayib Bukele offered to accept deportees of any nationality, including violent American criminals currently imprisoned in the U.S.

- President Trump began transferring criminal illegal aliens to Guantanamo Bay ahead of their repatriation back to their own countries.

- President Trump re-established the successful "Remain in Mexico" policy.

- President Trump restarted construction of the border wall.

- The Trump Administration officially declared Tren de Aragua, MS-13, the Sinaloa Cartel, the Jalisco New Generation Cartel, the United Cartéls, the Gulf Cartel, the Northeast Cartel, and the Michoacán Family as Foreign Terrorist Organizations.

- New York City Mayor Eric Adams (D) agreed to allow federal immigration officials to operate on Rikers Island and deport illegal alien criminals following his meeting with Border Czar Tom Homan.

- Mexico announced a deployment of 10,000 troops to the border to combat illegal immigration and fentanyl trafficking, while Canada announced a flurry of measures to combat fentanyl manufacturing and trafficking following President Trump's imposition of tariffs on the two countries.

- President Trump implemented an additional 10% tariff on imports from China in order to stem the flow of illegal aliens and fentanyl.

- President Trump ordered an end to birthright citizenship.

- President Trump suspended the U.S. Refugee Admissions Program.

- The Department of Justice filed suit against the State of New York and some of its elected officials over their willful failure to follow federal immigration law and announced that it will take action against so-called "sanctuary cities" for their obstruction of U.S. law.

- The Department of Homeland Security "clawed back" tens of millions of dollars in funds paid by rogue FEMA officials to house illegal aliens in luxury New York City hotels.
- President Trump reinstated the death penalty for federal capital crimes.

PROTECTING AMERICAN WORKERS AND FOSTERING ECONOMIC GROWTH:

- President Trump restored a 25% tariff on steel imports and elevated the tariff to 25% on aluminum imports to protect these critical American industries from unfair foreign competition — a move praised by the Steel Manufacturers Association, the Aluminum Association, and businesses across the country.
  - Robert Simon, CEO of JSW Steel USA, praised President Trump's steel and aluminum tariffs, celebrating them "as a project that will flood the U.S. with jobs as trading partners move their industries to U.S. soil to avoid tariffs."
- Makoto Uchida, the CEO of global automaker Nissan, said President Trump's tariffs could push the car manufacturer to move its production from Mexico to the U.S.
- President Trump unveiled a plan for fair and reciprocal trade, making clear to the world that the United States will no longer tolerate being ripped off.
- President Trump secured hundreds of billions of dollars in new investments.
  - President Trump announced the largest artificial intelligence infrastructure project in history, securing $500 billion in planned private sector investment — with major CEOs agreeing it would not have been possible without President Trump's leadership.

- ◦ Saudi Arabia declared its intention to invest $600 billion in the United States over the next four years.
- ◦ President Trump secured a $20 billion investment by DAMAC Properties to build new U.S.-based data centers.
- ◦ Taiwan pledged to boost its investment in the United States.
- ◦ Electronics giants Samsung and LG "are considering moving their plants in Mexico to the U.S." now that President Trump is back in office.
- In February, forecasters from the Federal Reserve Bank of Philadelphia revised their economic growth projections for the first quarter of 2025 up from 1.9% to 2.5%, and their unemployment rate projections for the quarter down from 4.2% to 4.1%.
- After a meeting with President Trump, Stellantis announced it will reopen its assembly plant in Belvidere, Illinois — putting 1,500 employees back to work — and build its next-generation Dodge Durango in Detroit, Michigan. The company also announced new investments in their Toledo, Ohio, and Kokomo, Indiana, facilities.
- President Trump laid out a visionary plan to establish a Sovereign Wealth Fund to maximize the stewardship of the $5+ trillion in assets held by the United States.
- Following President Trump's victory, the S&P 500 set a new record as the stock market surged to record highs — while major Wall Street firms like JP Morgan Chase posted their highest ever annual profits.

LOWERING THE COST OF LIVING:

- President Trump directed the heads of all executive departments and agencies to "deliver emergency price relief ... to the American people and increase the prosperity of the American worker."

- President Trump established the National Energy Dominance Council to maximize use of the U.S.' extensive energy resources, thereby enabling lower energy prices.
- Crude oil prices have fallen over 5% since President Trump took office.
- The Department of Energy postponed burdensome Biden-era efficiency standard rules for the following appliances, saving American consumers large sums:
  - Central air conditioners: Biden rules were slated to make air conditioners $1,100 more expensive, according to Alliance for Consumers.
  - Gas water heaters: Biden rules were slated to make water heaters $2,800 more expensive.
  - Clothes washers and dryers: Biden rules were slated to make washers $200 more expensive.
  - Light bulbs: Biden rules were slated to make light bulbs $140 more expensive.
  - Walk-in coolers and freezers, commercial refrigeration equipment, and air compressors.
- The total cost of federal regulations in 2023 was a record-breaking $2.1 trillion, or $15,788 per U.S. household, according to the Competitive Enterprise Institute. By requiring agencies to identify at least ten existing rules, regulations, or guidance documents to be repealed for every one rule they promulgate, President Trump has put the U.S. on track to severely reduce regulatory costs for everyday Americans.
  - The National Associations of Manufacturers found the cost of federal regulations was even greater — at $3.079 trillion in 2022.
- Secretary Sean Duffy's very first action at the Department of Transportation was to initiate rulemaking resetting Corporate Average Fuel Economy (CAFE) standards — effectively eliminating the Biden-era electric vehicle mandate.

- NBER economist Mark R. Jacobsen "estimates that a one-mpg increase in CAFE standards costs consumers of all income levels approximately 0.5% of their income in the first year of the increase. By the 10th year following the increase, however, this cost becomes regressive, as the increase drives up the price of used cars. A one-mpg increase in CAFE standards costs consumers earning less than $25,000 per year 1.12% of their income, but only costs consumers earning more than $75,000 per year 0.41% of their income."

RE-ESTABLISHING AMERICAN STRENGTH:

- President Trump secured the release of six American hostages in Venezuela, two Americans in Afghanistan, an American-Israeli citizen in Hamas captivity, a Pennsylvania teacher in Russian captivity, and an American citizen in Belarus — bringing the total number of American hostages released under President Trump to 11.
- President Trump spoke with Russian President Vladimir Putin and Ukrainian President Volodymyr Zelenskyy in pursuit of finally securing peace as negotiations get underway.
- President Trump restored maximum pressure on Iran, "sanctioning an international network for facilitating the shipment of millions of barrels of Iranian crude oil worth hundreds of millions of dollars to the People's Republic of China."
- President Trump redesignated the Iran-backed Houthis as a Foreign Terrorist Organization.
- President Trump hosted Israeli Prime Minister Benjamin Netanyahu for a visit where he proposed a bold vision for securing lasting peace in Gaza.
  - Former U.S. Ambassador to Israel David Friedman described the proposal as "brilliant, historic and the only

idea I have heard in 50 years that has a chance of bringing security, peace and prosperity to this troubled region."

- President Trump hosted Japanese Prime Minister Shigeru Ishiba, who announced his intention to "elevate Japan's investment in the United States to an unprecedented amount of $1 trillion," import "historic" quantities of LNG from Alaska, and open new auto plants in the U.S.
- President Trump hosted Jordan's King Abdullah II, who announced that the Kingdom will accept 2,000 sick children from Gaza "as quickly as possible."
- President Trump hosted Indian Prime Minister Narendra Modi for a visit where they announced new deals between the two countries on immigration, trade, energy, and artificial intelligence.
- President Trump banned funding to UNRWA — a United Nations agency that employed hundreds of Hamas and jihad operatives.
- President Trump imposed sanctions on the International Criminal Court, which has illegitimately asserted jurisdiction over internal U.S. matters and baselessly targeted Israeli Prime Minister Benjamin Netanyahu.
- President Trump reinstated the Mexico City Policy to ensure no taxpayer dollars support foreign organizations that perform, or actively promote, abortion in other nations.
- The Department of State ordered embassies worldwide to only fly the American flag — not activist flags.
- President Trump declared all foreign policy must be conducted under the President's direction, ensuring career diplomats reflect the foreign policy of the United States at all times.
- The Department of State declared that U.S. foreign policy will be America First going forward.
- Following a visit from Secretary of State Marco Rubio, Panamanian President José Raúl Mulino agreed to withdraw from China's Belt and Road Initiative, a debt-trap diplomacy scheme

the Chinese Communist Party uses to gain influence over developing nations.

- The U.S. rejoined the Geneva Consensus Declaration, which promotes and strengthens opportunities for women and girls around the world, and protects the family as the fundamental unit of society.
- President Trump cracked down on anti-Semitism by canceling visas for foreign students who are Hamas sympathizers.
- President Trump ordered the immediate dismissal of the Board of Visitors for the Army, Air Force, Navy, and Coast Guard following years of woke ideologies infiltrating U.S. service academies.
- The U.S. Army barred transgender people from enlisting and stopped using taxpayer funds for sex change surgeries.
- President Trump reinstated, with backpay, U.S. service members who were discharged under the military's nonsensical COVID-19 vaccine mandate.
- Secretary of Defense Pete Hegseth restored Fort Liberty, North Carolina, to "Fort Bragg," in honor of a World War II hero.
- President Trump withdrew the U.S. from the World Health Organization.
- President Trump paused enforcement of the overregulation of American businesses abroad, which negatively impacted national security.
- President Trump proclaimed "Gulf of America Day" after the Department of the Interior officially established it on its mapping databases.
- President Trump initiated a process to build a next-generation missile defense shield over the United States.

UNLEASHING AMERICAN ENERGY:

- President Trump declared a National Energy Emergency to unlock America's full energy potential and bring down costs for American families.
- President Trump rescinded every one of the Biden Administration's job-killing, pro-China, anti-American energy regulations.
- President Trump empowered Americans with choice in vehicles, showerheads, toilets, washing machines, light bulbs, and dishwashers, and killed Biden-era regulations that restricted water flow and mandated inadequate light bulb standards.
- President Trump terminated the job-killing Green New Scam.
- President Trump withdrew from the disastrous Paris Climate Agreement, which unfairly ripped off our country.
- President Trump paused federal permitting for massive wind farms, which degrade our natural landscapes and fail to serve American consumers.
- President Trump reversed bureaucratic regulations that impeded Alaska's ability to develop its vast natural resources.
- President Trump re-opened 625 million acres for offshore drilling, which Biden banned in his waning days, in order to "drill, baby, drill."
- President Trump scrapped an Obama-era rule on greenhouse gases.
- President Trump ended the Liquefied Natural Gas pause and approved the first LNG project since the Biden Administration banned them last year.

BRINGING BACK COMMON SENSE:

- Health systems across the nation stopped or downsized their sex change programs for minors following President Trump's "Protecting Children from Chemical and Surgical Mutilation" executive order.

- In Illinois, Chicago's Lurie Children's Hospital paused sex-change surgeries for patients under 19 as it "work[s] to understand the rapidly evolving environment."
- In Colorado, Denver Health announced it would stop performing sex change surgeries on minor children, while UCHealth said it was ending so-called "gender-affirming care" for all minors.
- In Washington, D.C., Children's National Hospital "paused" prescribing puberty blockers and hormone therapies for minors, while Northwest Washington Hospital did the same.
- In Virginia, VCU Health and Children's Hospital of Richmond "suspended" providing transgender-related medication and surgeries for minors, while UVA Health also "suspended" transgender-related services for minors.

• President Trump ended the unfair, demeaning practice of forcing women to compete against men in sports — which resulted in the NCAA changing its rules.

- The Department of Education launched investigations into the California Interscholastic Federation and the Minnesota State High School League over their failures to comply.

• President Trump made it the official policy of the U.S. government that there are only two sexes.

• President Trump banned COVID-19 vaccine mandates at schools that receive federal funding.

• President Trump rolled back the Biden-era push to mandate paper straws.

• President Trump instructed the Secretary of the Treasury to stop production of the penny, which cost 3.69 cents each to make.

- President Trump directed full enforcement of the Hyde Amendment, which bars taxpayer dollars from being used to fund or promote elective abortion.
- The Department of Transportation terminated the approval for New York City's burdensome "congestion pricing" scheme.

RESTORING ACCOUNTABILITY AND TRANSPARENCY IN GOVERNMENT

- President Trump established the Department of Government Efficiency (DOGE) to maximize government productivity and ensure the best use of taxpayer funds — which has already achieved billions of dollars in savings for taxpayers.
- President Trump commenced his plan to downsize the federal bureaucracy and eliminate waste, bloat, and insularity.
  - President Trump ordered federal workers to return to the office five days a week.
  - President Trump ordered federal agencies hire no more than one employee for every four employees who leave.
  - President Trump ended the wasteful Federal Executive Institute, which had become a training ground for bureaucrats.
  - President Trump ordered the termination of all federal Fake News media contracts.
- President Trump ordered the Consumer Financial Protection Bureau — the brainchild of Elizabeth Warren, which funneled cash to left-wing advocacy groups — to halt operations.
- President Trump ordered an end to anti-Christian bias in the Federal Government.
- President Trump ordered an examination of all regulations to assess any infringements on Americans' Second Amendment rights.
- The Environmental Protection Agency canceled tens of millions of dollars in contracts to left-wing advocacy groups, an-

nounced an investigation into a scheme by Biden EPA staffers to shield billions of dollars from oversight and accountability, and put 168 "environmental justice" employees on leave.

- President Trump stopped the waste, fraud, and abuse within USAID — ensuring taxpayers are no longer on the hook for funding the pet projects of entrenched bureaucrats, such as sex changes in Guatemala.
- President Trump ordered an end to the weaponization of the Federal Government against American citizens.
  - The Department of Justice immediately began rooting out politically motivated lawfare that occurred in the Biden Administration.
- President Trump reversed the massive over-expansion of the IRS that took place during the Biden Administration.
- President Trump eliminated discriminatory DEI offices, employees, and practices across the bureaucracy alongside a return to merit-based hiring — including at the Federal Aviation Administration, where the Biden Administration specifically recruited individuals with intellectual disabilities and psychiatric issues.
  - As a result, taxpayer-funded PBS closed its DEI office, Disney dropped two of its DEI programs, Goldman Sachs ended its DEI policy, and Institutional Shareholder Services announced it would no longer consider diversity of company boards when making its voting recommendations.
  - The Federal Communications Commission opened an investigation into discriminatory DEI policies at Comcast, an entity it regulates.
- President Trump ordered an end to all censorship of Americans by the federal government.
- President Trump ordered a review of funding for all non-governmental organizations, so taxpayers are no longer funding those that undermine America's interests.

- ○ The Department of State issued a "pause" on existing foreign aid grants to ensure accountability and efficiency.
- President Trump lifted last-minute collective bargaining agreements issued by the Biden Administration, which sought to impede reform.
- President Trump overrode bureaucratic red tape that limited water availability in California following the failure of the state's water system during the devastating wildfires.
- President Trump terminated the Biden-era electric vehicle mandate.
  - ○ President Trump suspended the Biden-era EV charging program, which had resulted in just eight charging stations despite $7.5 billion earmarked for the program.
- President Trump shut down the wasteful Biden-era "Climate Corps" program.
- The Federal Communications Commission took action against a Soros-backed radio station that leaked sensitive information about ICE operations.
- President Trump ordered the declassification of documents related to the assassinations of President John F. Kennedy, Jr., Robert F. Kennedy, and Rev. Dr. Martin Luther King, Jr.
- President Trump opened the White House Press Briefing Room to non-legacy media outlets as the White House sets a new standard for transparency in the digital age.
- President Trump reinstated press privileges for roughly 440 journalists who the Biden Administration sought to silence.
- President Trump fired members of The Kennedy Center's Board of Trustees amid their obsession with perpetuating radical, left-wing ideology at taxpayer expense.
- President Trump revoked the security clearances of the 51 "spies who lied."

EMPOWERING THE AMERICAN PEOPLE

- President Trump established the Make America Healthy Again Commission, which redirects the national focus to promoting health rather than simply managing disease.
- President Trump took executive action to expand access to in vitro fertilization (IVF).
- President Trump established the White House Faith Office to protect Americans' religious liberty.
- President Trump ordered an end to the radical indoctrination of children in K-12 schools that receive federal funding.
- President Trump took executive action to support parents in choosing the best education for their children.
- President Trump established the Presidential Working Group on Digital Asset Markets to strengthen U.S. leadership in digital finance.
- President Trump granted full and unconditional pardons to 23 pro-life Americans who were unjustly persecuted by the Biden Administration.
- President Trump pardoned two Washington, D.C., police officers who were imprisoned simply for doing their jobs of apprehending criminals.
- President Trump has had his cabinet confirmed by the Senate at a far faster pace than his predecessors, with a majority of his cabinet earning confirmation in his first month.

| 4 |

The Media

On 7 January 2025, Mark Zuckerberg, owner of Meta (parent company of Facebook), posted a video to Threads about how content will be handled on Facebook. On 26 February, Jess Bezos, the owner of Amazon who purchased the Washington Post, declared changes in editorial inclusion (and exclusion). He was explicit about following Musk's approach to 'free speech'.

Marty Baron, former editor of the Washington Post, decried the Post's shift as motivated by a fear of Trump, which included the Post not running a presidential endorsement in 2024. He claims David Shipley "was perceived as an enemy of Trump for one reason and one reason only: the coverage by The Washington Post — not just the news coverage but also the editorials."

Along with Elon Musk, who bought Twitter and reinstated Trump's suspended account, they make up three of the four richest individuals in the world as of the writing of this book. They represent media consumed by nearly everyone in America. And they all sat in the front row with Trump for his inauguration.

Zuckerberg Video

Hey everyone. I want to talk about something important today because it's time to get back to our roots around free expression on Facebook and Instagram. I started building social media to give people a voice. I gave a speech at Georgetown five years ago about the importance of protecting free expression, and I still believe this today, but a lot has happened over the last several years.

There's been widespread debate about the potential harms from online content. Governments and legacy media have pushed to censor more and more. A lot of this is clearly political, but there's also a lot of legitimately bad stuff out there. Drugs, terrorism, child exploitation. These are things that we take very seriously, and I want to make sure that we handle responsibly. So we built a lot of complex systems to moderate content, but the problem with complex systems is they make mistakes even if they accidentally censor just 1% of posts.

That's millions of people, and we've reached a point where it's just too many mistakes and too much censorship. The recent elections also feel like a cultural tipping point towards, once again, prioritizing speech. So, we're going to get back to our roots and focus on reducing mistakes, simplifying our policies, and restoring free expression on our platforms. More specifically, here's what we're going to do.

First, we're going to get rid of fact-checkers and replace them with community notes similar to X starting in the US. After Trump first got elected in 2016, the legacy media wrote nonstop about how misinformation was a threat to democracy. We tried in good faith to address those concerns without becoming the arbiters of truth, but the fact-checkers have just been too politically biased and have destroyed more trust than they've created, especially in the US. So, over the next couple of months, we're going to phase in a more comprehensive community notes system.

Second, we're going to simplify our content policies and get rid of a bunch of restrictions on topics like immigration and gender that are just out of touch with mainstream discourse. What started as a movement to be more inclusive has increasingly been used to shut down opinions and shut out people with different ideas, and it's gone too far. So, I want to make sure that people can share their beliefs and experiences on our platforms.

Third, we're changing how we enforce our policies to reduce the mistakes that account for the vast majority of censorship on our platforms. We used to have filters that scanned for any policy violation. Now, we're going to focus those filters on tackling illegal and high-severity violations, and for lower-severity violations, we're going to rely on someone reporting an issue before we take action. The problem is that the filters make mistakes, and they take down a lot of content that they shouldn't. So, by dialing them back, we're going to dramatically reduce the amount of censorship on our platforms. We're also going to tune our content filters to require much higher confidence before taking down content. The reality is that this is a trade-off. It means we're going to catch less bad stuff, but we'll also reduce the number of innocent people's posts and accounts that we accidentally take down.

Fourth, we're bringing back civic content. For a while, the community asked to see less politics because it was making people stressed, so we stopped recommending these posts, but it feels like we're in a new era now, and we're starting to get feedback that people want to see this content again. So we're going to start phasing this back into Facebook, Instagram, and Threads while working to keep the communities friendly and positive. Fifth, we're going to move our trust and safety and content moderation teams out of California, and our US-based content review is going to be based in Texas. As we work to promote free expression, I think that will help us build trust to do this work in places where there is less concern about the bias of our teams.

Finally, we're going to work with President Trump to push back on governments around the world. They're going after American companies and pushing to censor more. The US has the strongest constitutional protections for free expression in the world. Europe has an ever-increasing number of laws, institutionalizing censorship, and making it difficult to build anything innovative there. Latin

American countries have secret courts that can order companies to quietly take things down. China has censored our apps from even working in the country. The only way that we can push back on this global trend is with the support of the US government, and that's why it's been so difficult over the past four years when even the US government has pushed for censorship.

By going after us and other American companies, it has emboldened other governments to go even further. But now we have the opportunity to restore free expression, and I'm excited to take it. It'll take time to get this right, and these are complex systems. They're never going to be perfect. There's also a lot of illegal stuff that we still need to work very hard to remove. But the bottom line is that after years of having our content moderation work focused primarily on removing content, it is time to focus on reducing mistakes, simplifying our systems, and getting back to our roots about giving people voice. I'm looking forward to this next chapter. Stay good out there, and more to come soon.

Author's Response to Video

{Published under the title "America's Brave New Media" on 11 January on the author's blog, ConsiderReconsider.Com}

At first I thought it was AI. My wife wondered if it was AI. It looked and felt like it; the content seemed so carefully structured. Zuckerberg's video on January 7th was welcomed by those who felt their rights have been infringed, while others scratched their heads or didn't care. Personally, I found it terrifying.

"It's time to get back to our roots around free expression. We're replacing fact checkers with Community Notes"

The message by itself seemed innocuous, but it was immediately cheered or jeered according to political preferences. Why? Because in spite of being framed with free speech as the issue, the substance of the message was nothing but a very telling laundry list of what (who) would be censored less and what (who) would be censored more. The appeal to very specific agendas could have been right off any far-Right website.* And it was CLEVER. His choice of expressions and omissions expertly veiled implications yet dog whistled to those who are eager to shift public narratives in their direction. To untrained ears, it seemed harmless and even sincere, if not a bit bizarre.

Some of us knew it was coming and could connect the dots. How? History is not a collection of things that just happens. It's causes and effects, evolving fads and sentiments, reactions and counter-reactions, cyclical progressions, and ever-shifting agendas. And of course, it's about propaganda and control. When we understand the history and evolution of control as connected to the history and evolution of communication and the public sphere, we can see what is happening RIGHT NOW is a pivotal point in history. So let's rightfully start the story before the story.

The advent of social media is the first time in human history where most of us have a voice and can have discourse with almost anyone, anytime, anywhere, on any subject. We can express opinions, which even before this time was mostly reiterating what we heard elsewhere. But now we can hear it from anywhere, and propagate (share) it like a virus, with non-expert and non-factual voices easily shouting down experts and journalists. It brought us a "freedom" we never had before, but had no precedence or understanding of how to use responsibly. Yelling fire in an online theater seems fine, and the power of this medium — often more full of cats than fury — is underestimated. Facebook was the shiny new weapon in Obama's first presidential campaign arsenal. Message boards were the platform by which the Church of Scientology was protested worldwide, crushing their stranglehold over journalists and critics. Iranian protests during the Jasmine Revolution were organized on Twitter, and even the Libyan dictator lost his head shortly after blocking the public from their Internet access.

In America, the average person didn't do more than grumble at the idea of our government having a "kill switch" for the Internet — if they followed that news at all. Yet we undeniably use it as a public commons like an always-open town square, coffee shop, family and friend reunion, and town hall meeting all rolled into one. We don't see it as a replacement for traditional journalism, but Elon Musk does. He openly proclaims that legacy media and journalism is dead. On November 6th, 2024, he declared the New Media Order.

"You are the media now."

The king is dead. Long live the king. The genie isn't going back in the bottle. The landscape of news, information, and rhetoric is completely different from previous generations. This ought to usher in a new era of freedom of speech, press, and by extension, truth. But scratch that last one off. As the web brought us a False Egalitarianism of Ideas, social media has made truth itself "democratic". In the Orville episode "Majority Rule" (similar to the Black Mirror episode "Nosedive"), a news anchor reports an industrial waste problem, but then reports that it must not be true because 74% of the population voted it was an incorrect assessment. This is not fiction to us. It's human nature to have fact-irrelevant beliefs and make fact-irrelevant decisions. But a truly post-truth society started in 2015 with the mantra of "fake news", then "alternative facts" sent down by the highest office, and culminating in the vilification of experts during a pandemic.

We are now entering the age of digital populism, and these are its fruits. But let's be clear — it wasn't caused by social media. In fact, social media companies were under pressure to stave off misinformation and its effects, in part to reduce platform companies' liability for user content. They did a horrible job, automating the process instead of hiring an army of service agents. The algorithm seemed to victimize some and give others a free pass. It was akin to haphazard censorship with no human at the helm. Everyone (regardless of their politics) cried fowl under the conspiracy theory that their posts and those of people like them were being personally targeted for their ideology. Fear-mongers played on this. Conspiracists played on this.

Online media was flooded with nonsense that cost thousands of un-necessary deaths and almost a civil war in America. And it may be true that (those considering themselves) Conservatives found content "hidden" or tagged with fact checks more than others because statis-tically they were the ones parroting the most false and misleading in-formation, much of it later found to originate from Russian bots. It got so bad, the President of the United States was suspended and then banned from Twitter, just to have those who couldn't see the harm he was causing cry foul even louder. Looking back, it may have saved the nation, at least for that time being.

Facebook avoided wholesale censorship by marking some content as possibly misleading or untrue, particularly with regards to misin-formation about COVID-19, vaccines, and Stop the Steal claims that nonetheless resulted in historic and tragic violence. The populist re-sponse? Fact checkers must be ignored and adding MORE speech by presenting conflicting views was somehow "censorship". (This harkens to other "liberties" being not defined by what one can do, but by what can do with impunity and without consequences. The rest of us call that "license".)

Algorithms, when left to their own devices (pardon the expres-sion), can have unintended inherent biases, usually subtle societal ones. But they don't outright lie or target people unless you make them do so. In 2020, it was determined that Donald Trump was the primary disseminator of false information on Twitter. This is consis-tent with determinations by teams of journalists that he had told tens of thousands of lies in a few short years. But it's not just him. In a twist of irony in November 2020, X's AI told one user "Elon Musk has been identified as one of the most significant spreaders of misin-formation on X since he acquired the platform". One must wonder if that digital whistleblower was sent to a "recodification camp". And we should consider the possibility that was the reason he acquired it — not to protect everyone's voice, but bring back hateful, libelous voices that cause real harm, including that of the previously-banned presi-dent. Musk himself relishes dangerous and prejudicial conspiracies. In another instance, AI was having trouble differentiating between content from the Republican Party and White Supremacists. I can only say here that subjectively, one person's bias is another person's honesty. In recent years, GOP rhetoric has transgressed lines not previously crossed by either party and perhaps doth protests too much.

As with traditional news, vast Right-leaning media notwithstanding, existing AI is being accused by some of being inherently "Liberal" and therefore "Conservative" AIs must be established as an alternative for Right-leaning people. Bubble, anyone? As one acquaintance of mine says we have too many "Liberal fact checkers", people seem unclear of the concept. It's only a matter of time before we need two versions of the Periodic Table. The human nature problem is that individuals only see things that affect them, so it is natural that they feel and acknowledge when they have the appearance of being censored while ignoring the similar instances that do affect those with opposing views. As I had to say to another acquaintance, just because it rains five days in a row and it's reported doesn't make the weatherman "pro-rain". And when reality isn't on your side, it is easier and more natural to stomp your foot than change your mind. Am I being unfair? I can only say that I have Liberal friends who have had content removed or flagged (justified and unjustified) and while many Conservative friends were not hit at all, some regularly were, and it was no surprise why — not due merely to some "political incorrectness".

Psychology and backstory established, this brings us up to date ...

In principle, it doesn't matter if the problem is worse on one side or the other. It's not even really about that. But the fact is that one party has been taken over by people currently establishing the country's first state-run media. Musk spent an enormous amount of money to ensure Trump was elected, even with bragging about handing him swing states. (Investigations are now underway to determine Musk's influence in numerous European elections.) In MAGA, he became overnight the stage-sharing celebrity, and even before the administration changes hands is speaking and acting as an unelected, unhired de facto American bureaucrat and diplomat. And now enters Zuckerberg, donating a fortune to the inauguration ceremony (as if it will be spent there), followed by this video announcement to fall in line with Musk's mandates for X. It vows to 'open up' speech regarding existing targets of hate speech, particularly immigrants and the LGBTQ+ community, dialogue that has not truly been curbed anyway. Meanwhile lip service is given regarding "hate speech", a likely exception (or the true intention) being a euphemistic use — where in current Republican terms means specifically anything that can be labeled antisemitic due to criticizing or not unquestionably supporting Israel. This was virtually never allowed in traditional media and will become forboden again.

So where is the propaganda or control? Orwell wrote without the notion of the Internet or social media. He understood the nature of man, of power, and of propaganda. But he didn't see the modern world we actually have coming and how we got there. America has never had state-controlled media, and I don't think in any obvious form anyone would accept it. Even before a broadening of choices through cable television, government had to overtly censor information and it was usually obvious and known. Regardless of a small number of companies governing most channels, almost no politician or policy can go without the challenge of criticism or dissenting voices, ESPECIALLY with the crowdsourced citizen journalism we see online. Sure, there have been limitations in underlying assumptions that in turn limit HOW we frame issues. And we are at the mercy of advertising dollars flowing from ratings and audience numbers, where we ourselves choose junk media over real news. And of course, we also demand not to have basic assumptions challenged — anything that knocks too hard upon our patriotic fragility. That is the main reason foreign news reports things ours does not.

Traditional censorship will not do the trick. The medium requires other methods, and technology provides them. Algorithms don't even have to censor, or "fact-check", or expose people to opposing views. It requires the opposite of such things, hence the threat we all but recognize. It requires that the APPEARANCE of general consensus

("Community Notes") be shifted to whatever views those behind the platform wish to push. All that must be done is to control levels of exposure between users. Us humans will follow the crowd more than we realize. It determines what is not just socially acceptable to do and say, but what to think. So the concepts of algorithms used to read the crowds can be reversed and make the crowds read them. In such a general, amorphous way, what becomes majority and minority opinion is no longer predictable but GUIDABLE simply by convincing people it is so.

Musk is a genius with vision, though perhaps more of a Lex Luthor than Tony Stark. He knows he has that power, and clearly has worked to obtain it. Zuckerberg must know it, too, though he comes off more as having one of his children hostage and being given a script to follow or else. He's jumping on the bandwagon to either profit or be steamrolled by the richest man and the most powerful one at his side. The Three Muskovites are pretending to save us from a "technocracy" that did not exist by implementing one right before our screens. They are playing 3-D chess while the rest of us are hoarding our checkers.

This should have scared us sooner. The richest man is the world, someone who controls one of the most important media-communication commons in history, was declared a governmental right hand man to the incoming president. Musk is being given full reign as head of "DOGE" to oversee all aspects of government as a "department" under Trump but without the accountability of an official federal agency. And if that isn't enough of a dystopic narrative that will not end well, Musk says he plans to make one robot for every person on Earth, after years of telling us not to trust AI and the robots will come for us. It reads like he's living out his own global domination fantasies, and yet it's not entirely impossible he may succeed. We are well past a satire singularity at this point. Perhaps that's why the Muskovites are publicly open about what they are doing — because it's a deception so big it's unimaginable, and perhaps too late.

"We aren't just the media here now. We are also the government."

Donald Trump Jr.'s words from December 19, 2024, could be interpreted as the ultimate empowerment of We the People. We know almost half of America is applauding that, or at least will not question it. But some of us perceive the foundation, the gameplan, and execution of a fundamentally new 21st Century oligarchy. We fear — and not without good reason — that "we" the media and "we" the government are at best whoever falls compliantly into the algorithm set by a technocratic few by which the United States government and all its power will be beholden.

*In the context of this article, it just as well could have been reversed, appealing to far-Left agendas, with a far-Left government, and would be just as bad. The point being made here is that curating content in any form should not be so blatantly biased or partisan, especially when directly wedding the powers behind an administration with those who have ultimate influence and control over discourse in the public commons.

Note added 16 February:

A side addendum of sorts. from Chomsky's "Responsibility of Intellectuals" (50 year anniversary edition):

There was also a different view, but it did not enter the debate: that the war was 'fundamentally wrong and immoral', not 'a mistake'. Though that position didn't make it into the mainstream hawk–dove debate, it was in fact held: namely, by a large majority of the public, as was found in the investigations of the Chicago Council on Foreign Relations, which conducts regular studies of popular attitudes on a wide range of issues. The figures held steady until 1999, after which it seems that the question was dropped. These are quite astonishing figures for an open question, particularly when respondents are drawing the conclusion in virtual isolation, the conception being inexpressible and unthinkable in mainstream discussion. One can only guess what the figures would be if the rigid doctrinal framework were penetrable.

This shows us that even with a Free Press, there are limitations and assumptions as to how any issue may be discussed.

Bezos Tweet

I shared this note with the Washington Post team this morning:

I'm writing to let you know about a change coming to our opinion pages.

We are going to be writing every day in support and defense of two pillars: personal liberties and free markets. We'll cover other topics too of course, but viewpoints opposing those pillars will be left to be published by others.

There was a time when a newspaper, especially one that was a local monopoly, might have seen it as a service to bring to the reader's doorstep every morning a broad-based opinion section that sought to cover all views. Today, the internet does that job.

I am of America and for America, and proud to be so. Our country did not get here by being typical. And a big part of America's success has been freedom in the economic realm and everywhere else. Freedom is ethical — it minimizes coercion — and practical — it drives creativity, invention, and prosperity.

I offered David Shipley, whom I greatly admire, the opportunity to lead this new chapter. I suggested to him that if the answer wasn't "hell yes," then it had to be "no." After careful consideration, David decided to step away. This is a significant shift, it won't be easy, and it will require 100% commitment — I respect his decision. We'll be searching for a new Opinion Editor to own this new direction.

I'm confident that free markets and personal liberties are right for America. I also believe these viewpoints are underserved in the current market of ideas and news opinion. I'm excited for us together to fill that void.

Jeff

| 5 |

Project 2025

Donald Trump denied any connection between Project 2025 of the Heritage Foundation and his 2024 presidential campaign. However, many of his previous staff were associated with the Foundation and many contributors to that project became cabinet members after reelection. Russell Thurlow Vought, considered the architect of Project 2025, was director of the Office of Management and Budget the last year of Trump's previous administration, and was again appointed to that position.

Kevin Roberts, president of the Foundation, sees the organization's role as "institutionalizing Trumpism". Project 2025 is the current version of the Foundations "Mandate for Leadership", and it may be no coincidence that the rhetoric surrounding his second term is that he received a "mandate" from the people to do a laundry list of things that, if his executive orders are any indication, are right out of the "2025 Playbook".

The well referenced Wikipedia article on Project 2025 summarizes the plan, as well as the views of opponents that it is "an authoritarian, Christian nationalist plan that will steer the U.S. toward autocracy" and that legal experts say "it would undermine the rule of law, separation of powers, separation of church and state, and civil liberties".

The Project itself cannot be reproduced here (it is available for sale on their site), but the following is offered as an overview of its content and relationship to Trump's second administration.

Wikipedia Entry

{Captured 3 March 2025 from https://en.wikipedia.org/wiki/Project_2025. Its extensive citations can be found there, and at the time of this writing, very few parts were uncited or contested in any way. Only a handful of those were omitted here.}

Project 2025 (also known as the 2025 Presidential Transition Project) is a political initiative to reshape the federal government of the United States and consolidate executive power in favor of right-wing policies. The plan was published in April 2023 by The Heritage Foundation, an American conservative think tank, in anticipation of Donald Trump winning the 2024 presidential election.

The ninth iteration of the Heritage Foundation's Mandate for Leadership series, Project 2025 is based on a controversial interpretation of the unitary executive theory that states that the entire executive branch is under the complete control of the president. Proponents of Project 25 say it will dismantle a government bureaucracy they say is unaccountable and mostly liberal. Critics have called it an authoritarian, Christian nationalist plan that will steer the U.S. toward autocracy. Legal experts say it would undermine the rule of law, separation of powers, separation of church and state, and civil liberties.

The project calls for merit-based federal civil service workers to be replaced by people loyal to Trump, to take partisan control of key government agencies, including the Department of Justice (DOJ), Department of Commerce (DOC), and Federal Trade Commission (FTC). Other agencies, including the Department of Homeland Security (DHS) and the Department of Education (ED), will be dismantled or abolished. The president will then be free to implement Project 25's agenda, including reducing taxes on corporations and capital gains, instituting a flat income tax on individuals, cutting Medicare and Medicaid, and reversing President Joe Biden's policies. Project 25 calls for reducing environmental regulations to favor fossil fuels and proposes making the National Institutes of Health (NIH) less independent and defunding its stem cell research. It proposes criminalizing pornography, removing legal protections against anti-LGBTQ+ discrimination, and ending diversity, equity, and inclusion (DEI) programs while having the DOJ prosecute anti-white racism instead. The project recommends the arrest, detention, and mass deportation of illegal immigrants, and deploying the military for domestic law enforcement. The plan also proposes enacting laws supported by the Christian right, such as criminalizing those who send and receive abortion and birth control medications and eliminating coverage of emergency contraception.

Most of Project 2025's writers and contributors worked either in Trump's last administration or on his election campaign. Trump campaign officials maintained contact with Project 2025, seeing its goals as aligned with their Agenda 47 program. Trump later attempted to distance himself from the plan. After he won the 2024 election, he nominated several of the plan's architects and supporters to positions in his administration. Four days into his second term, analysis by Time found that nearly two-thirds of Trump's executive actions "mirror or partially mirror" proposals from Project 2025.

Background

Heritage Foundation president Kevin Roberts established the Project in 2022.

Kevin Roberts, president of the Heritage Foundation, established Project 2025 with the goal of "building a governing agenda, not just for next January but long into the future".

The Heritage Foundation, a conservative think tank founded in 1973, has had significant influence in U.S. public policy making. In 2019, it ranked among the most influential public policy organizations in the United States. It coordinates with many conservative groups to build a network of allies.

Heritage president Kevin Roberts sees the organization's current role as "institutionalizing Trumpism." The Heritage Foundation is closely aligned with Trump. At a 2022 Heritage Foundation dinner, Trump endorsed the organization, saying it was "going to lay the groundwork and detail plans for exactly what our movement will do ... when the American people give us a colossal mandate." Roberts said in April 2024 that he had talked to Trump about Project 2025; the Trump campaign denied this.

Vice President JD Vance wrote the foreword to Roberts's book Dawn's Early Light: Taking Back Washington to Save America.

Project 2025 was established in 2022 with Paul Dans as director to provide the 2024 Republican presidential nominee with a personnel database and ideological framework. According to the Johnson Amendment, 501c3 organizations like Heritage cannot explicitly promote a particular election candidate. The Heritage Foundation spent $22 million preparing staffing recommendations for a conservative government in 2025. This was much more than what the group typically does for its staffing recommendations because President Trump said he had terrible staff during his first term. Citing the Reagan-era maxim that "personnel is policy", some political commentators have argued that personnel is the most important aspect of Project 2025.

The Mandate for Leadership series has had updated editions released in parallel with United States presidential elections since 1981. Heritage calls its Mandate a "policy bible", claiming that the implementation of almost two-thirds of the policies in its 1981 Mandate was attempted by Ronald Reagan, and similarly, the implementation of nearly two-thirds of the policies of its 2015 Mandate was attempted by Trump.

In April 2023, the Heritage Foundation published the 920-page Mandate, written by hundreds of conservatives. Nearly half of the project's collaborating organizations have received dark money contributions from a network of fundraising groups linked to Leonard Leo, a major conservative donor and key figure in guiding the selection of Trump's federal judicial nominees.

The 2024 Trump campaign said no outside group speaks for Trump and that Agenda 47 is the only official plan for a second Trump presidency. Policy suggestions from groups in Project 2025 reflected Trump's own words. His campaign said it appreciated these groups' policy suggestions. On July 5, 2024, Trump denied any knowledge of Project 2025. Political commentators including Robert Reich, Michael Steele, and Olivia Troye dismissed Trump's denial.

Heritage briefed other 2024 Republican presidential primaries candidates on the project, but focused on policies Trump could implement.

Project 2025 is not the only conservative program with a database of prospective recruits for a potential Republican administration, though these initiatives' leaders all have connections to Trump. In general, these initiatives seek to help Trump avoid the mistakes of his first term, when he arrived at the White House unprepared. By reclassifying tens of thousands of merit-based federal civil service workers as political appointees in order to replace them with Trump loyalists, some fear they would be willing to bend or break protocol, or in some cases violate laws, to achieve his goals.

Advisory board and leadership

Partner network

By February 2024, Project 2025 had over 100 partner organizations. The Southern Poverty Law Center identified seven of these as hate or extremist groups.

In May 2024, Russell Vought was named policy director of the Republican National Committee platform committee. The Center for Renewing America (CRA), founded by Vought, is on Project 2025's advisory board. CRA drafted executive orders, regulations, and memos that could have laid the groundwork for rapid action on Trump's plans when he won. The CRA identified Christian Nationalism as one of the top priorities for the second Trump term. Vought claimed that Trump blessed the CRA, and that his effort to distance himself from Project 2025 was just politics. Vought was Trump's director of the Office of Management and Budget during his first term.

In July 2024, Stephen Miller, a former Trump advisor, sought to remove his company, America First Legal, from the Project 2025 list of advisory board members. Before leaving Project 2025, he appeared in a promotional video for it. In November 2024, he was appointed as an advisor to the White House for Trump's second term.

Connections to Trump

Project 2025 partners employ over 200 former Trump administration officials. Trump was not personally involved in drafting or approving the plan. Six of his cabinet secretaries are authors or contributors to the 2025 Mandate, and about 20 pages are credited to his first deputy chief of staff. By summer 2023, the project was seen as a fitting organization for Trump's young and loyal advisors.

John McEntee, a senior advisor for Project 2025 and former Trump aide, said the project was doing valuable work in anticipation of Trump's second term.

Christopher Miller, who was secretary of defense for the last month of Trump's first term, wrote the Mandate's chapter on the Department of Defense.

Before his second term, many Project 2025 contributors were expected to have positions in the second Trump administration, and the administration was expected to use the database of potential federal employees the project recruited and trained. Peter Navarro, one of Mandate's authors, was appointed Senior Counselor for Trade and Manufacturing.

Leadership

Associate project director Spencer Chretien, associate director of presidential personnel during Trump's first term, said it was "past time to lay the groundwork for a White House more friendly to the right".

On July 2, 2024, Heritage Foundation president Kevin Roberts created controversy by saying, "we are in the process of the second American Revolution, which will remain bloodless if the left allows it to be." Shortly afterward, the Foundation released a statement adding, "Unfortunately, they have a well established record of instigating the opposite."

Project 2025 released a statement on July 5 saying the project "does not speak for any candidate or campaign" and that it is up to "the next conservative president" to decide which of its recommendations to implement. In July 2024, Trump reiterated his disavowal of Project 2025, but in the same month Project 2025 Director Paul Dans confirmed that his team had ongoing connections with Trump's campaign. During the week of July 29, Dans told Project staff that he would step down as director in August to focus on the election campaign. Kevin Roberts assumed leadership of the project.

Roger Severino is vice president of domestic policy at The Heritage Foundation. He, Roberts, and Dans wrote much of the Mandate.

Philosophical outlook

The Mandate for Leadership outlines four main aims: restoring the family as the centerpiece of American life; dismantling the administrative state; defending the nation's sovereignty and borders; and securing God-given individual rights to live freely. Roberts writes in the Mandate's foreword: "The long march of cultural Marxism through our institutions has come to pass. The federal government is a behemoth, weaponized against American citizens and conservative values, with freedom and liberty under siege as never before."

Roberts interprets the phrase "pursuit of happiness" in the Declaration of Independence as "pursuit of blessedness". According to him, "an individual must be free to live as his Creator ordained—to flourish." The Constitution, he argues, "grants each of us the liberty to do not what we want, but what we ought". Project 2025 plans to infuse every aspect of federal government with Christian nationalism. Roberts writes that the U.S. in 2024 is a place where "inflation is ravaging family budgets, drug overdose deaths continue to escalate, and children suffer the toxic normalization of transgenderism with drag queens and pornography invading their school libraries". Roberts also expressed concern over crime in the U.S.

Dans, also an editor of the project's guiding document, described Project 2025 as preparing a staff of conservatives to fight the deep state with their training from partner organizations. He wrote that Project 2025 has four pillars:

- The Mandate for Leadership
- A personnel database, open to submissions from the public that Heritage can share with Trump's team
- The Presidential Administration Academy, an online educational system
- A secret playbook for creating teams and plans to activate in case the president says "so help me God".

Policies

The plan contains some culture war issues and broad policies that depart from past Republican orthodoxy.

Economy

Project 2025 provides a range of options for economic reform that vary in their degree of radicalism. It is critical of the Federal Reserve, which it blames for the business cycle, and proposes abolishing it; it advocates instead that the dollar be backed by a commodity like gold. It recommends eliminating full employment from the Federal Reserve's mandate, instead focusing solely on targeting inflation.

The Project envisions eventually moving from an income tax to a consumption tax, such as a national sales tax. In the interim, the Project seeks to extend the Tax Cuts and Jobs Act of 2017 (TCJA). It further recommends simplifying individual income taxes to two flat tax rates: 15% on incomes up to the Social Security Wage Base ($168,600 in 2024), and 30% above that. An unspecified standard deduction would be included, but most deductions, credits and exclusions would be eliminated. The proposal would likely increase taxes significantly for millions of low- and middle-income households.

It aims to reduce the corporate tax rate from 21% to 18% because the Mandate authors see it as the most harmful tax. The 2017 TCJA cut the rate from 35% to 21%. It proposes reducing the capital gains rate for high earners to 15% from the 2024 level of 20%. After these reforms are implemented, it recommends that a three-fifths vote threshold be required to pass legislation that increases individual or corporate income tax. The constitutionality of such "legislative entrenchment" is debated, but most legal scholars agree it is not allowed.

The project proposes merging the Bureau of Economic Analysis, the Census Bureau, and the Bureau of Labor Statistics into a single organization, and aligning its mission with conservative principles. It recommends maximizing the hiring of political appointees in statistical analysis positions. It also recommends that Congress abolish the Consumer Financial Protection Bureau. It plans to abolish the FTC, which is responsible for enforcing antitrust laws, and shrink the role of the National Labor Relations Board, which protects employees' ability to organize and fight unfair labor practices. Some of the authors worked for Amazon, Meta, and Bitcoin companies directly or as lobbyists. One expert claimed inconsistencies in the plan are designed for fund-raising from certain industries or donors that would benefit.

Project 2025 suggests abolishing the Economic Development Administration (EDA) at the Department of Commerce, and, if that proves impossible, having the EDA instead assist "rural communities destroyed by the Biden administration's attack on domestic energy production". Project 2025 also seeks to facilitate innovations in the civilian nuclear industry.

The project declares that "God ordained the Sabbath as a day of rest" and recommends legislation requiring that Americans be paid more for working on Sunday. It also aims to institute work requirements for people reliant on the Supplemental Nutrition Assistance Program, which issues food stamps. It recommends that OSHA be more lenient on small businesses and that the overtime exception threshold be kept low enough not to burden businesses in rural areas.

Project 2025 is split on the issue of foreign trade. Mandate author Peter Navarro advocates what he calls a fair trade policy of reciprocal, higher tariffs on the European Union, China, and India, to achieve a balance of trade, though not all U.S. levies are lower than those of its major trading partners. On the other hand, Mandate author Kent Lassman of the Competitive Enterprise Institute promotes a free trade policy of lowering or eliminating tariffs to cut costs for consumers, and calls for more free trade agreements. He argues that Trump's and Biden's tariffs have undermined not just the American economy, but also the nation's international alliances.

Regarding banking regulation, Mandate recommends combining the Office of the Comptroller of the Currency, the Federal Deposit Insurance Corporation, the National Credit Union Administration, and parts of the Federal Reserve that perform regulatory and fiscal supervision. The document says deposit insurance undermines bank depositors' incentive to monitor their banks' balance sheet.

Education and research

A major concern of Project 2025 is what it calls "woke propaganda" in public schools. In response, it envisions a significant reduction of the federal government's role in education, and the elevation of school choice and parental rights. To achieve that goal, it proposes closing the Department of Education, and giving states control over education funding and policy. Programs under the Individuals with Disabilities' Education Act (IDEA) would be administered instead by the Department of Health and Human Services. The National Center for Education Statistics (NCES) would become part of the Census Bureau.

The federal government, according to Project 2025, should be no more than a statistics-keeping organization when it comes to education. Federal enforcement of civil rights in schools should be significantly curtailed, and such responsibilities should be transferred to the Department of Justice, which would then be able to enforce the law only through litigation. The federal government should no longer investigate schools for signs of disparate impacts of disciplinary measures on the basis of race or ethnicity. Project 2025 blames federal government overreach for schools prioritizing "racial parity in school discipline indicators—such as detentions, suspensions, and expulsions—over student safety".

Project 2025 further advocates that Title I of the Elementary and Secondary Education Act of 1965 be allowed to expire, removing $18 billion in federal funds for schools in low-income areas. Public funds for education should be available as school vouchers with no strings attached, even for parents sending their children to private or religious schools. Cuts should be made to the funding for free school meals. The Head Start program that provides services to children of low-income families should be ended. Roger Severino claimed the program does not provide value, but never provided evidence for his claims. For the project's backers, education is a private rather than a public good. Project 2025 criticizes any programs to forgive student loans.

Project 2025 encourages the president to ensure that "any research conducted with taxpayer dollars serves the national interest in a concrete way in line with conservative principles". For example, research in climatology should receive considerably less funding, in line with Project 2025's views on climate change.

Environment and climate

Mandate's climate section was written by several people, including Mandy Gunasekara, whom Trump previously chose as the EPA's chief of staff, and Bernard McNamee, whom Trump appointed to the Federal Energy Regulatory Commission. Four of the report's top authors have publicly engaged in climate change denial. McNamee dismisses climate change mitigation as progressive policy. Gunasekara acknowledges the reality of human-made climate change but considers it politicized and overstated. She claimed to have been an instrumental advocate for the United States withdrawal from the Paris Agreement in 2017. On the other hand, project director Paul Dans accepts only that climate change is real, not that human activity causes it.

The manifesto advises the president to go further than merely nullifying Biden's executive orders on climate change, to "eradicate climate change references from absolutely everywhere". It proposes abandoning strategies for reducing greenhouse gas emissions responsible for climate change, including by repealing regulations that curb emissions, and abolishing the National Oceanic and Atmospheric Administration (NOAA), which the project calls "one of the main drivers of the climate change alarm industry". One scientific expert said these policies would endanger lives, are shooting the messenger, and serve the climate change denial movement.

The Inflation Reduction Act increased the Department of Energy's Loan Programs Office's loan budget from $40 billion to $400 billion. Project 2025 supports repealing the Inflation Reduction Act and closing the Loan Programs Office. McNamee advocates that the DOE reorient funding at the national labs it sponsors from climate change and renewable energy research to making energy more affordable. He advocates entrenching these changes by closing the DOE's Office of Energy Efficiency and Renewable Energy and Office of Clean Energy Demonstrations.

Project 2025 advocates downsizing the EPA. In particular, it seeks to close the EPA's Office of Environmental Justice and External Civil Rights. Heritage Foundation energy and climate director Diana Furchtgott-Roth has suggested that the EPA support the consumption of more natural gas, despite climatologists' concern that this would increase leaks of methane (CH_4), a greenhouse gas more potent than carbon dioxide (CO_2) in the short term. Project 2025 wants to reverse a 2009 EPA finding that carbon dioxide emissions are harmful to human health, preventing the federal government from regulating greenhouse gas emissions. It also advocates preventing the EPA from using private health data to determine the effects of pollution. Under its blueprint, the expansion of the national electrical grid would be blocked, the transition to renewable energy stymied, and funding for the DOE's Grid Deployment Office curtailed. Nonpartisan experts said renewable energy projects will have to slow down if the electrical grid is not expanded.

The project further advocates that states be prevented from adopting stricter regulations on vehicular emissions, as the state of California has, and that regulations on the fossil fuel industry be relaxed. For example, restrictions on oil drilling imposed by the Bureau of Land Management could be removed.

Project 2025's manifesto includes eliminating climate change mitigation from the National Security Council's agenda and encouraging allied nations to use fossil fuels. It declares that the federal government has an "obligation to develop vast oil and gas and coal resources" and supports Arctic drilling.

Project 2025 recommends incentives for members of the general public "to identify scientific flaws and research misconduct" and to legally challenge climatology research.

Republican climate advocates have disagreed with Project 2025's climate policy. Joseph Rainey Center for Public Policy president Sarah E. Hunt considered the Inflation Reduction Act crucial, and U.S. Representative (now U.S. Senator) John Curtis said it was vital that Republicans "engage in supporting good energy and climate policy". American Conservation Coalition founder Benji Backer noted growing consensus among younger Republicans that human activity causes climate change, and called the project wrongheaded.

The project abandons the habitat conservation goal of 30 by 30, and advocates that the National Flood Insurance Program be replaced by private insurers. The League of Conservation Voters has criticized this as a giveaway to private industry.

Expansion of presidential powers

Project 2025 seeks to place the federal government's entire executive branch under direct presidential control, eliminating the independence of the DOJ, the FBI, the Federal Communications Commission, the Federal Trade Commission, and other agencies. The plan is based on a controversial interpretation of unitary executive theory, "an expansive interpretation of presidential power that aims to centralize greater control over the government in the White House." Kevin Roberts said that all federal employees should answer to the president. Since the Reagan administration, the Supreme Court has embraced a stronger unitary executive led by conservative justices, the Federalist Society, and the Heritage Foundation, and overturned some precedents limiting Project 2025's vision of executive power.

Project 2025 proposes that all Department of State employees in leadership roles should be dismissed no later than January 20, 2025. It calls for installing senior State Department leaders in "acting" roles that do not require Senate confirmation. Kiron Skinner, who wrote the State Department chapter of Project 2025, ran the department's office of policy planning for less than a year during the Trump administration before being forced out of the department. She considers most State Department employees too left-wing and wants them replaced by those more loyal to a conservative president. When asked by Peter Bergen in June 2024 if she could name a time when State Department employees obstructed Trump policy, she said she could not.

If Project 2025 were implemented, Congressional approval would not be required for the sale of military equipment and ammunition to a foreign nation, unless "unanimous congressional support is guaranteed".

Trump said in 2019 that Article Two of the U.S. Constitution grants him the "right to do whatever as president", a common claim among supporters of the unitary executive theory. Similarly, in 2018, Trump claimed he could fire special counsel Robert Mueller. Trump is not the first president to consider policies related to the unitary executive theory. The idea has seen a resurgence and popularization within the Republican Party since the 9/11 terrorist attacks in 2001.

In 2023, Stephen Miller proposed immediately mobilizing the military at the start of second Trump administration for domestic law and immigration enforcement under the Insurrection Act of 1807. Jeffrey Clark, a senior fellow at CRA and Project 2025 contributor, has investigated using the Insurrection Act for other purposes, including suppressing protests like the George Floyd protests. The Heritage Foundation denied Project 2025 planned to use the Insurrection Act, but Mandate has a single line that says it is possible to use the Insurrection Act to secure the southern border. Russell Vought said the CRA was working to keep legal and defense communities from preventing use of the Insurrection Act.

Clark also promoted making the Department of Justice less independent of the president in order to let Trump prosecute his political rivals. For his alleged acts while working at the DOJ during the end of Trump's term, Clark has become a co-defendant in the Georgia election racketeering prosecution and an unnamed co-conspirator in the federal prosecution of Trump for alleged election obstruction.

Media Matters reported that several Project 2025 partners praised the 2024 Supreme Court decision Trump v. United States, which grants broad immunity from prosecution for acts committed in the course of a president's official duties.

Federal staffing

Project 2025 proposes reclassifying tens of thousands of federal civil service workers as political appointees in order to replace them with Trump loyalists. It established a personnel database shaped by the ideology of Donald Trump. Throughout his first term, Trump was accused of removing people he considered disloyal, regardless of their ideological conviction, such as former attorney general William Barr. In 2020, White House Presidential Personnel Office employees James Bacon and John McEntee developed a questionnaire to test potential government employees' commitment to Trumpism. Bacon and McEntee joined Project 2025 in May 2023. The project uses a similar questionnaire to screen potential recruits for adherence to its agenda. For Trump's second term the project recommends that a White House Counsel be selected who is "deeply committed" to the president's "America First" agenda.

In 2020, Trump established the Schedule F job classification by executive order. Biden rescinded this classification at the beginning of his presidency. Russell Vought, who worked on Schedule F during Trump's first term, joined Project 2025. He said that Trump's second term would destroy the administrative state and fire and traumatize federal workers. He advocated reviving Schedule F during Trump's second term. Kevin Roberts said: "People will lose their jobs. Hopefully their lives are able to flourish in spite of that. Buildings will be shut down. Hopefully they can be repurposed for private industry." On January 20, 2025, Trump signed an executive order to that effect.

In response to Schedule F's reinstatement, several unions sued and took other protective measures to prevent its full implementation. At the end of Biden's term, about 4,000 government positions were deemed political appointments. If fully implemented, Schedule F will affect tens of thousands of professional federal civil servants who have spent many years working under both Democratic and Republican administrations. According to Georgetown University professor of public policy Donald Moynihan, while apolitical and meritocratic selection of public servants is vital to administrative functioning, the Republican Party increasingly views them and public sector unions as threats, or resources to be controlled. Political scientist Francis Fukuyama has said that while the federal bureaucracy is in dire need of reform, Schedule F would "dangerously undermine" the government's functionality.

Project 2025 encourages Congress to require federal contractors to be 70% U.S. citizens, ultimately raising the limit to 95%. It also calls for the president to reinstate Executive Orders 13836, 13837 and 13839, which relate to how federal agencies address labor unions, grievances, and seniority.

By June 2024, the American Accountability Foundation, a conservative opposition research organization led by former Senate aide Tom Jones, was researching certain key high-ranking federal civil servants' backgrounds. Called Project Sovereignty 2025, the undertaking received a $100,000 grant from Heritage. Its objective was to post online the names of 100 people who might oppose Trump's agenda. Announcing the grant in May 2024, Heritage wrote that the research's purpose was "to alert Congress, a conservative administration, and the American people to the presence of anti-American bad actors burrowed into the administrative state and ensure appropriate action is taken." Some found Project Sovereignty 2025 reminiscent of McCarthyism, when many Americans were persecuted and blacklisted as alleged communists.

Foreign affairs

In Mandate, Christopher Miller derides the Biden administration for letting the USA's military capabilities decay. Mandate's preface says, "For 30 years, America's political, economic, and cultural leaders embraced and enriched Communist China and its genocidal Communist Party while hollowing out America's industrial base." Miller also focuses on China strategy, warning that China is building up its military and its nuclear arms could potentially rival the United States'. He discusses the need to maintain a balance of power that prevents China from becoming a regional hegemon. He suggests that China is a belligerent state best countered by an expanded nuclear arms program and raised expectations of regional allies like South Korea and Japan.

On the campaign trail, Trump avoided giving specific foreign policy plans, but Kiron Skinner, who wrote Project 2025's State Department chapter, considers China a major threat, and is critical of any conciliatory move toward it.

in Mandate, Max Primorac suggests significant changes to the U.S. Agency for International Development (USAID)'s mission due to "divisive political and cultural agenda that promotes abortion, climate extremism, gender radicalism, and interventions against perceived systemic racism". Mandate recommends the word gender be purged from all USAID programs and documents. It also mentions specific United Nations agencies the U.S. should cease to support financially and suggests the president be given more power to allocate U.S. foreign aid.

Project 2025 favors neither interventionism nor isolationism, instead insisting that all decisions related to foreign policy prioritize national interests.

Nuclear policy

The Mandate argues that the U.S. should maintain its nuclear umbrella only for member nations of the North Atlantic Treaty Organization (NATO), and that these countries should be responsible for deploying their own conventional forces to deter Russian aggression. As of June 2024, 24 of the 32 NATO members had allocated at least 2% of their Gross Domestic Product (GDP) to defense.

Christopher Miller advocates that the U.S. replace all its Cold War nuclear capabilities and infrastructure and develop the LGM-35 Sentinel. He also promotes testing more weapons in violation of the Comprehensive Nuclear-Test-Ban Treaty. The Biden administration also promoted the Sentinel's development.

More specifically, the Mandate calls for a speech shortly after inauguration to "make the case to the American people that nuclear weapons are the ultimate guarantor of their freedom and prosperity", to be followed by additional funding for nuclear weapons modernization programs to develop and produce new warheads such as W87-1 Mod and W88 Alt 370 and deploy as-yet-unproven directed-energy and space-based weapons and a "cruise missile defense of the homeland". The plan advocates continuing the B61-12 and W80 modernization programs, which began in 2013 and 2014 respectively and have been continued by each administration since. It also advocates restarting funding for nuclear armed submarine-launched cruise missiles. The Obama administration retired similar missile programs in 2010. Trump restarted funding these SLCM-N in 2018, but the Biden administration canceled the funding in 2022.

Plans include placing multiple warheads on each Minuteman III ICBM and its Sentinel replacement by 2026, putting nuclear warheads on Army ground-launched missiles, adding nuclear capabilities to hypersonic missile systems, directing the Air Force to investigate a road-mobile ICBM launcher, expanding the pre-positioning of nuclear bombs and weapons in Europe and Asia, and directing the National Nuclear Security Administration (NNSA) to "transition to a wartime footing". This would be funded by directing the NNSA to submit monthly briefings to the Oval Office and separate budget requests from the Energy Department, along with directing the Office of Management and Budget to submit a supplemental budget request to Congress.

The Bulletin of the Atomic Scientists called Project 2025's nuclear policy "the most dramatic buildup of nuclear weapons since the start of the Reagan administration" and the beginning of a new global nuclear arms race. It includes the prioritization of nuclear weapons development and production over other security programs, rejecting Congressional efforts to find cost-effective alternatives for the plans, increasing the number of nuclear weapons above treaty limits, rejecting current arms control treaties, expanding the NNSA's capability and funding, preparing to test new nuclear weapons despite the Comprehensive Nuclear Test Ban Treaty, and accelerating all missile defense programs.

Healthcare and public health

Roger Severino wrote Mandate's chapter on health care. He accuses the Biden administration of undermining the traditional nuclear family, and wants to reform the Department of Health and Human Services (DHHS) to promote this household structure. According to Project 2025, the federal government should prohibit Medicare from negotiating drug prices and promote the Medicare Advantage program, which consists of private insurance plans. Federal healthcare providers should deny transgender people gender-affirming care.

Project 2025 suggests a number of ways to cut funding for Medicaid, such as caps on federal funding, limits on lifetime benefits per capita, and letting state governments impose stricter work requirements on beneficiaries of the program. Other proposals include limiting state use of provider taxes, eliminating preexisting federal beneficiary protections and requirements, increasing eligibility determinations and asset test determinations to make it harder to enroll in, apply for, and renew Medicaid, providing an option to turn Medicaid into a voucher program, and eliminating federal oversight of state Medicaid programs. The project also advocates cutting funding to the Department of Veterans Affairs (VA).

Project 2025 aims to alter the National Institutes of Health (NIH) by making it easier to fire employees and to remove DEI programs. Conservatives consider the NIH corrupt and politically biased. Severino says the CDC should not publish health advice, because it is inherently political.

Immigration reforms

This Mandate for Leadership suggests abolishing the Department of Homeland Security (DHS) and replacing it with an immigration agency that incorporates Customs and Border Protection (CBP), the Transportation Security Administration (TSA), Immigration and Customs Enforcement (ICE), the U.S. Citizenship and Immigration Services (USCIS), and elements of the departments of Health and Human Services and DOJ. Other tasks could be privatized. The admission of refugees would be curtailed, and processing fees for asylum seekers would increase, something the Project deems "an opportunity for a significant influx of money". Immigrants who wish to have their applications fast-tracked would have to pay even more.

In April 2024, Heritage said that Project 2025 policy includes "arresting, detaining, and removing immigration violators anywhere in the United States".

Stephen Miller, a key architect of immigration policy during the Trump presidency, is a major figure in Project 2025. In November 2023, Miller told Project 2025 participant Charlie Kirk that the operation would rival the scale and complexity of "building the Panama Canal". He said it would include deputizing the National Guard in red states as immigration enforcement officers under Trump's command. These forces would then be deployed in blue states.

Miller considered deputizing local police and sheriffs for the undertaking, as well as agents of the Bureau of Alcohol, Tobacco, Firearms and Explosives and the Drug Enforcement Administration. He said these forces would "go around the country arresting illegal immigrants in large-scale raids" who would then be taken to "large-scale staging grounds near the border, most likely in Texas", to be held in internment camps before deportation. Trump has also spoken of rounding up homeless people in blue cities and detaining them in camps. Funding for the Mexico–United States border wall would increase.

Project 2025 encourages the president to withhold federal disaster relief funds granted by the Federal Emergency Management Agency (FEMA) should state or local governments refuse to abide by federal immigration laws, by, for example, not sharing information with law enforcement.

Identity

Project 2025 opposes what it calls "radical gender ideology" and advocates that the government "maintain a biblically based, social-science-reinforced definition of marriage and family". To achieve this, it proposes removing protections against discrimination on the basis of sexual or gender identity, and eliminating provisions pertaining to diversity, equity, and inclusion (DEI)—which it calls "state-sanctioned racism"—from federal legislation. Federal employees who have participated in DEI programs or any initiatives involving critical race theory might be fired.

Public school teachers who want to use a transgender student's preferred pronouns would be required to obtain written permission from the student's legal guardian. Project 2025's backers also want to target the private sector by reversing "the DEI revolution in labor policy" in favor of more "race-neutral" regulations. Project 2025 is part of a trend of intensifying backlash against DEI in the early 2020s.

The White House's Gender Policy Council would be disbanded. Government agencies would be forbidden from instituting quotas and collecting statistics on gender, race, or ethnicity. Project contributor Jonathan Berry explains, "The goal here is to move toward colorblindness and to recognize that we need to have laws and policies that treat people like full human beings not reducible to categories, especially when it comes to race." The U.S. Census Bureau would be reformed according to conservative principles.

Journalism

Project 2025 proposes reconsidering the accommodations given to journalists who are members of the White House Press Corps. It proposes defunding the Corporation for Public Broadcasting, a private, nonprofit corporation that provides funding for the Public Broadcasting System and National Public Radio, as "good policy and good politics" because it accounts for "half a billion dollars squandered on leftist opinion each year". It also entertains the idea of revoking NPR stations' noncommercial status, forcing them to relocate outside the 88–92 range on the FM dial, which could then be taken by religious programming. Brendan Carr, who wrote the article on the Federal Communications Commission in Project 2025, was appointed by Trump to lead the FCC, and subsequently launched an investigation into NPR and PBS, in accordance with Project 2025.

The Project also proposes allowing more media consolidation by changing FCC rules that would allow for the converting local news programs into national news programs.

The project pushes for legislation requiring social media companies to not remove "core political viewpoints" from their platforms and proposes banning TikTok. It also would prevent the Federal Elections Commission from countering misinformation or disinformation about election integrity.

Law enforcement

In the view of Project 2025, the Department of Justice (DOJ) has become "a bloated bureaucracy with a critical core of personnel who are infatuated with the perpetuation of a radical liberal agenda" and has "forfeited the trust" of the American people due to its role in the investigation of alleged Trump–Russia collusion. It must therefore be thoroughly reformed and closely overseen by the White House, and the director of the Federal Bureau of Investigation (FBI) must be personally accountable to the president.

A DOJ reformed per Project 2025's recommendations would combat "affirmative discrimination" or "anti-white racism", citing the Civil Rights Act of 1964. Former Trump DOJ official Gene Hamilton argues that "advancing the interests of certain segments of American society... comes at the expense of other Americans—and in nearly all cases violates longstanding federal law." Therefore, the DOJ's Civil Rights Division would "prosecute all state and local governments, institutions of higher education, corporations, and any other private employers" with DEI or affirmative action programs. Hamilton was also general counsel for America First Legal, a Project 2025 partner organization.

Legal settlements called "consent decrees" between the DOJ and local police departments would be curtailed. According to Project 2025, if the responsibilities of the FBI and another federal agency, such as the Drug Enforcement Administration (DEA), overlapped, then the latter should take the lead, leaving the FBI to concentrate on (other) serious crimes and threats to national security.

Project 2025 acknowledges that capital punishment is a sensitive matter, but nevertheless promotes it to deal with what it considers an ongoing crime wave and for "particularly heinous crimes" such as pedophilia, until the U.S. Congress legislates otherwise.

Like Trump, Project 2025 believes that the District of Columbia is infested with crime and as such suggests authorizing the Uniformed Division of the Secret Service to enforce the law outside of the White House and the immediate surroundings.

National security

Project 2025 would require the U.S. Department of Defense to abolish its DEI programs and immediately reinstate all service members discharged for not getting vaccinated against COVID-19. The United States Armed Forces would not be authorized to take climate change into account in evaluating national security threats.

Project 2025 identifies all communist and socialist parties and states, including China, as threats to U.S. national security. It also expresses concern over China's influence on American society, and recommends banning the social network TikTok (which it accuses of espionage) and the Confucius Institutes (which it accuses of corrupting American higher education). The Project also expresses concern over Chinese intellectual property theft and accuses Big Tech of acting on the behalf of the Chinese Communist Party to undermine the U.S.. American pension funds would be encouraged to avoid Chinese investments and American companies seeking to invest in sensitive sectors in China would face restrictions or denial of permission.

Pornography and adult content

In the foreword of Project 2025's Mandate, Kevin Roberts argues that pornography promotes sexual deviance, the sexualization of children, and the exploitation of women; is not protected by the First Amendment to the United States Constitution; and should be banned. He recommends the criminal prosecution of people and companies producing pornography, which he compares to addictive drugs. Previously, the Supreme Court has ruled against attempts to ban pornography on First Amendment grounds. Roberts has said that despite Trump's past of appearing in Playboy magazine and having an affair with a porn actor, he could still be a powerful advocate against pornography because "our lord works with imperfect instruments". When the Republican Party nominated him for president in 2016, Trump signed a pledge to examine the "public health impact of Internet pornography on youth, families and the American culture". He did not fulfill this promise. The American Principles Project, part of the Project 2025 advisory board, has advocated for state laws that reduce pornography's accessibility.

Transportation infrastructure

Project 2025 recommends curtailing the Bipartisan Infrastructure Law of 2021, which authorizes funding for de-carbonizing transportation infrastructure. It views the Federal Transit Administration (FTA) unfavorably, calling it a waste of money. It suggests cutting federal funding for transit agencies nationwide in the form of the Capital Investment Grants (CIG) program. It wants the FTA to conduct "rigorous cost–benefit analysis" even though the agency already scrutinizes projects before allocating funding.

Women's reproductive health

Project 2025's proponents maintain that life begins at conception. The Mandate says that the Department of Health and Human Services (HHS) should "return to being known as the Department of Life", as Trump HHS secretary Alex Azar nicknamed it in January 2020, voicing his pride in being "part of the most pro-life administration in this country's history". Project 2025 said Trump should align federal organizations with the policy that abortion is not health care and promote American health "from conception to natural death".

In 2022, the Supreme Court ruled in Dobbs v. Jackson Women's Health Organization that, contrary to Roe v. Wade, state abortion bans are constitutional, but Project 2025 encourages the next president "to enact the most robust protections for the unborn that Congress will support".

Severino told a Students for Life conference that Project 2025 was developing executive orders and proposing regulations to roll back Biden's abortion policies and solidify a new environment in the wake of Dobbs. For example, the Reproductive Healthcare Access Task Force Biden created would be replaced by a dedicated pro-life agency that would advocate for health of unborn children and women with newfound authority.

The project opposes any initiatives that in its view subsidize single parenthood. It encourages the next administration to rescind some of the provisions of the Family Planning Services and Population Research Act of 1970, enacted as Title X of Public Health Service Act, which offers reproductive healthcare services, and to require participating clinics to emphasize the importance of marriage to potential parents.

Severino writes in the project's manifesto that the Food and Drug Administration should reverse its approval of the abortion pills mifepristone and misoprostol on ethical grounds. Project 2025 proposes eliminating insurance coverage of the morning-after pill Ella, which insurance companies are required to cover under the Affordable Care Act (ACA). Severino also recommends that the Centers for Disease Control and Prevention "update its public messaging about the unsurpassed effectiveness of modern fertility awareness-based methods" of contraception, such as smartphone applications that track a woman's menstrual cycle. He says that the HHS should require states to report the method and motivation of each abortion, the gestational age of the fetus, and the mother's state of residence.

The project seeks to restore Trump-era "religious and moral exemptions" to contraceptive requirements under the ACA, including emergency contraception (Plan B), which it deems an abortifacient, to defund Planned Parenthood, and to remove protection of medical records involving abortions from criminal investigations if the records' owners cross state lines. Project 2025 contributor Emma Waters told Politico, "I've been very concerned with just the emphasis on expanding more and more contraception." According to her, Project 2025's policy recommendations constitute not restrictions but rather "medical safeguards" for women. Waters said she wanted the NIH to investigate contraception's long-term effects.

In Project 2025's "Department of Justice" section, Gene Hamilton calls for enforcement of federal law against using the U.S. Postal Service for transportation of medicines that induce abortion. Project 2025 seeks to revive provisions of the Comstock Act that banned mail delivery of any "instrument, substance, drug, medicine, or thing" that could be used for an abortion. Congress and the courts have narrowed Comstock laws, allowing contraceptives to be delivered by mail.

Project 2025 aims to enforce Comstock more rigorously at the national level to prohibit sending abortion pills and medical equipment used for abortions through the mail. The project proposes criminal prosecution of senders and receivers of abortion pills. It does not explicitly advocate banning abortion, but some legal experts and abortion rights advocates said adopting the Project's plan would cut off access to medical equipment used in surgical abortions to create a de facto national abortion ban.

To prevent teenage pregnancy, Project 2025 advises the federal government to deprecate what it considers promotion of abortion and high-risk sexual behaviors among adolescents. It also seeks to remove HHS's role in shaping sex education, arguing that this is tantamount to creating a monopoly.

Other initiatives

Database

To be admitted to the "Presidential Personnel Database", a recruit must respond to several prompts about their ideologies. One is "name one living public policy figure whom you greatly admire and why". A recruit's social media accounts will be scrutinized. The key people involved with the database are former Trump administration officials, including John McEntee.

Heritage claims to have nearly 20,000 profiles as of July 2024, though those could simply be empty after someone started the process and did not finish. Staffers have privately questioned how many of the people in the database could actually work in a future administration.

Once the second Trump presidency began, White House screening teams fanned out to federal agencies to screen job applicants for their loyalty to the president's agenda. On his first day in office, Trump signed an executive order to restore merit-based federal hiring practices and "dedication to our Constitution".

Training modules

The training modules that members in the database had access to were relatively light on substance and heavy on ideology. The database and modules were low-budget productions. ProPublica has published 23 of the videos Project 2025 created to support the training. According to ProPublica, 29 of the 36 speakers in the videos worked for Donald Trump in some capacity, including on his 2016–2017 transition team, in his administration, or in his 2024 reelection campaign.

Draft executive orders

Project 2025 and the CRA have also helped draft executive orders that are not public. Draft orders include invoking the Insurrection Act to deploy the military for domestic law enforcement, which the Heritage Foundation denied. At least 38 Democratic members of Congress have called on Project 2025 to release the draft executive orders, also known as the "180-Day Playbook", saying it is in the public interest to know what is being planned. In July 2024, Micah Meadowcroft, the director of research at CRA, said in a secretly recorded interview that the orders would be distributed during the presidential transition in such a way that they would never be made public.

Dawn's Early Light

On September 24, 2024, Heritage Foundation president and Project 2025 architect Kevin Roberts was due to release the book Dawn's Early Light: Taking Back Washington to Save America, with a foreword by Republican vice-presidential nominee JD Vance. The book was initially subtitled Burning Down Washington to Save America.

In the book, Roberts "outlines a peaceful 'Second American Revolution' for voters looking to shift the power back into the hands of the people". In a review of the book, Vance wrote: "We are now all realizing that it's time to circle the wagons and load the muskets. In the fights that lay ahead, these ideas are an essential weapon." Colin Dickey of the New Republic says the book reveals paranoid, Stalinist tactics like using conspiracy theories to violently enforce their vision for the world. Roberts criticizes birth control and law enforcement (preferring a more heavily armed frontier-like society), while promoting public prayer as a key tool in the competition with China.

On August 6, 2024, the book's release was postponed until after the November election.

Roberts held book release events in Manhattan and Washington, D.C. On November 13, 2024, The Guardian published an account of the hostile reception its reporter encountered at one of the events. Although invited to attend the event, the reporter was expelled.

Implementation

After Trump won the 2024 election, he nominated several Project 2025 contributors to positions in his second administration. Some nominees need confirmation by the U.S. Senate, as required by the Appointments Clause of the U.S. Constitution. His choice to lead the FCC, Brendan Carr, wrote the manifesto's chapter about the agency. Tom Homan, picked by Trump to act as a "border czar", also contributed to the Project 2025 document. Trump also nominated Russell Vought to direct the Office of Management and Budget. After these selections, Karoline Leavitt issued a statement saying "President Trump never had anything to do with Project 2025"; Leavitt herself is an instructor for Project 2025's "Conservative Governance 101" training program and was chosen by Trump as White House Press Secretary.

Other authors or contributors to Project 2025 who have been nominated or appointed to roles in the second Trump administration include Michael Anton (contributor, appointed Director of Policy Planning); Paul S. Atkins (contributor, nominated for Chair of the Securities and Exchange Commission); Steven G. Bradbury (contributor, nominated for Deputy Secretary of Transportation); Troy Edgar (contributor, nominated for Deputy Secretary of Homeland Security), Jon Feere (contributor, appointed Chief of Staff at ICE), Pete Hoekstra (contributor, nominated for ambassador to Canada), Roman Jankowski (contributor, appointed Chief Privacy Officer and Chief Freedom of Information Act Officer for the Department of Homeland Security), and Peter Navarro (author, appointed Senior Counselor for Trade and Manufacturing).

Aspects of the project implemented in the first days of Trump's second term include executive orders to reopen large areas of Alaska, including the Arctic National Wildlife Refuge, to oil drilling, and the withdrawal of a pending Biden administration ban on PFAS in drinking water. Trump's executive orders on immigration and federal implementation of the death penalty went further than Project 2025 recommended. His policy on TikTok diverged from Project 2025's call to ban the app.

Metadata show that United States Office of Personnel Management memos sent to federal workers were written by Peter Noah and James Sherk, both associated with the Heritage Foundation. Time magazine found that, as of January 24, more than 60% of the executive actions Trump had issued "mirror or partially mirror proposals from Project 2025".

Trump's early executive actions closely mirrored Project 2025's outline, reinforcing concern that his administration is rapidly enacting a pre-planned right-wing playbook. His executive orders on gender policies, federal hiring, and foreign aid reflect the project's policies, signaling a shift toward more autocratic governance. Paul Dans has expressed satisfaction that Trump's early executive orders align with the project's Mandate for Leadership. One executive order diverts funding from public schools to private school vouchers, a move directly aligned with Project 2025's goal to reshape the education system. Project 2025 advocated changes to foreign aid, including a foreign aid freeze; in January 2025, Trump initially signed an executive order freezing new foreign aid for 90 days, and later in January the administration sent a notice requiring that stop-work orders be issued for all existing foreign aid.

Trump's early budget freezes and spending cuts reflected Project 2025's aggressive push to downsize government programs and shift power to conservative institutions. In addition, his push to weaken FEMA is part of a broader Project 2025 strategy to reduce the federal government's role in disaster relief and shift responsibility to state and private entities. Trump's policy actions reignited scrutiny of Project 2025, with critics warning that his administration is actively implementing its agenda across multiple sectors.

On February 7, 2025, the National Institutes of Health (NIH) announced that it would change its maximum indirect cost rate for university research grants from 50% in some cases to 15%, as recommended by Project 2025.

Reactions and responses

Supporters of Project 25 say it will dismantle a government bureaucracy that is, they believe, unaccountable and biased toward liberalism. Critics of the project have called it authoritarian, Christian nationalist and autocratic. Legal experts say it would undermine the rule of law, the separation of powers, the separation of church and state, and civil liberties. The project has also been criticized for its language, which has been called warlike and apocalyptic—for example, describing the "battle plan" to regain control of the government, which some have interpreted as threatening political violence.

Critics have also criticized the project's aims and professionalism, with an August 2024 profile in Politico calling it underfunded, disorganized, and "self-hyped". Some critics have suggested Project 2025 is based on personal vengeance, or that its proposals for "national conservatism" are merely an "attempt to intellectually retrofit a rationale for Trumpism". Political journalist Michael Hirsh says Project 2025 is anti-intellectual, citing scholar Matthew Continetti, who says it embraces "a furious reaction against elites of all stripes".

Allegations of authoritarianism

Democracy experts, political scholars, and other commentators have described the project as dangerous, risking authoritarianism, and apocalyptic. Many legal experts have said it would undermine the rule of law, the separation of powers, the separation of church and state, and civil liberties. Snopes says "people across the political spectrum" are worried the plan is a precursor to authoritarianism.

Ruth Ben-Ghiat, a scholar of fascism and authoritarian leaders at New York University, wrote in May 2024 that Project 2025 "is a plan for an authoritarian takeover of the United States that goes by a deceptively neutral name". She said the project's intent to abolish federal departments and agencies "is to destroy the legal and governance cultures of liberal democracy and create new bureaucratic structures, staffed by new politically vetted cadres, to support autocratic rule". She continues:

Appropriating civil rights for white Christians furthers the Trumpist goal of delegitimizing the cause of racial equality while also making Christian nationalism a core value of domestic policy. Doing away with the separation of church and state is the goal of many architects of Trumpism, from Project 2025 contributor Russ Vought to far-right proselytizer Michael Flynn, who uses the idea of "spiritual war" as counterrevolutionary fuel ... Bannon, Roberts, Stephen Miller, and other American incarnations of fascism are convinced that counterrevolution leading to autocracy is the only path to political survival for the far right, given the unpopularity of their positions (especially on abortion) and their leader's boatload of legal troubles.

Political experts have said Project 2025 represents significant executive aggrandizement, a type of democratic backsliding involving government institutional changes made by elected executives that has been seen in Russia, Hungary, Turkey, and Venezuela. Cornell University political scientist Rachel Beatty Riedl says this global phenomenon represents threats to democratic rule not from violence but rather from using democratic institutions to consolidate executive power. She says, "if Project 2025 is implemented, what it means is a dramatic decrease in American citizens' ability to engage in public life based on the kind of principles of liberty, freedom and representation that are accorded in a democracy." Phillip Wallach, a senior fellow studying separation of powers at the American Enterprise Institute, characterized the project as visions that bleed into authoritarian fantasies.

Donald B. Ayer, the deputy attorney general under George H. W. Bush, said,

Project 2025 seems to be full of a whole array of ideas that are designed to let Donald Trump function as a dictator, by completely eviscerating many of the restraints built into our system. He really wants to destroy any notion of a rule of law in this country ... The reports about Donald Trump's Project 2025 suggest that he is now preparing to do a bunch of things totally contrary to the basic values we have always lived by. If Trump were to be elected and implement some of the ideas he is apparently considering, no one in this country would be safe.

Michael Bromwich, who was Justice Department inspector general from 1994 to 1999, remarked,

The plans being developed by members of Trump's cult to turn the DOJ and FBI into instruments of his revenge should send shivers down the spine of anyone who cares about the rule of law. Trump and rightwing media have planted in fertile soil the seed that the current Department of Justice has been politicized, and the myth has flourished. Their attempts to undermine DOJ and the FBI are among the most destructive campaigns they have conducted.

Max Stier of the Partnership for Public Service is among those who have voiced concern the project would revive the early-American spoils-and-patronage system that awarded government jobs to those loyal to a party or elected official rather than by merit. The Pendleton Act of 1883 mandated that federal jobs be awarded by merit. Former Trump campaign and presidency senior advisor Steve Bannon has advocated for the plan on his War Room podcast, hosting Jeffrey Clark and others working on the project.

Spencer Ackerman and John Nichols in The Nation and Chauncey DeVega of Salon.com have called Project 2025 a plan to install Trump as a dictator, warning that Trump could prosecute and imprison enemies or overthrow American democracy altogether. Longtime Republican academic Tom Nichols wrote in The Atlantic that Trump "is not bluffing about his plans to jail his opponents and suppress—by force, if necessary—the rights of American citizens".

In Mother Jones, Washington bureau chief David Corn called Project 2025 "the right-wing infrastructure that is publicly plotting to undermine the checks and balances of our constitutional order and concentrate unprecedented power in the presidency. Its efforts, if successful and coupled with a Trump (or other GOP) victory in 2024, would place the nation on a path to autocracy."

Peter M. Shane, a law professor who writes about the rule of law and the separation of powers, wrote:

> The Times quotes Vought's impatience with conservative lawyers in the first Trump administration who were unwilling to do Trump's bidding without hesitation. Criticizing the timidity of traditional conservative lawyers, Vought told the Times: "The Federalist Society doesn't know what time it is." As for making the Justice Department an instrument of White House political retribution, Vought would unblinkingly jettison the norm of independence that presidents and attorneys general of both parties have carefully nurtured since Watergate. "You don't need a statutory change at all, you need a mind-set change," Vought told the Post. "You need an attorney general and a White House Counsel's Office that don't view themselves as trying to protect the department from the president."

For his 2023 book The Undertow: Scenes from a Slow Civil War, Dartmouth College professor Jeff Sharlet spent years traveling to meet Trump supporters. He writes that his initial "objections to describing militant Trumpism as fascist have fallen away". He says Project 2025 is influenced by the New Apostolic Reformation, a rapidly growing evangelical and charismatic movement aligned with Trump. Sharlet says that the Project's first mandate to "restore the family as the centerpiece of American life and protect our children" is "Q-coded—it's 'protect the blood,' it's the 14 words, it's all this stuff".

In a June 2024 column for the libertarian magazine Reason, Steven Greenhut criticized Project 2025 for increasing governmental power, and risking authoritarianism and abuse, by centralizing control of the executive in the president.

In July 2024, Donald Moynihan of Georgetown University wrote that:

> [Project 2025] would add measurably to the risks of corruption in American government. President Trump talks a lot about the deep state. Again, that is very similar to what authoritarians in other countries have tended to do to justify taking more direct control over civil service systems. So I think there is a dangerous pattern here, where it would not just reduce the quality of government. It would also open the door for abuses of political power.

In July 2024, Reed Galen said that "Project 2025 is Maga's endorsed blueprint for turning America into an authoritarian state".

LGBTQ+

LGBTQ+ writers and journalists have criticized Project 2025 for its proposals to remove protections for LGBTQ+ people and to outlaw pornography by claiming it is an "omnipresent propagation of transgender ideology and sexualization of children". Writing for Dame magazine, Brynn Tannehill argued that The Mandate for Leadership in part "makes eradicating LGBTQ people from public life its top priority", while citing passages from the playbook linking pornography to "transgender ideology", arguing that it related to other anti-transgender attacks in 2023.

Guthrie Graves-Fitzsimmons, the author of Just Faith: Reclaiming Progressive Christianity, criticized Project 2025 for appealing to Christian nationalism. In particular, Graves-Fitzsimmons criticized Severino's chapter on the U.S. Department of Health and Human Services and his opposition to the Respect for Marriage Act that repealed the Defense of Marriage Act and codified the federal definition of marriage to recognize same-sex and interracial marriage.

On July 10, 2024, hacktivist group SiegedSec announced it had hacked the Heritage Foundation and acquired 200 gigabytes of user information, citing opposition to Project 2025 and the organization's general opposition to transgender rights as the group's primary motivation.

Political

Several conservatives and Republicans have criticized the plan for its stances on climate change and trade. Ron DeSantis embraced Project 2025 in August 2023.

In June 2024, Democratic Congressman Jared Huffman announced the formation of The Stop Project 2025 Task Force. He warned that the project would hit "like a blitzkrieg" and said: "if we're trying to react to it and understand it in real time, it's too late. We need to see it coming well in advance and prepare ourselves accordingly." He and others have called the project "dystopian". The Biden campaign launched a website critical of Project 2025 hours before his June 27 debate with Trump. In August 2024, an oversize copy of The Mandate was used as a prop during the 2024 Democratic National Convention.

After Trump won the 2024 United States presidential election, many Republicans, Trump allies, and other right-wing commentators, including right-wing podcast host Matt Walsh, said on social media that Project 2025 was the official plan. On his podcast, former White House advisor Steve Bannon praised Walsh's comment, and Texas official Bo French tweeted, "So can we admit now that we are going to implement Project 2025?"

Other reactions and responses

In April 2024, historian Emma Shortis wrote:

> The Mandate's veneer of exhausting technocratic detail, focused mostly on the federal bureaucracy, sits easily alongside a Trumpian project of revenge and retribution ... [plans] more broadly aim for nothing less than the total dismantling and restructure of both American life and the world as we know it. ... The Mandate doesn't specify who the next conservative president might be, but it is clearly written with Trump in mind ... Project 2025's Mandate is iconoclastic and dystopian, offering a dark vision of a highly militaristic and unapologetically aggressive America ascendant in "a world on fire". Those who wish to understand Trump and the movement behind him, and the active threat they pose to American democracy, are obliged to take it seriously.

In April 2024, responding to criticism of the project, Heritage released a document titled "5 Reasons Leftists HATE Project 2025". Restating many of its previously published objectives, the document said that "the radical Left hates families" and "wants to eliminate the family and replace it with the state"; that leftist "elites use the 'climate crisis' as a tool for scaring Americans into giving up their freedom"; that the "radical Left wants our country to travel down [the] same dark path" toward becoming the Soviet Union, North Korea, or Cuba; and that "woke propaganda" should be eliminated at every level of government.

In July 2024, Oren Cass, author of the labor chapter, criticized the project's leadership: "Gaining productive power requires focusing on people's problems and explaining how you are going to solve them, not pounding the table for Christian nationalism or a second American revolution."

Reading Project 2025 as a Manifesto

{Written by Ruth Houghton and Aoife O'Donoghue; published 26 February on the website Verfassungsblog on Matters Constitutional. Used under Creative Commons license, https://verfassungsblog.de/reading-project-2025-as-a-manifesto/}

Manifestos have very often prefigured constitutional crisis, revolution, the overthrowing of legal orders, and set the terms of what follows. Project 2025, or the 2025 Presidential Transition Project, can be read as a manifesto, and one that is now well on its way to being implemented. Examining it through the lens of constitution (re)making sets out some of the terms in which it could be opposed, including by counter-manifesto.

Constitutional Change and Manifestos

The US started with a manifesto. The US Declaration of Independence is a firm articulation of a claim to have the necessary constituent power to make a new state. It throws off the legitimacy of the old legal order – the British constitutional imperial structure – and sets out the basis for the "new world" it was seeking to create.

Manifestos are more common in law than we may presuppose. War Manifestos were long part of the apparatus of legality in warfare in international law. The French Declaration of the Rights of Man and of the Citizen, for instance, remains part of French constitutional law. The Haitian Declaration of Independence was key to establishing black sovereignty. There are also the manifestos that challenge exclusionary practices of constitutional law; for example, feminist manifestos such as Olympe de Gouges' which claimed that the Citizens in the French Declaration must include women, as they too fought the revolution, claimed in other words constituent power on behalf of women to make the new state.

These types of political manifestos (and the constitutions they go on to inspire) are a form of utopian legal blueprint for the imagined state they are demanding and creating. They pre-figure the legal order that they wish to come into place. Where manifestos might outline how power should be wielded, how citizenship will be bestowed and how human rights will be guaranteed in this 'better place', the constitutions that follow set up these terms. The liberal utopianism of the US Constitution was not utopian for all, of course. The two-thirds solution embedded racist citizenship into its roots while the continued absence of the Equal Rights Amendment has meant that women's bodily autonomy and equality of citizenship are continuously bombarded and reliant on the judiciary for their protection.

What Frankenberg describes as the 'constitution as political manifesto' turns what were revolutionary, political or normative claims into mere statements to be confirmed, declared or reaffirmed in constitutional form. Through legal performance, they take on a form of apparent immutability. If we are in a 'post-constitutional moment' (as Russell Vought argues), or witnessing the counter-constitution (as Kim Lane Scheppele labels it), then it is imperative that constitutional scholars expose this myth of immutability and start to critique the claims to constituent power that are emerging. What then can we learn from reading Project 2025 as a constitutional manifesto and the ways in which it aims to remake the state?

Reading Project 2025 as a Manifesto

Project 2025 is very much a manifesto. It lays out a vision that is both backward looking, in that it claims to be bringing the US constitution back to its roots, while also forward looking in laying out a very clear utopian blueprint. Blueprint utopias (in contrast to, for instance, feminist utopias which tend towards a "critical" model, that rejects an end state) are very often invoked in imperial or authoritarian projects. They are the utopias that people most often are referring to when they talk about oppression.

While both Donald Trump and J.D. Vance distanced themselves during the election campaign from Project 2025, and Project 2025 says all over the front page of its website that it is not a Trump plan, the first few weeks in office suggest its contents certainly are one of the blueprints for the re-ordering of the US Constitutional system. Many of the document's authors either worked with previously or are now part of the administration.

The document was put together by the Heritage Foundation, a US right-wing think tank. It describes itself as a 'historic movement' to 'take down the Deep State and return the government to the people.' Now, that phraseology might make some immediately sceptical, but then again, calling George III a tyrant probably did in 1787 also. To construct a potential constituency from its audience, it states

> "If we are going to rescue the country from the grip of the radical Left, we need both a governing agenda and the right people in place, ready to carry this agenda out on day one of the next conservative administration."

The use of "we" is a common tactic employed by manifesto writers to attract likeminded individuals and/or to construct legitimate constituent power. These can be read as prefigurative claims to have the power to bring about these fundamental changes to the constitutional structure of the US. It established a collective "we" that is positioned against an 'other', here that 'other' are those who they describe as radical Left, but also the many others targeted in the Project.

Reading Project 2025 as a manifesto exposes how in today's legal reality, it is a blueprint for what is happening. A quick comparison between the demands and recent Executive actions suffices. It is a long document, but the elements they themselves highlight is a good starting place.

A Gendered Pattern

The website's front-page states that one aim is to '[b]an biological males from competing in women's sports'. Of course Trump's Executive Order goes further, but in the main text of Project 2025 there is a clear link made between trans people and pornography and what it describes as 'radical gender ideology'. If we place that alongside the Project's aim to dismantle Diversity, Inclusion and Equity (DEI), and Trump's Executive Orders to 'maintain a biblically based, social-science-reinforced definition of marriage and family' a gendered pattern emerges.

The project claims that they are '[r]estoring the family as the centerpiece of American life'. But what we get here, is an almost stereotypical move from making trans people non-citizens by removing their identity, then moving into family, and from here of course, undermining the rights of all women. A return to social-science and biblical definitions of the family is one where women, and their bodies, are confined and controlled. The definition of women and men contained in another Executive Order, is one that begins, biologically inaccurately, from conception, where, according to Project 2025, life begins.

Reading Project 2025 as a utopian manifesto facilitates and necessitates an exploration of the underpinning fundamental values at the core of the project. In her approach to utopia, Ruth Levitas reminds scholars to be "archaeological" in their study of utopian projects; to ask who is included and who is excluded, and to consider the harms and exclusions that ground the political demands. The gender ideology is not hidden beneath the surface in Project 2025. Blueprint utopias might invoke an inevitable final destination, but what Levitas and theories of utopianism provide are the tools to interrogate how these blueprints are constructed, disseminated, and ultimately to start to expose their hideous harms that inform their "dreams".

Project 2025 is also deeply sceptical of climate change, promoting, for instance oil and gas exploration in Alaska and ending wind energy development. Another Trump Executive Order goes about 'Unleashing Alaska's Extraordinary Resource Potential' while rescinding a Biden Executive Order that supported offshore wind.

Overthrowing the Constitution

Many of the Executive Orders are being challenged before US Courts, the Just Security blog has an excellent tracker for keeping up to date on these cases. The reaction of the Executive to the judiciary is important. The Executive Order that denies birthright citizenship, guaranteed under the 14th Amendment to the US Constitution, is being held up across four courts. The order itself is damaging to ideas of the rule of law, to introduce an Executive Order that quite obviously contradicts the constitution.

But J.D. Vance's reaction to the judiciary holding up executive orders was to state that '[j]udges aren't allowed to control the executive's legitimate power'. Project 2025 argues there is a duty to protect the powers and privileges of the President from encroachments by Congress, the judiciary, and the administrative components of departments and agencies. Dismantling the notion of the separation of power as a fundamental commitment within US constitutional law and creating an all against the President scenario.

Project 2025 emphasises the need for political appointees to be answerable only to the President. The Ensuring Accountability for All Agencies Executive Order partially brings that into place; it removes vast swathes of oversight and accountability, leaving just the President. Project 2025 is also clear that it wishes the administrative state to be dismantled. For instance, it wanted the Centre for Disease Control (CDC) to be 'prohibited from taking on a prescriptive character'. The CDC is now delaying releasing information on, for instance, bird flu.

Project 2025 is very clear on what it sees as the extent of power the Executive Office ought to hold, stating 'the overall situation is constitutionally dire, unsustainably expensive, and in urgent need of repair. Nothing less than the survival of self-governance in America is at stake.' This is a manifesto call to action, and we should take seriously how far they will go to implement this plan

Stop Project 2025

What we have seen over the past few weeks is the implementation of a manifesto that aims to completely alter the US legal order while adamant that it is returning to its roots. In 'dismantling the administrative state; defending the nation's sovereignty and borders; and securing God-given individual rights to live freely', Project 2025 foreshadows the basis on which the Trump Administration is acting. And whilst it might not offer *the whole basis*, thus far it has given us a fair indication of travel.

Reading Project 2025 as a manifesto heralds a warning of what is potentially to come, it offers a blueprint for the US Constitutional structure it seeks to prefigure. But what reading these sorts of texts as manifestos also highlights is the need to be alert for the counter-manifestos that are emerging – in other words, the resistance to Project 2025, which was present even before Trump's election – whether that is in the form of women's magazines outlining their projections for the state of women's rights if Project 2025 is implemented, to the (albeit overly commercialised) t-shirt people can buy in support of "Stop Project 2025".

Manifestos as prefigurative constitutional documents are more common than we imagine. Though Project 2025's handbook for constitutional re(making) is rare in both its detail and the speed at which it is being implemented. Regarding it as such, enables the possibility of opposition on its own terms, a counter-manifesto to prefigure a new and different constitutional future to one currently being constructed.

| 6 |

DOGE

The United States Digital Service (USDS) was renamed and re-purposed as the Department of Government Efficiency (DOGE) by Executive Order on 20 January 2025. The name is a nod to the "Doge" Internet meme. The cryptocurrency Dogecoin paid homage to the meme, which experienced a temporary surge in price when mentioned by Elon Musk back on 20 December 2020. Musk's subsequent tweets proffered it as "the people's crypto", but he has no known direct involvement in the currency as of the writing of this book.

The biggest concern voiced by opponents is that Musk is an unelected official with unprecedented powers. Trump said that Elon Musk is "in charge" but not an employee. Amy Gleason was named as administrator of DOGE (rumored to be surprised herself when asked), but the White House admits that Musk is still the senior White House adviser who oversees the Department.

There is much confusion over the authority of the department's degree of access, employee vetting, and security clearances. Under Musk's direction, employees have been locked out of offices and emails, and millions of dollars have been "turned off" for myriad programs, with some turned on again. His team of mostly young men (one of whom resigned over unapologetic racist comments) is criticized because of their expertise in technology and not forensics or accounting, as would be expected if trimming waste was the intention of the efforts. Wired Magazine is treating its journalistic coverage of DOGE explicitly as a technology issue.

Musk himself has acted as a de facto representative of the administration since before the inauguration, even meeting with officials from other nations. Ever since the inauguration, he has been seen in many instances of coverage of the President, giving rise to criticism that he is in charge rather than the President himself.

Concerning, but downplayed, were the comments of Musk's four-year-old son (named 'X Æ A-Xii') toward President Trump during an Oval Office interview. "You're not the president and you need to go away" was followed by "I want you to shut Your fucking mouth up!" Interestingly, an image was posted on social media of Elon's son by the Resolute Desk alongside the image of President Kennedy's son playing beneath the desk, captioned "history repeats itself". Some have proffered the idea that Musk has one of his children with him at all times in public, using them as a human shield given concerns over Luigi Mangione's recent murder of a CEO.

Social media has branded his Tesla Cybertruck as the "Swasticar" or "WankPanzer", as well as the "Incel Camino", "Deplorean", and "ClusterTruck". Portuguese editorial cartoonist Zez Vaz created an image showing 'Tank Man' (Tiananmen Square, 1989) standing in front of Cybertrucks instead of tanks. Sheryl Crow sold her Tesla and donated proceeds to NPR, whose funding is being threatened. California Governor Newsom countered the revocation of federal credits for buying electric vehicles by proposing a state-level credit for EVs, one that was interpreted as excluding Tesla products. Sales are plummeting in Europe, over 40% down from last year. Government monitors in some offices were hacked, displaying an AI video of Trump licking Musk's bare feet. In short, he's a rock star to those who support Trump, but for the rest of the country, not so much.

Layoffs and Buyouts

Approximately two million federal employees were offered the incentive to resign or retire with most of a year's severance. Many were discouraged by their departments from taking the deal under the belief they may not get paid, and in the end about four percent of those offered the deal took it. The White House target was 5-10%. Trump said he plans to have layoffs to make up the difference. This process was first blocked then allowed by the courts on 12 February.

As he had done with Twitter (now known as X), Musk let go large percentages of the workforce of several agencies, including those responsible for monitoring the nuclear arsenal — and is scrambling to get back those who are needed to function.

Wall of Receipts

Musk admitted there were and will be mistakes in his reckoning, but a list of hundreds of such mistakes -- including a false claim of millions of dollars of condoms sent to Gaza -- would take too long to detail here. According to NPR, referring to DOGE's website's ever-retracting "wall of receipts",

> DOGE deleted more than $2.5 billion from its initial batch of savings claims. This includes an adjustment to a triple-counted U.S. Agency for International Development (USAID) project worth up to $655 million, as highlighted by multiple media outlets. Savings from that USAID project are now listed as an estimated $18 million — less than 1% of the nearly $2 billion claimed at the tracker's launch.

Perhaps the biggest gaffe was touted by Trump, saying,"We identified and stopped $50m being sent to Gaza to buy condoms for Hamas ... They used them as a method of making bombs. How about that?" The White House press secretary reiterated the claim, saying DOGE and the Office of Management and Budget (OMB) "found that there was about to be 50 million taxpayer dollars that went out the door to fund condoms in Gaza ... a preposterous waste of taxpayer money". DOGE later retracted the claim, which is believed to have actually referred to $83M sent to Mozambique, one of the provinces being called Gaza.

It would be negligent to omit that, in the words of LeMonde, the Washington Post discovered that Musk, through his various business interests, "has benefited from $38 billion in contracts and government aid" in the last two decades. There is talk of billions more to come.

An Ultimatum

On 22 February, Musk put everyone on notice: "Consistent with President Donald Trump's instructions, all federal employees will shortly receive an email requesting to understand what they got done last week. Failure to respond will be taken as a resignation." The actual e-mail said "Please reply to this email with approx. 5 bullets of what you accomplished this week and cc your manager" and the deadline was 11:59 PM on Monday, 24 February.

It was met by a wave of abusive responses, including ridicule of Musk himself. Department heads told their employees not to answer, particularity the Department of Defense and the FBI, citing security concerns and existing chains of command regarding terminations. The "order" was then restated by Musk to have employees follow the previous instructions but report to their department heads.

ESTABLISHING AND IMPLEMENTING THE PRESIDENT'S "DEPARTMENT OF GOVERNMENT EFFICIENCY"

{Executive Order, 20 January}

By the authority vested in me as President by the Constitution and the laws of the United States of America, it is hereby ordered:

Section 1. Purpose. This Executive Order establishes the Department of Government Efficiency to implement the President's DOGE Agenda, by modernizing Federal technology and software to maximize governmental efficiency and productivity.

Sec. 2. Definitions. As used in this order:

(a) "Agency" has the meaning given to it in section 551 of title 5, United States Code, except that such term does not include the Executive Office of the President or any components thereof.

(b) "Agency Head" means the highest-ranking official of an agency, such as the Secretary, Administrator, Chairman, or Director, unless otherwise specified in this order.

Sec. 3. DOGE Structure. (a) Reorganization and Renaming of the United States Digital Service. The United States Digital Service is hereby publicly renamed as the United States DOGE Service (USDS) and shall be established in the Executive Office of the President.

(b) Establishment of a Temporary Organization. There shall be a USDS Administrator established in the Executive Office of the President who shall report to the White House Chief of Staff. There is further established within USDS, in accordance with section 3161 of title 5, United States Code, a temporary organization known as "the U.S. DOGE Service Temporary Organization". The U.S. DOGE Service Temporary Organization shall be headed by the USDS Administrator and shall be dedicated to advancing the President's 18-month DOGE agenda. The U.S. DOGE Service Temporary Organization shall terminate on July 4, 2026. The termination of the U.S. DOGE Service Temporary Organization shall not be interpreted to imply the termination, attenuation, or amendment of any other authority or provision of this order.

(c) DOGE Teams. In consultation with USDS, each Agency Head shall establish within their respective Agencies a DOGE Team of at least four employees, which may include Special Government Employees, hired or assigned within thirty days of the date of this Order. Agency Heads shall select the DOGE Team members in consultation with the USDS Administrator. Each DOGE Team will typically include one DOGE Team Lead, one engineer, one human resources specialist, and one attorney. Agency Heads shall ensure that DOGE Team Leads coordinate their work with USDS and advise their respective Agency Heads on implementing the President 's DOGE Agenda.

Sec. 4. Modernizing Federal Technology and Software to Maximize Efficiency and Productivity. (a) The USDS Administrator shall commence a Software Modernization Initiative to improve the quality and efficiency of government-wide software, network infrastructure, and information technology (IT) systems. Among other things, the USDS Administrator shall work with Agency Heads to promote inter-operability between agency networks and systems, ensure data integrity, and facilitate responsible data collection and synchronization.

(b) Agency Heads shall take all necessary steps, in coordination with the USDS Administrator and to the maximum extent consistent with law, to ensure USDS has full and prompt access to all unclassified agency records, software systems, and IT systems. USDS shall adhere to rigorous data protection standards.

(c) This Executive Order displaces all prior executive orders and regulations, insofar as they are subject to direct presidential amendment, that might serve as a barrier to providing USDS access to agency records and systems as described above.

Sec. 5. General Provisions. (a) Nothing in this order shall be construed to impair or otherwise affect:

(i) the authority granted by law to an executive department or agency, or the head thereof; or

(ii) the functions of the Director of the Office of Management and Budget relating to budgetary, administrative, or legislative proposals.

(b) This order shall be implemented consistent with applicable law and subject to the availability of appropriations.

(c) This order is not intended to, and does not, create any right or benefit, substantive or procedural, enforceable at law or in equity by any party against the United States, its departments, agencies, or entities, its officers, employees, or agents, or any other person.

THE WHITE HOUSE,
    January 20, 2025.

First DOGE Subcommittee Hearing

{26 February}

Marjorie Taylor Greene: Which grows bigger and bigger every year. In 2025, interest payments are projected to be $952 billion, which is more than our entire military budget. In 2026, it will be $1 trillion. And by 2035, $1.8 trillion. Over the next decade, total interest payments are projected to be $13.8 trillion. These interest payments don't serve a single American. They don't build a bridge, a road, provide disaster relief or fund a single part of the behemoth that is the federal government. These interest payments pay our masters who own our debt, and the American people are in debt slavery to everyone who owns our debt. Our crippling national debt and massively growing interest on our debt will destroy us, not destroy one political party or the other, it will destroy all of us together. It drives inflation, making life unaffordable for Americans struggling to financially survive. It is crippling small businesses struggling to be successful. Our massively growing debt and interest are the chains and shackles harnessed to every American and their children and every generation to come.

But first, let us be brutally honest about how this massive debt came to be in the first place. It came from Congress and from elected presidential administrations, and I believe enslaving our nation in debt is one of the biggest betrayals against the American people by its own elected government. The American people's anger over this betrayal is what gave birth to the concept of DOGE, the Department of Government Efficiency. In fact, DOGE became a major part of President Trump's campaign and led to his overwhelming victory in November. Every day Americans go to work, they run businesses, they have to earn their paycheck. No one guarantees it. And if they don't do a good job, they get fired. They also have to pay their bills, credit card debts, balance their checkbooks and scrap and save every penny they can in order to plan for that rainy day and hopefully retirement one day.

Private businesses only survive on hard-earned income by serving their customers so well that their customers pay them for the services and products they consume. If that business fails, its employees lose their jobs and paychecks and the owners lose their business and everything they risked along with it. Many go bankrupt in this process and lose everything. No one bails them out. They only survive by excellent customer service and smart financial management. This is the real world that most Americans live, work, and survive in every day. This is the pursuit of happiness, and this is how you pursue the American dream.

However, the federal government, government employees and unelected bureaucrats do not live by the same rules as the great American people and private businesses. The federal government's income is the American people's hard-earned tax dollars, their literal blood, sweat, and tears, and taxes are collected by law at gunpoint, don't pay your taxes and you go to jail. The federal government does not have to provide excellent customer service to earn its income. It takes your money whether you like it or not, and federal employees receive their paycheck no matter what, whether veterans receive their benefits or not, whether your mail shows up or not, and whether your tax dollars are used to help Americans in need or sent to foreign countries, for foreign people, for foreign causes. No matter how bad the federal government fails the American people, it still takes your money. It still pays its own federal employees and it never ever goes out of business. There are no consequences for bad customer service, total failure, and for enslaving the American people against their will. In the ever-growing and future all-consuming national debt,

Congress has a dismal approval rating that ranges between 12 and 20%. I don't blame the American people one bit for their sentiment and disgust. The American people will be watching this committee and how we tackle one of the biggest problems of our time. While we are a committee made up of the opposite far-reaching corners of Congress, we were each elected to serve and represent the American people and how their hard-earned tax dollars are spent. We as Republicans and Democrats can still hold tightly to our beliefs, but we are going to have to let go of funding them in order to save our sinking ship. This is not a time for political theater and partisan attacks. The American people are watching. The legislative branch can't sit on the sidelines. In this subcommittee, we will fight the war on waste shoulder to shoulder with President Trump, Elon Musk and the DOGE team. This week we turn our attention to improper payments by the federal government, including in Medicaid and Medicare. I'm looking forward to what we find out and how to solve this crisis.

I now yield to the Ranking Member Ms. Stansbury for her opening statement.

Melanie Stansbury: All right, well good morning everyone. Thank you Madam Chair, and welcome to the very first Subcommittee on Government Efficiency. As was said, this committee is tasked under the Oversight committee with ensuring that the government and the vital services that it provides from healthcare to national security actually work for the American people. And this is certainly a topic that we have worked on for many, many years here in the Oversight committee in which I personally have worked on as a former civil servant who worked at the Office of Management and Budget. And in fact, for anyone who has ever worked on these issues, you know that there is ample ground for bipartisan work to make the government work better for the American people and to ensure that it operates in a more efficient manner.

And in fact, all of us here on the Democratic side are ready to roll up our sleeves and to get to work. And just last week I had the opportunity to sit down with the Chairwoman and to discuss these very issues and opportunities to work across the aisle. And like the Chairwoman who shared some of her background with me, I grew up in a working family. I grew up working for small mom and pop family businesses and understand the necessity of balancing the books, making sure we can deliver and fiscal responsibility. And that's why today's hearing is focused on making sure that the federal government is doing what it's supposed to and digging into the more than $236 billion in improper payments that we see going out the door every single year. And we need to get to the bottom of that. And we need to make sure that we're putting into place rigorous oversight and controls to prevent fraud and abuse. And of course, to go after bad actors.

And that is why myself and the Oversight Ranking Member Connolly and other Democratic members of the committee sent a set of bipartisan ideas that we'd like to work on together that would root out waste fraud and abuse and modernize and streamline how our agencies deliver vital programs for the American people. These are programs that are important for our seniors and our families and healthcare and the education system, and we need bipartisan solutions to get across the finish line. And we've been trying over the last several years to get these ideas out of this committee, but unfortunately, the committee's priorities have been elsewhere under the current majority. So I hope we can fix that this Congress.

But we can't just sit here today and pretend like everything is normal and that this is just another hearing on government efficiency. I mean, all you have to do is look across this room and see that it is not a normal hearing because while we're sitting here, Donald Trump and Elon Musk are recklessly and illegally dismantling the federal government, shuttering federal agencies, firing federal workers, withholding funds vital to the safety and well-being of our communities and hacking our sensitive data systems.

In fact, while we were here discussing government waste on the House floor yesterday, Elon Musk was standing behind the Resolute Desk in the Oval Office with the President and the administration was making emergency court appeals to try to unlock his team's access to the Treasury payment system, which they claim they are using to study improper payments, which is the topic of this hearing. But here's the thing, the Treasury payment system, which includes social security information and bank accounts for millions of Americans and data that's critical to national security and the operation of the US government and payments that go out the door annually equal to almost a fifth of the US economy is not where the payment decisions are made because that happens inside the agencies that are currently being dismantled. And the people who actually investigate waste, fraud and abuse at these agencies are the inspector generals who Donald Trump fired his first week in office in a midnight massacre.

So we have to ask ourselves, what is really going on here? Why did Republicans block Elon Musk from appearing before this very committee last week? Why is the administration so eager to allow Elon Musk and his hackers to have access to proprietary and private information in the Treasury payment systems? Why are our colleagues across the aisle shielding them as they are clearly breaking the law? And why is the Vice President trying to rewrite the US Constitution by tweet and undermine the judiciary?

So obviously, we're in the Oversight committee and we have a lot of questions and so do the American people, especially while our colleagues across the aisle are trying to scoop up the savings from the dismantling of these agencies to pay for the largest permanent tax break in American history for billionaires and the folks that they're helping on their side of the aisle.

So let me close by saying this directly to Mr. Elon Musk. We are well aware that you are eager to engage with members of Congress on social media, but we're not here to play. If you have serious desire to engage in democracy and transparency, we welcome you to the Oversight Committee. Come and testify in front of the American people under oath because we want to know what you're up to. So if you're interested in talking to us, then please join us here in The People's House, in the House of Representatives. And with that, I yield back

Marjorie Taylor Greene: The Gentle lady yields. President Trump signed an executive order on his first day in office called Establishing and implementing the President's Department of Government Efficiency. The EO simply renamed an office in the White House that was actually established by President Obama in 2014 called the US Digital Service. President Trump can have Elon Musk into his Oval Office anytime he likes. I now recognize the chairman of the Oversight Committee Chairman James Comer.

James Comer: Well, thank you Chairwoman Green for holding today's hearing. To launch a war on waste. President Trump won an electoral landslide with a clear mandate from the American people to eliminate Washington waste and stop the theft of American tax dollars, and he is delivering on his promise. President Trump has empowered Elon Musk and DOGE to conduct a government-wide audit to identify solutions to curb waste and protect tax dollars. That's exactly what the mission of this committee is supposed to be, and I'm glad that my colleagues on the other side of the aisle have found a newfound interest in waste, fraud, and abuse.

With a staggering $37 trillion in national debt, we have no time to lose. A key place to start is improper payments. Since 2003, the government has lost $2.7 trillion because of improper payments, fraudsters, organized, criminals, hostile foreign actors, and even government employees have siphoned money away from those who truly qualify for assistance. For years, republicans and Democrats on Oversight committee have condemned this waste. But now that DOGE is taking real action, Democrats are choosing to defend the bureaucracy and status quo instead of standing up for the American people. I want to thank Chairwoman Green for holding this very important hearing, not only to expose the problems, but to find solutions. We stand with President Trump and DOGE in the fight to end waste, fraud and abuse in Washington.

With that, I yield back to Subcommittee Chairwoman Green and congratulations again, Chairwoman on holding this first hearing of the DOGE Subcommittee.

Marjorie Taylor Greene: Thank you, Mr. Chairman. The gentleman yields back. I now recognize the Ranking Member on Oversight, Mr. Connolly.

Gerald Connolly: Excuse me. Thank you, Madam Chair. And thank you for having this first hearing on DOGE. Improper payments is not a new subject. I remember joining Steve Lynch and then Todd Platts, Republican member from Pennsylvania in my freshman year talking about improper payments. At that time, improper payments were in the range of 30 billion a year. They're now in the range of $280 billion a year and times 10, we could cut almost $3 trillion from the debt if we addressed improper payments in a deliberative way, which GAO has called for in the high-risk category for years.

We can also secondly enforce the tax code. It's estimated that at least a half a trillion dollars a year is left on the table uncollected, but owed because of lack of resources in the IRS, again, times 10 is $5 trillion over a decade. And finally, we can modernize federal IT systems, which we've championed for years on this committee. We know that legacy systems alone could save hundreds of millions of dollars a year in operating and maintenance costs. So if we want to be serious about it, let's be serious about it. But the way not to do it is to fire the people charged with the remit of waste, fraud and abuse, namely, inspectors general. President Trump has already now fired 19, including most recently, the USAID Inspector General who dared to warn that we could lose a half a billion dollars of food aid because it's in warehouses not being moved because of the funding freeze that was imposed in AID. That's a cost we need to avoid. And for doing his job that idea was fired.

If we want to be serious, we've got to have objective neutral inspectors general who are monitoring government waste fraud and abuse and expenditures, and I think you would find Democrats more than willing partners in that kind of enterprise if we're going to be serious. But a wrecking crew, a wrecking crane, a wrecking ball is not going to do it, and we're not going to support that approach to waste fraud and abuse in the federal government. I yield back. Thank you.

Marjorie Taylor Greene: The gentleman yields. The President of the United States has the prerogative to fire anyone that has overseen $36 trillion in debt enslaving the American people, and rightfully so.

I'm pleased to welcome today's expert panel of witnesses who each bring unique experience and expertise that will be valuable to today's discussion. I'd first like to welcome Mr. Haywood Talcove, the Chief Executive Officer for Government at LexisNexis Risk Solutions, Inc. His commitment to customers needs allows LexisNexis to develop market-leading solutions that have enabled customers to stop fraud, waste, and abuse.

Next, we have Mr. Stewart Whitson, the Senior Director of Federal Affairs at the Foundation of Government Accountability. Stuart was previously a special agent in the FBI, a US Army veteran, and now spends his time at FGA, advocating to improve welfare, the workforce, and other policy.

Next, we have Ms. Dawn Royal, a certified welfare fraud investigator in the state of Wyoming and Director for the United Council of Welfare Fraud. She advocates for investigating and preventing fraud of government benefits and has done so over the past 16 years.

Finally, we have Mr. Dylan Hedtler- Gaudette, the director of Government Affairs at the Project on government Oversight. Dylan leads advocacy efforts and policy reforms to a wide range of good governance. I thank each of our witnesses for being here today, and I look forward to your testimony.

Pursuant to committee Rule 9G, The witnesses will please stand and raise their right hand. Do you solemnly swear or affirm that the testimony you are about to give is the truth, the whole truth, and nothing but the truth, so help you God?

Witnesses: I do.

Marjorie Taylor Greene: Let the record show that the witness has answered in the affirmative. Thank you. You may take a seat. We appreciate you being here today and look forward to your testimony. Let me remind the witnesses that we have read your written statement and it will appear in full in the hearing record. Please limit your oral statement to five minutes. As a reminder, please press the button on the microphone in front of you so that it is on and the members can hear you. When you begin to speak. The light in front of you will turn green. After four minutes, the light will turn yellow. When the red light comes on, your five minutes have expired, and we would ask that you please wrap up. I now recognize Mr. Talcove for his opening statement.

Haywood Talcove: Chairwoman Green Ranking Member Stansbury and distinguished members of the committee. For over a decade, a silent war has been waged against American taxpayers, not with bombs or guns, but with data and technology. Outdated government systems permit criminals to access unlimited sums of money. During the pandemic, they stole $1 trillion. 70% of those dollars went overseas. Shockingly, it's just not criminals exploiting the system. It's the flawed system itself acting as the accomplice.

If left unchecked, the US government will continue to lead the world in funding cyber criminals. This is a data and technology problem and it demands a data-driven response. Criminal syndicates have turned benefit programs into their personal ATM machines, exploiting those in need who wait months for benefits that may never come. These ruthless crooks use our money to fund child trafficking, disperse drugs in our communities and terrorism. For years, criminal networks have stolen personal information from the public and private sector. They exploit real identities to manipulate antiquated government systems, siphoning up billions and taxpayers hard-earned money. We continue to pay benefits to deceased and incarcerated individuals. Direct money to bad actors flagged on the Do Not Pay list and overlook duplicate social security numbers by not following best practices. During the pandemic, a simple cross-check of PPP loan recipients against IRS records would've exposed massive fraud and prevented payments to transnational criminals who sold their "sauce" on the dark web. To stop this, we must reclaim control of our systems, not just from the criminal syndicates, but the flawed systems enabling them. Smarter technology data and identity verification are not optional. Their necessity is to protect taxpayers and ensure aid reaches those who truly need it. Now, the use of AI is fundamentally changing society, but in the hands of criminals, it has become a weapon. Lawbreakers are now using it to supercharge the award on taxpayers.

They use AI to create fake identity documents that pass biometric verifications, bots, flood portals with thousands of fraudulent claims per second, and deep fakes that mimic real applicants bypass the outdated NIST 800-63 standards from 2017. Honest and deserving people seeking access to government benefits suffer through endless application forms that are nearly impossible to navigate, but criminals from Russia, China, and Romania gain access with ease. The private sector has fraud rates below 3%. Meanwhile, the public sector operates at a 20% fraud rate. The solution is clear. It's already used every day to protect consumers. You seamlessly interact with your bank through an app that verifies your identity in milliseconds.

There's no excuse for the government to lag if we do the following. Number one, implement identity verification on the front end. Criminals should never receive a dime. Eliminate self-certification. No more honor system for billion dollar programs and continuous auditing. Keep verifying because criminals never stop adapting. Pay and Chase does not work. Of the $250 billion stolen in pandemic unemployment fraud, less than 5 billion has been recovered. The idea in government that you cannot have speed and security is fiction.

I urge Congress to consider making the following legislative changes. Number one, update the 1974 Privacy Act to allow for data sharing and matching. Number two, fund a budget for fraud prevention in each Appropriation Bill, the USDA spends one 20th of 1% on fraud. Mandate that individuals caught stealing from entitlement programs, pay hefty fines, and are removed from the program permanently. And finally, eliminate broad-based categorical eligibility. This committee has a choice. Continue losing this war against criminal cartels in nation states or fight back and save $1 trillion annually. Fraud prevention is not benefit prevention, it's the key to ensuring that every dollar reaches those who truly need it. Hard-working. Americans rely on these programs not just to survive, but to build better lives for their families. When criminals exploit the system, they just don't steal money. They steal opportunities. Stopping fraud isn't about denying benefits. It's about protecting them. This crime has two victims. The first are the taxpayers, and the second are those seeking benefits. The fraudsters, cartels, and criminal syndicates are watching this hearing. I'm sure of it. It's time to show them that America will not fund its own destruction. Thank you and I look forward to your questions.

Marjorie Taylor Greene: Thank you, Mr. Talcove. I now recognize Ms. Royal for her opening statement.

Dawn Royal: Good morning, Chairwoman Green, Ranking Member Stansbury and Committee members. My name is Dawn Royal. I'm a certified welfare fraud investigator, two-term past president and a current director of the United Council on Welfare Fraud. The United Council on Welfare Fraud is a national professional organization dedicated to protecting the integrity in our nation's public assistance programs. We are the only national organization singularly focused on the detection, prevention and prosecution of welfare fraud.

For too long, agency bureaucrats have pitted citizens access to welfare programs against the integrity of those programs. Access versus integrity should never be an either-or dichotomy. We can all agree that access to public assistance is crucial. America's citizens should not be hungry or deprived of medical care because of their inability to pay. However, making sure vulnerable citizens have access to these welfare programs should not mean that we simply turn a blind eye to integrity. If we do not pursue the prevention, detection and prosecution of fraud, taxpayers become the victims as the welfare programs become slush funds for anyone wanting to supplement their income with SNAP benefits, absolve themselves from the financial responsibility of medical bills, and using Medicaid to further taxpayer exploitation by taking advantage of cash assistance, energy assistance, child care, and other social welfare programs.

One example of a welfare fraud is a case that I investigated that was criminally prosecuted last year. The applicant mother failed to disclose her children's father as well as his employment and income on multiple applications she submitted for Medicaid, SNAP and Low Income Energy Assistance. The co-defendant father worked a steady job earning a six-figure salary and provided an enviable lifestyle for his family, including vacations, luxury vehicles, snowmobiles, motorhomes, lavish gifts, including one from the wife to the husband, which was a $1,200 bottle of bourbon. Evidence we presented at trial included a candidate registration forms filed by the defendant father when he ran for town council and later mayor of the town where he declared he lived at the same address provided by his wife on her public assistance programs.

This was a case of greed, but it emphasizes how easy it was for these criminals to make false statements on applications in order to receive benefits from multiple programs that they were never eligible for. I could spend the rest of my day providing countless examples of how taxpayer-funded programs are exploited and the message would be the same. Investigators continue to be hamstrung by antiquated regulations, conflicting directives from federal agencies, and the lack of access to technology. Sadly, investigators have also found themselves at odds with the career bureaucrats who recite watered-down facts about fraud in order to promote their political agendas. Specifically, we can look to the career bureaucrats who have historically claimed that the fraud rate in SNAP is less than 1%. The disregard for the value of integrity is evidenced by the less than one 20th of 1% of the SNAP budget spent on the prevention, detection and prosecution of fraud. As part of Medicaid unwinding debacle, the bureaucrats specifically directed states that they, I quote, "Cannot recover or recoup the cost of services from a beneficiary, even if they have been found after an administrative hearing or criminal proceeding to have committed Medicaid beneficiary fraud or abuse."

Sadly, it is already apparent that career bureaucrats are not being totally transparent as they attempt to protect spending and broken programs. We fail to understand how mitigating the rampant fraud in Medicaid SNAP and other welfare programs stands up or strengthens the welfare programs. Fact is the opposite is true. Ignoring fraud and gaslighting fraud statistics erodes the very foundations of the programs that are essential to their future viability.

There are things this committee can do to help the investigators fighting the war on fraud. Number one, eliminate self-attestation in the application process for all programs. Number two, funding for technology. That includes identity verification tools that will help prevent fraud. The current pay and chase model is not sustainable. Number three, immediately implement the National Accuracy Clearinghouse, the NAC, that will provide data to states to prevent duplicate in all of the social welfare programs. And four, allocate direct funding with mandates restricting the use of the funding to the prevention, detection and prosecution of fraud.

In closing, we're at a crossroads. Those of us who have firsthand knowledge of the degree in which public welfare programs are being attacked, know that reform is absolutely necessary. Reform to the recipient application process, the billing process, and Medicaid, and how SNAP benefits are processed and how providers and retailers are authorized. We thank you for the opportunity for UCOFF to participate in this hearing. We feel that the investigators who are on the front lines fighting the daily battle against the war on fraud need to be at the table and participating in the development of action plans that will make a difference in protecting the programs and defending the taxpayers.

Marjorie Taylor Greene: Thank you, Ms. Royal. I now recognize Mr. Whitson for his opening statement.

Mr. Whitson: Chairwoman Greene, Ranking Member Stansbury, members of the subcommittee thank you for the opportunity to testify today.

On the campaign trail, president Trump promised to take on the bloated bureaucracy in DC, rebuild trust in the DOJ and the FBI, crack down on waste, fraud and abuse and restore common sense. And on day one, he started delivering on those promises with a wave of executive orders and the official launch of DOGE, which he of course tasked Elon Musk to lead. Already DOGE efforts have brought to the public's attention countless examples of wasteful spending, including $59 million paid to luxury hotels in New York to house illegal immigrants, 1.5 million to advance DEI in Serbia's workplaces, $32, 000 for a transgender comic book in Peru. The list goes on, but rather than applauding the work of DOGE, the left has launched a coordinated campaign to try to demonize Mr. Musk with the hope of shifting focus away from the disastrous waste, fraud, and abuse that occurred on Biden's watch. Guess what? It's not working, because no matter what political party people hail from, the vast majority of Americans agree that $10 million worth of food funneled to al-Qaeda was probably not the best use of taxpayer money.

There's another source, a key source of wasteful spending that DOGE and the subcommittee should set their sights on next, and that's Medicaid waste and fraud. While initially meant as a program for the truly needy Medicaid has bloated into a massive welfare program for millions of able-bodied adults lured into the trap of government dependency. As Medicaid has grown, so too has mismanagement. Today, more than one in $5 spent on Medicaid is improper. In Medicaid alone fraud and mismanagement is on track to cost US taxpayers, get this, more than $1 trillion over the next 10 years. When it comes to the problem of improper payments, the Medicaid program is the biggest culprit and culpice encompassing nearly one-third of all federal improper payments. More than 80% of Medicaid improper payments are due to one thing, eligibility errors. If Congress wants to help President Trump address wasteful spending, then targeting eligibility errors in Medicaid should be one of your top priorities.

Bottom line, to address this challenge, Congress can take three decisive actions. First, Congress can strengthen the Medicaid program through legislative action. That would include repealing Biden's disastrous Medicaid streamlining rule, which ties the hands of states trying to remove ineligible enrollees. You can, and should, do this through reconciliation and it will produce $164 billion in savings, if you do. You can also strengthen verification requirements to ensure only eligible individuals receive benefits and ensure a nationwide NAC is implemented without delay.

Second thing Congress can do is to help President Trump's DOGE effort by ensuring that entrenched partisan bureaucrats don't stand in the way of reform. Musk and his DOGE team have already found hundreds of billions of dollars funneled into wasteful, fraudulent and flat-out insane projects, but they've only scratched the surface. If this much fraud has been exposed in just a few weeks, imagine what else is buried under layers of red tape and government excuses.

Guess what? All of these insane projects have one thing in common, they were all approved and funded by unelected bureaucrats. These and other entrenched bureaucrats are already pledging to fight against President Trump's efforts to improve government accountability and efficiency. Personnel is policy and without competent staff to faithfully execute the President's agenda, the DOGE project will fail. This is where Congress can help. Congress can support the President and carrying out his DOGE effort by making all executive branch employees at will codifying the President's authority to fire unproductive or insubordinate agency employees as needed. At the same time, Congress can grant the President authority to permanently eliminate vacant positions and consolidate non-essential positions across agencies and departments to help promote efficiency and put the right people in the right seat.

The third thing Congress can make President Trump's DOGE cost-cutting and deregulatory reforms permanent by passing the Reigns Act. There's only one big problem with the DOGE effort; most of its work can be undone by a future president with a stroke of a pen. To make President Trump's DOGE reforms permanent Congress must act, and the best way to do this is to pass the Reigns Act. This would return Article One, Budgetary Power of the Purse to Congress while promoting deregulation. It would also help lock in the DOGE reforms and cement President Trump's legacy as the most consequential, deregulatory and cost-cutting president in US history.

The American people are watching it's time for Congress to act. Thank you. I look forward to your questions.

Marjorie Taylor Greene: Thank you, Mr. Whitson. I now recognize Mr. Hedtler-Gaudette for his opening statement.

Mr. Hedtler-Gaudette: Thank you, Chairwoman Greene, Ranking Member Stansbury and members of the subcommittee. My name is

Dylan Hedtler-Gaudette and I'm the director of Government Affairs at the Project on Government Oversight or POGO. I appreciate the opportunity to be with you here today to talk about the critical issue of bringing more accountability and transparency to federal spending, including; rooting out waste, fraud and abuse.

Since our founding in 1981, POGO has been focused on promoting more accountability and rooting out wasteful spending and promoting efficiency, especially at the Department of Defense. We have a long and well-established track record on these issues and we take a back [inaudible 00:36:29] when it comes to promoting a better and more effective government, which necessarily includes a federal government that is a good and responsible steward of taxpayer dollars.

Let's take a moment to pause here to talk a little bit about terms that we're going to hear a lot today and the difference between them. Waste is different from fraud. Fraud is different from abuse, and abuse is different from both. When we talk about improper payments, they are a subset of those other three categories, but that doesn't tell us the whole picture either. Sometimes improper payments are a function of bad record keeping, sometimes they are a function of outdated information technology systems. Sometimes they come about through human error and sometimes they come about through negligence. There are a variety of reasons why improper payments happen. It just simply is not the case that improper payments are only a function of bad people, doing bad things, with bad intent. That doesn't mean we shouldn't focus on trying to mitigate improper payments, and that certainly doesn't mean that the American people should not be concerned with how their tax dollars are used.

The good news is that there are some time-tested solutions and tools to help mitigate these problems. For example, when we think about the independence of inspector general, we're talking about a resource that is extraordinarily valuable to the American people. In fiscal year 2023 alone, Inspector General identified over $93 billion worth of potential savings to taxpayers. Whistleblowers are also an incredible resource to the American taxpayer. Through the IRS's whistleblower program alone, billions of dollars have been recouped from tax cheats since the inception of that program in 2007. Whistleblowers have also played an instrumental role in helping the Department of Justice pursue False Claims Act cases that have resulted in billions of dollars in reclaimed settlement costs. It seems to me that if an administration were serious about wanting to root out waste, fraud and abuse, they would support and resource whistleblowers and inspectors general. They would not demonize them and they would certainly not fire them en masse in an unlawful midnight purge.

There are other reforms we can think about too, reforms that are more technical but just as important. Key statutes such as the Federal Funding Accountability and Transparency Act, the Data Act and critical platforms like USASpending.gov were really important improvements and innovations when they came about, but they're in need of overhaul and reform. Currently, the status quo is that we have an extraordinarily hard time tracking federal dollars from end-to-end. This is due in large part to a broken chain of data collection, of reporting information, and the ability to monitor and track in real-time what is happening with federal dollars.

This informational black hole is where a lot of impropriety happens. It's where waste, fraud and abuse live. Yes, this is where improper payments often happen. More importantly, we also don't have a good, clear and consistent way of understanding what is happening with tax dollars at the end point. What is the impact that we're having? What is the return on investment that we're having? We now have an annual budget of close to $7 trillion a year. We can't say, with any degree of clarity and consistency, what we're getting for all of that money.

We have some more good news though; there are bipartisan efforts and there have been for years to try and clean up this situation. We at POGO have had the privilege and pleasure of working on some of those initiatives. We were a part of the federal taxpayers right to no act being passed into law just a couple of years ago, which created, for the very first time, a program inventory of all the programs in the federal government and that would be available to the public.

We have worked with a member of this very committee, the House of Oversight and Accountability Committee, to introduce a piece of legislation that would bring more transparency to federal sub award reporting. We have supported and endorsed multiple pieces of legislation that take direct aim at the improper payments issue. We also have additional ideas that don't yet have congressional champions. One proposal is to clean up, and modernize, and standardize the award descriptions that are available in USA Spending to make them more useful and relevant. We have another proposal to harmonize the amount of data and information we collect between contract spending and non-contract spending. We stand ready, willing and able to work with anybody who wants to work with us on these common-sense solutions.

Lastly, I want to put in a quick word for Congress and specifically I want to ...

Marjorie Taylor Greene: The gentleman's time has expired.

Mr. Hedtler-Gaudette: Apologies.

Marjorie Taylor Greene: Yes.

Mr. Hedtler-Gaudette: I can't see the flashing light.

Marjorie Taylor Greene: That's okay. Thank you, Mr. Hedtler-Gaudette. We appreciate your testimony.

I now recognize myself for five minutes of questions. I'd like to thank our witnesses today for your testimonies and the suggestions that you have brought before this committee. I'd also like to thank Chairman Comer for this opportunity to chair the Historic Oversight Subcommittee on DOGE.

Americans are shocked to learn that $2.7 trillion of their hard-earned tax dollars have been stolen or wasted in improper payments since 2003. You see, in the private sector, companies can't continue to run if they keep employees that allow waste and abuse with their resources, but that has continued for decades here in the federal government.

Mr. Talcove, do private sector companies have a lower rate of improper payments than the federal government?

Haywood Talcove: Yes. The fraud rate that the criminals are taking advantage of in the public sector is around 20%. In the private sector, it's around 3%. It's really because the tools that are used in the private sector aren't used in the public sector; front-end identity verification, self certification and then, finally, making sure that individuals are who they say they are. If we start using these tools, you will see the fraud rate go down dramatically because, for the most part, this fraud isn't taking place by real individuals. It's individuals whose identities have been stolen on the dark web, they use that information pretending to be somebody else, and because of the antiquated systems, processes and technologies in place, in government programs, they're able to steal at scale.

Marjorie Taylor Greene: Right. Mr. Talcove, we would say that private companies that pretty much have to exist on a 20% profit rate, they're not allowed. They can't continue to be successful if they were to allow their customers data to be stolen like that and used by criminals. However, the federal government, who can continue printing checks and continue in operation, never fixes its problems because it can't be forced to go out of business. Would you agree with that? Yes or no?

Haywood Talcove: Yes. One of the things I noticed during Covid was the criminals learned that government was the mark, because it never runs out of money and they focus on it at scale. Then, the likelihood of getting caught is virtually zero.

Marjorie Taylor Greene: I think it's outrageous for Americans to know that their identity can be stolen and then used for child trafficking, drug trafficking and terrorism, like you stated in your opening statement.

Ms. Royal, your testimony states that many programs operate under essentially an honor system in which applicants need not verify their identity, income, residency or other key eligibility factors. You call this a trust everyone instead of a trust by verify approach. Does this mean the federal government, in some states, are giving out billions of dollars to individuals without verifying who they are, or whether they meet program eligibility requirements?

Dawn Royal: Yes, ma'am. That's correct.

Marjorie Taylor Greene: That's outrageous. Do states have enough incentive to prevent fraud and to recover improper payments?

Dawn Royal: No. In fact, states are hesitant to spend their state dollars to protect federal dollars.

Marjorie Taylor Greene: Would greater investment in program integrity efforts yield a positive return for taxpayers?

Dawn Royal: Yes. It could easily be self-funding.

Marjorie Taylor Greene: Amazing. Mr. Whitson, your testimony states that both the Biden and Obama administrations issued rules and guidance that made it harder for states to verify eligibility for Medicaid. You say that repealing Biden's Medicaid streamlining rule would save 164 billion over 10 years, because the rule restricts eligibility verification that states can perform. Can you explain why this rule is so costly?

Mr. Whitson: Yeah. The rule does a number of things, but for instance, it prohibits states from verifying eligibility more than once a year. For non-disabled folks to just go in and look and say, "Hey. Are you still eligible for the program?" It says you are forbidden from doing that any more often than once a year. Obviously people's lives change and so they may become ineligible, and so it's designed to keep them on the program. Another thing, it prohibits in-person or phone interviews to verify their identity. People apply for it and then the person on the other end says, "Well, I just want to call and make sure this is a real person, not someone in another country or whatever." The rule prohibits that. There's a number of other provisions. It also opens a lengthy reconsideration periods, and this is where illegal immigrants are able to obtain the benefits. Basically it says once you get these benefits, you can't interfere with it for a 90-day period or longer. There's a number of horrible things,

Marjorie Taylor Greene: So we can't verify if someone is illegal or legal receiving ... Just to correct that, yes or no.

Mr. Whitson: A state has to wait at least 90 days. Actually, what we're seeing is it's led some states to wait as long as 13 years on the program.

Marjorie Taylor Greene: Unbelievable. My time has expired. Thank you very much. I now recognize Mr. Lynch from Massachusetts for five minutes.

Mr. Lynch: Thank you very much, Madam Chair. First of all, let me congratulate you, and also Ms. Stansbury on your new positions. I want to thank the witnesses for your testimony. We've already heard some good ideas about how to work together. Mr. Hedtler-Gaudette,

I, for one, would be most open to working with POGO and trying to work on some of the legislative ideas that you have to actually get at some of this waste, fraud and abuse.

Since this is my first opportunity to speak in this new subcommittee as the representative for the Eighth Congressional District in Massachusetts, I want to first of all make clear that my primary purpose, in seeking appointment to this subcommittee, is for the singular and sacred purpose to defend our democracy, which I believe is under attack in this country, and to uphold my oath to support and defend the constitution against those who might secretly or openly seek its destruction.

Make no mistake, this is a moment for representative democracy. This is a test of our resolve. In the coming days and weeks, we will all get to decide whether we stand with a couple of billionaires who, despite their own financial successes, still harbor such grievances in their hearts that after all that democracy has provided to them, they remain animated by the desire to dismantle this democratic government and to punch down at some of the weakest and most vulnerable in our society. Two men who clearly understand that the easiest way to incite large numbers of people is to use social media to exploit the dynamic forces of hatred and fear.

Madam Chair, if we're going after waste, fraud and abuse, let's start with abuse. Abuse of power. As of yesterday, there were 55 lawsuits under consideration by the federal courts across our nation as a result of Elon Musk's and President Trump's unlawful acts. Many of those lawsuits have already been sustained by the federal district courts and orders have been rendered to undo those unlawful acts. This is just the beginning and Congress has an important role to play. I, for one, look forward to that opportunity. This is a moment of great consequence for our country and for our democracy, and I remain grateful to the good people of the Eighth Congressional District of Massachusetts who sent me here.

Mr. Hedtler-Gaudette, again, happy to join you on some of your efforts. POGO has worked very closely with our IG community. Is that right? The inspector general's?

Mr. Hedtler-Gaudette: Yeah. That's correct, congressman,

Mr. Lynch: I know your work is very much similar to what we ask our inspector generals to undertake. I want to ask you, what do you think ... In the most recent report from the Inspector Generals, and this is the Council of the Inspector Generals, a nonpartisan group on integrity and efficiency in government, they identified more than $93 billion in potential savings. The first thing that President Trump did, coming into office, was to fire 17 agency inspectors general. From POGO's standpoint, what does that do to our ability to identify and root out waste, fraud and abuse?

Mr. Hedtler-Gaudette: Thank you, Congressman.
I would say, to put it simply, it completely undermines our ability to root out waste, fraud, and abuse. Inspector General exists for essentially one purpose, and they were originally created in the immediate aftermath of Watergate. I think you all probably do not need me to give you a history lesson at all on what happened in the Watergate era. There's a reason they were created at that time because there was a lot of waste, fraud and abuse happening, and there were not cops on the beat that were internal, that were independent, that were situated in agencies to be able to find these things and expose them and do something about them. That's what Inspector General exists to do. It's completely, I'd say, anathema to any stated mission to find cost savings and to root out waste, fraud and abuse to fire Inspector General and to undermine them. It makes no sense. Those two things do not add up.

Mr. Lynch: Thank you very much. The firings that occurred when President Trump came to the office included the Special Inspector

General for Afghan Reconstruction, Mr. Sopko. I actually did over 20 trips to Afghanistan working with him. He actually uncovered $4 billion in savings in rooting out American taxpayer waste being conducted in Afghanistan. The IG at the Department of Defense, the agency ...

Marjorie Taylor Greene: The gentleman's time has expired,

Mr. Lynch: Okay. Thank you, Madam Chair. I yield back. Thank you.

Marjorie Taylor Greene: Okay.

Mr. Lynch: Appreciate that.

Marjorie Taylor Greene: Thank you.

Mr. Lynch: Thank you.

Marjorie Taylor Greene: I now recognize the gentleman from Texas, Mr. Cloud.

Mr. Cloud: Thank you, Madam Chair.

For far too long, DC politicians have gotten away with measuring their personal value and worth by how much of other people's money they give away. For far too long, they self-righteously have opined that the spending was for altruistic purposes given out of care and compassion. For far too long, they've been more concerned with looking like they cared than having enough care and concern to actually do the due diligence to ensure that the tax dollars were being used wisely and effectively. For far too long, those of us who've worked to uncover waste, fraud and abuse have had to deal with what amounts to an unconstitutional force branch of permanent bureaucracy that has too often worked to ignore, obfuscate, delay and frustrate our efforts to bring transparency and oversight.

Over the last few weeks, the DOGE effort has begun to uncover not only how massive the waste, fraud and abuse is, but also the extent at which DC politicians, and too many obstinate bureaucrats, have coordinated to create what is essentially the largest money laundering scheme in history. While Americans have been working to make ends meet, they have been using taxpayer dollars to fund unnecessary, egregious, and even evil things, here at home and around the world.

Thankfully, in DOGE, we have a president bringing the leadership needed and a focused effort along with the talent, technology, tools and transparency to this waste, fraud and abuse. To those who would stand opposed to this effort, I would just point out, while it's understandable to find waste, fraud and abuse that has grown and metastasized in this government even over decades, certainly accelerated over the last few years, to continue to protect it is corruption.

I want to thank the chair for beginning this war on waste on this side of Pennsylvania Avenue and bringing together this committee. This effort is so important as we work to relieve the American people of this burden of waste, fraud and abuse.

Mr. Talcove, you mentioned in your written statement and talked about it in your statement at the beginning, that this waste, fraud and abuse is a national security threat. Certainly one of the challenges facing us, it is a national security threat, is our fiscal situation. We have got to find ways to find savings to the American people in order to bring confidence to the bond markets, to put our country on a fiscal footing and to reverse the curse, so to speak, that we are placing on our children and our grandchildren.

You mentioned a couple threats though. You mentioned internal threats. You said that these cases involve government employees, individuals entrusted with administering benefits, who instead of using their positions to approve fraudulent claims, override security controls, or even sell sensitive claimant information for profit. Now, this is not every federal employee, for sure, but within the context of people who are trying to give their best effort, we have an internal threat. You also mentioned transnational fraud rings, terrorist organizations, nation states, North Korea, nuclear weapons programs funded by our tax dollars, China, Nigeria, Iran, Romania, Russia, not our friends necessarily that are being funded by taxpayer dollars. Could you give us some examples of how this is happening?

Haywood Talcove: God. Yeah. When you think about what happened during the pandemic, $1 trillion was stolen. 70% of that money went overseas, and I can give you some examples. In a western state, they had more people applying for unemployment insurance benefits than they had individuals over 18. The people that were stealing the money from Romania were using it to facilitate other fraud schemes that include fentanyl, that include doing things to impact our democracy.

On the insider threat, the first thing I have to say, and my dad was a public servant, is 99% of people that work in the public sector are honest, hardworking individuals, but there are some. What you need is data and technology to root that out. There were examples during the pandemic, there were some examples even of last week where people got into the Medicaid system in a western state and stole $50 million in less than four months. You have to have these controls in place. These aren't individuals stealing, Mr. Cloud, these are organized criminal groups, both domestic and transnational.

Mr. Cloud: As you mentioned, taxpayers are being forced to fund the demise of our own country.

Mr. Winston, I wanted to ask you, because there's a lot of talk about reconciliation right now. You mentioned Medicaid and what could be done to bring a pretty substantial amount of savings. This is without affecting those who truly need Medicaid and for what the purpose of the program was extended for ...

Marjorie Taylor Greene: The gentleman's time has expired. Does the witness want to answer the question?

Mr. Whitson: No. Only to say that, yes, there's a tremendous amount of savings that can be found from the streamlining rule, but also work requirements in the program is another big area that can be done in reconciliation. That could save a significant amount as well, 241 billion in federal spending over 10 years.

Mr. Cloud: Thank you.

Marjorie Taylor Greene: Thank you.

Mr. Cloud: Thank you, Madam Chair.

Marjorie Taylor Greene: You're welcome. I now recognize the gentleman from California, Mr. Garcia.

Mr. Garcia: Well, thank you. Thank you to all of our witnesses for being here. I want to just start off by making something clear. I think we're all here to fight against the lies, the corruptions and the attacks on our social safety net. Now, we should in no way be cooperating with House Republicans who want to shut down the Department of Education and destroy Medicare and Medicaid. We should not stand by as the richest man on the planet gives himself and his companies huge tax cuts while the American people get absolutely nothing.

Now, I find it ironic, of course, that our chairwoman, Congresswoman Greene, is in charge of running this committee. Now, in the last congress, Chairwoman Greene literally showed a dick pic in our oversight congressional hearing, so I thought I'd bring one as well. Now, this of course, we know, is President Elon Musk. He's also the world's richest man. He was the biggest political donor in the last election. He has billions of dollars in conflicts of interest, and we know that he's leading a power grab, also abided by and encouraged by Donald Trump, and of course the chairwoman, Congresswoman Greene.

I also want to run through what DOGE actually is going to do. It's a demolition plan that's going to run through our government. DOGE is trying to abolish the Department of Education. That means opportunities denied to kids. It means you're ripping away opportunities for children with disabilities who are dependent on this money. You are also halting medical research, which is also critical, which we have to also stop the idea that we are going to eliminate or destroy the Department of National Institutes of Health, NIH is crazy.

Let's talk about the Department of Labor. We're talking about protections for working people across this country where people can actually complain about abuses their companies are making against them, and their co-workers. Workers are now going to be in danger. Let's also talk about the Consumer Financial Protection Bureau. Another huge issue for us, think about the scammers and fraudsters that'll be empowered across this country because Elon Musk wants … Essentially, these companies have more power over consumers and over people across this country. Look at the Centers for Medicare and Medicaid services. That is actually what's being discussed, partly today. Healthcare we're talking about being denied to millions of poor people, working-class people across this country. And now of course they're onto their largest target, the US Social Security Administration. We're talking about the destruction of the actual social safety net in this country. We know that one in five Americans collect social security. Seniors, disabled people. This entire plan is about hurting the American social safety net and destroying our institutions, and it's important that we actually call out what is happening at this subcommittee. This is not about working with the richest man on the planet. This is actually about empowering. This committee wants to empower the richest person in the world to hurt people so they can take all of this money that they so-called want to save and then give it to themselves, their companies, and their billionaire friends. That is the attack that is happening in this committee and across this country, and it's important that we call it out.

We also know, of course, that Elon Musk is sending his unqualified DOGE staff to carry out this agenda across all these agencies, and in some cases actually teenage staffers. No accountability, no experience, and problematic records. They're trying to rob you and they're probably a minor. Thank you and I yield back.

Marjorie Taylor Greene: The gentleman yields and I now recognize the gentleman from South Carolina, Mr. Timmons for five minutes.

Mr. Timmons: Thank you, Madam Chair. I find it sad that my colleagues across the aisle can't take this seriously. We have $36 trillion in debt. We run an annual almost $2 trillion deficit. When I got elected six years ago, we had 21 trillion in debt, so in six years, we've added over $15 trillion to the debt. And guess what? President Trump ran on fixing this problem. President Trump told the American people he would right the ship financially, and he said during the campaign that Elon Musk was going to be the person to lead this charge, the man that has turned business after business around. He's the richest man on the planet because he succeeds at his endeavors, and that's why President Trump has appointed him the head of this effort.

This is a very serious problem and it's incredibly hypocritical that my colleagues across the aisle are complaining about this because Joe Biden, Joe Biden signed his name and wanted the American people to believe that he had the ability to forgive $250 billion with a signature. Guess what? Supreme Court ruled he did not. That's our system of checks and balances.

The President, Biden, he clearly was experiencing cognitive decline. He didn't even have the ability to be charged with a crime as determined by his own Department of Justice, but he signs his name and he thinks it gives a quarter of a trillion dollars away, redistributes taxpayer dollars. It's just crazy that we can't come together to address the greatest national security threat facing this country, our debt.

Now to the task at hand, Medicaid fraud. Mr. Talcove, if we implement enhanced identity verification and enhanced income verification, what will happen? How much money will we save?

Haywood Talcove: You'll save hundreds of billions of dollars. Identity verification, elimination of self-certification and monitoring beneficiaries will prevent these transnational criminal groups from accessing those systems at scale, so legitimate people who need the benefits can get them in a timely fashion.

Mr. Timmons: So we're going to get actual benefits to people, to American citizens that are in need, faster because if you do it electronically through a web-base like they did in Missouri, where the pilot program saved almost 20% of Medicaid dollars. So all we have to do is adopt what has already been proven in Missouri, and we'll save 20%.

To the people out there listening, we spend almost $900 billion every year on Medicaid, and if 20% of that is saved, that's almost $200 billion. We've got a $1.8 trillion annual deficit, we just knocked off 200 billion, let's keep this train going.

The fact that the Democrats are filing lawsuit after lawsuit to impede the efforts of President Trump to right our fiscal ship is unforgivable. It's unforgivable.

Mr. Talcove, you talked about pandemic fraud. I have a bill that would cause the IRS to share data with the Small Business Administration and the FBI and the Department of Justice that would show that you were ineligible for PPP loans and you got them. I think that would save probably a hundred billion. Do you think that we should go back and take money away from people that fraudulently got COVID money?

Haywood Talcove: During the pandemic, the PPP program was a virtual buffet for fraudsters. It was because of that 1974 Privacy Act where data sharing and matching is virtually impossible. Congress needs to change that.

Mr. Timmons: But we can do it retroactively. We can do it retroactively. We can find the people that stole this money, hold them accountable, probably get some of the money back. So I already have that bill filed. That bill, I think would probably get $100 billon. So now we got enhanced identity verification, enhanced income verification that has been proven in Missouri. It does work. So I'm working on that bill, we're going to drop it soon. That's $200 billion. There's a competition in Congress. I think we should have a competition on this committee. I got $300 billion in savings proposed. We got to all pull our weight because we have such a massive problem right now, but I would just ask my colleagues across the aisle to get out of the way if you don't want to help. If you don't want to help right the fiscal ship in this country, get out of the way. Stop filing lawsuit after lawsuit. We do not have the financial ability to continue down this path, and we're going to save this country with or without you. You can kick and scream all the way or you can get out of the way. I prefer the former. Thank you Madam Chair.

Marjorie Taylor Greene: The gentleman yields. I now recognize the gentleman from Texas, Mr. Casar.

Mr. Casar: This subcommittee is supposedly about looking into waste, fraud and abuse, so I'd like to start talking about independent inspector generals who are supposed to be looking into waste, fraud and abuse. Mr. Talcove, do you know how many inspector generals at agencies that were investigating Elon Musk's companies have been fired by the Trump-Musk administration?

Haywood Talcove: No.

Mr. Casar: It is five. Ms. Royal, the Inspector General of the Department of Labor had 17 open investigations into Tesla and SpaceX. Do you know what the Trump-Musk administration did to that inspector general?

Ms. Royal: No.

Mr. Casar: They fired him, and I think y'all know. Mr. Whitson, the Inspector General of the Department of Transportation was investigating Tesla. Do you know what the Trump-Musk administration did to that inspector general?

Mr. Whitson: No.

Mr. Casar: They were fired. The Department of Defense's Inspector General was looking into SpaceX. Mr. Hedtler, do you know what the Trump-Musk administration did to that inspector general?

Mr. Hedtler-Gaudette: I believe he was fired.

Mr. Casar: Thank you. I think everybody on the panel knows what the answer to these questions were. The US Department of Agriculture Inspector General was investigating Musk's Neuralink. Mr. Talcove, now, I'll ask you again under oath, do you know what Mr. Trump did to that inspector general that was looking into one of Musk's companies?

Haywood Talcove: No.

Mr. Casar: He was fired. The inspector general at the EPA was repeatedly taking on Tesla. Mr. Hedtler, since it seems that you're answering the questions that everyone knows the answer to, do you know what the Trump-Musk administration did to that inspector general?

Mr. Hedtler-Gaudette: I believe he was also fired.

Mr. Casar: Also fired. At least five inspector generals that were looking into Elon Musk's companies were fired by the Trump-Musk administration. These inspector generals who are independent, protected by law. They are the people that find the waste, fraud and abuse and found many of the cases of waste, fraud and abuse that have been brought up today. Fired because they were looking into Elon Musk.

At the NLRB, the National Labor Relations Board, which is supposed to protect workers from getting their unions busted by folks like Elon Musk made functionally broken by the so-called Department of Government Efficiency that really is the Department of Government Efficiency for Elon Musk, not for you.

They are trying to shut down the Department of Education, the Department of Labor. You know what Elon Musk doesn't seem to be looking into? His own contracts. Again, I'll ask you, Mr. Talcove, do you know how much money a day Mr. Musk will receive from the federal government for his contracts?

Haywood Talcove: No.

Mr. Casar: The answer is $8 million a day. Just last year, Elon Musk was promised $3 billion from close to 100 contracts with the federal government. Ms. Royal, do you know how much the average person in this country who survives on Social Security, one of our seniors who's worked their entire life, about how much they have to survive on a day?

Ms. Royal: I do not.

Mr. Casar: $65 a day. We're not looking into Elon Musk's $8 million a day. This subcommittee chaired by Marjorie Taylor Greene and the House Republicans is looking into your grandmother's $65 a day.

Let me be clear. I think we would all support taxpayer savings. Look into money we might needlessly send to billionaires and big corporations, find taxpayer savings and send it back to your hardworking family. But instead, what House Republicans and the Trump-Musk administration want to do is they want to look into your kids' lunch money, your kids' teacher's salary, into your grandparents' social security. They want to take that money and give it out in billionaire tax cuts, and they're talking about that in committee tomorrow, in Budget Committee tomorrow. They just released their plan.

So let me be clear. When Republicans talk about government efficiency in this Congress, they're not looking into billionaires who don't pay their taxes. They're not looking into billionaires who get rich off of government contracts. They're not looking into Elon Musk firing watchdogs who are supposed to keep them accountable. They're looking at cutting your public schools. They're going straight for your social security. They're coming straight for cancer research. They're coming straight for the Department of Education. They're not looking at big tech. They're not looking at big Pharma because those people fund their campaigns. If this committee we're serious about rooting out waste from our federal government, then today's whole hearing would be about how Musk and Donald Trump are firing the independent watchdogs who've done this work for decades. Instead, my Republican colleagues' actual goal on this committee is to distract from Trump and from Musk's corrupt war on accountability. This will not be a subcommittee dedicated to making government efficient for everyday people. It's about helping Elon Musk and Donald Trump be as efficient as possible in robbing our government and handing out our government services to the rich. So this seems that this subcommittee is just going to be-

Marjorie Taylor Greene: The gentleman's time has expired.

Mr. Casar: ... Like the agency it's named after-

Marjorie Taylor Greene: The gentleman's time has expired.

Mr. Casar: A sham. A total sham.

Marjorie Taylor Greene: The American people are $36 trillion in debt, it certainly seems reasonable that someone has been fired. I now recognize the gentleman from Tennessee-

Mr. Casar: You're going to put us further in debt with your billionaire taxes.

Marjorie Taylor Greene: ... Mr. Burchett. You're not recognized. Mr. Burchett, you're recognized for five minutes.

Mr. Burchett: Thank you, Chair Lady. The gravy train for a lot of these folks, it's been on biscuit wheels and it's about to run off the dadgum tracks and it's about time. Could you imagine standing up here and defending waste, fraud and abuse? But I think that's what we're seeing. When people squeal and don't ask questions I think it shows the American public what the heck's going on, and that little gravy train is getting ready to run out. The spigot is getting ready to be turned off. Mr. Talcove, that's correct how you say your name, brother?

Haywood Talcove: Yes, sir.

Mr. Burchett: All right. How can the federal government improve identity verification for these entitlement programs?

Haywood Talcove: Yeah, it's doing what the private sector does every single day, whether you use your bank, you go to Amazon, using those tools and moving away from some of the dated compliance standards that the federal government uses. NIST IAL863, 2017 before there was anything called deep fakes and generative AI tools.

Mr. Burchett: Also, I was informed that PayPal has never been, they've never been able to crack into that and steal people's vital information. Are they using those systems that you would be favorable towards, that government seems to be shying away from?

Haywood Talcove: Yes, sir.

Mr. Burchett: And describe that, how that works.

Haywood Talcove: There are systems that are based on encryption. They use technology and they use data to validate you are who you say you are. The people that are stealing right now, I believe a lot of them are actually ghosts from China, Russia, Nigeria, and Romania.

Mr. Burchett: I read a report today that North Korea was involved in this and some of that as well.

Haywood Talcove: They are.

Mr. Burchett: And those people are enemies. Again, they'll hate us for free, we don't have to give them taxpayer money. And are there loopholes that can be closed to avoid these improper payments? And I wish you'd describe those to me.

Haywood Talcove: All right. The biggest, most important thing, particularly in the benefit program space is the use of self certification. As Mr. Timmons noted, the state of Missouri is using a solution called Steady IQ to validate wages and wealth. You cannot allow individuals to provide the information based upon what they think. It has to be based on what you know, and that will stop the ghosts from using people's identities to steal money from US taxpayers.

Mr. Burchett: How much money do you calculate is wasted... Due to waste, fraud and abuse in the entitlement programs each year?

Haywood Talcove: Yeah. My number right now between federal, state and local government is you can save $1 trillion a year by simply putting in front-end identity verification, eliminating self-certification and monitoring the back end of the programs that are providing the benefits. Those three things.

Mr. Burchett: You said you could eliminate that, but there are others you feel like some more low-hanging fruit.

Haywood Talcove: I would start with those three things because they're simple. That'll take that 20% fraud rate that you're seeing in the public sector, down below 5%.

Mr. Burchett: Chair lady, I would suggest that we adopt Mr. Timmons legislation and get that out of the committee as fast as possible. What actions also could Congress take to fix these problems quickly?

Haywood Talcove: I think the first thing is updating and redoing the 1974 Privacy Act. That is virtually impossible to do data matching. It's very difficult to have data shared, and when you look back at the pandemic, data sharing and data matching would've stopped probably 50% of the trillion dollars that was stolen from taxpayers.

Mr. Burchett: Do any of y'all like to add anything to that?

Mr. Whitson: Congressman, I would just add that rather than accepting self-attestation, that states should have to be required to actually verify people's identities. And here's the key part, before they get enrolled. They shouldn't get enrolled and then eventually come later on down the road.

Mr. Burchett: It's amazing to me. A doctor's appointment back in Knoxville and the verification process is very extensive. It's more so than the federal government requires for any of this. What type of computer systems are these agencies using and do they need updating?

Haywood Talcove: They're using very dated technology, but they're also burdened. I look at the USDA, 6.2 million words in a 10,000 page document that shows how to implement the rules of the program. Nobody can figure that out. So one of the things that I think has to happen is the simplification of these processes and systems and then just use the technology that we use every day in the private sector.

Mr. Burchett: Okay. Thank y'all so much for being here.

Marjorie Taylor Greene: Gentleman's time has expired.

Mr. Burchett: Thank you, Chair Lady.

Marjorie Taylor Greene: I now recognize the gentlewoman from Texas, Ms. Crockett for five minutes.

Ms. Crockett: Thank you, Madam Chair. And Mr. Talcove, I'm just going to go ahead and pick up where you left off really quickly. Just to be clear, the upgrades that you're talking about as it relates to our data processes, these aren't things that would be free are they? They would cost some kind of money. Not looking for a number, but they will cost, correct?

Haywood Talcove: Some are free and some would cost money.

Ms. Crockett: Okay. All right. So I just want to leave it there because we've had a number of these hearings. So I do want to be clear before the Trump administration came in, this committee did exist in the form of the Oversight Committee, and our task is to root out waste, fraud and abuse. In that vein, we had a number of hearings, at least last term, I can't speak for any other term as I'm only in my sophomore term, and we dealt with improper payments. And interestingly enough, our chairwoman, who is so passionate about this today, she missed every single one of those improper payment hearings. But just to be clear, I was there. So I don't want anyone to believe that Democrats just come to work and don't plan to do work.

In fact, I'm trying to figure out exactly what it is that the Republicans believe our job is. Because right now they have relinquished their constitutional duties over to an unelected bureaucrat, someone who no one went out to vote for, and absolutely he is occupying the Oval Office, as we saw yesterday, and that is a first for me, to see someone occupying the Oval Office who's never actually been elected to the Oval Office and actually answering more questions than the person that allegedly got elected. But for whatever reason, this is the first time we're having a DOGE subcommittee hearing, and that guy's not here. Instead we have y'all, so I do want to thank you for coming.

But I will say this, it's also interesting to me that in the first few days of DOGE existing, we know that they are trying to get rid of the Department of Education, USAID, Consumer Financial Protection Bureau. They're laying off FAA workers. They are going after the FDA, the CDC, the HHS, the FBI agents, and they're talking about getting rid of FEMA and they brought y'all in. And I am going to say that I actually was shocked that there was only one person that seemed like he was an overt Trumper, as you laid out your opening remarks, because I anticipated that at least one of y'all would say, "Yes, what Elon is doing is exactly what we were prescribed." But instead, I will applaud you because you actually were focused. You talked about what the American people are looking for us to do. We've actually consistently on this side of the aisle promoted this idea of making investments into technology so that we can do things such as, say, look at the Department of Defense.

The Department of Defense that takes up approximately oh, 50% of our discretionary income, or our discretionary spending, approximately 50% goes to Department of Defense. Department of Defense has not been able to pass an audit in the last six audits, and we're not talking about pennies. I understand that we want everything to be perfect, and if we could get all waste, fraud and abuse out, that would be fantastic. But let me talk about the big numbers.

The big numbers are on that side. When we look at, say, our entire workforce, our federal workforce, as we're trying to somehow fire all of them, they don't even make up a total of 5%. It's even less than that when we look at our budget.

But let's talk about defense. That just happens to be the same side of the ledger that Mr. Musk gets the vast majority of his money from. In fact, at the same time that they were unlawfully, and we will stay in court because on this side, we believe in law and order. We believe in, I mean, a number of us are actually lawyers, but nevertheless, we understand the Constitution. We believe in that as well. And so there's things such as impoundment. Because as Mr. Whitson said, he said, "We need to return the power of the purse to Congress." It never left. According to the Constitution, that's where it's at.

Now, I know that people are confused right now because for whatever reason, we had a guy that went in, and you talk about people invading our data, listen, people said that they were upset about TikTok, but I'm upset about the guy that runs Twitter, who for sure is doing nefarious things. Because I don't understand, if you are trying to conduct audits and figure out where the waste, fraud and abuse is, I don't know why you would go to some tech guy. In fact, it was only techies that were sitting there in inauguration. We didn't have auditors. I would welcome auditors to come in and do forensic audits. In fact, he sat there in the Oval Office yesterday and he admitted that he was lying and he was using his propaganda machine to do it when he said that we sent millions of dollars to Gaza for condoms. That was a lie. So let me tell you something. We were duly elected-

Marjorie Taylor Greene: The Gentle Lady's time has expired.

Ms. Crockett: ... and it is time for-

Marjorie Taylor Greene: The Gentle Lady's time has expired.

Ms. Crockett: ... Us to do our job. To reign in this rogue actor known as Elon Musk.

Marjorie Taylor Greene: The Gentle Lady's time has expired. I now recognize the gentleman from Missouri, Mr. Burlison.

Mr. Burlison: Thank you, Madam Chair. I just want to speak frankly at first to the American people. We are nearing $37 trillion in national debt. What does that mean? That means that each and every US taxpayer owes over $323,000. What does that mean? That means when the EPIC, which is the Economic Policy Innovation Center, says we have 18 trillion left. That's it. 18 trillion left to take out, and we're spending $2 trillion in debt every year. Folks, we are at the precipice of a debt... A debt cycle. We are literally at a point in which the dollar will be worth nothing. What does that mean? I mean, we know Social Security goes bankrupt in eight years. Medicare goes bankrupt in 10 years. And then 15 years from now, the dollar is completely devalued and worth nothing. So what does that mean? That means your pension, the money in your bank, your savings is nothing. It's worthless.

So what are we doing? We're trying to save this country. We're trying to save your pensions. We're trying to save your bank accounts. We're trying to save this country for the next generation. And it would be nice if we had help, but instead, we have people that are fighting us on this. And I think that I would hate to be in the Democratic Party right now because you're in a really bad bind. You're having to defend all of this crazy spending, all of this crazy waste. So how do you do it? You do ad hominem attacks. You attack the messenger.

Oh, Elon Musk, he's rich. He must be evil. That's the attacks. Really, you can't do any better than that?

Let's talk on the policy. On the policy. Help us. We're trying to save this country. This is what an Elon Musk who's making no money doing this is trying to save this country. Why? Because he is invested in the United States of America more than anybody. So I think that we should embrace it. In fact, not a single company, governor of any state would ever turn down Elon Musk and his team of DOGE from coming in and providing free services to right the course financially in any state or organization. It's ridiculous that we would demonize someone that loves this country so much.

Mr. Whitman, the formation of agencies via the executive action is not new. The formation of DOGE is not new. Are you familiar with any other previous presidencies where they've formed organizations like DOGE via executive action?

Mr. Whitson: Yeah, so actually the agency that DOGE is occupying is one that was created in a previous administration so it is something that happens routinely. But I don't know if that answers your question.

Mr. Burlison: Yeah. There's been the Office of Budget Management was created, Environmental Protection Agency was created, the US Digital Service, which is now DOGE, was created all by executive order.

Mr. Whitson: And actually one other I'd add is USAID was originally created through an executive order by President Kennedy and then later formalized.

Mr. Burlison: And then Madam Chair, I have a video I would like to end with. That just... Let's review. If we could cue that. I want to remind my democratic friends at a point in which you once had the majority of the American people on your side, this is what your party believed in.

> *Al Gore: This report tells us how to cut waste, cut red tape, streamline the bureaucracy, change procurement rules, change the personnel rules, and create a government that works better and costs less.*

> *Bill Clinton: I've read it. And where it says the president should, the president will.*

> *Speaker 1: Among the 800 recommendations, eliminating 12% of the federal workforce, merging some government agencies like the FBI, the DEA, and the Bureau of Alcohol, Tobacco and Firearms, closing hundreds of government offices outside Washington.*

> *Barack Obama: From the day I took office, one of the commitments that I made the American people was that we would do a better job here in Washington in rooting out wasteful spending. We thought that it was entirely appropriate for our governments and our agencies to try to root out waste, large and small, in a systematic way. It means cutting some programs that I think are worthy, but we may not be able to afford right now. A lot of the action is in Congress and legislative. But in the meantime, we don't need to wait for Congress in order to do something about wasteful spending that's out there. We haven't seen as much action out of Congress as we'd like, and that's why we launched on our own initiative, the campaign to cut waste. And we're going to keep on finding every possible way that we can do that, even if Congress is not acting.*

There you go. I think it speaks for itself. My time has expired.

Marjorie Taylor Greene: The gentleman's time has expired. Thank you. I now yield to the gentlewoman from the District of Columbia, Ms. Norton for five minutes.

Ms. Norton: Thank you. Our Republican colleagues and the Trump administration continue to demonize our friends and neighbors who work for the federal government and swear an oath to protect the Constitution and serve the public. Thousands of civilian federal employees have given their lives in the line of duty for their country. The administration seems intent on dismantling much of the federal government in violation of the Constitution statutes and regulations, and our Republican colleagues are letting them do it. They want to gut the nonpartisan civil service and to convert a significant portion of the remaining civil service into political appointees. Depriving the federal government of employees' expertise and experience will harm the services that the government provides to all Americans.

Mr. Hedtler-Gaudette, the administration is attempting to cause a mass exodus from our federal workforce. Will this increase or decrease waste, fraud and abuse?

Mr. Hedtler-Gaudette: Thank you, Delegate Norton. I think it's pretty clear that chaos is not the friend of efficiency. If you undermine the very functionality of the government, you're not going to make it more efficient. You're going to make it worse, and it's going to cost even more money to recoup or to fix things that go wrong in the interim. So again, I mentioned earlier that if you care about waste, fraud, and abuse, firing inspector general doesn't add up. I think if you care about government being more efficient, I think intentionally creating chaos is the opposite of that.

Ms. Norton: Well, Mr. Hedtler-Gaudette, do federal employees operate without oversight or rules and regulations?

Mr. Hedtler-Gaudette: No, absolutely not. They are governed by plenty of rules and regulations.

Mr. Hedtler-Gaudette: ... and when there are independent Inspector General at the agency they're supposed to be at, they also have a cop on the beat making sure that they do so.

Ms. Norton: I want to highlight some stories demonstrating exactly the kind of federal workers the administration is trying to force out. How about Chris Mark at the Department of Labor whose pioneering work on mine safety has reduced miners' safety deaths from roof collapses to almost zero today? Or Jarod Koopman at the Internal Revenue Service who pioneered new methods for tracking criminal cybersecurity currency transactions that led to the rescue of 23 children from rape and assault, as well as a seizure of hundreds of millions of child abuse videos and 370 pedophile arrests? This work also prevented funding from going to terrorist groups. Or Ronald E. Walters who manages the 155 national cemeteries around the country and tends to the resting places of almost 4 million veterans. These are just a few of the federal workers who serve Americans every day. The workers are wild land firefighters, border guards, doctors, nurses, food inspectors, air traffic controllers, and law enforcement that do their civic duty often despite the fact that they could make such more in the private sector. Thank you and I yield back.

Marjorie Taylor Greene: The gentlelady yields. I now yield to the gentleman from Georgia, Mr. Jack.

Brian Jack: Thank you very much, Madam Chair. And I want to also thank you for convening this hearing. I think it's incredibly important and I want to thank our witnesses for appearing before us today. Like another member of this committee, I too was once an employee of the executive office of the President. I worked in President Trump's White House from the very first to very last day of his first term and I saw firsthand how entrenched and resistant the federal bureaucracy was to his agenda. So it's no surprise that today a few of my Democrat colleagues have continued that trend by using their time to bash Elon Musk instead of discussing ways to work together to advance a bipartisan cornerstone of President Trump's agenda, the mission to finally eliminate waste, fraud, and abuse. And I just took a rudimentary count of the Dems' testimony or rather comments today, and I've got 27 mentions of Elon Musk and three mentions of waste.

And I don't know if that's in fact the right count, encourage anybody to fact check me, but I think it illuminates and illustrates one of the problems that we're facing, which is a lack of bipartisan effort to address these critical things. Waste, fraud, and abuse is something that should be bipartisan. The chair noted that in her opening remarks. Now, Madam Chair, you know how much I enjoy studying public opinion. So with your approval, I'd like to enter into the record the CBS News poll from this past weekend conducted February 5th to 7th, 2025. And I'd also like to illuminate two findings. First, 70% of Americans, Democrats and Republicans included, believe President Trump is already doing the job that he was elected to, which is interesting because I have an article here from CNN from September, 2024 that notes, "Trump says Elon Musk has agreed to lead proposed government efficiency commission as ex-President unveils new economic plants."

So he is doing exactly what he said he would do by empowering his administration to root out waste, fraud, and abuse. And that's exactly what we're trying to do here today. I'd also like to note one interesting statistic from that. 62% of Americans want Democrats in Congress to work with us to advance the priorities that President Trump was elected to govern on. So I think those are two stats that I hope everyone pays attention to. But to ask questions of our witnesses, I'd first like to start with Mr. Talcove. One of the things that I've found very interesting from your opening testimony is you talked, and I think you engaged with Mr. Burchett on the 1974 Privacy Act, and I had some interesting folks visit my office yesterday who noted that one-third of all prior authorizations are still done manually by phone, fax, or direct post mail. First off, would love your comments on that. And

I'd also like for you to expound upon some of the solutions that we can deliver to this Congress and modernizing that 1974 Privacy Act.

Haywood Talcove: Yeah, these aren't people problems, these are technology problems. You can't process the number of individuals that are accessing our systems person by person. It just takes too much time. So by updating the 1974 Privacy Act and allowing for digital matching, you would've very quickly realized that a large portion of the PPP loan funds were going to the wrong person. You would've been quickly able to match... And I think the number was 20% were on the Do Not Pay list. You can't expect people to do what a machine and especially AI can do today.

Brian Jack: Fair enough. Thank you very much for that. And if I can also ask, Mr. Whitson, I think we share a common interest, which is to move departments and agencies outside of Washington DC. It's something that I campaigned on, something that I helped President Trump effectuate in his first administration. And I have to imagine that if we have departments and agencies outside of DC, if we've got a workforce that's more reflective of the balance that America is, we at the same time too could potentially root out some of this waste, fraud, and abuse by enabling other Americans, other citizens of our country to help advance some of these issues. So would love your commentary on that before my time expires.

Mr. Whitson: No, I think you're exactly right, Congressman Jack. So I think A, you'd save a lot of taxpayer money, so building a headquarters in downtown DC versus Huntsville, Alabama, you're going to be able to save a lot of money. Number two is you're actually going to make life better for the employees as well. So that's a point that's also missed a lot, but commuting into DC versus being able to go somewhere else where it's a better cost of living and things like that might be better for the folks. And then lastly, these areas where you set up a headquarters are going to be populated by people that live in the area to fill the rank and file of staff positions. And so if you plant these federal agency headquarters in the heart of any area that's overwhelmingly one party or the other, then you're going to naturally get that sway versus something that's more representative of the people as a whole.

Brian Jack: Well, thank you very much to our witnesses. Mindful of my time, I want to finish before my time expires. I yield back to our chairwoman, Marjorie Taylor Greene.

Marjorie Taylor Greene: Thank you.

Greg Casar: And Chair Woman, I would like to ask for unanimous consent to enter something into the record.

Marjorie Taylor Greene: What is it?

Greg Casar: It is a report from the Congressional Research Service, nonpartisan CRS that lays out the rules and the law for firing Inspectors General, which of course look into waste, fraud, and abuse and-

Marjorie Taylor Greene: Without objection.

Greg Casar: Thank you. And that rule requires for the law to be followed, for Congress to be notified with 30 days and a reason for firing Inspectors General to give Congress a chance to overrule that and that's the law. So thank you for entering that into the record.

Melanie Stansbury: Madam Chair-

Marjorie Taylor Greene: Without objection, the materials Mr. Jack cited are also submitted for the record. I now recognize-

Melanie Stansbury: Apologies. While we're on it, I'd also like to ask for unanimous consent to submit for the record two items. One is a statement from the AFL-CIO, department of people who work for a living with views on working people to make the government work. And the second is a statement from the Center for Responsibility and Ethics in Washington on ways to combat waste, fraud, and abuse in the federal government.

Marjorie Taylor Greene: Without objection, so ordered. I now recognize the gentlelady from New Mexico and Ranking Member, Ms. Stansbury, for five minutes.

Melanie Stansbury: All right. Well, thank you, Madam Chairwoman, and thank you once again to all of our witnesses for being here to testify. Thank you to my colleagues. We are going to have so much fun in this committee this Congress. I actually appreciate the video that was shown just a few moments ago because when I worked at the Office of Management and Budget, I actually worked on the waste EO that was referenced that President Obama signed. But there is one fundamental difference between the Presidents and Vice Presidents that were shown on that video and what's happening today, and that is that they followed the law. So my colleagues across the aisle who are asking us to get out of the way and stop trying to block things in the courts, let me tell you, we do not work for an unelected billionaire like apparently this guy does.

We work for the American people. And so if an unelected, unvetted individual private citizen is hacking our government systems, breaking the law, firing federal employees, dismantling statutorily created agencies, withholding funds, we are going to fight you in the courts. And I'm actually really sad that my dear friend Mr. Burchett left because I want to talk about that gravy train on biscuit wheels that he just talked about because that gravy train is not the federal workforce, it's the billionaires that are trying to hack that system right now in which unfortunately, my colleagues right now are working on a reconciliation deal to cut Medicaid, to cut Medicare, and use that money to give to tax breaks to their billionaire buddies. That is the gravy train that is actually going on here.

But because this is the Oversight Committee, let's do a little bit of oversight. For the last several weeks, I've been talking to Treasury and OMB officials to try to get to the bottom of why Elon Musk and his team are trying to hack the Treasury payment system because this is a completely non-partisan system that literally just pays the bills of the federal government. So why are they so eager to hack this system? And I have to say that over the last several weeks, we have literally received thousands of calls in every single congressional office.

In fact, we know that our friends across the aisle are also receiving these calls because this system pays the bills of the US government, it pays our soldiers, it pays for the work that we do overseas. It pays your Social Security benefits, it pays your tax refunds. So why is Elon Musk and his hackers trying to access that system and why did a senior civil servant who had overseen the system for over 30 years get asked to stand down after a 25-year-old intern working for Elon Musk tried to get access to the code for that system? Now, Thankfully, they were shut down in the court system, but Musk has installed with the President's blessing one of his Silicon Valley buddies, who I want to point out and which the media has not paid a lot of attention to is the CEO of a private IT company, including Citrix that has millions of dollars in IT contracts with the federal government.

And not only is he still operating as the installed DOGE person at Treasury, he is actively still the CEO of this private company. How is that even legal? Is it legal? I don't think it's legal because the federal court is trying to shut this down. We also know that that 25-year-old software engineer in violation of the court order was actually given access to modify the code. So what is going on here and why is this such a threat to the American people? Why are thousands of people calling us? It's because of the size and the significance of these payments, because it is an invasion of the privacy and security of the American people, because it could threaten our ability as a country if there was a default in the debt ceiling, and because it contains highly classified information that our foreign adversaries are trying to cyber attack us regularly for.

So why is a private citizen being given access to this system? We know they're trying to shut down payments. They're trying to shut down agencies. What's next? Are they going to shut down your Social Security payments? We don't know because they have no oversight and Elon Musk will not come in front of this committee. And in fact, the Treasury folks are saying this is the biggest insider threat they've ever seen in the history of the agency. So we are sounding the alarm, and no matter how many executive orders that Donald Trump signs or how many tweets that the VP sends, you cannot rewrite the Constitution and we are going to hold you to account. I yield back.

Marjorie Taylor Greene: The gentlelady yields and I now recognize... Oh yes.

Eric Burlison: I have three documents I want to submit for the record. The first document is the Constitution Article 2. I would like to submit that for the record that clearly spells out the President's authority. I would also like to submit for the record, 5 US Code 31 61, the Employment Compensation of Employees, which clearly spells out his authority to create DOGE. And then I want to submit for the record the executive order that Trump issued on January 20th, 2025 establishing DOGE officially.

Marjorie Taylor Greene: Without objection, so ordered. I now recognize the gentleman from Texas, Mr. Gill, for five minutes.

Brandon Gill: Thank you, Madam Chair, and thank you for hosting this committee. If we've learned anything so far, it's that Republicans want to cut waste, fraud, and abuse from our federal government and save taxpayer dollars, and Democrats want to grandstand and play politics. We can see right now even of the six Democrats on this committee, only one can even be bothered to stay for the duration of this hearing. All we've heard about for most of this hearing from the other side of the aisle is Elon Musk, Elon Musk, Elon Musk, unelected bureaucrat. And I'd like to ask if Democrats really care about unelected bureaucrats making decisions over our lives, where were they whenever their God, Anthony Fauci, was forcing vaccine and mask mandates on the American people for four years during the Covid crisis? Where were they whenever unelected Alejandro Mayorkas was facilitating the invasion of our country by illegal aliens who were murdering and raping and pillaging our people?

Where were they whenever the Secretary of Education, unelected, Cardona targeted states and schools and people who disagreed with his view of the radical Left's transgender ideology? Where were they whenever Gary Gensler, former chairman of the SEC, also unelected, was lawlessly thwarting the development of financial markets, particularly in the crypto space, by lawlessly pursuing regulation via enforcement? They were nowhere to be seen because they don't care because all of those things benefited their side of the aisle at the expense of ours. And perhaps that's also why they don't seem to be very interested in rooting out improper payments from our federal government. If you wonder why so many people are cynical about American politics, this is it. This is exactly why. The reality is that Elon Musk serves as an employee of the President and we were given a massive mandate to carry out what he's been doing. His job is to carry out the will of the American people as expressed through the executive.

That's exactly how the Constitution is supposed to work. The Constitution did not create an unelected, unaccountable fourth branch of government in the administrative state. The American people know this. My colleague, Brian Jack, discussed some of the opinion polls recently. We are doing and President Trump is doing exactly what he was elected to do, and that's why he is polling at a 53% approval rating, higher than he was at any point during his first administration. Even Elon Musk and his DOGE efforts now are polling at a

49% approval rating, which just to point out is 16 points higher than President Biden was polling at whenever he finished his term in office. The Democrat Party has for decades systematically grown and weaponized the administrative state against the American people, and the American people have had enough of it. Right now, we're talking about $2.7 trillion in improper payments since 2003.

We are uncovering what could be the biggest money-laundering scandal in American history, and the other side of the aisle could care less. They have no concern about where this money went, to what entities it went, to what governments, to what people or groups? Nothing. All they want to talk about is Elon Musk incessantly. So it does make me wonder if they don't care about where it's going, do they have an idea? Because what we've uncovered so far is that so much of the waste, fraud, and abuse of our federal government is actually funding their side of the aisle.

It's funding media outlets that are running cover for Democrats routinely, the NPR, PBS, the BBC, Politico. It's going to fund Left-wing NGOs that are facilitating the invasion of our country. It's going to fund Left-wing transgender activism and sex changes all over the globe. This is money that's being used... Taken from the American people and used against their interests. If you care about rooting out waste, fraud, and abuse, we should be serious about this. I'm very excited to be on this committee. I'm excited to expose what's being going on. Thank you, Madam Chair. And with that I yield.

Marjorie Taylor Greene: The gentleman yields. In closing, I want to thank our witnesses again for their testimonies today. I now yield to the Ranking Member for closing remarks.

Melanie Stansbury: Thank you, Madam Chairwoman. Well, I never thought so many conspiracy theories and wild accusations could be wound into one five-minute speech, but I appreciate my friends across the aisle. First of all, let's talk about this massive mandate that supposedly brought Donald Trump into office. Donald

Trump did not run on putting an unelected billionaire in charge of dismantling the federal government. He ran on lowering prices for Americans, and I think it's interesting that while we're sitting here this morning, the top of the New York Times is reporting that inflation has risen unexpectedly as food and energy prices have soared. What's going on, guys? I thought you were going to tackle inflation in food and energy prices. Isn't that what the executive orders were supposed to do? Oh, wait. Or is dismantling diversity, equity, and inclusion in our federal agencies and putting an ideological agenda and trying to fire the federal workforce your actual agenda?

Have you been too busy trying to actually address the fiscal health of this country? Because the numbers are telling us that you have. So let's be real about what's going on here. I also want to point out that literally while we've been sitting here for the last almost two hours, getting lectured on fiscal responsibility, literally the Republicans just released their plan to raise the debt limit while we were sitting here and they want to raise it by $4 trillion. Okay, guys, literally, I am just without words. Inflation is going up. You want to raise the debt ceiling by $4 trillion. You want to gut Medicare, you want to gut Medicaid. You're talking about going after Social Security after promising that you wouldn't. I mean, really, what the heck is going on here? We're not trying to take down Elon Musk as a businessman. This dude is literally breaking the law inside of the federal government.

And for a party that is supposed to be the party of law and order, in quotes, I really do not see you holding him accountable and doing your most basic constitutional responsibility in the separation of powers. So I want to end where I started. We are the Oversight Committee. We are the People's House for the United States of America. We represent the American people and so, Mr. Elon Musk, if you would like to appear in front of the Oversight Committee, you have been duly invited. Please come tell us what you're doing, come testify in front of the American people, and please come hold yourself to account. With that, I yield back.

Marjorie Taylor Greene: The gentlelady yields. I now recognize myself for closing remarks. President Trump was elected with a mandate to rein in unaccountable bureaucracy in Washington and to wage war on waste. I know that because I campaigned alongside him and so did my colleagues. This hearing was the first battle of that war. And in the coming days, the subcommittee will release a report with legislative solutions to the problems we have identified here today. We aren't going to wait all the way until the end of this Congress. We're going to get to work immediately. The bureaucrats who have run Washington for decades are beyond the point of forgiveness. Their sheer incompetence and pure spite for the hard-working American people have resulted in total failure. The federal government has made over $2.7 trillion in improper payments since 2003, including $236 billion in 2023 alone. Those are trillions of dollars that honest Americans have paid in taxes at gunpoint over the years.

As we approach April 15th, Americans are once again preparing to do their taxes and fork over their unfair share of money it takes to run this country. And I have to tell you, the American people have not been getting their money's worth for a long time. Most improper payments in recent years were issued through five programs, Medicare, Medicaid, the Earned Income Tax Credit, pandemic unemployment insurance, and the Paycheck Protection Program. But a total of 16 federal programs had improper payment rates of 10% or more in 2023. That includes SNAP, the federal food stamp program, which paid out $10 billion taxpayer dollars improperly. To get their arms around this problem, Elon Musk and the DOGE team went straight to the source. They went to the Treasury Department's fiscal service, which makes about 90% of the trillions in federal payments issued annually. The audit of these payment systems was long overdue.

Treasury Secretary Scott Bessent gave DOGE employees working for the government read-only access to these systems so they could conduct that initial audit. That audit is already paying dividends. Musk learned that the databases federal agencies are supposed to check to prevent payments to fraudsters, crime rings, and dead people are not being kept up to date. Going forward, we are going to get more mileage out of these do-not-pay databases. That means fewer improper payments and less fraud and waste of taxpayer dollars. Despite this fraud that's already been revealed, a federal judge in New York issued a ruling last Friday that ran totally contrary to the will of the people. The judge blocked not only DOGE, but the Treasury Secretary himself from accessing his own agency's payment systems. That's absurd. Only career Treasury Department unelected bureaucrats can access the system the judge ruled. This turns the Constitution on its head.

We will hold this judge and others who try to stop the will of the people and their elected leaders accountable. As is written in the Federalist Papers, the judiciary has no influence over either the sword or the purse, no direction either of the strength or the wealth of the society. It may truly be said to have neither force nor will, but merely judgment and must ultimately depend upon the aid of the executive arm for the efficacy of its judgments. But the whole DC swamp is freaking out that the unelected officials from DOGE were allowed access to these systems. That makes no sense. Federal judges were not elected, the Treasury bureaucrats were not elected, and they have failed to fix the problem that is enabling American taxpayers to be robbed. So why not bring in skilled outside experts like private companies and private citizens who are successful in the real world to do everyday work that we need to get done here like audits?

Of course, federal payment systems are only one link in the improper payment chain. We need to look at other links in the chain. We need better front-end identify verification to screen out fraudsters, and we need to close eligibility loopholes. That means not letting applicants self-attest to their own eligibility and it means ending categorical eligibility, which lets someone who fraudulently qualifies for one federal benefit automatically get other federal benefits. Finally, we need to better coordinate fraud prevention efforts between federal governments and the states. These are all issues that we will be taking a hard look at in this committee and coming up with solutions to, including legislation and referrals to committees of jurisdiction that will deliver for the American people. With that and without objection, all members have five legislative days within which to submit materials and additional written questions for the witnesses, which will be forwarded to the witnesses. If there is no further business without objection, the subcommittee stands adjourned.

| 7 |

Two Weeks In ...

I don't think anyone could have taken in all the news each day. Some suggested that Steve Bannon's "flood the zone" theory was in play, where by design, so many things are put into play that the system can't respond to it all. Some will get through no matter what, at least too quickly for the judiciary to halt it all. After two weeks, the picture was coming into focus.

Dictator on Day One ... and Two ... and Three ...

{Written by the author, published on 4 February on Consider-Reconsdier.Com, the writing of this became the idea behind this book, as it seemed every day there was more to add, another piece of the puzzle as to what was going on and the implications thereof.}

Donald Trump promised to be a "dictator on day one". Two weeks in and there's no end in sight, as I made note of over 40 steps in the march to illiberal madness and complete control by one faction of one party. The Constitutional challenges and lawsuits from states to unions are mounting. Some are even suggesting all this is happening so fast to keep the public and lawmakers off-balance, as per tactics espoused by Steve Bannon. The term "coup" is now on the table, though some of us recognize it started in 2020. Others have noted that the majority of his executive orders are directly out of the Project 2025 playbook — as are so many of his cabinet picks from the Heritage Foundation in spite of pre-election denials of connections. The MAGA faithful have continued to cheer while telling the rest of us we are just being crybabies, and should just sit back and watch how wonderful the next four years will be. This article is for the future, as no doubt historians will study these times carefully to see what went horribly wrong so fast.

Please note I have put less-than-usual effort here into curbing my own biases. However, every point is based on fact-checkable truths, most of which I did so myself. Also, this is not an exhaustive list. I am not going into tariffs or ridiculous bids and threats to buy, steal, or invade Panama, Greenland, and Canada. The Epstein-worthy list of appointments going before Congress is too much to even address here, although even before his inauguration, plans to bypass the usual FBI background checks were underway.

Pardoning His Insurrectionists

The first of these steps was to pardon those who tried to seize, kidnap, and kill members of Congress — and even his own Vice President — to keep him in power after losing a lawful and exhaustingly-demonstrated fair election. This is where, you, the reader, will be separated as wheat or chaff. If you don't see this as a treasonous conflict of interest, please just stop reading now. You are simply not armed to process any other facts or logic here. For the rest of us, this arguably marks the end of the rule of law with regards to political violence. We must also note that the new top prosecutor for DC advocated for the insurrectionists and parroted Trump's false election claims.

The worst of it is that Trump explicitly said the militia group Proud Boys should have a voice in politics. These are the people Trump told to "stand back and stand by" as the election certification neared, the leader of which was given the longest sentence for his orchestrated, tactical assault on the Capitol, since pardoned and lounging at Mar-A-Lago. {Update: There are rumors that the new Attorney General, Pamela Bondi, plans to go after those who prosecuted or were involved in the arrests of the January 6th criminals.}

Dismantling Safeguards, Stacking the Deck, Political Retribution

The big news here are the buyouts offered to federal employees across multiple agencies, including the FBI, where leaders have been told to leave the bureau or be fired. In the Justice Department, the plan is immediate termination of employees who worked on criminal prosecutions of President Trump (now with hints of clemency for those "just following orders"). Dozens of senior aid officials were placed on leave, citing possible resistance to Trump's orders. Also ...

- Trump "granted" top secret security clearances to White House staff without going through traditional vetting.
- House Speaker Mike Johnson has removed Republican Rep. Mike Turner as Intelligence Committee chair because of orders "from Mar-A-Lago".
- Two top security chiefs at USAID were placed on leave after they refused to turn over classified material in restricted areas to Musk.
- Federal payments were suspended, then reinstated after lying about it, with some systems still down "for maintenance".
- Prohibitions on executive branch employees accepting major gifts from lobbyists was rolled back, and bans on lobbyists seeking executive branch jobs or vice versa are gone.
- Security protection was removed for past political opponents, including those who were targets of violence due to his own attacks and spreading conspiracies.
- An executive order restores a category (Schedule F) of federal workers which would lack job protections ordinarily afforded career civil servants.

Of particular interest to the reader should be a pause on the ban of TikTok, something he attempted his first term and now claims to be saving. His plan is to have United States become half-owner. This vague statement was originally interpreted by some as meaning American companies, but he is now proposing the creation of US sovereign wealth fund to be 50% owner. This fits perfectly well with Musk's control of X and Zuckerberg's capitulation to the new order of things, ushering in America's first mass media controlled by a combination of state and state-aligned oligarchs. (See my article "America's Brave New Media".)

The Most Powerful Man in the World

Without any Congressional approval or consent, Musk attempted to access Treasury infrastructure. After those attempting to prevent him were removed from their offices, he and his team were given full access February 1st. He immediately locked out senior government officials, websites vanished, and employees are now locked out of the building. Contrary to assertions otherwise by the President's Press Secretary, multiple employees have reported that some members of his team do not have sufficient clearance to legally access some records — including ones that listed employees' security clearance levels. {People have noted that there would not have been sufficient time for Musk himself to have been given security clearances, along with his college-age assistants.}

The ever-naive apologists are saying it's about time someone goes in and cuts all the waste and reduce government bureaucracy. Well, we've all wanted this for a LONG time. We know there will be countless finds and things worthy of scandal done over many years and administrations by both parties. But this is being done under an authoritarian with no regard for constitutional restraints, fanatical partisan intentions, an agenda of vendettas and far-Right extremists, and the ability to take complete control of the government if he isn't stopped no matter how benign anyone wants to believe. The very possibility of data breaches and back-door controls by the richest man in the world to every system and dollar is not merely concerning, but utterly insane.

On more sensational matters, was he just "sending his love" when he gave what so many are calling a "Roman salute"? A hand-gesture doesn't make someone a Nazi, but dog-whistle or not, American Neo-Nazis are throwing parades in support of the new normal. But let's stick to the man himself. As he pumped a record-breaking insane amount of cheddar ($277 million) into our presidential election, he is speaking to and funding fascist parties in European elections. The Union is pursuing criminal action for such interference at this point. But wait, there's more! Trump declared that aid will be cut off to South Africa over policies called "racist" by their far-Right, pro-Apartheid party. {Update: It is rumored that Visas for many countries will be limited, the exception being WHITE citizens of South Africa.}

Interestingly we come to the topic of Artificial Intelligence. Previously something Musk warned the world as being a threat, guidelines restricting AI use have now been removed. In response to cancelling investments in childhood Cancer research, Press Secretary Karoline Leavitt argued that AI will provide the answers, there being planned a HALF TRILLION DOLLARS in AI development. This is in part a response to China releasing an open-source AI it developed for comparative pennies. One can only wonder how much of that "investment" will go to Musk, whose technology depends heavily on AI. Ironically, he is using AI to crawl governmental administrative systems "looking for cuts".

Culture War

Obsessed with all things "woke" as the scapegoat for a fear-mongered collapse of White, Christian, English-speaking America, the language of reverse-discrimination is now absolute. Somehow, the term DEI became associated with political opponent Harris to the point where using the word "equitable" in a sentence makes one a radical Leftist. So what happened so far?

- All Federal DEI-related staff have been terminated.
- The Spanish-language page and social media channels for the White House were shut down
- Videos with ASL interpreters were eliminated (because 'captions should be enough').
- Trump's anti-DEI order resulted in Air Force videos of Tuskegee Airmen and female pilots to be removed from training (since restored after protest)
- Executive order overturned the Equal Employment Opportunity order from 1965
- The Justice Department dropped a case against a Texas doctor charged with leaking transgender care data
- Trump reversed EPA guidelines for environmental justice, eliminating help for Black and Latino communities hit harder by pollution
- The Defense Department intelligence agency has paused identity-related observances, such as federal holiday Martin Luther King Jr. Day. Defense Secretary Pete Hegseth himself declared the end of 'Cultural Awareness Months'.
- Trump blamed diversity and people with disabilities for a plane crash with no evidence whatsoever, falsely claiming that pilots and air traffic controllers could be mentally disturbed or disabled, or possibly a dwarf (no, I can't make this up).
- The Army pulled its sexual assault regulations off its websites
- Education Department employees were threatened to be placed on leave for attending diversity training. (One employee reported they were literally on an airplane when informed the training conference they were going to was cancelled.)
- Measures to protect and improve justice for rape victims on college campuses were repealed.

- The CDC was ordered to retract or censor research papers submitted to journals based on now-forbidden gender language.
- An actual federal mandate that only two genders be legally recognized
- Threatened to withhold school funding based on teachers acknowledging pronouns

The Primary Scapegoat

Trump and the news(ish) outlets that prop him up have successfully convinced America that an immigrant "invasion" is not only real, but the biggest threat to America. This sentiment is nothing new, as the Fentanyl issue rhymes with Reefer Madness in terms of creating associations between Mexicans and criminals who wantonly rape our White women. Prolific talking head Tucker Carlson parrots White Nationalist and Supremacist language into the public's ear regularly, and those south of the border are always the biggest threat to poison the blood of America (Trump's words) and replace us White folks (Tucker's words). This propaganda is so effective, this specific issue radicalized an otherwise Liberal woman killed trying to break into the Speaker's Lobby on January 6th — a Democrat living in a FOX-saturated household.

Now the promises to mass incarcerate and deport are being kept, and doesn't stop at those who have committed crimes — or even those BORN HERE.

- An open arrest of migrants in churches and schools is being flaunted, hotline and all.
- Trump has declared birthright citizenship invalid.
- Trump is questioning the legitimacy of Native American citizenship.
- Plan to reopen Guantanamo was proposed, supposedly housing 30,000 inmates. The current facility is meant for under a thou-

sand people. Cuba rejected this plan, but people have already been shipped there.
- The DOJ has halted legal programs for detained immigrants and cut off advocates' access to facilities.

Anti-Science, Anti-Health, Anti-Environment, Anti-Consumer

He, of course, immediately withdrew the United States from both WHO and the Paris Accords. Other actions in terms of government norms are more concerning.

- Health Agencies have been ordered to stop publishing bird flu warnings, and even scientific reports in journals.
- An independent EPA advisory board was fired.
- Prescription drug price controls were lifted.
- Trump fired the director of the Consumer Financial Protection Bureau.

The States

The states haven't been sitting still these past four rears, particularly in squeezing out anyone associated with stopping the attempts to overturn the election. Trump loyalists have been pushed into primaries across the board to displace anyone who contradicted The Big Lie. During these two weeks it continues, locally and in Congress. Elon Musk promised that he will use his wallet to remove any legislator who does not support Trump by replacing them at their re-election. And many states have passed or at least introduced myriad regressive, even draconian laws.

- In Tennessee, it is now a Class E felony for a legislator to vote against any measure that contradicts Trump's policies on immigration. This is the first time in American history where a lawmaker could suffer legal action for their vote.

- Oklahoma dissolved its Department of Mental Health and Substance Use Services, with everything to be turned over to the Department of Corrections. (This is reminiscent of Alabama using $400 million of COVID relief funds to build prisons.)
- With Federal blessing, various law enforcement investigations have been cancelled.

But let's not forget interference in State issues — where it's convenient, of course. Disaster relief funds for California are being held back under political conditions (demands), namely the turning on of a non-existent water flow to the areas hit by wildfires, and passing voter ID laws. Various states (and cities) are now striking back at both federal anti-sanctuary policies and interstate lawsuits against doctors and patients regarding reproductive services.

Are We There Yet?

Most of these authoritative changes are prefaced as childishly framing everything as Biden and/or Obama's fault. (If anyone wonders why he never let's a chance go to attack Obama, we must remember Trump's Birther roots and consider the possibility that it was his racism coupled with a Black President that induced him into becoming a Republican and running for office in the first place.) And here also enters doublespeak phrases like "Gender Ideology Extremism", "illegal and immoral discrimination programs" (DEI), "Climate extremism", all from the White House's website.

The bottom line is that this is not normal. This is not just pushing an agenda that's allowable under MAGA's new catchphrase "we won, deal with it". Trump promised to completely overhaul an office that no one man owns, and ignores all laws and limitations in the hope they can now win Supreme Court challenges. Not enough? Not to worry, Rep. Andy Ogles of Tennessee introduced the measure proposing a constitutional amendment to allow a third presidential term.

ADDENDUM {8 February}

In the few days it took to write this, a slew of other steps have been taken toward oblivion, including...

- Trump signed an order imposing sanctions on the International Criminal Court over investigations of Israel
- The Senate confirmed Project 2025 architect Russell Vought to lead the Office of Management and Budget
- Trump removed the head of the Federal Elections Commission.
- At the National Prayer Breakfast, Trump announced the coming creation of task force to "eradicate anti-Christian bias", a term even he admitted he had never herd of before.
- Trump started a conspiracy-scandal about subscription payments to news agencies.
- USAID executives were removed with plans to shut it down, along with the Department of Education (as promised) and other departments.
- NPR and PBS (and existing public media in general) are being targeted for defunding (and outside money may be prohibited, effectively shutting them down).
- Trump ended Biden's intelligence briefing access, likely in retaliation for having had it done to himself over his actions and unlawful possession and sharing of classified documents.

ADDENDUM {9 February}

Closing OSHA is now being discussed, and a new headline today, "Ed Martin, an advocate of Jan. 6 rioters who was in the mob outside the Capitol in 2021, now runs the U.S. attorney's office in Washington that investigated them."

ADDENDUM {10 February}

More every day, of course, but here's the most important IMO: "Fired head of the agency that protects whistleblowers sues Trump, saying he was ousted illegally". Okay, I was wrong. THIS is the worst ... "The White House has designated Mr. Musk's office, the United States DOGE Service, as an entity protected from public records requests and most judicial intervention until at least 2034, by classifying its documents as presidential records."

At least we have the National Park Service and the AMA to give us updates and hope.

ADDENDUM {12 February}

Okay, once a day is apparently not enough. Between a war on paper straws and declaring the Gulf of Mexico the "Gulf of America" (and kicking out the AP from press briefings because they use the correct name), DEI is now being attacked in the private sector, with the Attorneys General of 19 states demanding Costco end their programs or face criminal investigations.

At least masses of judges are blocking some of Trump's (and DOGE's) actions and making them put back up websites and removed content. However, the White House is saying the courts are instigating a Constitutional crisis by them trying to curb his powers — as is their job.

Concerning if intentional ... https://www.npr.org/2025/02/11/nx-s1-5293447/jan-6-evidence-captiol-riot-donald-trump

Also ... "The Department of Homeland Security, as part of an evaluation of its election security mission, said on Tuesday that personnel focused on misinformation, disinformation and foreign influence operations aimed at U.S. elections have been placed on administrative leave."

ADDENDUM {Final}

Two actions of interest added to this list at the writing of this book: the Justice Department deleted a database started in 2020 to track federal police misconduct; preparations are underway to "dissolve the leadership" of the U.S. Postal Service, and bring it under the President's control rather than maintain its independence.

| 8 |

CPAC

C PAC, the Conservative Political Action Committee, had its annual convention February 19-22 in National Harbor, Maryland.

Trump's Address

Thank you very much. Thank you. Thank you. And a very special hello to CPAC. It's been a long time.

We've loved being back, and it's hotter than ever. This place is packed. You got to see outside. They can't—they don't know what's happening. They have no idea what's happening.

And a friend is here from Argentina, and a friend is here from Poland. Stand up. Great job. Thank you. Thank you very much.

Welcome back to the nation's capital where our movement is thriving, fighting, winning, and dominating Washington like never before. Nobody's ever seen anything like this before. They used to have a little smaller crowds here. It was a little bigger.

The fraudsters, liars, cheaters, globalists, and deep state bureaucrats are being sent packing. The illegal alien criminals are being sent home. We're draining the swamp, and we're restoring government by the people, for the people.

For years, Washington was controlled by a sinister group of radical left Marxists, warmongers, and corrupt special interests who drained our wealth, attacked our liberties, obliterated our borders, and sucked our country dry—not any longer. But on November 5th, we stood up to all the corrupt forces that were destroying America. We took away their power. We took away their confidence. They lost their confidence. You know? Do you ever watch? They lost their confidence.

Oh, it's so nice to watch. And we took back our country, and we must be doing something right because we've got the highest poll numbers that I've ever had and that any Republican president has ever had.

And our approval rating is now the highest ever across all demographics. Rasmussen just came out at 56%, Insider Advantage, 56%, RMG Research, 57%. And we have many polls in the mid-sixties, one at 71%. We like that 71%.

And according to YouGov, a big deal, 70% of Americans believe that what we are doing is right, and we are keeping our promises. That's all we're doing when you think is keeping our promises. That's all we had to do, And, their promises weren't worthwhile to go and vote for. They loved men playing in women's sports, open borders, little things like that.

But don't tell them. Don't tell them. Keep it quiet. We'll tell them about a week before the next election. Now keep it quiet. Let them think it's a great thing what they're doing.

You saw Maine yesterday, right, the governor of Maine? She's fighting to keep men in women's sports. You ever see what happens to a woman when a woman boxes a man who transitioned to womanhood? Did you ever see what happened? It's not pretty. It's not pretty. Let her do that fight. Let them all do that fight because I think that's about a 90-10 issue, and I can't figure out who the 10% are. Nobody can.

So today, I want to say thank you to all of the incredible patriots of CPAC and all of the incredible patriots in our country. Seventy-seven million, and it's actually much more than that because despite that, they cheated like hell. It was just too big to rig. It was too big to rig. Seventy-seven million.

Remember you used to go? I said, look. We're leading in the polls by a lot. Don't believe the polls. Just go and vote. You got to vote. We're going to make it too big to rig. And they tried, but it was too big to rig. One of the great statements. We love it because everybody won and voted.

We fought through hell together, but in the end, we achieved the great liberation of America. We're liberating our country right now. We're doing all these things that you're reading about. We're liberating our country.

I first spoke to this gathering fourteen years ago, and I won your straw poll. I didn't know anything about a straw poll. They took this big straw poll, and I won by, like, 27 points. And I figured, you know, that's good. Maybe I should keep doing it, and I did. And I became president. Isn't that great? Who would think? Who would think?

But he became president too. He's a MAGA guy too. Make Argentina great again. Right? Make Argentina great again. I kept hearing about this man. I kept hearing about this man in beautiful Argentina, and it is beautiful, but boy, did it have inflation. Inflation made it less beautiful. I hear you're doing fantastically. We're very proud of you, actually. And make Argentina great. Thank you very much. Great honor to have you.

But now it's my honor to address you for the first time as your 47th president of the United States.

I want to begin by thanking Matt and Mercedes Schlepp for the incredible job they do and everyone—everyone they put together. They put together an amazing team, the American Conservative Union for organizing this event along—oh, you have some big players here, Senator Ted Cruz, Eric Schmidt, Jim Banks of Indiana. Where's Eric? Where is Eric? Is it—hello, Eric. You can see Eric anywhere. He's right in the back of the room. He stands up.

They're all good. These are great people. Representatives Riley Moore, James Comer, Harriet Hageman, Byron Donalds, our great attorney general. It's going to be great. Pam Bondi. Where's Pam? I don't know where she is. So many people. So many people.

Secretary Doug Bergam. Secretary Chris Wright, oh, he's going to get that energy out of the ground, Secretary Scott Turner. Our next ambassador to the United Nations, Elise Stefanik, who just gave a great speech, by the way. A very good friend of mine is this—is this guy central casting, though? Tom Homan. Is he central casting? Where is—hello, Tom. I yield—well, I love that. How can I love a guy like that? But I do. He's doing a great job. Thank you, Tom, very much. Thank you. I appreciate it.

Arkansas governor, Sarah Sanders. Thank you, Sarah. Thank you. And Pennsylvania attorney general, Dave Sunday. I love that name.

We're also honored to be joined by President Duda of Poland who's a fantastic man and a great friend of mine. And we got 84% of the Polish people that voted for us, so you must be doing something right. Hanging out with Trump.

And again, President Milei of Argentina, thank you very much. Thank you very much. What a great guy.

And the Prime Minister of Slovakia, Robert Fico. Robert? Thank you, Robert. Thank you. Nice to see you.

The leader of the UK Reform Party who, by the way, did really well in that last election. I've been his friend for a long time, and I wasn't sure. Am I supposed to be his friend or not? But it never mattered to me if he did well or not. I always liked him, but it's easier to like him when he got the kind of votes he got. Really took—he took it by storm, and they say he's going to do even better this time. Nigel Farage. Where is Nigel? Thank you, Nigel. Thank you. What a great guy.

The leader of Spain's Vox party, Santiago Abascal. Thank you, Santiago. Thank you. Thank you very much. I thought that was you. Thank you very much. Great job you're doing.

And a friend of mine, Eduardo Bolsonaro of Brazil, the Chamber of Deputies. Thank you. Thank you. Say hello to your father. Thank you very much. Great family. Great gentlemen of your great family.

First Lady Melania Trump

And our great first lady, Melania, is watching us right now on television, so give her a hand. Give her a hand. Woah. Thank you. Thank you. Oh, she's going to be happy. That's so nice. We love our first lady. Everybody does.

With the help of so many incredible supporters here today, we're going to forge a new and lasting political majority that will drive American politics for generations to come. I think we're going to do fantastically well in the midterms. You know, in theory, the one that wins the presidency does not do well in the midterms, but I think this is going to be a change. We're at a level I don't think we've been at this level maybe ever as the Republican Party. We're a bigger, better, stronger party than ever before. More people in our party than ever before.

But the people have given us a resounding mandate for dramatic change in Washington, and we are going to deliver it. We're going to use it, and we're going to make America great again by using it.

So it's going to be something. But think of it, at the presidential level, we won the popular vote by millions and millions of votes. We swept all seven swing states, Michigan, Wisconsin, Pennsylvania, North Carolina, Georgia, Arizona, and Nevada, all by great margins. We won 85% of all of the counties in America. That means that map was red. Did you ever see the map? Did you see the certified map? Where is it? I want to see a certified map. It's all red. You can hardly find the blue.

Think of this. They won 525 counties, and we won 2,600 counties. It's the biggest margin ever recorded. And incredibly, for the first time ever, all 50 states shifted toward the Republican Party. It's never happened before. So it was indeed too big to rig.

We won the largest number of African American votes in Republican history by far. We won the largest number of Hispanic American votes, any Republican ever. Hispanic Americans, we love you. The energy, the brilliance of Hispanic Americans.

We won all of the cities and towns along the Texas border, whereas before I ran, we won none. We never used to win any. I got a call from our great governor of Texas who said, "President, you just won every single town along the Texas border to Mexico." I said, "Oh, is that good?" He said, "It hasn't happened since Reconstruction." I said, "Define Reconstruction for me." He said, "That means essentially the Civil War." That's a long—that's a long time. But that was, when I first heard about it, actually.

Our party has become the proud voice of hardworking citizens of every race, religion, color, and creed. And I think one of the main reasons, not that we're conservative or not that we're anything else, we are the party of common sense. It's about common sense. Right? It's all about common sense.

Over the past month, we've confirmed an all-star team of warriors, patriots, visionaries, and put the America First agenda into action. I see Doug Bergam sitting right over there. I'd say he was so good. I looked at him. I said, I got to have him here. I got to have him. He's—you know, he was a great—he was a great governor. He's involved with little thing called energy. He's got the Department of Interior, and Chris Wright has the Department of Energy.

So Chris has no energy, and Doug has all of the energy. Chris has more interior, but he doesn't have—so I merged them. So now you have an energy guy, and you have the guy with all the energy. And you're going to drill baby drill, aren't you? Drill baby drill.

And, Catherine, stand up. This wife is incredible. She is such an incredible woman. Incredible woman. You got very lucky, Doug. It's good to be successful, isn't it, Doug? She's an incredible woman. He's an incredible guy.

In addition to the great cabinet secretaries we have here today, we confirm Secretary of Defense, Pete Hegseth, to end the woke insanity and rebuild our military. Pete is fantastic. Thank you.

To stop the weaponization of federal law enforcement, I know about that, I think, better than any human being on earth. This week, we swore in a new director of the FBI, somebody that everybody wanted, Kash Patel. Kash is great. He's a popular guy. He went through. He went through with a blessing of a lot of good people too. I'll tell you, it was great.

To end the politicization of our intelligence agencies, we confirmed Director of National Intelligence, Tulsi Gabbard, who is something very respected, highly respected.

And to make America healthy again, we confirm Secretary of Health and Human Services, Robert F. Kennedy Jr. Great guy. We need him. We need him.

You know, there's a number on autism as an example with children, autism. And you go back fifteen years, it was from 10 to 20,000. You had, like, one in 10 to 20,000. Some say 10, some say 20, but it was in that vicinity. That's a big vicinity. Now it's one in 36 babies of autism. One in 36. Think of it. It was one in probably 20,000 people. Now it's one in 36. There's something wrong. Something's wrong, and Bobby is going to find it. Working with Dr. Oz, by the way. Working with Dr. Oz.

Together, we've achieved more in four weeks than most administrations achieve in four years. We made—we made a lot of progress. I heard O'Reilly last night say Donald Trump for the first four weeks is the greatest president ever in the history of our country. That was O'Reilly. Bill O'Reilly is alright. You know who he said second was? George Washington. That's not bad. I beat George Washington. I love beating George Washington. Thank you, Bill.

On our first day in office, we declared a national emergency at our southern border. After years of politicians using our military to defend foreign borders while leaving our country defenseless and helpless, we deployed—we deployed a group of people, active duty troops to defend our border and repel the invasion of our country. This was an invasion.

You know, we had a great first term, a really great first term, and I called it an invasion. And we had great numbers, but now we have the best numbers we've ever had. We've never had numbers like this. We've done it all in four weeks. Think of it. That was Tom Homan, Kristi Noem, the whole group.

When day one, I ended the catch and release. I reinstated remain in Mexico when I signed an order that will end birthright citizenship for the children of illegal aliens. Because it wasn't meant for these children. It wasn't meant for people that escaped or invaded, came into our country illegally. It was meant for the children of slaves. Because when it was done many, many years ago, it was during a very tough period in this country's history, and that was meant for the children of slaves. I wish people would understand that so they could get this thing approved, and we don't have millions and millions of people coming into our country, and they shouldn't be here.

This week, I also canceled temporary protected status for migrants from Haiti pouring into our country.

Immigration and Border Security

Pouring in. If I weren't elected president, there'd be nobody in Haiti anymore. They were pouring in at levels from other countries too, all over Africa, the Congo, all over South America. And they were coming in from prisons and mental institutions and insane asylums, jails, and gang members. And, you just have to see gang members, drug lords, people that are drug addicted.

They were sending them all into our ridiculous and very stupid Biden open border. Our border czar was Kamala. Haven't said that name in a while. I haven't said that name. No. I haven't said that name in a while. Kamala. I'll bet nobody knows her last name. Nobody ever knows her last name. Even during the campaign, you'd have to say Kamala.

It's strange. You know? A little different name. Kamala because her last name was Harris. I used to say, Senator Harris. They nobody knew who the hell I was talking about. So I had to go Kamala. But think of it, I was beating Joe badly, really badly, and they changed him. I'm the only one that ever had to beat two people. I had to beat two. I had to beat two. We beat two. We—I didn't beat. You beat. You beat two people.

No. He was doing better. That's like the great Dana White. He has a fight, and one guy's doing really badly. So when they take him out, they put another guy in the fight, the same guy that's—I had that. Never happened before. A lot of things we do never happened before.

You ever noticed that? We've the first in everything. So we beat two candidates.

They said, who do you run against? Well, we ran against Biden, and we ran against Kamala Harris. But illegal border crossings now have plummeted by almost one hundred percent. The border czar never called the border, never called the great people of the border. They have unbelievable—I called them so much they couldn't take my calls. They hated me. But then they became to love me. You know what? Because the border people want to have great borders. But you have to call them on occasion.

"How are we doing today? Pete, how are we doing?" You have to call. And we called the right guys. I became friends. You know, the border patrol endorsed me. And, these people, you have no idea. They weren't supposed to because you're not supposed to do that. I don't think you're allowed to do it. Actually, they did it anyway. They said this is—this is crazy, but these are great people and ICE and our general law enforcement, and by the way, our great, great firemen and firewomen too. They were great. They all endorsed us.

With the police, we got high nineties in terms of—and many of them were unionized. You know? We have a young lady who's right now going for the Department of Labor, and she tends to be a little bit—a little bit on the, slightly left of center. And everybody said, why did I do that? I said, you know why I did that? Because unions like her and labor likes her and a lot of people like her, and she's very solid, very strong, and she's going to do the right thing. But they all voted for us.

They didn't vote for me. They voted for us. We got the teamsters. We got the firefighters. We got the police. We got the auto workers. We're so great. We had tremendous support. So I think it's nice to give them a person in the center because that's what she—she's going to be very good, I think. But a lot of people say, why'd you do that? I said, because they want to do something nice for these people that voted for me. Oh, gee. What a great political move that was. Now they're all saying, what a great political move. No. It's just—it's all common sense. Remember that. Remember that. Sean O'Brien was fantastic. The whole group, they were great.

Over the past few weeks, we've begun the largest deportation operation in American history, larger even than that of President Dwight D. Eisenhower, a very moderate man, but he was very strong in that. He didn't like people running into our country and taking over our country. I'll tell you, I had four years. I don't know if you had this.

I couldn't stand it. Don't get angry. Donald, don't get angry, please. I couldn't stand it. Watching these people come in from jails and mental institutions and and the worst criminals in the street, gang members being dropped off in buses and bused into our country. I couldn't stand it. So I said, I'm going to run for president again. And now we don't have that problem. Now we don't have that problem anymore. We don't have that problem anymore.

We now have the best border we've ever had. And by the way, if they can ever find my world's favorite chart ever in history, I'll show you what it was when I left, and now it's even slightly better. Can you drop that chart, do think? I don't know. I never tell them about this, but they used to drop it like magic. If they can, they'll drop it. Who the hell knows? But it's my favorite chart, my favorite chart in history.

We're liberating communities like Aurora, Colorado and Springfield, Ohio that have been occupied by illegal alien criminals from all over the world. We're rescuing the Americans whose jobs have been stolen, whose wages have been robbed, and whose way of life has been absolutely destroyed.

And under the Trump administration, our country will not be turned into a dumping ground. We're not going to do it. We're going to have a great country again. It's going to happen soon. A lot sooner than you're thinking.

We're going to have so much money coming in from tariffs. Oh, you're going to say your senators and your congressmen are going to say, "Please, sir, please. You're making us look so bad. We have so much money coming in. I didn't know this was going to happen. Please don't do this to us. We look very bad."

But they're great. They're doing well. I tell you the Republican senators just—they're sticking together. The republics—the Republican congressmen and women are sticking together. Every once in a while, you have one that wants a little action or something. I don't know what it is. It's so sad to see. I just hate to see it. I hate to see it, but they're sticking together.

One thing about the Democrats, they have rotten, horrible policy, the worst policy in history, but they stick together. We have great policy, but sometimes they don't stick, but they've been sticking for us. They've been sticking. And, I think the speaker and the leader have done a fantastic job. That's Thune and Johnson. And I think they've done—two guys really working hard and doing a—they're really doing a great job.

But we have a lot to stick with. We have a lot to stick together for because what we've done has never been done before. Nobody's ever seen anything like this, and nobody's ever seen four weeks like we've had, especially the four weeks, the first four weeks.

You know, that's like if you golf, when you sink that first four footer in the first hole, it gives you confidence on the next hole. You sink another one. Now you go into that third hole, and you can't—and by the time you get to the fifth hole, you feel you can't miss. Right? Like a baseball player, he gets up, and he hits our first one, and then the second at bat, he hits that one. And, you know, you get—and we have great confidence. And they've lost their confidence, as I said. They really lost their confidence. I watched them. They're really screwed up.

I watched this MSNBC, which is a threat to democracy, actually. They're—they're stone cold, but they're stuttering. They're all screwed up. They're all mentally screwed up. They don't know what—their ratings have gone down the tubes. I don't even talk about CNN. CNN sort of like, I don't know. They—they—they are pathetic, actually. But MSNBC was mean. Their ratings are absolutely down.

This Rachel Maddow, what does she have? She's got nothing. Nothing. She took—she took a sabbatical where she worked one day a week. They paid her a lot of money. She gets no ratings. I should go against her in the ratings because I'll tell you, she gets no rate. All she does is to talk about Trump, Trump, Trump, Trump, Trump, all different subjects. Trump this, Trump that. But these people are really—I mean, they lie. You—they shouldn't be allowed to lie every night. They are really a vehicle of the Democrat party. They should be paying.

Is that Gordon? Yes. Is that Gordon? The great Gordon Chang? Is that good? Stand up, Gordon. Wow. We have everybody here today. Thank you very much. How am I doing on China? Am I doing good? Am I doing good on China?

Tell you one thing, nobody's ever done like I've done on China. Nobody ever let people know what was happening with respect to China. And I happen to like President Xi, and I have tremendous respect for the people of China. Love the people of China. But, we've been treated very unfairly by China and many other countries, and, we're not being fairly treated anymore.

We had that down to a science in the first term, and then they lost it. You know, we lost over a trillion dollars to China this last year under Biden. Crooked Joe Biden. What do we like better? Crooked Joe or sleepy Joe?

Ready? Ready? Crooked Joe or sleepy? Ready? Crooked Joe. Yeah. Sleepy Joe. Got to stay with Crookie. He had one ability that I didn't have. He could do something that I couldn't do.

I don't say that because he was a horrible golfer. Remember he challenged me during the debate to a golfer? Man? He said, "I'm a six handicap." I said, "You're not a thirty-six handicap." He said he's a six. And then he said, "Well, I'm eight." Remember? I said, that was quick. Picked up two strokes.

We said nominate, but he was—he's not a thirty-six handicap, but he had one ability that was amazing. He could go with cameras on him, television, fake news on him, probably because he knows they wouldn't cover it badly. You know, they covered him as well as you can cover him. How the hell can you cover the guy? Well—but—but he had this incredible—he could barely walk in the sand.

Somebody thought he looked great in a bathing suit. And he'd walk in the stand pulling a thing that weighed about six ounces. You know those aluminums? The aluminums are very good. You can—a child—it's meant for children and very old people to lift. Right? So he—he would put it down, and he'd put it down, and he'd fall into it, and he'd immediately fall asleep in front of the media. I could never do that. That's the only thing. That's the only thing. I could never do it. No. He was sleepy Joe, but he was crooked as hell. You know? There's no question.

He was a sleepy crooked guy. Terrible, terrible president. He was the worst president in the history of our country. I don't—I'll say it. Jimmy Carter passed away recently, and he passed away a happy man. He was a happy man when he passed away because he said that it's not even close. Joe was the worst. And believe me, I have to clean up the mess. I'm cleaning up the mess, and it is a mess on the border with inflation. They go over—every single thing he touched turned to shit. Okay? Everything. True. It's true. That's true.

Now Franklin Graham's angry at me. They'd be better if you would never use foul language. And I told him, I said, Franklin, you know, Franklin Graham's a great guy, by the way. Does a great job. The son of the great Billy Graham. Right? But I said to Franklin, you know, sometimes you need it for emphasis. And he said, "No. No. They'd be even better if you wouldn't use any bad language."

That's not really a terrible word. You know? But that's a much more appropriate word, a better—what word would I use to describe? What word could I use? It's, so and we have to be truthful too.

So, you know, all countries are now taking their illegal aliens back even those that stated strongly, we will never take them back. Don't ever send them to us. But they said that during the Biden administration. They never said it during my administration. Venezuela's taken them back. They're all—Colombia's taken them back. Remember Colombia said, "We will not—we will not take them back," he said. And within about thirteen minutes, I think, "We would love to take them back. In fact, we will send our planes to pick them up." Remember?

And they said, what happened? What happened? And you see these Venezuelan planes loaded up with some real nice people. You wouldn't have wanted to be the pilot on any of those planes. But they know we're not playing games.

And just this week, I officially designated bloodthirsty cartels and murderers gangs as foreign terrorist organizations, something which Biden didn't want to do and nobody wanted to do. It's true. The full might and power of the federal government now be dedicated to eradicating MS-13, Tren de Aragua. That's the Venezuelan prison gangs. These are very nice fellows.

The only thing good about them is they make our criminals look like nice people. It's true. Remember when they used to say, people that come in from foreign countries are nice people. These are wonderful people. These are good people. They're not murderers. They're not terrible. They're—these people make us look like babies. Okay? You know the Hells Angels?

They're among the nicest people on earth when you compare them to these thugs. And the Hells Angels actually love our country, if you can believe that. They actually do. But their members and their leaders in the United States will be hunted down. I'm talking about MS-13.

They are hunting them down. We will—we removed tens of thousands. MS-13, Tren de Aragua, rooted out, arrested, and expelled from our soil like the savage monsters that they are. We don't have anybody coming up from Argentina. Nobody's coming up from Argentina to facilitate the mass removal of criminal aliens.

I also issued an executive order to make available the full capacity in detention. We're going to use Guantanamo Bay. We have a detention facility that's actually massive. Nobody even knew it existed. Holds thousands of thousands of prisoners.

We never used it. For four long years, you had a president who put illegal aliens up in penthouse suites in beautiful hotels on Park Avenue, on Madison Avenue, on Fifth Avenue in Manhattan. Now you have a president who is stamping their ticket to Gitmo on a one-way trip back to the places from which they came, the wonderful places. Big difference.

My administration is also moving swiftly to save the U.S. economy from the train wreck of inflation and worse that Joe Biden created. I withdrew from the one-sided Paris climate accord. It was a disaster. It was a disaster. I terminated the Green New Deal scam. One of the greatest hoaxes ever played on this country is the Green New Deal scam. We spent trillions of dollars on this nonsense and, just a total hoax.

It really set back our country, I want to tell you, monetarily and every other way. And I canceled Joe Biden's insane electric vehicle mandate where everybody has to have an electric. And if you want an electric car, get an electric car. If you want a gasoline-powered car, if you want to have a hybrid, you get it. The only thing you can't do is a hydrogen-powered car.

You know why? They said it really works great, but when it doesn't work, you never find the body. It's a bad—that's a bad sign. You know, when it doesn't work, you've—they found the body on a tree about two hundred and fifty yards up the road. It's seriously bad.

So we'll leave hydrogen out of it for a little while, I think, or maybe permanent. I'd say permanently. To crush inflation by slashing spending, I imposed an immediate federal hiring freeze, a federal regulation freeze, and a foreign aid freeze. We're giving to countries that hate us. We're giving billions and billions of dollars to countries that hate us, and I signed an order creating the Department of Government Efficiency.

You probably haven't heard of it, which is now waging war on government waste, fraud, and abuse. And Elon is doing a great job. He's doing a great job. We love Elon, don't we? He's like, I—he's a character with his—with his son, X.

We love X. He's the only one kid get away. His son's really named X. He's the only one can get away with naming his son X. We haven't—did it this day. You're crazy. But he's great. He's doing a great job, and he doesn't need this. He doesn't need it, but he's—he wants to see—you know, he's a patriot. People said, well, what official position does he have? He said, patriot. Oh. They didn't know. They said, that was good. He's a patriot.

Here are some of the flagrant scams that, as an example, they've spent money on, and we've been able to recapture for a large dose of it, at least.

$520 million for a consultant to think of that. Five hundred and twenty million dollars. Five hundred and twenty million. You know, when I hired consultants and they—they just take advantage of you, it's a horrible thing to watch. And I give them twenty-five thousand dollars. I feel I'm overpaying. These guys got five hundred and twenty million dollars.

$25 million to promote biodiversity conservation and socially responsible behavior in Colombia. This is Colombia South America, not Columbia University. Of course, that might be worse actually, based on their actions.

$40 million to improve the social and economic inclusion of sedentary migrants. Nobody knows where, who are they, where do they come from, just sedentary migrants. Nobody even knows what a sedentary migrant is. If they were sedentary, they wouldn't be a migrant. Right? They wouldn't move. No. They wouldn't move. They'd stay in the same place. Right, Doug?

$42 million for social and behavior change in Uganda

$10 million for Mozambique medical male circumcisions. Why are we going to Mozambique to do circumcisions? It's a lot of money.

$14 million for improving public procurement in Serbia is a beauty.

$486 million to a consortium of elections and political process strengthening ideas, of which $22 million goes to inclusive and participatory political process in Moldova. $29 million goes to strengthen the political landscape and help them out so that they can vote for a radical left communist in Bangladesh. You had to see who they supported. You wouldn't—yeah. You would believe it. Nobody in this room would be in that group.

$20 million for fiscal federalism and $19 million for biodiversity in Nepal.

$47 million for improving learning outcomes in Asia.

$18 million for helping India with its elections. Why the hell—why don't we just go to all paper ballots, let them help us with their elections. Right? Voter ID. Wouldn't that be nice? We're giving money to India for election. They don't need money. They—they take advantage of us pretty good. The high—one of the highest tariff nations in the world. We try and sell something. They have a two hundred percent tariff, and then we're giving them a lot of money to help them with their election.

$32 million for the Prague Civil Society Center.

$14 million for social cohesion in Liberia

$9.7 million to develop a cohort Cambodian youth with enterprise-driven skills. Think of that.

Millions of dollars for sex change operations in Guatemala

$20 million for Sesame Street in Iraq. They put out a little play on the street. Twenty million dollars. You could do it on Broadway and have nineteen million dollars left over. No. It's a scam. They—they get kickbacks and all sorts things out. It's a scam. Whoever heard of it. Think of it. Twenty minute Sesame Street play.

We're also uncovering outrageous incompetence and fraud in the Social Security. We have, look. Let's assume that people, generally speaking, in our case and everybody in this room, we're going to all live way over a hundred, but this is a little ridiculous because not too many people are going over a hundred. Everybody, hopefully, in this room will. But there are in the Social Security ranks and files. And what we're doing now is finding out, do they get paid? Do they get paid?

In other words, is somebody taking all of this money? So they have over one hundred to a hundred and nine, 4.7 million Social Security numbers, think of that, from people whose age is over one hundred. 3.6 million people whose age is over one hundred and ten years, 3.47 million people who are over one hundred and twenty years of age, 3.9 million people whose age goes from one hundred and thirty to one hundred and thirty-nine years of age. 3.5 million whose age goes from one hundred and forty to one hundred and forty-nine years old. 1.3—see, it's coming down now slowly.

No. It's all a scam. The whole thing is a scam. 1.3 million people. 1.3 who are over one hundred and fifty years of age.

And over 130,000 people are listed on our Social Security roles as over one hundred and sixty years of age. Now the final is at 1,039. So now we're down into reasonable numbers. 1,039 people are listed between the ages of two hundred and twenty years old to two hundred and twenty-nine. And we have one person who's listed at two hundred and forty-one years of age.

And we have one person listed at three hundred and sixty years of age, an all-time record, and our country's two hundred and fifty years old. So that person's substantially older than our country.

Under our administration, there will be no tolerance for Social Security fraud. We will not allow anyone to cheat our seniors, and those who will do that will be prosecuted by Pam Bondi and others.

We are also going to Fort Knox. I'm going to go with Elon. And would anybody like to join us? Because we want to see if the gold is still there. We want to see. Wouldn't that be terrible if we open up this Fort Knox?

It's got—it's just solid granite that's five feet thick. The front door, you need six muscle men to open it up. I don't even think they have windows. Wouldn't that be terrible if we opened it up and there was no gold there? Like, so we're going to open those doors.

We're going to take a look. And if there's twenty-seven tons of gold, we'll be very happy. I don't know how the hell we're going to measure it, but that's okay. We want to see lots of nice, beautiful, shiny gold in Fort Knox. Don't be totally surprised. We open the door. We'll say, there's nothing here. They sold this too. Now we have a very corrupt group of people in this country, and we're finding them out.

We're removing all of the unnecessary, incompetent, and corrupt bureaucrats from the federal workforce. That's what we're doing. And under the buyouts, we offered federal employees more than seventy-five thousand federal bureaucrats, think of that, have voluntarily agreed to surrender their taxpayer-funded jobs. We want to make governments smaller, more efficient. We want to keep the best people, and we're not going to keep the worst people. And, you know, we're doing another thing.

If they don't report for work, we're firing them. In other words, you have to go to office. Right? Right? Look at her.

If you don't report to work, you know, that's another scam. You know, who the hell—if I'm staying home, I'm going to—let's see. My golf handicap would get down to very low number. You—so you'd be shocked if I told you the real number, but I would be so good. I'd—I'd try and get on tour.

I'd get—I would be so good. I'd call up. I'd say, listen. I'm really working here. Where are my gloves? Where are my gloves? Either that or, in many cases, they have second jobs while they're getting paid by us. So one of the reasons they're leaving is because they don't want to have to show that, and, we're demanding to see that information. How many jobs have you had? Who paid you while you were working for the government?

And, all—and we are demanding that people, if they work for the government, they have to show up and sit in an office and do their job. Right?

And we've also effectively ended the left-wing scam known as US-AID, the agency's name, has been removed from its former building, and that space will now house agents from customs and border patrol. Beautiful.

And at the ultra-left CFPB, it said which was terrible. So many people have been hurt by that. I used to call—I used to get calls from lending offices, from owners of small banks, and they were almost crying. What they did to those people, they destroyed them, put them out of business. They established—it was established by Elizabeth "Pocahontas" Warren. Does anyone know—remember the Pocahontas scam?

"I'm an Indian. Therefore, I'm entitled to be a senator. I'm an Indian," she said. "Could we see proof of that, please?" She said, "Well, the only proof I have is my mother said I have high cheekbones." Oh, that's fine. That's no good. Right? Remember she went out? I just really spooked her, I tell you.

Remember she went out? She couldn't take it anymore. Was going to Pocahontas. Pocahontas. Everyone knew she was not an Indian.

I had more Indian blood than her, and I have no Indian blood. I'd—I'd had—I'd be honored to, but I don't have—anybody had more than her. Do you remember she went out and she had a blood test? And it came back, and she was so happy because it said one-thousand twenty-fourth. That means everybody in this room had more than her.

But because there was even the scant—in other words, you know, one million years ago, something could've happened. And she was so happy that she released it, and she got killed. That was the end of her presidential career. She does not like me very much, but she's a—she's a very angry person. Do you notice the way she is?

She's always screaming, and she's crazy. These people are crazy. The radical left is meaner. Yes. I don't know what it is, Doug. They're meaner than us, aren't they? We're like normal people. You know? We're smart. We get our word, but we don't go crazy.

Of course, they'll take my little red from fifteen minutes ago. The fact is, he lost control on the stage. He lost control. And they'll have me screaming having to do with Franklin. Poor Franklin.

He lost control. I don't get it. You know, you think they'd want to love our country. They have no ratings anymore. Nobody listens to them. Nobody believes the fake New York Times. Washington Post is doing no business. They're losing all their business. Nobody believes them.

But we've escorted the radical left bureaucrats out of the building and locked the doors behind them. We've gotten rid of thousands.

International Organizations

I withdrew the United States from the corrupt World Health Organization. I withdrew from the anti-Semitic UN Human Rights Council. The council is horrible, and I withdrew from the terror-supporting UN Relief and Works Agency. The UN has such great potential, but not the way it's run now. It's terrible the way it's run now.

We stopped all taxpayer money to these corrupt institutions. And by the way, just so—because who the hell knows—we got to talk about something very important, the war between Russia and Ukraine. People are being killed, mostly young men, mostly Russian and Ukrainian men at levels you've never seen before. Thousands of people are weakened.

I've spoken to President Putin, and I think that thing is going to end, but it's got to end. It's a horrible, horrible thing to watch. I'm dealing with President Zelensky. I'm dealing with President Putin. I'm trying to get the money back that, or secured because, you know, Europe has given one hundred billion dollars.

The United States has given three hundred and fifty billion dollars because we had a stupid, incompetent president and administration. Three hundred and fifty. But here's worse. Europe gave it in the form of a loan. They get their money back.

International Aid and Negotiation

We gave it in the form of nothing. So I want them to give us something for all of the money that we put up, and I'm going to try and get the war settled, and I'm going to try and get all that death ended. So we're asking for rare earth and oil, anything we can get, but we feel so stupid. Here's Europe. And you know, it affects Europe.

It doesn't really affect us except we don't like to see two things. Number one, how Biden got us into this thing in the first place. Terrible. But why is it that he didn't ask for equalization? Europe should put up more money than us.

But even if you said the same thing, how come we went so far out front? And he didn't know that Europe gets his money back. They did it in the form of a loan. We don't get our money back. We get nothing.

So we're getting our money back. We're going to get our money back because it's not—it's not fair. It's just not fair. And we will see, but I think we're pretty close to a deal, and we better be close to a deal because that has been a horrible situation. It would have never happened if I were president.

And by the way, October 7th, Israel would have never happened if I was president. It would have never happened. Iran was broke. They had no money for Hamas or Hezbollah. They had no money to give.

Everybody knows that. Jewish people in the audience know that Iran was broke. They were not giving money around. And when I got out, they took all the sanctions off Biden, and Iran became rich very quickly. With oil, you can become rich very, very quickly.

And, the rest is history. What a horrible thing. Even though the hostages are coming back, I saw it this morning where we got six more back. Biden got none back, by the way, just so you understand. None. Zero. He would have never gotten any of them back, but they're coming back in pretty bad shape. It's a horrible thing, and many are dead. Many are dead.

So we'll see how that all ends up, but it's a—it's a horrible thing. But I just want you to know we're working on that. That's a very big part of it. And I don't like talking about it because we're in the middle of negotiations, but it's, it's very, very sad. It's a very sad. It would have never happened.

There was no way Russia was never going to go in, and they went in because of a lot of reasons. And, so many people are dead. Far more people are dead than you're reading about. You know, when they blow up all these cities, all those cities are—they look like demolition sites. Every single building is down.

All of those beautiful golden towers at a thousand years old, They're lying on the ground in smithereens—blown to smithereens. There's nothing left of them. They're just lying on the ground, never to be rebuilt again, not possible to rebuild them again. And, all of that heritage—heritage is gone. People have done a really horrible job that would have never—if I were president, zero chance that a shot would even have been fired. Wouldn't have happened. So sad.

To further turbocharge our economy, we have launched the most aggressive deregulation program in any nation's history, and we're also going to be seeking the largest tax cuts in American history. Again, we—we brought them down, as you know, from close to forty percent down to twenty-one percent. Now we're bringing them down to fifteen percent if you make your product in the United States of America.

We're defending the American worker like never before, and that's why the auto workers and the union workers and the teamsters and so many others, they supported us, the firemen, policemen, so many others, whether they were union or nonunion, they all supported us. They supported—they're called workers, and they supported us at levels that nobody's ever seen before.

Weeks ago, I imposed a ten percent tariff on all goods coming from China because of the fact that they're sending fentanyl into our country through Mexico, by the way. I'm not happy with Mexico or I'm not happy with Canada either. I imposed twenty-five percent tariffs on all foreign steel and aluminum, and I will soon impose reciprocal tariffs on any country that charges us.

And by the way, the reciprocal means they charge us, we charge them. Same thing. So nobody can be upset. Right? But we have countries charging us two hundred percent, and we charge them nothing. They charge us, we charge them. Our country's going to become rich again, very rich.

I always say it's my favorite word in the dictionary. The word tariff is my favorite word in the dictionary. You know, we were richest, the richest relatively from—think of this. From 1870 to 1913, that was our riches because we collected tariffs from foreign countries that came in and took our jobs and took our money, took our everything. But they charged tariffs, and we had so much money. They set up the 1887—you think of that long time ago. 1887 tariff commission. It was a commission of very important people to determine where we should spend all of the tremendous vast wealth that we had.

We had so much wealth. Wouldn't it nice today? Of course, now we give it away to transgender this, transgender that. Everybody gets a transgender operation. It's just wonderful.

Now we give it away like, to crazy things. But in those days, it was different. It was a different world. It was a different country, but we were very rich because of tariffs. And I get myself in trouble because I say that tariff is my favorite word, and the fake news went crazy.

"What about god? What about wife and family? What about love?" I said, okay. Tariff is now my fourth favorite word.

I got myself into a lot of trouble with that. You can't believe it. I said tariff is my favorite word in the dictionary, and I got killed by the fake news. So I say now, it doesn't sound good. Tariff is—it's my fourth favorite word.

I go, tariff is my fourth favorite word. It sounds so terrible, but this way, I'm free. I write free. You know? I don't get clobbered by the fake news.

But tariffs are also a powerful tool of diplomacy, and all around the world are moving quickly to bring back peace through strength. We have the greatest—you know, I rebuilt our entire military in the first term. We left a lot of it, although a lot of it, but very small relatively, in Afghanistan. The Taliban has it. You know, they have their parade every year where they take our military vehicles and run them up some little street and, like, it's their form of a military parade, and it makes me angry when I see that.

Angry. When I see that, I get angry. You know, we give them—I don't think anyone knows this. We give Afghanistan about two or two and a half billion dollars a year. Do you know that?

For aid. Aid. We need aid ourself. We give and I'm going to go back. And, I told them yesterday, I want to look at it, but if we're going to give them money, it's okay.

But I want them to give us back our military equipment that they have. They're selling it. Doug, would you take that, please? Alright. Write something up.

No. I want them to give back. If we're going to give them that kind of money, let them give back the military equipment, which, they have where they have tanks and trucks and guns and goggles. They have goggles. They have night goggles better than we have.

Brand new right out of the box. It's unbelievable. So I want to do that, and I want the, if we're going to pay them, I want to get that equipment back. Okay? Doug can do it.

He's one of the guys. He's a business guy. To hear me sitting there saying, how the hell did this ever happen? Right? Can you believe it?

We give them billions of dollars, and we gave them our military equipment. Just tremendous numbers of billions of dollars worth of mill—billions and billions.

We have a ceasefire in Gaza, and we're joined today by several survivors of the captivity under Hamas, including Noah Arghamani and Ilana Gretusky. Britt Uski. Wow.

Look at that. How beautiful. What a beautiful group of people. Wow. Thank you very much.

Thank you very much. And you're sitting next to a great guy, Sebastian Gorka, who's also now in the administration. From day one. Right, Sebastian? He's been—he's been a loyalist from day one. We love Sebastian. Thank you very much, Sebastian. Thank you, everybody. That's very nice. Beautiful.

We're going to make it work somehow. You know? We're doing the best we can. We started—it should've never happened. That's the sad part. Would've never happened. If I were president, then I should've been. If I were president, it would've never happened, but it did so. We're doing the best we can with it. Thank you very much. Thank you.

Also with us are family members of some individuals who are still hostages, and we will not rest until all of the hostages have been returned back home. Some of them are coming home in, very bad condition, and some of them are coming home only as bodies. They're—they're dead. We have a lot of them coming home now.

They're dead. And these are largely young people. Young people don't die. Young people are young people. They don't die like this, but they're dead.

And the parents come to me, and they say, "Please, sir, could you get my son back?" How old is he, sir? "My son is dead." It's important just as important as if that son were alive to get the body back. It's amazing, actually.

Amazing. Just as important. Thank you. It's amazing, though, that the parents—these—the parents are strong. I mean, look strong.

What does strong mean? Strong is their life is ruined. Really, it's ruined. I see the people. But they come up to me, and it's so important to get the body back.

They know. And some are—are not sure. They're eighty percent sure he's dead or she's dead, but they have that little glimmer of hope. And I say, let him have that hope. Right?

Let him have that hope. But getting the body back is just as important as getting the son back healthy or the daughter back healthy. It's amazing to see when I—when I see the level of intensity and love and, sorrow and tragedy.

As I said in my inaugural address, it's my hope that my greatest legacy will be as a peacemaker, not a conqueror. I don't want to be a conqueror.

Under the Trump administration, every day brings more good news for America. I've ended all of the so-called diversity, equity, and inclusion programs across the entire federal government and the private sector. And notified every single government DEI officer that their job has been deleted. They're gone. They're fired.

You're fired. Get out. You're fired. I made it the official policy of the United States government that there are only two genders, male and female. That was easy.

I banned men from competing in women's sports. And I also proudly banned the use of—now, thank you. We banned the use of puberty blockers, hormone injections, and other chemical and surgical mutilation of your youth. Could you imagine making a speech like this ten years ago? People would say, what the hell is he talking about?

Right? This is a sickness that came along with critical race theory and all of the other things that we had to put up with. And it's all out now, critical race theory and transgender insanity. It's all gone from our schools and from our military. And I believe it's gone too.

I think we've—we've turned the heads of even the people that if—if you can believe they're believers, I don't know if they were, but I believe that it's all gone. And I've directed the reinstatement of any service member who is expelled from the armed forces due to the COVID vaccine mandate. They will be returned to their former rank with full back pay. Full back pay. I banned government censorship from your voices and brought back free speech in America.

We have free speech. We didn't have free speech. We do have it now, actually. Now this was a very vicious regime. You know?

I was put under investigation more so than the late great Alphonse Capone, one of the great killers of the world. Trump, my father would look down—my mother. How the hell did this happen to my boy? This was his—no. I was under investigation at a far greater level than Al Capone or anybody else, probably in the history of our country.

These people are sick. They're sick. They're bad people. I ended Joe Biden's weaponization soon as I got in. I said I'm going to hit him with the same stuff.

But I ended his whole weaponization of our government and removed his handpicked radical left Marxist prosecutors from the Department of Justice. I was so happy to do that. They weaponized government. They weaponized government. I pardoned and hundreds of Biden's political prisoners, including Christians, pro-life activists, and the J6 hostages who were treated terribly for years.

We even got rid of people like Pete Buttigieg, who did the worst job of anybody in the history of transportation. What a bunch of losers. I revoked the security clearances of Anthony Blinken, Jake Sullivan, John Brennan, James Clapper, and every non-patriot who lied to cover up Hunter Biden's laptop from hell. We took away their security clearance. And they're not allowed to enter any government building either.

I also revoke Joe Biden's security clearances, the Biden prime family security clearances, and they'll no longer be allowed to access state secrets while selling themselves all around the world. Oh, well. Now these were bad people. These were bad people. And I do that because this should never be allowed to happen again.

What happened to me in this administration, what happened on J6, what happened on all of the things they did that were so bad should never ever be allowed to happen again.

And on a friendlier note, I renamed the Gulf of Mexico, the Gulf of America. And we are restoring the name of a great president, William McKinley, to Mount McKinley in Alaska. And as you know, many years ago, Jimmy Carter gave away the Panama Canal. And Panama started the process of giving the Panama Canal, by the way, the most expensive development ever in the history of our country, relatively.

It would have been one and a half trillion in today's dollars. Thirty-eight thousand people died from our country building the Panama Canal. They died from mosquitoes and snakes. Think of it. They paid them five times their salary. They brought them to Panama, and they had a twenty-five percent chance of dying. They dug under nets so the mosquitoes wouldn't get them. But we lost thirty-eight thousand, mostly men, laborers, construction workers because it was such a harsh way to live. It was very brutal. They died—thirty-eight thousand.

Again, it was the most expensive thing we ever built, and they gave it away for one dollar to Panama. And last year, made five billion dollars. Also, that's one of the most successful projects ever built in terms of money monetarily, and it's the eighth wonder of the world. It connects two oceans with one being sixteen feet higher than the other. Think of it, the Pacific and the Atlantic.

Think of what that is. You're going through dikes and canals. Amazing what they did. It was really a wonder of the world. We gave it away for nothing.

But we didn't give it to China. We didn't give it to China. We gave it to Panama. We're going to take back the Panama Canal.

In a matter of weeks, we have restored America's pride, America's confidence, and America's spirit.

According to a brand new poll from Rasmussen, the number of Americans who believe we are in the right track now exceeds the number who think we're on the wrong track. This is the first time in twenty-three years. That's hard to believe. And we had one poll where we're at eighty-one percent right track, wrong track. I guess it depends on who, but that one poll because Rasmussen's been a good poll.

First time in over twenty years that we've had a positive number on that. That's great. That's great.

November 5th, 2024 will go down as one of the most important days in the history of our country. I'm pointing to Mike Lindell.

That man suffered. That man suffered. The FBI thugs went up to him, and they took away everything he had. He suffered. And Mrs. Lindell is a great—a great guy. They went after him. It was just terrible. This was a vicious weaponization of your government. But he's all—I'll tell you, he stood up. He's all man. He stood up. He stood up strong, and nothing was going to faze him. And I want to thank you on behalf of everybody, Mike. You put up with a tremendous amount. And he never changed his mind.

He said that election of 2020 was rigged, and he's more of a believer today than he was even four years ago. But now it's okay to say it, Mike. Now it's fine. Now that's why, you know, when it comes to a day where you can't challenge crooked elections, we've got a real problem in this country.

And as of January 20th, 2025, the dark days of high taxes, crushing regulations, rampant inflation, flagrant corruption, government weaponization, and total incompetence, those days are over. They're over.

But we cannot stop now. We're going to push forward every single day. In the immortal words of that great American hero, Captain John Paul Jones, "I have not yet begun to fight." And neither have you.

So together for the next four years, we are going to stand strong. We are going to work hard. We are going to fight, fight, fight, and win, win, win. Thank you to CPAC. Thank you, Matt. Thank you. Thank you, Mercedes. Thank you very much. Thank you, everybody. God bless America.

Thank you very much. God bless America. Thank you.

Elon Musk Interview

{Introduced by Rob Schmitt, host at Newsmax. And yes, he had a huge chainsaw.}

Schmitt: Man. That is a big crowd. And they are not here for me. How you guys doing? Nice vibe this month, right? After the best month we've ever had. Nice to see you. Thanks for coming out. It's good to see you. Let's not kill any more time, let's bring out Elon Musk ... We've got one more surprise, in case this wasn't enough.

Musk: Well, President, uh, President Milei has a gift for me.

Schmitt: Javier Milei from Argentina, you guys know who that is, right?

Musk: This ... is ... the chainsaw for bureaucracy. CHAINSAW!

Schmitt: Mr. President, thank you so much. Nice to meet you. I love it. We love it.

Musk: Where should we put this?

Schmitt: They want it right here. A little stage prop.

[Crowd cheers]

Musk: I love you guys, too!

Schmitt: Thanks guys. Have a seat.

The two men settle into the armchairs.

Schmitt: So, uh. Heheh. That was something.

Musk: I am become meme. Yeah. Pretty much. I was living the meme. It's just — I was living the dream, and I was living the meme, and that's, pretty much what's happening. I mean, DOGE started out as a meme. Think about it! [laughs] Now it's real! Isn't that crazy!

Schmitt: It is, it is crazy.

Musk: But it's cool. I was living the dream, and I was living the meme, and that's, pretty much what's happening.

Schmitt: Let me ask you this. A year ago, if someone had told you you'd be at CPAC and working with the president to absolutely shred [dramatic pause] the government — the swamp — whatever you want to call it. Would you believe that?

Musk: No. But it's cool! This is awesome. And I just wanna say, thanks for your support, I mean. You guys are. You know. We're, you know, we're trying to get good things done, but also, like, you know, have a good time doing it and, uh, you know, and have, like, a sense of humor. You know. So, like, I mean, the sort of the left wanted to make comedy illegal, you know, you can't make fun of anything. So this is, like, comedy sucks. It's like, nothing's funny. You can't make fun of anything. It's like, LEGALIZE COMEDY! YEAH! Legalize Comedy!

Schmitt: And we've shifted the entire culture in just the last few months, the whole culture of this country has shifted dramatically just because of that election.

Musk: Yeah, exactly. Freedom of speech, having fun again, it seems like we should... We should have a good time. You know?

Schmitt: I mean, it's a great time. Everybody in this place is so excited, and I haven't, I mean, when you talk to conservatives, everybody's happy.

Musk: Yeah.

Schmitt: And everybody feels this great sense of relief, because we were going to hell for about four years.

Musk: Yeah.

Schmitt: It really felt bad, especially toward the end, it felt really bad.

Musk: Yeah. I mean, I thought, I thought we were sort of heading for a point of no return really, you know, until, um, that's why it was so essential that President Trump win the election and, and that there, there be a Republican majority in the House and Senate, which, thanks to you [gestures generally at CPAC audience] that, that has been accomplished. Yeah.

Schmitt: I want to ask you, one of the biggest questions I have for you is — you've been, you know, politically, you weren't really on one side or the other for a long time. You were a businessman, a lot of people, they stay away from it now. You're on a side, you've chosen a side. You're sitting here in a MAGA hat. How did that happen? What was the moment?

Musk: It's like, you know, dark gothic MAGA. [Calls attention to hat, with MAKE AMERICA GREAT AGAIN in gothic]

Schmitt: That's a good one. Was there a specific moment? Was there a moment that it all changed?

Musk: Yeah, when I realized I was a fool. But no, I was, I guess, uh... yeah, I mean, I'd say, I was like, politically neutral for, for quite a while. You know. You know, leaning a little Democrat. You know...

Schmitt: So then how do you go from that to this? [points at CPAC audience]
Musk: Well, uh, it --

Schmitt: Did they go crazy?

Musk: Yeah, they did — they did go crazy. I mean that whole cancel culture and, you know, trying to, trying to stop freedom of speech, and um, infringe upon, just in general, infringe upon people's personal freedoms. You know, they just want state control, state control of what you say... They wanna, they wanna, you know, take away your guns, and the reason they wanna take away your guns, is like, so there's nothing you can do to oppose them. So it's sort of like, you know, I just, I just, I just like. We, we, we, we just need to restore the fundamental elements of what made America great, which is, uh, freedom and opportunity.

Schmitt: We're seeing a lot of these freedoms disappearing in the West. It's not just about America. We're watching, we're all watching Europe and knowing that they're about 50, 100 years ahead of us, right? Because they got an early start, and we're watching how they're devolving, and you're trying to save it from happening here.

Musk: I mean, in Europe, they put people in prison for memes. Yeah. You know, I'm like, that's insane.

Schmitt: They're collapsing. They're a collapsing society. It feels that way.

Musk: It ... feels ... like ...

Schmitt: France was nicer 50 years ago than this.

Musk: Yeah.

Schmitt: I don't think you can question it.

Musk: Yeah. Um. so. Yeah. So. Yeah. I mean. Really.

Musk: [Turns to crowd] Yeah, I love you too! I mean. I really, I really, I really just want to do useful things, like, you know, basically build products, you know, provide products and services that are that are good and I wasn't really that interested in being political. It, just, like, there was a certain point, no choice. Yeah. So, yeah.

Schmitt: Can I ask you — on the same side of that coin — what's it like going from neutral to being vilified, largely vilified by the media? I think you're --

Musk: What? No. Really? [Laughs]

Schmitt: I mean, turn on some of these channels, brother. I mean, they're angry at you. Does it bother you at all?

Musk: I mean, were they chanting for my death? I suppose that's a little, you know... like, the song's not even that good. And it's like, it's like, you call that a death chant? That's nothing, please.

Schmitt: They've been singing a lot lately. There's a lot of music lately. It's not good music either. Yeah, yeah. I would say that they're, you know, watching what you're doing with DOGE is just that — people love it.

Crowd cheers.

Schmitt: I mean, I've always looked at the government and... I've always looked at the government. I've seen this big machine that, and you just know that they waste because they don't care. Nobody could. There's more money coming. They don't care. You're cutting all this out. Everybody in this country knows that the government is full of waste, fraud, and abuse, and you're doing the work, and the Americans love it. Watching their reaction politically to this, I can't believe how bad they are responding to this. I don't know how you're going to sit there and scream and complain because they're cutting waste out of the government and try to win another election. How do you try to win on that?

Musk: Well, at this point, I'm like, I'm not sure how much of the left is even real.

Schmitt: Like, how much was propped up by our money?

Musk: Yeah, you see, like, these, these sort of fake rallies with hardly any people and the media will, like, frame it, and like, you know, get all six people you know, in the frame, but it's like, nobody else is there, like, just, it doesn't have popular support, um. But there's, but then, but then you learn that, like, there's hundreds of billions of dollars going to these so-called NGOs, and that, and it's your tax dollars that are funding things that are fundamentally anti-American.

Schmitt: And they're propping up their narrative. A lot of that government money has been propping up a left that I don't think is, I don't think is as strong as they made it seem.

Musk: In fact, a massive amount of your tax dollars is going to legacy media companies, directly from the government.

Schmitt: The government wants to take over media.

Musk: Yeah, it's terrible.

Schmitt: Yeah, that's why we have X.

Musk: Yeah! And that's --

Schmitt: That's why you spent $44 billion — I mean, there's a lot of money. More than it was probably worth, but it had, there was a message.

Musk: Freedom is priceless. Probably one of the most important investments this country's ever seen. If you gotta protect the First Amendment, it's not much more important than that.

Musk: Yeah. I mean, I got a lot of criticism, and people, people, said, well, that proves he's a huge idiot from a, you know, like, look, he bought it for like whatever, $44 billion and now it's worth, like, eight cents.

Schmitt: And it's not worth eight cents!

Musk: You know, there's that, but, but yeah, it was essentially to, you know, buy ... freedom... of expression. And --

Schmitt: Once's that's gone it's all over, all over, yeah, tyranny is really quick after that.

Musk: Yeah. I mean, like, you know. All the sort of federal money going to media companies is what, what helps explain why the legacy media all says the same thing at the same time. Yeah, like, isn't it, like, it's like, weird, like, you put them up with, like, you know, like, when --

Schmitt: They're mouthpieces for...

Musk: For the state! Yes.

Schmitt: That's what we've come to know. Yeah, scary.

Musk: Yeah. I like the theme with it, where, where, where, because they're always saying, like, threat to our democracy, threat to our democracy, but if you just replaced democracy with bureaucracy.... It makes a lot of sense.

Schmitt: Makes perfect sense.

Musk: Big threat to the bureaucracy.

Schmitt: That's exactly right. Let's talk about, let's talk about these DOGE dividend checks that everybody's talking about this week. And I know you tweeted out that you're gonna because ... Does everybody want, like, a $5,000 check in the mail? That sounds kind of good, right? And the best part about it would be knowing where it came from, that that's five grand that you sent them last year.

Musk: Totally, it's money that's taken away from, from things that are destructive to the country, that and from organizations that hate you, to you. That's awesome.

Schmitt: Does it seem like --

Musk: I mean that's like, glorious. The spoils of battle, you know?

Schmitt: Is there traction on that?

Musk: Yeah, yeah. So yeah. [inaudible] ... the president. He's supportive of that. And so it sounds like, you know, that's something we're going to do. So as we're finding savings, that's going to translate directly to reductions in tax. Yeah.

Schmitt: I mean, I think they fired 6,000 people at the IRS today, and I think, they said last night that they're talking about shutting down the IRS. I think it's fair. I think people should realize this is, I mean, the amount of money that we said we send Washington, like five or six trillion a year, that is such an ungodly amount of money. I mean, like, a trillion seconds, is like 30 years or something like that. I mean, that's how much we send them. And they seem to never have enough. There must be a lot you can cut.

Musk: No, absolutely. People ask me, What's the most surprising thing that you've encountered when you go to DC? You know, we're in DC. And I said, well, the most surprising thing is the scale of the expenditures, and actually, uh, how easy it is to with a just, just when you add caring and competence, where there was absent before you can actually save billions of dollars sometimes in, in an hour. Yeah, like, it's wild.

Schmitt: And then they scoff at it and say, oh, a few billion here there. I mean, the way they're talking about it, they, you can see they don't care. It's so it's such little money compared to how much they're used to wasting. That's what's really scary.

Musk: Um, yeah, no, exactly. But obviously it's, it's, it just shows that they really lack empathy for the average taxpayer who's working hard, paying, paying taxes, and then, and then they say, oh, a million dollars doesn't matter. I'm like, I think it matters a lot to people you know. So what are you talking about?

Schmitt: I'd like to have it. Let me ask you a question. You know, I know the President fairly well. Watched him survive two assassination attempts. The second, had the first one not happened, the second one would have gotten him, because without those extra guys, they would have never seen that gun poking through the fence at the golf course.

Musk: Isn't it mind blowing that this has happened? I mean, and just and what? By the way, why do we still know nothing about that guy in Butler, what's going on? But uh Kash is gonna get to the bottom of it! Yeah! Woo!

Schmitt: Just a couple hours ago, I saw that the security detail that you had come in with is enormous.

Musk: It's not that enormous, maybe it should be bigger.

Schmitt: It might. I think you could probably afford it. But, I mean, how concerned are you about your safety? I mean, it's you. Are you? You are a wanted man. Are you? Are you?

Musk: So I look, I'm open to ideas for improving security. I have to tell you. Like I don't actually have a death wish. I think. But, you know, it's not that easy. So, yeah, I mean, but I have like that, even like people like President Bukele from El Salvador, who managed to put in prison like a 100,000, like, murderous thugs. And he was like, he called me. He's like, I'm worried about your security. I'm like, YOU'RE worried about my security? Okay, you know. I mean, yeah.

Schmitt: Talk about guts to do that down there.

Musk: I mean, yeah, totally.

Schmitt: And then survive.

Musk: Like, I'm like, I was like, how did you put all those thugs in prison without dying, because things like that would have been not easy. You know.

Schmitt: Well, there's the President, as one of his top attorneys is now investigating, I guess Chuck Schumer, for threats against SCOTUS. Congress, on the Democrats' side, for saying, you know, basically saying he's gonna bring a war to you, like a fight to you. I mean, the rhetoric... you guys are screwing with things that are not supposed to be messed with.

Musk: We're fighting [inaudible]

Schmitt: A lot of people that really don't want that to happen.

Musk: We're fighting Matrix big time here. It has got to be done.

Schmitt: Yeah, and it certainly does. What's going on with — tell us about Fort Knox. Kentucky. It's a military base. It's a ton of gold, tons and tons and tons.

Musk: 5,000 tons of gold, something.

Schmitt: 5,000 are there in the ground and like this. I mean, it's a very secure thing.

Musk: I think we all want to see it.

Schmitt: I'd love to see it like this.

Musk: This is your gold, by the way. It's the public's gold.

Schmitt: Do you think it's not there?

Musk: I don't know, but I think I just want to see it. Yeah, we want to go see it and just make sure. Like, make sure, like, did somebody spray paint some lead or something, you know, yeah, like, is this real gold? You might have to bite the bar. You know. But I think, honestly, you know, part of this also is just like, let's, you know, let's have some fun. And, you know, like, like, I said, this, all this gold at Fort Knox. It's the public's gold. It's your gold. So, like, I think you have, like, a right to see it.

Schmitt: And take a tour.

Musk: Yeah, I think we should have a ... do a tour. And the President last night was like, that's, I think he's in favor of it. That would be cool. And then we, like, it should be like a live tour, like, you'll see what's going on, open the door, like, what's behind it, well, and there's, you know, I think I'd watch that. Yeah.

Schmitt: I mean, what is, what is 5,000 tons of is it? Is it the size of this --

Musk: Gotta be pretty big, you know. It's gotta be a lot of other stuff in there, like, around, like, I don't even... got some other stuff in there.

Schmitt: Are you thinking about auditing the Federal Reserve as well, which is obviously --

Musk: Yeah, sure.

Schmitt: -- regulatory economy. I imagine you think the waste has got to be everywhere.

Musk: Yeah, no, waste. Waste is pretty much everywhere. People ask, like, how can you find waste? And, like, in DC, I'm like, look, it's like being in a room, and this target, the wall, the roofs and the floor are all targets. So it's like, you're gonna close your eyes and go shoot in any direction, you can't miss, you know. So it's, it's pretty wild, like, like, you just push on things a little bit, and you save billions of dollars, like, just a little bit, you know, it's wild.

Schmitt: Scary, isn't it?

Musk: It's why I say like, it really is underrated, if you add caring and competence, how much things improve. Yeah, and, you know, and we just find so many totally crazy things, which, you know, obviously we're sharing with the public. We post everything we learn, you know, just you know, so you can see it, you know.

Schmitt: What do you --

Musk: It's like, isn't it? Like, it's totally wild. Like, we did just, we just did, like, a check on the database on Social Security. Like, says, how many, a lot Americans, alive Americans eligible for Social Security, are there? And according to the database, it's over 400 million. And we're like, wait a second, and how many are you again? Yeah. And then, like, we found, like, one person in there is, like, 306 years old. I'm like, [inaudible from crosstalk] I mean, yeah, you know this, America doesn't exist before at that time. Like, so, why? So, you know, maybe it's just me, but I think it's a red flag. I don't know.

Schmitt: But are there indications that there were checks going to those people, or any of those people?

Musk opens his mouth and pauses.

Musk: Well ... yeah.

Schmitt: I guess that's the question.

Musk: That's...

Schmitt: I get the Social Security Administration is dumb, but are they paying these people? Are they that dumb? I don't know.

Musk: A bunch of money is going out from the Social Security Administration, and, in fact, from all entitlement programs.

Schmitt: $72 billion in waste in like seven years. It's $10 billion a year.

Musk: Well, I think the rough estimate from General ... Government Accountability offices, there's over $500 billion in 40 years.

Schmitt: Sorry, five?

Musk: Five hundred billion.

Schmitt: Over how long?

Musk: Per year, per year.

Schmitt: On Social Security?

Musk: No, no, on all, on all--

Schmitt: On all government?

Musk: On all entitlements, all entitlements. Yeah, it sort of actually makes sense. When you look at the thing from a top level and say, like, okay, there's $7 trillion of spending by the government. What percentage do you think is fraudulent? Okay, exactly like a conservative estimate of the $7 trillion would be 10 percent. Conservative.

Schmitt: Probably higher than that, yeah, exactly like a quarter every dollar, right?

Musk: But if the fraud is only 10 percent of $7 trillion, you've got $700 billion of fraud, and by the way, so it's like, really easy to take advantage of the federal government. Very easy.

Schmitt: Look at COVID! Look at all these scams! I mean, it's unbelievable!

Musk: It looks like, for, in terms of covid payments, yeah, there was something like $200 billion of covid payment fraud taken by fraudsters out of the country. That's like, I think, listen, if there's going to be fraud, it should at least be domestic so, you know. But they managed to get $200 billion out of the country. I'm like, what! Why didn't we notice that?

Schmitt: Let me ask you, let's do immigration here for a second. You know, there's this move now that Trump's latest thing is that he cut, he's going to cut funding any kind of money that ends up in the hands of illegal immigrants. So if you're funding these sanctuary cities and states, that's how they thrive, right? They're paying for these hotels. That's all federal money. If you got a hotel in your city in New York, you got all these hotels full of migrants. That's not state money. That's the feds are covering that, he's going to cut all that. It's really hard to deport 15 million people. And it seems like the move now is, let's make it so that they leave on their own. If there's no longer a dole system for them, if they can't get their hands on hotel rooms and money, they're going to go back, especially if there's no work.

Musk: Well, I think it's really important for people to understand that the Biden administration sent any possible money that they could, they could, if there was money they could send to facilitate and amplify illegal immigration, they sent it. Okay. They took money from FEMA meant for helping Americans in distress, and sent that money to luxury hotels for illegal immigrants in New York. That is an outrage.

They actually did that, and not only that, even after the President signed an executive order saying it has to stop, the FEMA, the whatever deep state bureaucrats still pressed send on $80 million last week to go to the Roosevelt Hotel in New York and other places last week. And now, and now, they're mad that they've got stopped, and they're like trying to sue to have it be restored. It's like, the gumption.

Schmitt: You think they're creating a new voter class? You think that was the goal? When they opened up the borders for four years, create a new voter class, get them citizenship, get them in.

Musk: Yeah, a lot of these things like, you don't actually have to assume some grand conspiracy. You just need to look at basic incentives. So if the incentives, fundamentally, if the probability that an illegal is going to vote Democrat at some point, whether it's cheating, but eventually they can become citizens. But if probability is like 80, 90 percent just look at California, which is super majority Dem. And then the incentive is to maximize the number of illegals in the country. That is why the Biden administration was pushing to get as many illegals as possible and spend every dollar possible to get as many. Because every one of them is a customer. Everyone is a voter. So the whole thing was a giant voter importation scam.

Schmitt: Pretty obvious.

Musk: Very obvious. And then, moreover, then, they actually created the CBP One border app thing where they were, which is, like, where they could, they would literally fly people in. It's not like, like, at the point at which you know, people being flown in at your expense--

Schmitt: Sending planes--

Musk: Like building a wall up doesn't work.

Schmitt: They're literally flying them in. No other country in the world would do something like this. Nobody is this stupid.

Musk: Yeah. And then we found that there was, like $100 million contract given to some guy in London, actually, while, you know, yeah, well, the CBP One app. So, so then, so they're flying illegals into the swing states. And if you've got like, a margin of victory of maybe 20,000 people, and you fly 200,000 illegals into that state, it's not gonna be a swing state for long.

Schmitt: Change the numbers. Maybe in four, eight years.

Musk: Exactly.

Schmitt: It's a long game. It's just a matter of time.

Musk: So it might take, like, a year for an asylum seeker to get on the green card and five years for the citizenship, it's an investment that is guaranteed to pay off. It's just a question of when.

Schmitt: They all remember who brought them in and who left them here.

Musk: Exactly, exactly. I want to go back. I want to talk about my big deal like, I think a lot of people like, don't quite appreciate that this was an actual, real scam at scale to tilt the scales of democracy in America.

Schmitt: Treason.

Musk: Treason.

Schmitt: One more Biden question. I remember when, you know, when they would do the electric car stuff, they would always try to box you out, even though you have the only electric car anybody wants.
Musk: Yeah.

Schmitt: You said, I think this week that you think that Biden left these astronauts up in space because he didn't want to give you an opportunity to save them. Make NASA look bad, make the private sector look better, make you look good. You believe that?

Musk: Yeah, no, absolutely. So, of course.

Schmitt: I kind of agree. Why would he want to let you help them come down when you're supporting the president?

Musk: The Biden administration was, was attacking me next level. I mean, the Department of Justice — or Injustice, under the Biden administration — was, I mean, they were suing SpaceX. They're suing SpaceX for not hiring asylum seekers. And we're like, but it's actually illegal for us to hire asylum seekers because we're... rocket technology is covered under ITAR rules, which that means it's an advanced weapons technology, yeah. And so we can only hire permanent residents or green card or citizens, right? Like, so we're damned if we do, damned if we don't. We said like, so how can they sue us for not hiring asylum seekers when it's actually illegal for us to do so. But nonetheless, there was a big Department of Justice or Injustice case about this against SpaceX, so obviously it was an antagonistic situation, and those astronauts were supposed to be up there for eight days, and now they're up for eight months. Does that make any sense? And we, we, we, obviously could have brought them back sooner, but they didn't want anyone who could support President Trump to look good. Basically.

Schmitt: Yeah.

Musk: That's the, that's the issue.

Schmitt: A lot of them are saying right now that the reason that you want to get into Social Security, that you want to get into all of these different — into Treasury and things like that, is that you're looking for personal information and you're trying to make more money.

Musk: Yeah.

Schmitt: I've never met anybody as rich as you that cared less about money in my life. Every time I hear a story about you, you're sleeping on a couch of some other guy in a city that you could buy the entire thing. I don't think you care about money, dude.

Musk: I mean, I, I, I ... Listen, like if I steal Social Security, I can finally buy nice things. Yeah?

Schmitt: And on that same question, they're also talking about, you guys are going to end Social Security, you're going to end Medicare, you're going to end these things. I don't imagine that conversation has been had with the President, and that's the plan.

Musk: No, in fact, the actions that we're taking with the support of the President and the support of the agencies, is, what will save Medicare? What will save Social Security?

Musk: And and, because if the country goes insolvent, if all, if all the money is just spent on paying interest on debt, there's no money left for anything. Yeah, so that's, that's the reason I'm doing this, is because I looked at the big picture here, and it's like, man, our debt's getting out of control. The interest payments, interest on the national debt now exceeds the entire defense department budget.

Schmitt: A trillion a year. In interest, just to carry the money that we owe, is a trillion a year.

Musk: Yes.

Schmitt: Unbelievable.

Musk: Rising rapidly. So like, I mean, a country's no different from a person. Country overspends, country goes bankrupt. Same with, same as a person who overspends goes bankrupt. So it's not like optional to solve these things. It's essential.

Schmitt: So we're gonna go bankrupt.

Musk: Yes.

Schmitt: We are. Couple minutes left here. Russia, there's a huge push --

Musk: Oh, yeah, yeah. People like, sort of like, the end, like, yeah, you know, I'm a, I'm a bought asset of Putin, yeah, I'm like, he can't afford me.

Schmitt: Yeah, I think, I think you're worth more than Russia.

Musk: Think about it!

Schmitt: So you're trying to end, you're trying to end a war. Ending a war always means you have to compromise. You have to negotiate with an enemy or an adversary. That's just what it is. And right now, they are lambasting the president for trying a different method to war that they haven't been able to end for three and a half years. Three years. Yeah, they, you know, they're saying Trump's blaming Zelensky for the invasion. How do you, how do you process all of the negativity toward him for trying to end this war?

Musk: Well, first of all, I think we should have empathy for the people dying at the front lines. That's the most important thing. If people have been dying, you know, like, how many more years is this supposed to go on? And imagine if that was your son, your father, you know, what are they dying for? What exactly are they dying for? That line has, the line of engagement has barely moved for two years. There's a whole bunch of people dead in trenches for what. And I'll tell you what for, what it's like for the biggest graft machine that I've ever seen in my life, that's for what. It's unreal, like the amount of money that is being taken in graft and bribery is disgusting. And so what's actually happening is that those, those you know, people, those poor guys, are getting sent into a meat grinder for money. That's what's actually going on. And needs to stop.

Schmitt: Trump is so pragmatic on this. He just, he's just looking at it, and he's saying it's Ukraine, it's not our country, it's not a NATO ally. I just want to see people not dying. I want to see, on both sides, I mean, think about how many young — so many young men have died in Ukraine that the army is starting to age out. The military is aging out. You get 40 and 50 year old guys fighting in a war because there's nobody left that's not killed or maimed in their 20s. That's the reality. Think about how many people that is, if you're a humanitarian at all, you just got to end the war, like, no matter what, just get it over with.

Musk: Yes, people, they need to stop dying and the graft machines got to stop, you know, so, and I think people that don't, a lot of people out there don't realize, like, the president has a lot of empathy. He really cares. You know, he's good, he's a good man.

Schmitt: I got one more for you. I've been fascinated by you for a very long time.

Musk: Thanks.

Schmitt: I've just, I just, I've never seen anybody that can, you know, do so many things at the same time. I mean, you've got the rockets, you got the cars. I've always wanted to ask you, what is it like inside your mind, like, this, is it just 1,000 miles an hour? I mean, are you --
Musk: Yeah.

Schmitt: Is it just not? I mean, just, does it ever stop? Do you sleep? How much do you sleep? Paint us a picture of inside of the mind of a genius? Like, how do you... can you answer that question? It's not an easy question.

Musk: I mean... My mind is a storm. So. It's a storm. But, but, I mean, let me maybe tell you something like, you didn't ask the question, but, but I think it's worth nonetheless, maybe just elaborating on something, which is, you know, I grew up in South Africa and... but my morality was informed by America. I read comic books, you know, played Dungeons & Dragons. And I watched American TV shows and, like, it seemed like America cared about being the good guys, you know, about doing the right thing and, and that's actually pretty unusual, by the way.

Schmitt: In the world, it's very unusual. Yeah, it's not like, actually, countries don't do that.

Musk: No, they don't, no. And so I was like, Yeah, you know, you want to be this good. You want to be on the side of good. You want to care about what's right. And, and uh, yeah. So that's, that's, yeah, what I believe in.

Schmitt: I gave you, I gave you a tough one at the end.

Musk: Yeah.

Schmitt: So yeah, that's great. That's great. [looks to crowd] Elon Musk.

Musk: All right.

Schmitt: Thank you. Thank you so much. Appreciate you.

Musk: Thanks, guys!

Steve Bannon's Remarks

Yo!
What a glorious day!

Hold it. How did I draw the card to follow Elon Musk? Come on, Man!

You bring out the world's filthy cash super man and I'm supposed to follow it? I'm just a crazy Irishman! This is a glorious day! Do you know why it's glorious? Kash Patel's head of the FBI!

Confirmed by the United States Senate!

As was Bobby Kennedy Junior! Tulsi Gabbard! Pete Hegseth!

Didn't they tell you it couldn't be done? Didn't they all right there? Didn't the mainstream media say it couldn't be done? none of them? Right? It's a glorious day!

Mitch McConnell! Mitch McConnell's gone, he retired. Right? You did that!

Remember? On the Ukraine vote? Remember that? you broke? He broke his pick on that. You delivered that. Just like you delivered Tulsi and bobby and Pete and cash!

They said Trump wouldn't get any of his cabinet members key. He got 'em all. Why? Because of you. Scott Bessent today said Elon's group in the first thirty days found fifty-five billion dollars of waste, fraud, and abuse. Right? Fifty-five billion dollars. That's gonna add up to six- seven-hundred eight-hundred million dollars in one month. They've done that and President Trump, he's so excited he says hey, I think we balanced the budget. Right? President Trump, hang on for a second. Let's get it down under a trillion. Let's start there.

Zelenskyy's been put in his place. Right? Right?

And the J6ers are here at CPAC.

All of 'em!

From the medium-high security prisons to the US penitentiaries, the men that got [indistinct], all of them are here! right? They don't like that up there. They don't like the J sixers being here. The J6 are here and hey let me tell you something else i talked to Ambassador Rick Renell last night and the J sixers i think the J6 choir is going to play the Kennedy Center for a night in honor of their families and in fact, I got an idea that the night that they play the J6 choir plays and opens the new, you know, the new, uh, the new you with Richard

Grenell and President Trump as chairman we have the j6 choir and we invite all the families they try to destroy the j6ers and they get to sit in the boxes where the elite right and we take the elite for just one night and we take him down to the DC gulag right for one night

Think they can, think they can handle that? No, I don't think so either. Game likes game, right? Game knows game right? I tell you it's game the gentlemen sitting in White House, Donald J. Trump, it's a glorious day, days of thunder, days of thunder, and years of lightning. Every day is Christmas Day, every day you get more executive voice, more executive actions. It's not going to stop.

But you know what's the most important thing of all that it's, um, you. You're here today at CPAC! You represent the tip of the tip of the spear of the populist nationalist movement. All of that from Kash Patel to McConnell leaving to the J6 being free! right? To Zalinski being put in his place and Elon just said right there, it's been nothing but grift. The parents and the kids and Ukraine didn't want him to die. Who wants him to die? The globalists wanted him to die. Who said stop it? You said stop it, you gave voice to President Trump.

No, what, why was it so important that all the media is here and the world's here and the financial ties of London and the New York Times and all these? Why, why are they all here? There're not here to see me. They can see me every day on Real America Voice screaming like a mad man at a microphone. They can see, they can see rob Schmidt and Elon Elon's everywhere, right? It's great he's everywhere, right? JD Vance gave a great speech and you can see JD all the time. President Trump's gonna give a magnificent speech on Saturday, is he not?

But they get enough of President Trump every day, don't they? Hell yeah! He calls them in to the Oval Office, he signs Executive orders and they're sitting there throwing these questions, baboom! Baboom! He's like a Howitzer. If they get enough of President Trump, you know what they are really here for. They're here because of you. They can't defeat what they don't understand. They can't destroy what they don't understand, right? they can't contain what they don't understand. From Riyadh to Beijing to Berlin to the city of London to Buenos Ares, you name it, in every world capital every hedge fund, every political consultant, all the money, all the power, all the legislation, you know what they want? They want to understand MAGA.

You know why? You represent the best of the American People. In your righteous indignation you rose up! right? You rose up how many times I've been doin' this last two or three years what did I tell you last year on this very stage we're going to win we're going to win the primary we'll win the general election and Donald Trump's going to return to the white house and all these guys all the mainstream media the fake news mocked and ridiculed Trump's not going not going win the primary you right? right? You were right they had u who was it Nikki? Nikki? Had had governor and I like governor Sanchez life has governor Sanchez dropped out by then I don't I don't remember or was soon thereafter you had Trump's back you had Trump's back in those dark days of 2021 did you not? Remember he went to Mar-a-Lago and it was like a lion in winter and they all abandoned him except for you!

And the schleps had enough guts and courage to taking the CPAC in Orlando in March 47 days after he had gone into exile because guess what? They stole the 2020 election! Is there any doubt in your mind that they stole the 2020 election? They stole it! And they know they stole it! They thought you were finished they were going to de bank you they were deplatform you, you are nothing but trash, or nothing but garbage, and nothing but deplorables. Right? You surprised them with Hillary Clinton and guess what 11 more, 74 million, 11 more than we had in 2016 voted when you won the 2020 election. And the reason the J6ers are here and they're patriots is because that was a fedsurrection, totally set up by the FBI, by the justice department, by all of them, and we're going the receipts, were going to show the receipts, and they thought Trump's finished and you're finished.

No. I want you to look within yourself right now at that journey. Go back to 2021. Go back to your life, go back to the anxiety and man Trump won but they stole it! The system's so big, so corrupt, so powerful! Remember that? Back on our heels? Right? You didn't quit just like in any military contest we got a rally point, we dug the guide on in and say you regroup. Dust ourselves off, fix bayonets we're charging again. That is why Kash Patel is the director of the FBI! That is why Bobby Kennedy is the head of the HHS! That is why Tulsi Gabbard is a DNI that is why pet Hegseth is across the river in the Pentagon. Fix bayonets'! Fix Bayonets! You're not gonna stop! You know why they fear you and Riad you know what they fear you in Beijing you know what they fear you in berlin and the city of London because they know you're not stoppable. Right?

This time, what, almost 80 million votes 40% of black men in this country came and voted with you and supported you. Majority of Hispanics Hispanic families voted with you! Every Asian every Asian American in this country, come this is your home, is MAGA Right? Every member, everybody from India that's here in the United States as a citizen, come this is your home, MAGA right? The Make America Healthy Again! That do it like that we're going toward will to Maga you're unstoppable! You're unstoppable and they know that. You don't think in Riyadh they know that, you don't think in Rome they know that? You don't think in Berlin they know that? The righteous indignation of the American people just like every Patriot grave, just like the Revolution, the Civil War, and World War II, they understand when the American people with its common sense, isn't what President Trump say, a revolutionary common sense. Right? It's also a revolution of common decency! The decency, the grit, the determination, the courage of the American people unparalleled in world history. This is what we have. Our best and brightest on every battlefield, all throughout the world from the South Pacific to Europe. To North Africa. What other nation on earth ever done that? None. What other people have ever done that? None. Only you. And you rose up and you rose up and you said you know what? Trump is our guy.

Is President Trump perfect? No, he's far from perfect, he is an imperfect instrument. But I will tell you George General Washington was an imperfect instrument. Abraham Lincoln is an imperfect instrument. And he's the third, these come along every hundred years. Leaders that take us in a new direction and that's what Trump has done. It was the divine providence of won 2016 and it was divine providence hand that let them steal 2020 because we had to see how depraved they were. We had to see how demonic they were. We had to see what they were prepared to do to this country. And what did you do? Did you ever falter? No you did not! Did you ever doubt? No you did not! Did you ever question? No you did not and you know what it brought us? A glorious, a glorious, glorious victory!

The reason these phonies in the mainstream media were nothing but the propaganda department for the ruling class in this world, right? They fear you. They fear you, cuz they understand you're not beatable. You're not beatable. They've had every shot and right now and I want people to celebrate and to come together. Ww're going to do it the next couple of days. But understand the toughest part of this war is ahead of us. I've never promised you anything I've never promised you sunlit options. I said it's ahead of us. Maybe decades. But it's time in American history that people have to lay it all down. You're expendable to get to bridge the other side. You know that. You're not asking for a handout. You're not asking for a pat on the head, right? You're not asking for a 'thank you'. All you're asking for is where is my Musket, and where is my bayonet, and where do I go over the top?

The other question they all running around they're all running around, what's the future in MAGA? What's the future in 2028. We ain't worried about 2028, we're worried about today and tomorrow and the next day. That's how we won. We didn't go back to 2021, what's, what's going to happen in 2024, no it's every single day. You report for duty and we get it done. Action! Action! Action! So media don't have to come up and ask, I'm going to tell you right now. The future of America is MAGA. Ok? And the future of Maga is Donald J. Trump! We want Trump in 28 That's why they can't stand a man like Trump comes along once or twice a country-s history. right? We want Trump! We want Trump!

Crowd and Bannon: We want Trump! We want Trump! We want Trump! We want Trump! We want Trump!

Got to love you. No nothing's going to work him up like that. No, no, no, no, no, they want to say, oh 'Trump's a lame duck', Trump's this, Trump's that, Trump's now around 28, Trump is here. He's the leader of this movement. When they record the history of this age, ain't going to remember me or Elon Musk or Tucker Carlson or Sean Hannity, they will remember two things: Donald Trump and MAGA, ok?

And you know why? You know why they know they can't beat you? And why they're so upset? You're agency. Your human agency. You did this yourselves. You came, you worked though it, you said I'm going to put aside fear. I'm going to put aside questions of concern. I'm going to put aside my anxiety of the 2020 election being stolen. I'm going to get together. We're going to fight. We're not going to back off any day. Your agency. Your human agency. right?

They can come up with all the algorithms in Silicon Valley they want. They can take away half of the economy as far as economy goes. Human agency is what drives this world forward, right? This is the Holy Spirit working through us. Your agency. That's why Trump, General Washington and Lincoln and Trump, they come along every hundred years. Most nations never have them, we've had three. He is an instrument of divine providence, right? Of course he is! Look what he's run, look at what this capital has become. The revolutionary generation never anticipated this imperial capital, right? If they came back today, they would spit on the floor to see what we've allowed to do. What we've allowed to happen, right? With the lords of easy money and the oligarchs. They would say 'Hey, what we need a populist nationalist revolution' and guess what? Donald Trump gave them one, right?

its oging to to get so tough, its going to get so hard. Are you going to quit? or are you going to back Trump? Are you for prepared to fight? When he made the moral decision to come back from Maralargo understand they were going to put him iin prison for seven hundred years, right? They're going to bankrupt him. they're going to destroy his family. What did he do? He came back in 47 days and said I'm in, are you in? right?

When they tried to shoot him they tried to assassinate him and he was on the ground right there. They could have crawled off like any other politician in the world. What did he do, he got up, and what did he say?

Crowd: Fight. Fight. Fight.

I cannot hear you?

Crowd: Fight. Fight. Fight.

Are you prepared to fight for Trump?

Crowd: Yes!

Are you prepared to fight for this republic?

Crowd: Yes!

Are you prepared to fight for this country?

Crowd: Yes!

The hardest, toughest days are ahead, but you know what? Riyadh, Berlin, based -- Beijing, Moscow, the city of London. Right here ... this is not beatable. The only way they win is if we retreat and we're not going to retreat. We're not going to surrender. We're not going to quit.. Fight, fight, fight.

[Gives clear "Roman salute" and smirks]

Amen. God bless you. You are amazing. You've honored every patriot in this country. Every patriot grave. You have honored them through your agency. This is all you.

[Gives rough military salute]

NOTE

Jordan Bardella, a far-right leader in France, canceled his speech over Bannon's apparent Nazi salute.

Context

Steve Bannon was a founding board member of Breitbart News and then executive chairman, declaring in 2016 that the website was "the platform for the alt-right". He was co-founder of the Government Accountability Institute in 2012 and executive chair until 2016. As vice president of the board of Cambridge Analytica, described as a "psychological warfare tool" by one of its founders, he allegedly oversaw the collection of Facebook data which was used to target American voters.

He was appointed chief executive of Donald Trump's presidential campaign, and then chief strategist and senior counselor. According to a letter from members of Congress, his "ties to the White Nationalist movement have been well documented" and "sends a disturbing message about what kind of president Donald Trump wants to be". He denied the lable, calling himself an "economic nationalist". In February 2017, he was featured on the cover of Time, with the article's headline, "Is Steve Bannon the Second Most Powerful Man in the World?"

He left employment in the White House in August of 2017 and returned to being executive chairman of Breitbart.

In 2020, he was indicted for conspiracy to commit wire fraud and money laundering, inappropriately using funds collected for building the wall at the border with Mexico. He peladed guilty to one state felony count. Although Trump distanced himself, Bannon remained faithful in supporting him, and received a last minute pardon when Trump left office in 2021. He and some of his content was banned from social media channels following his call for the beheading of Anthony Fauci.

An Editorial Response

{From "Closer to the Edge" on Substack, used with permission}

There was a moment, right before Elon Musk fired up the chainsaw, when I thought: Maybe this isn't real. Maybe I'm trapped inside some sort of mass psychosis, a hallucination shared by every washed-up conservative grifter and bargain-bin dictator with a podcast. But then Musk yanked the cord, the engine roared, and the room erupted in a wild, feral cheer, and I realized—no, this is happening. This is real. This is CPAC 2025.

There was a time when CPAC was just an insufferable Republican networking event where men in navy suits argued about tax cuts and social security reform. That time is over. Now, it's a high-stakes reality show where billionaires wield power tools, insurrectionists show up expecting gift baskets, and Steve Bannon lumbers through the halls like a whiskey-marinated warlock, muttering about the "deep state."

It's no longer about politics. Politics requires strategy, ideas, the ability to form a coherent sentence. CPAC is something else. It's a doomsday cult in its final days, a sweaty, paranoid, backstabbing orgy of has-beens, never-weres, and soon-to-be-indicted felons clinging to the last fumes of Trump's bloated, wheezing presidency.

ELON MUSK AND THE CHAINSAW

There was no official announcement, no reason given. One moment, CPAC was just the usual swamp of dull speeches and aggressive flag-humping. And then, like a libertarian fever dream come to life, Argentina's wild-eyed, chainsaw-wielding president, Javier Milei, strutted onto the stage and presented Elon Musk—the world's richest reply guy—with a chainsaw.

A real one. Gas-powered. The kind you use to clear forests or dismember a political rival.

Musk, dressed like a middle-aged man trying to relive his frat boy years—aviators, MAGA hat, the unmistakable look of a man who has been awake for four days and is loving every second of it—yanked the cord. The engine sputtered, then roared to life.

"This is for bureaucracy!" he bellowed, waving the chainsaw around like a televangelist who had finally lost his grip on reality.

The audience exploded into applause. This was the most coherent policy statement of the entire conference.

What, exactly, Musk meant by this? Nobody knows. Does Musk think he can chainsaw through government red tape? Or is he just here for the vibes, like a billionaire Jackass stunt gone horribly wrong? It didn't matter. The crowd saw a chainsaw, heard a rich man say the word "bureaucracy," and decided this was the future of governance.

Somewhere in the back, JD Vance, America's most emotionally constipated vice president, nodded along.

THE GREAT JD VANCE CHARISMA VOID

Speaking of JD Vance—the Vice President of the United States, the man who, in theory, is next in line to lead the most powerful country on Earth—he took the stage like a man trying to suppress a particularly aggressive bowel movement.

This was his moment. His chance to prove that when Trump finally collapses into a pile of expired KFC and unfulfilled subpoenas, he's the natural heir to MAGA.

So he did what all insecure Republican men do when they need validation: he complained about the feminization of men.

"We must reclaim the soul of America," Vance intoned with the passion of a substitute teacher explaining long division. Then he dived headfirst into the Great Culture War, bemoaning the woke infestation of the military, the existential threat of non-traditional families, and whatever else had been trending in his Facebook comments that morning.

It was a speech so devoid of personality, so aggressively bland, that even the CPAC audience—a group that will clap for literally anything—seemed distracted. People checked their phones. Some wandered off for more bourbon. Even Elon Musk, still high on chainsaw fumes, looked like he was about to X out of this tab.

For a man positioning himself as the next Trump, JD Vance is deeply, profoundly boring. He has all the charisma of a frozen dinner and the pollitical instincts of a concussed duck. And deep down, he knows it. You could see it in his face—the realization that no one at CPAC actually gives a shit about him.

BANNON: DRUNK, DERANGED, AND DANGEROUSLY CLOSE TO A NAZI SALUTE

And then there was Steve Bannon.

The human embodiment of a discarded cigar took the stage, ranting about Trump, deep state conspiracies, and the impending apocalypse that, conveniently, only Trump can prevent.

"The future of MAGA is Donald Trump!" he bellowed, red-faced and sweating bourbon, his gut fighting a desperate battle against the constraints of his shirt.

Then, as he closed his remarks, his arm shot up in a gesture that was just a little too Nazi-adjacent for comfort.

Was it a wave? Was it a fascist salute? Was it the final, spasmodic twitch of a man whose liver has declared bankruptcy? Who can say?

But it landed. The crowd roared. The banners waved. And once again, CPAC had casually flirted with full-blown fascism like it was just another item on the agenda.

TRUMP 2028: THE KING WANTS MORE

And then, the inevitable. The biggest clown in this whole circus is on his way.

Donald J. Trump, the orange ball of grievance and confusion, is set to take the CPAC stage on Saturday. And the crowd is already demanding a third term.

Yes, they're openly chanting for Trump 2028. No, they do not care that it is illegal.

Steve Bannon, looking like a man who just crawled out of a whiskey barrel, is leading the charge.

"The future of MAGA is Donald Trump! We want Trump in '28!"

The crowd roars.

Never mind that the Constitution exists. Never mind that we are one month into Trump's second term, and he is already bored of being president. Never mind that he just spent three days in Miami golfing and posting deranged things about Volodymyr Zelensky.

None of it matters. CPAC 2025 has officially given up on reality.

The Republican Party is dead—replaced by a billionaire cosplay movement where chainsaws are policies, gold reserves are conspiracies, and democracy is just another speed bump on the road to Trump's dictatorship.

And Saturday is the grand finale. Will Trump declare himself king? Will Musk, now high on chainsaw fumes, launch DOGE-funded tax rebates? Will the Jan. 6 rioters storm the stage demanding backpay for their time in prison?

The only thing certain is that it will be stupid.

| 9 |

DEI and Airplanes

A headline reads, "Attorney General Bailey Files Suit Against Starbucks for Race-and-Sex Based Discrimination", but it's not what you think. Anything that resembles affirmative action is now being targeted as (reverse) discrimination, though the target term is now "DEI" — Diversity, Equity, Inclusion. His claim is that the workforce of Starbucks was "more female and less white" and therefore hurts consumers who will be subjected to "higher prices and wait longer for goods and services". Given the anti-DEI Orders and agenda from the White House removing protections, these legal battles in some states are likely to become the norm.

Appointed Under Secretary for Public Diplomacy in the State Department, Darren Beattie is a former Donald Trump speechwriter who was fired in 2018 after CNN revealed he spoke at a conference attended by White Nationalists. (He is also a January 6th conspiracist.) On 4 October 2024, he wrote:

> Competent white men must be in charge if you want things to work. Unfortunately, our entire national ideology is predicated on coddling the feelings of women and minorities, and demoralizing competent white men.

The event that perhaps brought DEI to the forefront was, oddly, a plane crash. An Army Blackhawk helicopter struck an American Airlines regional jet over the Potomac River on 29 January. Seemingly out of nowhere, the President suggested bad hiring practices were the problem, the discussion taking on a life of its own. The Press Secretary defended Trump's statements and read off a list of disabilities -- even dwarfism -- as being allowed for hire. The FAA employs large numbers of people who are not Air Traffic Controllers. The Controllers themselves must all meet the same physical and psychological standards. However, it was even implied this ought to be a concern with pilots, which are not FAA employees and have their own rigorous requirements.

Oddly, when asked if the public should be concerned, there was no admission of danger, only blame, and that Trump will fix it. Part of that fix turned out to be identifying tens of millions of dollars to fund a deal with Starlink (owned by Elon Musk) for upgrading air traffic control communications. The use of AI has also been mentioned. The staff was instructed to avoid paper trails and minimize documentation.

Here it must be noted that actual air traffic accident statistics do not reflect assertions by either side. There have not been significant increases of incidents in recent years, nor has there been a provable increase of incidents after Trump dismissed key FAA officials weeks before the crash in question.

Press Conference

Unidentified: Mr. President, welcome.

Donald Trump: Thank you very much. Thank you. I'd like to request a moment of silence for the victims and their families, please. Thank you very much. I speak to you this morning in an hour of anguish for our nation. Just before 9 PM last night, an American Airlines regional jet carrying 60 passengers and four crew collided with an Army Blackhawk helicopter carrying three military service members over the Potomac River in Washington, DC while on final approach to Reagan National Airport.

Both aircraft crashed instantly and were immediately submerged into the icy waters of the Potomac, real tragedy. The massive search and rescue mission was under way throughout the night, leveraging every asset at our disposal. And I have to say, the local state and federal military, including the United States Coast Guard in particular, they've done a phenomenal job -- so quick, so fast, it was mobilized immediately.

The work has now shifted to a recovery mission. Sadly, there are no survivors. This was a dark and excruciating night in our nation's capital and in our nation's history, and a tragedy of terrible proportions. As one nation, we grieve for every precious soul that has been taken from us so suddenly. And we are a country of -- really we are in mourning.

This has really shaken a lot of people, including people, very sadly, from other nations who were on the flight. For the family members back in Wichita, Kansas, here in Washington, DC and throughout the United States and in Russia, we have a Russia contingent, some very talented people, unfortunately, were on that plane, very, very, very sorry about that.

Whose loved ones were aboard the passenger jet, we can only begin to imagine the agony that you are all feeling, nothing worse. On behalf of the First Lady, myself and 340 million Americans, our hearts are shattered alongside yours, and our prayers are with you now and in the days to come -- we'll be working very, very diligently in the days to come.

We're here for you to wipe away the tears and to offer you our devotion, our love and our support, it's great support. In moments like this, the differences between Americans fade to nothing compared to the bonds of affection and loyalty that unite us all, both as Americans and even as nations. We are one family and today we are all heartbroken we're all searching for answers.

That icy, icy Potomac, it was a cold, cold night, cold water. We're all overcome with the grief for many who have so tragically perished will no longer be with us. Together we take solace in the knowledge that their journey ended not in the cold waters of the Potomac, but in the warm embrace of a loving, God. We do not know what led to this crash, but we have some very strong opinions and ideas.

And I think we'll probably state those opinions now, because over the years I've watched as things like this happen and they say, well, we're always investigating. And then the investigation, three years later, they announce it. We think we have some pretty good ideas, but we'll find out how this disaster occurred and will ensure that nothing like this ever happens again.

The FAA and the NTSB and the US military will be carrying out a systematic and comprehensive investigation. Our new Secretary of Transportation, Sean Duffy -- his second day on the job when that happened, that's a rough one -- will be working tirelessly. He's a great gentleman. A whole group is -- these are great people, and they are working tirelessly to figure out exactly what happened.

We will state certain opinions. However, I'm also immediately appointing an acting commissioner to the FAA, Christopher Rocheleau, a 22-year veteran of the agency, highly respected. Christopher, thank you very much, appreciate it. We must have only the highest standards for those who work in our aviation system.

I changed the Obama standards from very mediocre at best to extraordinary, you remember that. Only the highest aptitude, have to be the highest intellect and psychologically superior people were allowed to qualify for air traffic controllers. That was not so prior to getting there. When I arrived in 2016, I made that change very early on because I always felt this was a job that -- and other jobs too, but this was a job that had to be superior intelligence.

And we didn't really have that, and we had it. And then when I left office and Biden took over, he changed them back to lower than ever before. I put safety first, Obama, Biden and the democrats put policy first, and they put politics at a level that nobody's ever seen because this was the lowest level. Their policy was horrible, and their politics was even worse.

So, as you know, last week, long before the crash, I signed an executive order restoring our highest standards for air traffic controllers and other important jobs throughout the country. So it was very interesting. About a week ago, almost upon entering office, I signed something last week that was an executive order, very powerful on restoring the highest standards of air traffic controllers and others, by the way.

And my administration will set the highest possible bar for aviation safety. We have to have our smartest people. It doesn't matter what they look like, how they speak, who they are. It matters, intellect, talent, the word talent. You have to be talented, naturally talented geniuses. You can't have regular people doing that job.

They won't be able to do it. But we'll restore faith in American air travel. I'll have more to say about that. I do want to point out that various articles that appeared prior to my entering office, and here's one, the FAA's diversity push includes focus on hiring people with severe intellectual and psychiatric disabilities.

That is amazing. And then it says FAA says people with severe disabilities are most underrepresented segment of the workforce and they want them in and they want them -- they can be air traffic controllers. I don't think so. This was in January 14th. So that was a week before I entered office. They put a big push to put diversity into the FAA's program.

Then another article, the Federal Aviation Administration, this was before I got to office recently, the second term, the FAA is actively recruiting workers who suffer severe intellectual disabilities, psychiatric problems, and other mental and physical conditions under a diversity and inclusion hiring initiative spelled out on the agency's website.

Can you imagine? These are people that are -- I mean, actually their lives are shortened because of the stress that they have. Brilliant people have to be in those positions and their lives are actually shortened, very substantially shortened because of the stress where you have many, many planes coming into one target.

And you need a very special talent and a very special genius to be able to do it. Targeted disabilities are those disabilities that the federal government, as a matter of policy, has identified for special emphasis in recruitment and hiring, the FAA's website states. They include hearing, vision, missing extremities, partial paralysis, complete paralysis, epilepsy, severe intellectual disability, psychiatric disability, and dwarfism all qualify for the position of a controller of airplanes pouring into our country, pouring into a little spot, a little dot on the map, a little runway.

The initiative -- the initiative is part of the FAA's Diversity and Inclusion hiring plan. Think of that. The initiative is part of the FAA's Diversity and Inclusion hiring plan, which says diversity is integral to achieving FAA's mission of ensuring safe and efficient travel. I don't think so. I don't think so. I think it's just the opposite.

The FAA website shows that the agency's guidance on diversity hiring were last updated on March 23rd of '22. They wanted to make it even more so. And then I came in and I assumed maybe this is the reason, the FAA, which is overseen by Secretary Pete Buttigieg, a real winner. That guy is a real winner. Do you know how badly everything's run since he's run this Department of Transportation?

He's a disaster. He was a disaster. As a mayor, he ran his city into the ground and he's a disaster now. He's just got a good line of bullshit. The Department of Transportation, his government agency charged with regulating civil aviation. While he runs it, 45,000 people, and he's run it right into the ground with his diversity.

So I have to say that it's terrible. Then it's a group within the FAA, another story, determined that the workforce was too white, that they had concerted efforts to get the administration to change that and to change it immediately. This was in the Obama administration just prior to my getting there. And we took care of African Americans, Hispanic Americans, we took care of everybody at levels that nobody's ever seen before.

It's one of the reasons I won, but they actually came out with a directive. Too white. And we want the people that are competent. But now we mourn and we pray and would like to ask all Americans to join me in a moment of silence as we ask God to watch over those who have lost their lives and bring comfort to the loved ones.

And I just want to say God bless everyone in this room. This has been a terrible very short period of time. We'll get to the bottom of it. So we all saw the same thing. We've seen it many times. I've had the honor of hearing tapes. Tapes of scary -- very scary tapes. You had a airliner coming in, American Airlines.

He was doing everything right. He was on track. He was the same track as everybody else that came in. It's probably the same track as they've had for 25 years or more. He's coming in the path and for some reason, you had a helicopter that was at the same height, obviously, when they hit, but pretty much the same height and going at an angle that was unbelievably bad.

When the air traffic controller said, do you see, you know, he was talking about, do you see him? But there was very little time left when that was stated. And then also, he said follow him in and then almost immediately after that, you know, seconds after that, there was the crash that took place. Well, you follow him in, that means like everything's fine.

Follow them in. You had a pilot problem from the standpoint of the helicopter. I mean, because it was visual, it was very clear night. It was cold, but clear and clear as you could be. The American Airlines plane had lights blazing. They had all their landing lights on. I could see it from the Kennedy Center tape.

We had a tape up on the Kennedy Center that seems to be the primary thus far. I'm sure we'll see other tapes because it's such a -- an area where there are a lot of cameras, a lot of cameras looking up into the air, into space. So we'll probably see many other shots of it before too much time goes by. But we had a situation where you had a helicopter that had the ability to stop.

I have helicopters. You can stop a helicopter very quickly. It had the ability to go up or down. It had the ability to turn and the turn it made was not the correct turn, obviously, and it did somewhat the opposite of what it was told. We don't know that that would have been the difference because the timing was so tight.

It was -- so it was so little. There was so little time to think. But what you did have is you had vision, the helicopter had vision of the plane because you had vision of it all the way -- perfect vision of it all the way from at Kennedy Center where the tape was taken. And for some reason, there weren't adjustments made.

Again, you could have slowed down the helicopter substantially. You could have stopped the helicopter. You could have gone up, you could have gone down, you could have gone straight up, straight down, you could have turned, you could have done a million different maneuvers. For some reason, it just kept going and then made a slight turn at the very end.

And there was -- by that time, it was too late. They shouldn't have been at the same height because, if it wasn't the same height, you could have gone under it or over it. And nobody realized or they didn't say that it's at the same height. At the same height, it would -- still wouldn't have been great, but you would have missed it by quite a bit.

It could have been 1000 feet higher, it could have been 200 feet lower, but it was exactly at the same height and somebody should have been able to point that out. So all of this is going to be studied, but it just seems to me from a couple of words that I like to use, the words common sense, some really bad things happened and some things happened that shouldn't have happened.

So you had a helicopter going in identical direction. You had a helicopter that was at the exact same height as somebody going in essentially the opposite direction. You had a plane that was following a track, which is a track that every other plane followed. And I don't imagine, I know I've heard today that they might have been following the preceding plane, which was pretty close, but not that close, the preceding plane.

But you wouldn't have even been able to see that because of the direction that the helicopter was coming in at. So you had a confluence of bad decisions that were made, and you have people that lost their lives -- violently lost their lives. We're going to take a few questions. I'd like to ask our new Secretary of Transportation to say a few words, Sean Duffy, a great gentleman, just started.

It's not your fault, and I know you agree with me very strongly on intellect and even psychological well-being of the air traffic controllers. It's such an important position and I think I can emphasize stronger. I changed it. When I first ran in 2016, I changed it. We had the highest standard that you could have.

And then they changed it back, that was Biden, to a standard you just ... I read it to you, that was from one of your papers, one of the people in this room that actually wrote that. And then I changed it back a few days ago. And unfortunately, that was ... we'll see. We don't know that necessarily it's even the controller's fault.

But one thing we do know there was a lot of vision and people should have been able to see that. At what point do you stop? At what point do you say, well, that plane's getting a little bit close? So, this is a tragedy that should not have happened. Please, sure.

Sean Duffy: Thank you, Mr. President. And I would just note, the president's leadership has been remarkable during this crisis. We have had a whole-of-government response, local, state, federal. And when you see that kind of cooperation, it begins with the leadership in this body. So, thank you for that, Mr. President, you make our jobs a lot easier.

You made an important point that when we deal with safety, we can only accept the best and the brightest in positions of safety that impact the lives of our loved ones, our family members. And I think you make a really important point on that, Mr. President, that is the motto of your presidency, the best and the brightest, the most intelligent coming into these spaces.

I want to take a moment and extend my condolences to the families of the loved ones. We commit to them that we are going to get to the bottom of this investigation, not in three years, not in four years, but as quickly as possible with the NTSB who is here today as well as the FAA. What happened yesterday shouldn't have happened.

It should not have happened. And when Americans take off in airplanes, they should expect to land at their destination. That didn't happen yesterday. That's unacceptable. And so, we will not accept excuses. We will not accept passing the buck. We are going to take responsibility at the Department of Transportation and the FAA to make sure we have the reforms that have been dictated by President Trump in place to make sure that these mistakes do not happen again.

And again, I want to thank you for your leadership, Mr. President, and I appreciate the confidence you placed in me.

Donald Trump: Thank you very much. Pete, would you like to say something, please?

Pete Hegseth: Well, thank you, Mr. President. Again, I want to echo what the Transportation Secretary said about your leadership. From the moment we found out about this, we were in contact with the White House trying to determine exactly what happened. I would echo as well, no excuses, we're going to get to the bottom of this.

We, first and foremost, from the Defense Department want to pass our condolences to the 64 souls and their families that were affected by this -- never should happen -- and certainly the three service members, the three soldiers, a young, captain staff, sergeant and CW2 chief warrant officer, on a routine annual retraining of night flights on a standard corridor for a continuity of government mission.

The military does dangerous things, it does routine things on a regular basis. Tragically last night a mistake was made, I think the president is right. There was some sort of an elevation issue that we have immediately begun investigating at the DOD and Army level. Army CID is on the ground investigating, top-tier aviation assets inside the DOD are investigating, sir, to get to the bottom of it so that it does not happen again because it's absolutely unacceptable.

But I want to echo what the transportation secretary and you, Mr. President, said because it pertains to the DOD as well. We will have the best and brightest in every position possible. As you said in your inaugural, it is color blind and merit-based, the best leaders possible, whether it's flying Black Hawks, flying airplanes, leading platoons or in government.

The era of DEI is gone at the Defense Department, and we need the best and brightest, whether it's in our air traffic control or whether it's in our generals or whether it's throughout government. So, thank you for your leadership and courage on that, sir, and we'll stand by you on it. Thank you.

Donald Trump: Thank you very much. JD, please.

J.D. Vance: Thank you, Mr. President, for your leadership. I just want to re-emphasize something the president said, and you've heard from the secretary of transportation and of defense, there really was a whole of government response. We were all on the phone. We were all communicating yesterday trying to get to the bottom of this immediately but also try to communicate with the American people about what happened.

Something the president said that I think bears re-emphasizing, which is that when you don't have the best standards in who you're hiring, it means on the one hand you're not getting the best people in government. But on the other hand, it puts stresses on the people who are already there. And I think that is a core part of what President Trump is going to bring and has already brought to Washington, D.C. is we want to hire the best people because we want the best people at air traffic control, and we want to make sure we have enough people at air traffic control who are actually competent to do the job.

If you go back to just some of the headlines over the past 10 years, you have many hundreds of people suing the government because they would like to be air traffic controllers, but they were turned away because of the color of their skin. That policy ends under Donald Trump's leadership because safety is the first priority of our aviation industry.

Thank you, Mr. President.

Donald Trump: Thank you.

Question: Mr. President, on DEI and the claims that you've made, are you saying this crash was somehow caused and the result of diversity hiring? And what evidence have you seen to support these claims?

Donald Trump: It just could have been. We have a high standard; we've had a much higher standard than anybody else. And there are things where you have to go by brainpower. You have to go by psychological quality -- and psychological quality is a very important element of it. These are various very powerful tests that we put to use and they were terminated by Biden and Biden went by a standard that is the exact opposite.

So, we don't know, but we do know that you had two planes at the same level, you had a helicopter and a plane. That shouldn't have happened. And we'll see -- we're going to look into that and we're going to see. But certainly, for an air traffic controller, we want the brightest, the smartest, the sharpest.

We want somebody that's psychologically superior and that's what we're going to have.

Question: Mr. President?

Donald Trump: Yeah, please go ahead.

Question: Mr. President, you mentioned at the top of the briefing that there were several Russian nationals on the flight.

Donald Trump: Yes.

Question: Will the US government be willing to facilitate the transfer of their remains --

Donald Trump: Yes, we will.

Question: Considering the fact there is no direct air travel between the two countries?

Donald Trump: We've already been in contact with Russia and the answer is yes, we will facilitate. Yes, please go ahead.

Question: Thank you, Mr. President. The situation in the Democratic Republic of the Congo is getting worse. Even though President Joao Lourenco has been mediating the conflict between Rwanda and the Democratic Republic of the Congo because he wants to bring peace and stability. The situation is really bad right now. I want to hear from this president if you have any plan in the future to bring peace in the Democratic Republic of Congo.

Donald Trump: You're asking me a question about Rwanda, and it is a very serious problem, I agree, but I don't think it's appropriate right now to talk about it, but it is a very serious problem.

Question: Mr. President, do we yet know the names of the 67 people who were killed? And you are blaming Democrats and DEI policies and air traffic control, and seemingly the member of the US military who was flying that Black Hawk helicopter. Don't you think you're getting ahead of the investigation right now?

Donald Trump: No, I don't think so at all. I don't think -- with the names of the people -- you mean the names of the people that are on the plane? You think that's going to make a difference? They are a group of people that have lost their lives. If you want a list of the names, we can give you that -- we'll be giving that very soon. We're in coordination with American Airlines. We're in coordination very strongly, obviously, with the military. But I think that's not a very smart question. I'm surprised coming from you.

Please, please.

Question: Thank you, President Trump. Thank you for being here. Based on your analysis so far, do you have a sense of who is at fault? If it was the plane, the helicopter, air traffic control? And can you assure people that it is safe to fly in and out of DC?

Donald Trump: Well, I've given you the analysis and the analysis was -- it was based on vision. You had a lot of people that saw what was happening. You had some people that knew what was happening. There were some warnings, but the warnings were given very, very late. Those warnings were given very late. It was almost as they were given, a few seconds later there was a crash.

It should have been brought up earlier. But the people in the helicopter should have seen where they were going. I can't imagine people with 20/20 vision not seeing what's happening up there.

Again, they shouldn't have been at the same height. You're going in reverse directions or sideway directions, obviously, you want to be at different heights. I see it all the time when I'm flying. You have planes going in the opposite, they're always lower. We're higher or they're -- so if somehow there's a screw up, there's not going to be a tragedy.

It will be close, but you know there's never going to be a tragedy if you're at a different elevation. For whatever reason, they were at the same elevation. And also from the American Airlines standard,

he's along the track that every plane is along. You say what was a helicopter doing in that track? It's very sad.

But visually somebody should have been able to see and taken that
helicopter out of play and they should have been at a different height.
All right.

Question: On your executive order -- Thank you, sir. You mentioned the Russians that were on board that plane. What other na-
tionalities were on board that passenger --

Donald Trump: There were a couple of others. We're going to be
announcing it in about an hour. We have some very specific information. We're calling the countries. We've spoken to most of them, but
there were some other countries represented.

Question: Have you spoken to President Putin?

Donald Trump: I have not, no.

Question: Mr. President --

Donald Trump: Not about this.

Question: If I may, on your Executive Order, you've already issued
an Executive Order you say we'll restore aviation safety.

Donald Trump: Right.

Question: This crash happened after that. Was the Executive Order successful? And what more needs to change to keep people safe?

Donald Trump: Well, you know, we issued it three days ago and
we were -- we're in the process of making those changes. This is --
this is something that should have been done a long time ago. Actu-

ally, my original order should have never been changed and I think maybe you wouldn't have had this problem. Maybe.

Question: President Trump.

Donald Trump: Yeah, please go ahead.

Question: Yes, thank you. We see like everyday life that's very often the -- those diversity hires cause sometimes issues, as you just mentioned. So what plan do you have? Are we going to see some fire? Are you going to fire some of those diversity hires in the federal government? What's -- what's the plan do you have?

Donald Trump: I would say the answer is yes. If we find that people aren't mentally competent, you -- you see the language. The language is put out by them. And if you see that -- I'm not going to bore you by reading it again, but these are not people that should be doing this particular job. They'd be very good for certain jobs, but not people that should be doing this particular job.

Question: Mr. President, you have today blamed the diversity elements, but then told us that you weren't sure that the controllers made any mistake. You then said perhaps the helicopter pilots were the ones who made the mistake.

Donald Trump: Yeah. It's all under investigation.

Question: I understand that that's why I'm trying to figure out how you can come to the conclusion right now that diversity had something to do with this crash.

Donald Trump: Because I have common sense, OK? And unfortunately a lot of people don't. We want brilliant people doing this. This is a major chess game at the highest level. When you have 60 planes coming in during a short period of time and they're all coming in different directions and you're dealing with very high level computer -- computer work and very complex computers.

And one of the other things I will tell you is that the systems that were built, I was going to rebuild the entire system and then we had an election that didn't turn out the way it should have, but they didn't build the systems properly. They spent a lot of money renovating the system, spending much more money than they would have spent if they bought a new system for air traffic controllers, meaning the computerized systems.

There are certain companies that do a very good job. They didn't use those companies. They used companies that should not have been doing it. No, I think -- I think this -- I think it's very important to understand that for some jobs, and not only this, but air traffic controllers, they have to be at the highest level of genius.

Question: Sir, I want to ask you about the ice skaters in a moment because the US ice skating community was affected. But first, if I can, the cited FAA text that you read is real, but the implication that this policy is new or that it stems from efforts that began under President Biden or the Transportation Secretary Pete Buttigieg is demonstrably false.

Question: It's been on the FAA website --

Donald Trump: Who said that, you?

Question: No, I'm -- it's on the website, the FAA's website. It was there in 2013. It was there for the entirety --

Donald Trump: -- Take a look. What I read --

Question: It was there for the entirety of your administration, too --

Donald Trump: -- Nice and easy.

Question: So my question is why didn't you change the policy during your first administration?

Donald Trump: I did change it. I changed the Obama policy and we had a very good policy and then Biden came in and he changed it. And then when I came in, two days, three days ago, I signed a new order bringing it to the highest level of intelligence, OK?

Question: It was on the website --

Donald Trump: Please.

Question: It was on the website --

Donald Trump: Quiet. Quiet.

Question: Thank you. Welcome back to the -- I'm sorry. You mentioned that a vision was probably the problem that was at issue in this crash. There's been some reports that one of the pilots in the helicopter may have been using night vision equipment. Was there any --

Donald Trump: I heard that. We don't know. We're going to know that pretty soon. It may change your view plane if you do have the night vision. So it's very possible that could have happened. That would be -- that would be maybe a reason why you wouldn't actually see as well as on a clear night. You can see sometimes better without it.

Question: Mr. President, is it helpful to have your Secretary of Transportation confirmed and does this intensify your interest in getting other nominees confirmed quickly?

Donald Trump: Turn it -- go at -- what?

Question: Is it helpful to have your Secretary of Transportation confirmed, and does this intensify your interest in getting other nominees confirmed quickly as well?

Donald Trump: Well, sure. We want fast confirmations. And the Democrats, as you know, are doing everything they can to delay them. They've taken too long. We're -- we're struggling to get very good people that everybody knows are going to be confirmed, but we're struggling to get them out faster. We want them out faster.

It's a good question, actually. We -- we've been pushing Sean. Everyone knows Sean for a long time. He got many, many Democrat votes, but they want to take as long as they can. They ask questions like some of the questions that Peter would ask that were totally irrelevant and not very good questions. But they want to just keep it going.

They want to keep it going as long as possible. I was very honored, actually, that you got so many Democrat votes that was really good. That was really good.

Question: Mr. President. Mr. President. Mr. President, when are you trying to -- when are you trying to meet with the families? And the second question, is it your impression that little training was done during that time?

Donald Trump: The what?

Question: The training that the helicopter was involved in, is it anything you can tell us about --

Donald Trump: You don't know. These are the things that will come up with the investigation. You don't know, but the helicopter obviously was in the wrong place at the wrong time and a tragedy occurred. Please.

Question: I've got a question about --

Donald Trump: No, go ahead, please.

Question: Thank you, Mr. President. You've been critical of the current regulations and you've called for big reforms at FAA. I'm curious, sir, what --

Donald Trump: Well, I made the reforms, actually.

Question: What is your message --

Donald Trump: Three days ago, I made the reform.

Question: Yes, sir. What is your message then to the American public in the weeks and months ahead? Should they feel hesitant to fly? And if you could clarify perhaps something that the defense secretary said when he said that this helicopter was on a continuity of government mission?

Donald Trump: I don't know what that -- what that refers to, but they were practicing. They were -- they do that, they call it practicing and they were. And that's something that should be done. It's only continuity in the sense that we want to have very good people and that has to be in continuity and that's what they refer to. But it was basically practice and it was a practice that worked out very, very badly. OK?

Question: Should Americans feel hesitant to fly? Mr. President, yes, on his -- on his question, the first question, should people be hesitant to fly right now?

Donald Trump: No, not at all. I do not hesitate to fly. This is something that it's been many years that something like this has happened. And the collision is just something that we don't expect ever to happen again. We are going to have the highest level people. We've already hired some of the people that you've already hired for that position long before we knew about this.

I mean, long before from the time I came in, we started going out and getting the best people because I said it's not -- it's not appropriate what they're doing. I think it's a tremendous mistake. You know, they like to do things and they like to take them too far and this is sometimes what ends up happening.

Now with that, I'm not blaming the controller, I'm saying there are things that you could question like the height of the helicopter, the height of the plane being at the same level, going in opposite directions. It's not a positive. But no, we're already hiring people. No, flying is very safe. We have the safest flying anywhere in the world and we'll keep it that way.

Thank you all very much. Thank you very much, everybody.

Question: Were those people hired under DEI?

[leaves podium]

| 10 |

Health and Science

Nearly everything related to science is now a debate. From climate change and sexuality to vaccines and stem cells, the fields of science are influenced by funding but otherwise independent and scientist are accountable to each other globally. The following letters represent concerns from within and without these fields and the government agencies related to them.

Letter by Congressman Don Beyer

{Written regarding the National Science Foundation (NSF) firing workers illegally reclassified as probationary}

Dear Director Panchanathan,

I write to express deep concern and outrage over the National Science Foundation's (NSF) recent firing of NSF employees and the reclassification of hundreds of employees' employment status from permanent to a probationary status. The dismissal of some of our nation's top-notch scientists, as well as this arbitrary extension of the probationary period from one to two years undermines NSF's policy and statutory mission to promote scientific advancement in the United States.

By longstanding practice, NSF's probationary period for excepted employees has been one year, as clearly reflected in offer letters, SF-50 forms, and the agency's personnel manual. Many employees had their probation waived entirely through Direct Hire Authority negotiations, a discretionary power NSF exercised to fulfill urgent hiring needs. However, on January 20, 2025, the Office of Personnel Management (OPM) issued a directive requiring agencies to submit lists of probationary employees. In this guidance, OPM asserted that excepted-service employees must serve a two-year probationary period, disregarding agency-specific authority under applicable law. In direct response to OPM's directive, NSF unilaterally stripped permanent status from both bargaining unit and non-bargaining unit employees, including executives. Employees who had already completed a one-year probationary period—some of whom had their probation contractually waived—were suddenly reclassified as probationary, exposing them to termination without due process.

This sweeping policy shift was executed without prior notification for the affected employees—many learned of their status change through their union or a new SF-50 quietly placed in their personnel files. This was done without consultation or collective bargaining, violating NSF's obligations under the Federal Service Labor-Management Relations Statute, and without a formal agency memorandum clarifying the legal basis or rationale for disregarding established hiring policies.

On February 4, NSF signaled plans for a Reduction in Force, and on February 5, hastily renewed Intergovernmental Personnel Act appointments of visiting scholars, further jeopardizing career program officers. It is our understanding that NSF is now applying the definition of "employee" under 5 U.S.C. 7511 to prepare for adverse actions against its workforce. This is not an administrative technicality—it is an unjustified extension of probation and reversal of permanent employment status which contradicts Agency policy and undermines employees' ability to perform the mission of the agency. Finally, I learned earlier this week that over 168 probationary employees and expert appointments at NSF were dismissed from their roles.

NSF's actions have already inflicted serious harm. Before these cuts, NSF had a workforce of approximately 1,500 employees and 200 scientists from research institutions serving in temporary roles. The loss of approximately 10% of NSF's workforce will slow progress in our current science initiatives and severely hinder NSF's capacity for growth. In addition, employees have reported confusion and distress due to the Administration's unwarranted employment status reclassification. Alarmingly, the list of employees which NSF provided to OPM erroneously included permanent employees, putting them at risk for termination. The rushed nature of this decision and termination process has blindsided supervisors and added chaos to NSF's operational structure, not to mention risking U.S. scientific leadership, innovation and discovery.

It is absurd to mindlessly decimate the workforce that has led the world in science over the past 75 years, and to willingly give up excellent scientists and talent. I demand that NSF reinstate its employees who have been terminated and rectify the unlawful reclassification of permanent employees. The Administration must comply with labor agreements, recognize employee protections, and halt reclassifications.

I ask for a response in writing as to how you plan to comply with existing contractual obligations. NSF employees have dedicated themselves to advancing science, technology, and education in the United States, ensuring the nation remains competitive in STEM fields.

Sincerely,

Donald S. Beyer Jr.
Member of Congress

To the researchers, educators, and academics of the United States of America, your work is needed now more than ever.

{A letter coordinated by the American Psychological Association}

American science and innovation have advanced humanity for generations. The pursuit of science has led to humanity's greatest advances, improving people's lives and the health of our planet.

But today, science is under threat. The Pew Research Center found the share of Americans who say science has had a mostly positive effect on society has fallen and there's been a continued decline in public trust in scientists.

In this unpredictable time, we must remind ourselves of what remains the same. We need scientific research to support the health and safety of people and our planet. We need policy decisions that are grounded in research and data. We need researchers and educators who will seek scientific truths and prepare the next generation to carry on this critical work.

Science is at the core of our missions and we remain firmly committed to supporting, elevating, and fighting for science and those who further it.

This is our commitment to you.

- We will champion scientific integrity, including academic freedom, the inclusion of diverse perspectives, and policies grounded in scientific evidence.
- We will fight to ensure that research funding is stable and predictable, allowing scientists to pursue ambitious research and make meaningful discoveries.
- We will work to ensure experts like you have the resources they need to pursue research with autonomy and integrity, including critical datasets.

- We will continue to impress on others the importance of science as an objective, unbiased approach to understanding our world.

Scientific truths are nonpartisan. It has never been more important to recommit to scientific knowledge, and to ensure you have access to data, are free from censorship, and are able to do your valuable work.

We are committed to working every day to ensure that the researchers who have devoted their lives to discovery and truth can safely continue working to improve lives and benefit society.

Sincerely,

American Anthropological Association

American Association for Dental, Oral, and Craniofacial Research

American Association for Public Opinion Research

American Association for the Advancement of Science

American Association of Immunologists

American Association of Physics Teachers

American Geophysical Union

American Industrial Hygiene Association

American Institute of Biological Sciences

American Meteorological Society

American Physiological Society

American Political Science Association

American Psychological Association

American Psychological Association Services Inc.

American Society for Cell Biology

American Society for Microbiology

American Society for Pharmacology and Experimental Therapeutics (ASPET)

American Society of Civil Engineers

American Society of Plant Biologists

American Sociological Association

American Statistical Association

American Thoracic Society

Americans for Medical Progress

Association for Behavioral and Cognitive Therapies (ABCT)

Association for Computing Machinery (ACM)

Association for Psychological Science

Association for the Sciences of Limnology and Oceanography

Association for Women in Science

Association of Population Centers

Computing Research Association

Council on Undergraduate Research

Entomological Society of America

Federation of Associations in Behavioral & Brain Sciences

Gerontological Society of America

Linguistic Society of America

National Council on Family Relations

National Postdoctoral Association

Population Association of America

Population Researcher

Psychonomic Society

Society for Neuroscience

Society for Personality and Social Psychology

Society for Personality Assessment

Society for Research on Adolescence

Society for the Psychological Study of Social Issues

Society of Behavioral Medicine

The Association for Research in Vision and Ophthalmology (ARVO)

The Wildlife Society

| 11 |

The Gulf of America and Associated Press

Known locally by its native name Denali for centuries, a gold prospector named this Alaskan mountain "Mount McKinley" in 1896 in support of then-presidential candidate William McKinley. From 1917 until 2015, it was recognized by the federal government as Mount McKinley. The state of Alaska reverted to the native name in 1975, and in 2015, the United States Department of the Interior followed suit. On 20 January, President Trump issued an Executive Order restoring the federal designation of Denali to Mount McKinley, and designating the Gulf of Mexico as the Gulf of America.

The Gulf of Mexico, and international body of water, was named after a term for the Aztec people, appearing on maps as early as 1552. The Spanish territory in North America took its name when it became an independent nation in 1821. After Trump's order, designation as the "Gulf of America" was adopted by Google Maps, Apple Maps, Bing Maps, USA Today, Axios, Fox News, and other media outlets. Associated Press did not, resulting in the White House restricting access to press briefings, the oval office, and Air Force One. Interestingly, Fox News and Newsmax -- far-Right leaning media outlets -- objected to how AP was treated.

At a press conference on 12 February, White House Press Secretary Karoline Leavitt defended the decision, saying coverage was a privilege, and that "We reserve the right to decide who gets to go into the Oval Office ". She furthermore asserted that refusing the designation was telling a lie, and there will be consequences for whoever they deem is lying.

> If we feel there are lies being pushed by outlets in this room, we are going to hold those lies accountable. And it is a fact that the body of water off the coast of Louisiana is called the Gulf of America, and I'm not sure why news outlets don't want to call it that but that is what it is.

A lawsuit was brought by AP but temporarily denied by U.S. District Judge Trevor N. McFadden on 24 February. However, the judge said the situation was "uniformly unhelpful to the White House". A poster of the Gulf with the word "VICTORY" was the backdrop for a following press conference.

On 25 February, the White House "seized control of the press pool", replacing the Correspondent's Association as the body who decides access.

Restoring Names That Honor American Greatness

By the authority vested in me as President by the Constitution and the laws of the United States of America, it is hereby ordered:

Section 1. Purpose and Policy. It is in the national interest to promote the extraordinary heritage of our Nation and ensure future generations of American citizens celebrate the legacy of our American heroes. The naming of our national treasures, including breathtaking natural wonders and historic works of art, should honor the contributions of visionary and patriotic Americans in our Nation's rich past.

Sec. 2. Appointments to the U.S. Board on Geographic Names. (a) Within seven days of the date of this order, each agency head with authority to appoint members to the Board on Geographic Names (Board) pursuant to 43 U.S.C. 364a, shall review their respective appointees and consider replacing those appointees in accordance with applicable law.

(b) The Secretary of the Interior shall review and consider additional appointments to the Board to assist in fulfilling all aspects of this order, subject to all applicable laws.

(c) With respect to all applications for naming and renaming submitted to the newly constituted Board, the Board shall advance the policy established in section 1 of this order to honor the contributions of visionary and patriotic Americans and may update its principles, policies, and procedures as needed to achieve this policy.

(d) Where Congressional action is required to establish a renaming in public law, following Board approval on renaming, the Board shall provide guidance to all relevant Federal agencies to use the Board-approved name in the interim in federal documents and achieve consistency across the federal government.

Sec. 3. Renaming of Mount McKinley. (a) President William McKinley, the 25th President of the United States, heroically led our Nation to victory in the Spanish-American War. Under his leadership, the United States enjoyed rapid economic growth and prosperity, including an expansion of territorial gains for the Nation. President McKinley championed tariffs to protect U.S. manufacturing, boost domestic production, and drive U.S. industrialization and global reach to new heights. He was tragically assassinated in an attack on our Nation's values and our success, and he should be honored for his steadfast commitment to American greatness.

In 1917, the country officially honored President McKinley through the naming of North America's highest peak. Yet after nearly a century, President Obama's administration, in 2015, stripped the McKinley name from federal nomenclature, an affront to President McKinley's life, his achievements, and his sacrifice.

This order honors President McKinley for giving his life for our great Nation and dutifully recognizes his historic legacy of protecting

America's interests and generating enormous wealth for all Americans.

(b) Within 30 days of the date of this order, the Secretary of the Interior shall, consistent with 43 U.S.C. 364 through 364f, reinstate the name "Mount McKinley." The Secretary shall subsequently update the Geographic Names Information System (GNIS) to reflect the renaming and reinstatement of Mount McKinley. The national park area surrounding Mount McKinley shall retain the name Denali National Park and Preserve.

(c) The Secretary of the Interior shall work with Alaska Native entities and state and local organizations to adopt names for landmarks to honor the history and culture of the Alaskan people.

Sec. 4. Gulf of America. (a) The area formerly known as the Gulf of Mexico has long been an integral asset to our once burgeoning Nation and has remained an indelible part of America. The Gulf was a crucial artery for America's early trade and global commerce. It is the largest gulf in the world, and the United States coastline along this remarkable body of water spans over 1,700 miles and contains nearly 160 million acres. Its natural resources and wildlife remain central to America's economy today. The bountiful geology of this basin has made it one of the most prodigious oil and gas regions in the world, providing roughly 14% of our Nation's crude-oil production and an abundance of natural gas, and consistently driving new and innovative technologies that have allowed us to tap into some of the deepest and richest oil reservoirs in the world. The Gulf is also home to vibrant American fisheries teeming with snapper, shrimp, grouper, stone crab, and other species, and it is recognized as one of the most productive fisheries in the world, with the second largest volume of commercial fishing landings by region in the Nation, contributing millions of dollars to local American economies. The Gulf is also a favorite destination for American tourism and recreation activities. Further, the Gulf is a vital region for the multi-billion-dollar U.S. maritime industry, providing some of the largest and most impressive ports in the world. The Gulf will continue to play a pivotal role in shaping America's future and the global economy, and in recognition of this flourishing economic resource and its critical importance to our Nation's economy and its people, I am directing that it officially be renamed the Gulf of America.

(b) As such, within 30 days of the date of this order, the Secretary of the Interior shall, consistent with 43 U.S.C. 364 through 364f, take all appropriate actions to rename as the "Gulf of America" the U.S. Continental Shelf area bounded on the northeast, north, and northwest by the States of Texas, Louisiana, Mississippi, Alabama and Florida and extending to the seaward boundary with Mexico and Cuba in the area formerly named as the Gulf of Mexico. The Secretary shall subsequently update the GNIS to reflect the renaming of the Gulf and remove all references to the Gulf of Mexico from the GNIS, consistent with applicable law. The Board shall provide guidance to ensure all federal references to the Gulf of America, including on agency maps, contracts, and other documents and communications shall reflect its renaming.

Sec. 5. Additional Action. The Secretary of Interior may solicit public and intergovernmental input regarding additional patriots to honor, particularly in light of America's semiquincentennial celebration, and shall recommend action to me, through the Assistant to the President for Domestic Policy.

Sec. 6. General Provisions. (a) Nothing in this order shall be construed to impair or otherwise affect:

(i) the authority granted by law to an executive department or agency, or the head thereof; or

(ii) the functions of the Director of the Office of Management and Budget relating to budgetary, administrative, or legislative proposals.

(b) This order shall be implemented consistent with applicable law and subject to the availability of appropriations.

(c) This order is not intended to, and does not, create any right or benefit, substantive or procedural, enforceable at law or in equity by any party against the United States, its departments, agencies, or entities, its officers, employees, or agents, or any other person.

THE WHITE HOUSE,
January 20, 2025.

AP style guidance on Gulf of Mexico, Mount McKinley

President Donald Trump has signed an executive order to rename the Gulf of Mexico to the Gulf of America. The body of water has shared borders between the U.S. and Mexico. Trump's order only carries authority within the United States. Mexico, as well as other countries and international bodies, do not have to recognize the name change.

The Gulf of Mexico has carried that name for more than 400 years. The Associated Press will refer to it by its original name while acknowledging the new name Trump has chosen. As a global news agency that disseminates news around the world, the AP must ensure that place names and geography are easily recognizable to all audiences.

The AP regularly reviews its style guidance regarding name changes, in part to ensure its guidance reflects common usage. We'll continue to apply that approach to this guidance and make updates as needed.

There are other examples where the AP refers to a geographical place by more than one name. For example, the Gulf of California is sometimes referred to as the Sea of Cortez. The U.S. government has designated that body of water as the Gulf of California, while Mexico recognizes it as the Sea of Cortez.

President Trump also signed an executive order to revert the name of North America's tallest peak, Denali in Alaska, to Mount McKinley. Former President Barack Obama changed the official name to Denali in 2015 to reflect the traditions of Alaska Natives as well as the preference of many Alaska residents. Trump said in his executive order that he wanted to "restore the name of a great president, William McKinley, to Mount McKinley."

The Associated Press will use the official name change to Mount McKinley. The area lies solely in the United States and as president, Trump has the authority to change federal geographical names within the country.

The AP Stylebook will be updated to reflect both decisions.

AP statement on Oval Office access

{Executive Editor Julie Pace, 11 February}

As a global news organization, The Associated Press informs billions of people around the world every day with factual, nonpartisan journalism.

Today we were informed by the White House that if AP did not align its editorial standards with President Donald Trump's executive order renaming the Gulf of Mexico as the Gulf of America, AP would be barred from accessing an event in the Oval Office. This afternoon AP's reporter was blocked from attending an executive order signing.

It is alarming that the Trump administration would punish AP for its independent journalism. Limiting our access to the Oval Office based on the content of AP's speech not only severely impedes the public's access to independent news, it plainly violates the First Amendment.

Statement on White House Excluding AP from News Coverage

{Issued 11 February}

In the relationship between the press and the Office of the President, coverage and standards are entirely in the purview of individual organizations.

The White House cannot dictate how news organizations report the news, nor should it penalize working journalists because it is unhappy with their editors' decisions. The move by the administration to bar a reporter from The Associated Press from an official event open to news coverage today is unacceptable.

The WHCA stands with The Associated Press and calls on the administration to immediately change course.

Eugene Daniels, president of the WHCA

Statement from AP, Bloomberg News, Reuters on White House press pool access

{Joint statement, 26 February}

The three permanent wires in the White House pool, The Associated Press, Bloomberg News and Reuters, have long worked to ensure that accurate, fair and timely information about the presidency is communicated to a broad audience of all political persuasions, both in the United States and globally. Much of the White House coverage people see in their local news outlets, wherever they are in the world, comes from the wires.

It is essential in a democracy for the public to have access to news about their government from an independent, free press. We believe that any steps by the government to limit the number of wire services with access to the President threatens that principle. It also harms the spread of reliable information to people, communities, businesses and global financial markets that heavily depend on our reporting.

Julie Pace, Executive Editor, The Associated Press
Alessandra Galloni, Editor-in-Chief, Reuters

John Micklethwait, Editor-in-Chief, Bloomberg

Proclamation

{From White House website}

Today, I am very honored to recognize February 9, 2025, as the first ever Gulf of America Day.

On January 20, 2025, I signed Executive Order 14172 ("Restoring Names That Honor American Greatness"). Among other actions, that Executive Order required the Secretary of the Interior, acting pursuant to 43 U.S.C. 364 through 364f, to "take all appropriate actions to rename as the 'Gulf of America' the U.S. Continental Shelf area bounded on the northeast, north, and northwest by the State of Texas, Louisiana, Mississippi, Alabama and Florida and extending to the seaward boundary with Mexico and Cuba in the area formerly named as the Gulf of Mexico."

I took this action in part because, as stated in that Order, "[t]he area formerly known as the Gulf of Mexico has long been an integral asset to our once burgeoning Nation and has remained an indelible part of America."

Today, I am making my first visit to the Gulf of America since its renaming. As my Administration restores American pride in the history of American greatness, it is fitting and appropriate for our great Nation to come together and commemorate this momentous occasion and the renaming of the Gulf of America.

NOW, THEREFORE, I, DONALD J. TRUMP, President of the United States of America, by virtue of the authority vested in me by the Constitution and the laws of the United States, do hereby proclaim February 9, 2025, as Gulf of America Day. I call upon public officials and all the people of the United States to observe this day with appropriate programs, ceremonies, and activities.

IN WITNESS WHEREOF, I have hereunto set my hand this ninth day of February, in the year of our Lord two thousand twenty-five, and of the Independence of the United States of America the two hundred and forty-ninth.

| 12 |

Deportation

There are more stories than one can count about people being caught by ICE or other agencies. But these are anecdotal and hard to verify. It is unclear how often they are stopping people on suspicion due to racial profiling. There are reports of even Native Americans being detained. Are those with refugee status targeted? Will they ignore citizenship if they are presumed to have been "anchor babies"?

According to the website Accessible Law, "The right to legal counsel ... is limited to criminal cases. An undocumented immigrant facing deportation before the immigration court is not granted the right to legal counsel. This is because deportation proceedings are not a criminal proceeding."

A driving support for Trump has been with regards to addressing a perceived "invasion" with all the usual hallmarks of previous eras, with Fentanyl being the new Roofer Madness scare. Actual statistics and demographics are totally at odds with popular beliefs, and it is ironic that Biden deported more people than Trump in his first term. Clearly, this is about something else. We now hear openly White Supremacist rhetoric such as 'Great Replacement' theory (promulgated to wider audiences by former Fox host Tucker Carlson). But all this would be for another book. The point here is that whatever is happening out there as I write THIS book doesn't seem to be very transparent, although unclear numbers have been offered.

Instead, we find a promotional video of sorts, posted on X as "ASMR: Illegal Alien Deportation Flight" by the White House, showing a man being shackled and loaded on a military transport (identity or status unknown, though someone claims to have identified them as a U.S. citizen.). As a side note, India and other countries objected to people being sent back in shackles like prisoners. Many sent their own planes to pick up those to be deported.

The public's response? Many in the public are making references to Anne Frank when talking about the ethics of it all, while others, such as the Press Secretary, deem them all criminals by virtue of their migrant status. That won't be argued here, but it can be seen as a slippery slope, given that citizenship, or lack thereof rather, enabled the immediate conditions by which the Holocaust took place. That is why international law has standards to prevent nations from turning away those who seek asylum. I would refer the reader to the UN's "Convention relating to the Status of Refugees".

As this book is not primarily to debate these subjects, I offer a single anecdote.

Social Media Post, 24 February

{Adrian Baron, author of the legal blog The Nutmeg Lawyer and partner at Connecticut Law Firm Podorowsky Thompson & Baron}

If you think it's not happening in Connecticut. This was my experience today.

I'm a US Citizen. As a lawyer, I just left a US court house where I defended the Constitutional rights of 5 people. In view of that court house, several blacked out cars boxed me in on every side. That was followed by armed ATF and ICE officers in ski masks and tactical gear approaching my car as fellow lawyers and members of the public looked on in disbelief Then my client, in the company of his lawyer and guilty of a civil infraction, was taken out of the car by ICE and

ATF agents wearing ski masks. My morning in Connecticut. It's not normal.

You might have heard that ICE is only going after hardened criminals, drug dealers and gang members. It's simply not true. And in addition to ICE, they are repurposing DEA, FBI and ATF agents from their regular posts. So instead of ATF guys going after gun smugglers, DEA agents going after drug dealers, FBI going after terrorists, they are instead using these guys to go after undocumented immigrants. For example, a guy who overstayed a visa.

I'm an attorney. This morning I was giving my client a ride home after court in New Britain. He was not convicted of anything and has no criminal convictions on his record. As I began to reverse out of my parking spot; my car was suddenly blocked by 4 black vehicles. I was instructed to shut off my engine as my car was boxed in on three sides. ICE agents joined by ATF agents wearing black masks and tactical gear approached my car and removed my client.

My client is a Polish immigrant with a family. His violation was overstaying a legal tourist visa. He didn't sneak over the border. He entereed legally. His visa expired. Overstaying a visa is often considered a civil infraction.

If you overstay a tourist visa, there are ways you can fix your status. You may be eligible if you are an immediate relative of a U.S. citizen, such as a spouse, parent, or unmarried child under 21.

You must have entered the U.S. legally, even if your visa expired and you should not have any criminal offenses or other immigration violations.

This guy was in the process of adjusting his status.

My witnessing the incident is the only reason his family knows why he didn't come home. They still don't know where he was taken.

I'm not against deportations when warranted. I have no objection to gang members and criminals being deported.And yes, you can be deported for overstaying a visa. People need to obey our laws

But, even if you agree with these deportations, there was no reason for such a gross public display of force over a guy with an expired tourist visa. That means he entered the country lawfully with permission. He was legal until his visa expired. That is usually considered a civil infraction.

In my opinion, this was purely for optics and show. A waste of resources of multiple agencies.

Yes, ATF agents. The guys that go after gun smugglers and bomb makers. Like I'm Pablo Escobar or something. Thank God I dropped my 4 year old off at preschool earlier that morning.

Very disturbing.

| 13 |

Expansionism and Tariffs

Right out of the starting gate, Trump spoke of acquiring Greenland and the Panama Canal, purportedly because they are needed "for economic security". On 7 January, he even suggested the use of the military was an option to get them. Denmark, who owns Greenland, was not amused, with Anders Vistisen, a Danish member of the European Parliament responded,

---

Dear President Trump, listen very carefully. Greenland have been part of the Danish kingdom for 800 years. It's an integrated part of our country. It is not for sale. Let me put it in words you might understand: Mr. Trump, fuck off!

After the State of the Union address, Greenland responded that "We do not want to be Americans, nor Danes, we are Kalaallit (Greenlanders) ... The Americans and their leader must understand that." Panama responded to his claims about China running the Canal and America's progress in taking it over that "Once again, President Trump, is lying".

More bizarre was Trump's talk of annexing Canada, repeatedly referring to it as a "51st State", although he limited his intentions of coercion to "economic force". The buzzword before the election was "tariffs", not just for economic purposes and trade deficits, but to strong arm Mexico, Canada, and China into addressing other issues such as border security and Fentanyl. The initial threats early in the first forty days were calmed by "concessions" that amounted roughly to previous arrangements. But the tariffs are still on, and economists are panicking at the consequences, citing how they negatively affected America in his last term's trade wars.

Both Canada and Mexico are retaliating with tariffs of their own, and Canada has already been boycotting products such as liquor, which particularly hits Kentucky (which may be part of their effort to target "Red States"). Some steelmakers in Canada and Mexico have been refusing new orders going to the United States. China plans to ban the export of rare minerals to the United States, including gallium, germanium, antimony, and 'superhard materials'.

Canadian House of Commons

{Charlie Angus, Member of the House of Commons of Canada, 15 February}

Good morning and happy Valentine's Day.

I want to say this morning how much I love my country. We don't tend to do that in Canada. We think that that's gauche. We don't feel we need to say how much we love our country. But when we see the criminal gang that has taken control in Washington telling us we do not have a right to our nation, well, oh, not only am I going to love my country and its values and the people from one end of this beautiful nation to another, but I'm going to work with those ordinary Canadians to defend our right to continue to exist as an independent nation. And for this, on the eve of the 60th anniversary of the Canadian flag, I encourage Canadians to reflect what that symbol means, that symbol that has been in war zones, that symbol that has been as Canadians went to fight famines in other countries, that symbol of openness and inclusion that is the direct opposite to the politics of Elon Musk and Donald Trump. This week, we saw the shameful actions by Donald Trump to negotiate with Vladimir Putin, another gangster, to sell the people of Ukraine out.

Mr. Putin thinks that Vladimir Putin is a savvy genius, and he detests our country? Well, he's sending us a very clear message of the man he is.

Our neighbors are no longer our allies. We are dealing with a regime next door to us that is ignoring the international rule of law, and we have to take this dead serious, as a nation, with our political leaders, with ordinary Canadians.

So what do we do right now? Well, I'm extremely encouraged by the incredible response we've received from this pledge for Canada that's now just in the space of two weeks, had over 62,000 people sign up, people from across the political spectrum -- former Prime Minister, Kim Campbell, former Attorney General, Allan Rock, former Premier, Danny Williams -- but also the incredible artists and indigenous activists and labor activists and ordinary people across this country who said that there's a value to our nation that we're willing to defend. I also want to encourage and thank the ordinary people who, on their own, began the boycott of all things American. Now, some might think, Well, if you just choose not to go down to Tennessee this year, who's going to notice?

Well, right now, we're seeing the American tourism industry is in full on panic. There are now over $2 billion in travel that is at risk. That's 140,000 American jobs. That's if just 10 % of Canadians cancel their trips. It's still too early to say how many are canceling, but from the evidence that we are gathering, it's much, much higher than 10 %. It's about sending a message, sending a message to Texas governor, Greg Abbott, who said Canada was going to learn a lesson. Oh, really? Texas is going to teach Canada a lesson?

Well, we've got $400 million worth of travel that goes to Texas, Mr Abbott. How about we teach you a lesson and say, We got better places to go than Texas. If that's your attitude of Canadians, we will not go. Hell, no, we will not go. The boycott is going to target many, many areas of the United States that are very vulnerable right now. Kentucky has already started to speak up about the huge losses that they're facing in Kentucky Bourbon and Kentucky whiskey because their number one market is Canadians. When Canadians stop buying, it's sending a message. We know this is the only way right now that Americans are going to be able to put pressure on Donald Trump.

Because what's at risk here is the future of an international order where we respect the rights of countries to be independent. We respect the international rule of law. We respect our neighbors and borders, and this is something Mr. Trump is saying he will not respect. So, on this festival where we celebrate Canada as a nation and our flag, I am encouraged. I want to thank Canadians. I want to say we are strong, we do not bend, and we will never, ever, ever kiss the ring of that gangster from Mar-a-Lago. So let's celebrate the 60th anniversary for Canada and our flag in a way that we have never done before. Thank you. Merci. Thank you.

Canadian Prime Minister, March

{Prime Minister Justin Trudeau, 4 March, 2025, after the tariffs went into effect}

So today the United States launched a trade war against Canada, their closest partner and ally, their closest friend. At the same time, they're talking about working positively with Russia, appeasing Vladimir Putin, a lying, murderous dictator.

Make that make sense.

Canadians are reasonable and we are polite, but we will not back down from a fight — not when our country and the well-being of everyone in it is at stake. At the moment, the U.S. tariffs came into effect in the early hours of this morning, and so did the Canadian response.

Canada will be implementing 25 per cent tariffs against $155 billion worth of American goods, starting with tariffs on $30 billion worth of goods immediately, and tariffs on the remaining $125 billion of American products in 21 days' time.

Today we will also be challenging these illegal actions by filing dispute resolution claims at the World Trade Organization and through the USMCA.

But in the meantime, our tariffs will remain in place until the U.S. tariffs are withdrawn and not a moment sooner. And should these tariffs not cease, we are in active and ongoing discussions with provinces and territories to pursue several non-tariff measures, measures which will demonstrate that there are no winners in a trade war.

Now, just like I did a month ago, I want to speak first directly to the American people.

We don't want this. We want to work with you as a friend and ally, and we don't want to see you hurt either. But your government has chosen to do this to you. As of this morning, markets are down and inflation is set to rise dramatically all across your country.

Your government has chosen to put American jobs at risk at the thousands of workplaces that succeed because of materials from Canada, or because of consumers in Canada, or both. They've chosen to raise costs for American consumers on everyday essential items like groceries and gas, on major purchases like cars and homes and everything in between.

They've chosen to harm American national security, impeding access to the abundant critical minerals, energy, building materials and fertilizers that we have and that the United States needs to grow and prosper.

They've chosen to launch a trade war that will, first and foremost, harm American families.

They've chosen to sabotage their own agenda that was supposed to usher in a new golden age for the United States. And they've chosen to undermine the incredible work we've done together to tackle the scourge that is fentanyl, a drug that must be wiped from the face of the earth.

So on that point, let me be crystal clear: there is absolutely no justification or need whatsoever for these tariffs today. Now, the legal pretext your government is using to bring in these tariffs is that Canada is apparently unwilling to help in the fight against illegal fentanyl.

Well, that is totally false.

Let's look at the fact our border is already safe and secure. Far less than one per cent of fentanyl flows and less than one per cent of illegal crossings into the United States comes from Canada. But we acted, because we know we can always do better.

We responded to concerns, including from the president, by implementing an ambitious $1.3-billion border plan, a border plan that includes generational investments in new AI and imaging tools to stop the flow of fentanyl in its tracks, stronger co-ordination and information sharing with American agencies, along with the deployment of drones, helicopters and additional personnel to keep our border secure.

You know, a month ago, as part of an agreement with the United States that paused the tariffs, we made further commitments. We appointed Kevin Brosseau as our fentanyl czar, a man who dedicated his multi-decade career in law enforcement to combating organized crime networks and drug trafficking.

We designated seven drug cartels — sick, evil groups who cynically profit off the pain and suffering of people on both sides of the border — as the terrorist organizations that they are.

And just yesterday, we launched a new joint operations partnership, supported by a $200-million investment between Canada's security and law enforcement agencies, a partnership that will enhance the co-ordination of information and intelligence in order to thwart criminal gangs involved in the illegal fentanyl trade.

And critically, our actions are working as the U.S. Customs and Border Protection just acknowledged there was a 97 per cent drop in fentanyl seizure from January compared to December, to a near-zero low of less than half an ounce seized in January.

Now, I want to speak directly to one specific American.

Donald, in the over eight years you and I have worked together, we've done big things.

We signed a historic deal that has created record jobs and growth in both of our countries. We've done big things together on the world stage, as Canada and the U.S. have done together for decades, for generations. And now, we should be working together to ensure even greater prosperity for North Americans in a very uncertain and challenging world.

Now, it's not in my habit to agree with the Wall Street Journal. But Donald, they point out that even though you're a very smart guy, this is a very dumb thing to do.

We two friends fighting is exactly what our opponents around the world want to see.

And now, to my fellow Canadians. I won't sugarcoat it. This is going to be tough, even though we're all going to pull together because that's what we do.

We will use every tool at our disposal so Canadian workers and businesses can weather this storm. From expanding EI benefits and making them more flexible to providing direct supports to businesses. We will be there as needed to help.

But Canada, make no mistake. No matter how long this lasts, no matter what the cost, the federal government and other orders of government will be there for you.

We will defend Canadian jobs. We will take measures to prevent predatory behaviour that threatens Canadian companies because of the impacts of this trade war, leaving them open to takeovers. We will relentlessly fight to protect our economy. We will stand up for Canadians every single second of every single day. Because this country is worth fighting for.

You know we've been through tough spots before, but every time we've faced long odds and seemingly insurmountable obstacles, we've not only survived, we've emerged stronger than ever.

Because when it comes to defending our great nation, there is no price we all aren't willing to pay.

And today is no different. Thank you.

Mexican President's Response

{President Claudia Sheinbaum, 2 March, translated from Spanish}

Good afternoon. As you are probably aware, yesterday the United States government imposed a 25-percent tariff on the products we export to their country.

For 30 years, this hasn't happened because we have a free trade agreement. The most recent free trade agreement was signed by President López Obrador and President Trump, himself. This 25-percent tariff affects both countries, but it has particularly serious consequences for the U.S. economy, as it will dramatically increase the cost of all products exported from Mexico to the United States. It will add 25 percent to the cost.

Regarding these measures announced by the U.S. government, there are documents supporting them, which claim that one of the reasons for imposing this tariff is the fentanyl entering the United States from Mexico that is causing illness and deaths from overdoses.

But what is even more irresponsible - utterly irresponsible - is that the White House has issued a document claiming there are links between the Mexican government and organized crime.

I want to tell you about the statement I published on my social media yesterday, where I explain who truly have links to these criminal groups, and the reason for the overdose deaths among Americans, and where I also say that if they want to take action, they shouldn't focus on Mexico but on their own country, where they have done nothing to stop the illegal sale of this and other drugs.

First of all, as I said yesterday, we categorically reject the defamatory claims made by the White House accusing the Mexican government of having alliances with criminal organizations, as well as any attempts to interfere in our territory. Sovereignty is non-negotiable. If such alliances exist anywhere, they exist in the U.S. gun shops that sell high-powered firearms that are exclusively for military use to these criminal groups.

This was demonstrated - note this well - by the U.S. Department of Justice itself on January 8th of this year. I have here the document published on that date in which the Bureau of Alcohol, Tobacco, Firearms and Explosives, which operates under the Department of Justice - note this carefully - acknowledged that 74 percent of guns used by organized crime in Mexico come illegally from their country's military industry.

In just four months, our government has seized more than 40 tons of drugs, including 20 million doses of fentanyl. We have also arrested more than 10,000 people connected to these groups. We have a strategy, we are addressing the root causes, and we are fighting impunity. We are working every day to ensure the country's security. Now, if the U.S. government and its agencies want to address the severe fentanyl crisis in their country, why don't they start by cracking down on drug sales in the streets of their major cities?

How is it that people with addictions can buy these drugs? Why have we never heard of arrests of U.S. criminal groups in the United States? How is it that money laundering by criminal groups there is not investigated? Why don't they put all their intelligence to work to find the criminal groups that are selling fentanyl or other drugs in their territory?

They could also launch a large-scale campaign to prevent drug use and protect their young people, as we do in Mexico. The drug use and distribution is taking place in their country, and is a public health crisis they have never addressed. Why don't they ask themselves about the root causes behind so much drug use for so long in the United States?

Moreover, as I mentioned yesterday, the epidemic of synthetic opioids in the United States originates in the indiscriminate prescription of these medications, authorized by the Food and Drug Administration, the FDA, as shown by a legal case against a pharmaceutical company. There are television series that explain this. What's more, the drug that caused the synthetic opioid crisis is still being sold in their pharmacies with official authorization.

I want to you to know, and this is very important: Mexico does not want confrontation. We believe in collaboration between neighboring countries. Mexico wants to prevent fentanyl from reaching the United States or any other destination. Therefore, if the United States wants to combat the criminal groups and wants us to do it together, we must take comprehensive action, but always guided by principles:

The principles of shared responsibility, mutual trust, collaboration, and above all, respect for sovereignty. Sovereignty is non-negotiable. Coordination, yes; subordination, no. With this goal, yesterday in my statement I proposed to President Trump that we establish a working group with our best teams - both in security and public health. Problems are not solved by imposing tariffs, but through discussion and dialogue, as we have done.

And this I want to tell you about. This is what we have done in recent weeks with the State Department to address the issue of migration – in our case, always with respect for human rights. The graph that President Trump has been posting on his social media about the reduction in migration was created by none other than our team, which has been in constant communication with his.

To our Mexican brothers and sisters in the United States: I want to tell you that your president and an entire nation are here to defend you. If you want to return to Mexico, we welcome you with open arms. The Mexican people are brave and have great dignity. They are the most wonderful people on Earth. I tell you that your president is here for you. We have courage and determination, but, as I have said before, we must always act with a cool head and love for our people. Nothing we do will affect the dignity and interests of the Mexican people. I propose that we wait for President Trump's response to our proposal, and in tomorrow's morning press conference, in the People's Morning Press Conference, I will inform you of the first measures of what we call Plan B.

As Juárez said: Force accomplishes nothing; reason and law prevail. And between individuals, as between nations, respect for the rights of others means peace.

Other Responses

When Trump first declared his policies in January, officials from other countries gave mixed responses, from guarded concern and optimistic entreaties in Europe and Asia, to praise from Russia and Israel. However, his transactional negotiation style and easy jump to punitive actions, primarily tariffs and withholding aid, has not gone unnoticed.

> I've spoken to colleagues in the European Union, and there is unusual fear right now in the commission, because they don't know what's next ... I believe that Trump is going to choose his allies very carefully, and those who don't bend the knee will face the consequences of Trump's agenda. -- Georgios Samaras, lecturer in public policy at King's College London

| 14 |

Vance in Germany

A fter a visit to Hungary's right-wing nationalist Prime Minister Viktor Orbán, Vice-President JD Vance spoke in Munich on 14 February to the members of the far-Right party in Germany.

His Address

Well, thank you, and thanks to all the gathered delegates and luminaries and media professionals.

And thanks especially to the hosts of the Munich Security Conference for being able to put on such an incredible event. We're, of course, thrilled to be here. We're happy to be here.

And, you know, one of the things that I wanted to talk about today is, of course, our shared values.

And, you know, it's great to be back in Germany. As you heard earlier, I was here last year as a United States senator. I saw Foreign Minister—excuse me, Foreign Secretary David Lammy and joked that both of us last year had different jobs than we have now.

But now it's time for all of our countries, for all of us who have been fortunate enough to be given political power by our respective peoples, to use it wisely to improve their lives.

And I want to say that, you know, I was fortunate in my time here to spend some time outside the walls of this conference over the last

24 hours, and I've been so impressed by the hospitality of the people, even, of course, as they're reeling from yesterday's horrendous attack.

And the first time I was ever in Munich was with my wife, actually, who's here with me today, on a personal trip. And I've always loved the city of Munich, and I've always loved its people.

And I just want to say that we're very moved, and our thoughts and prayers are with Munich and everybody affected by the evil inflicted on this beautiful community. We're thinking about you, we're praying for you, and we will certainly be rooting for you in the days and weeks to come.

Now ... [Applause] Thank you. I hope that's not the last bit of applause that I get, but ...

We gather at this conference, of course, to discuss security. And normally, we mean threats to our external security. I see many great military leaders gathered here today.

But while the Trump administration is very concerned with European security and believes that we can come to a reasonable settlement between Russia and Ukraine, and we also believe that it's important in the coming years for Europe to step up in a big way to provide for its own defense, the threat that I worry the most about vis-à-vis Europe is not Russia, it's not China, it's not any other external actor. And what I worry about is the threat from within, the retreat of Europe from some of its most fundamental values—values shared with the United States of America.

Now, I was struck that a former European commissioner went on television recently and sounded delighted that the Romanian government had just annulled an entire election. He warned that if things don't go to plan, the very same thing could happen in Germany, too.

Now, these cavalier statements are shocking to American ears. For years, we've been told that everything we fund and support is in the name of our shared democratic values.

Everything from our Ukraine policy to digital censorship is billed as a defense of democracy, but when we see European courts canceling elections and senior officials threatening to cancel others, we ought to ask whether we're holding ourselves to an appropriately high standard. And I say "ourselves" because I fundamentally believe that we are on the same team. We must do more than talk about democratic values. We must live them.

Now, within living memory of many of you in this room, the Cold War positioned defenders of democracy against much more tyrannical forces on this continent. And consider the side in that fight that censored dissidents, that closed churches, that canceled elections. Were they the good guys? Certainly not, and thank God they lost the Cold War.

They lost because they neither valued nor respected all of the extraordinary blessings of liberty, the freedom to surprise, to make mistakes, to invent, to build.

As it turns out, you can't mandate innovation or creativity, just as you can't force people what to think, what to feel, or what to believe. And we believe those things are certainly connected.

And unfortunately, when I look at Europe today, it's sometimes not so clear what happened to some of the Cold War's winners.

I look to Brussels, where EU commiss—commissars warn citizens that they intend to shut down social media during times of civil unrest the moment they spot what they've judged to be, quote, "hateful content."

Or to this very country, where police have carried out raids against citizens suspected of posting anti-feminist comments online as part of, quote, "combating misogyny on the internet, a day of action."

I look to Sweden, where, two weeks ago, the government convicted a Christian activist for participating in Quran burnings that resulted in his friend's murder. And as the judge in his case chillingly noted, Sweden's laws to supposedly protect free expression do not, in fact, grant -- and I'm quoting -- "a free pass to do or say anything without risking offending the group that holds that belief."

And perhaps most concerningly, I look to our very dear friends, the United Kingdom, where the backslide away from conscience rights has placed the basic liberties of religious Britons, in particular, in the crosshairs.

A little over two years ago, the British government charged Adam Smith-Connor, a 51-year-old physiotherapist and an army veteran, with the heinous crime of standing 50 meters from an abortion clinic and silently praying for three minutes—not obstructing anyone, not interacting with anyone, just silently praying on his own.

And after British law enforcement spotted him and demanded to know what he was praying for, Adam replied, simply, it was on behalf of the unborn son he and his former girlfriend had aborted years before.

Now, the officers were not moved. Adam was found guilty of breaking the government's new "buffer zones" law, which criminalizes silent prayer and other actions that could "influence" a person's decision within 200 meters of an abortion facility. He was sentenced to pay thousands of pounds in legal costs to the prosecution.

Now, I wish I could say that this was a fluke—a one-off, crazy example of a badly written law being enacted against a single person. But, no, this last October, just a few months ago, the Scottish government began distributing letters to citizens whose houses lay within so-called "safe access zones," warning them that even private prayer within their own homes may amount to breaking the law.

Naturally, the government urged readers to report any fellow citizens suspected guilty of thoughtcrime.

In Britain, and across Europe, free speech, I fear, is in retreat.

And in the interest of comity, my friends, but also in the interest of truth, I will admit that sometimes the loudest voices for censorship have come not from within Europe but from within my own country, where the prior administration threatened and bullied social media companies to censor so-called misinformation—misinformation like, for example, the idea that coronavirus had likely leaped fr—leaked from a laboratory in China. Our own government encouraged private companies to silence people who dared to utter what turned out to be an obvious truth.

So, I come here today not just with an observation but with an offer. And just as the Biden administration seemed desperate to silence people for speaking their minds, so the Trump administration will do precisely the opposite, and I hope that we can work together on that.

In Washington, there is a new sheriff in town. And under Donald Trump's leadership, we may disagree with your views, but we will fight to defend your right to offer it in the public square, agree or disagree.

Now we're at the point, of course, that the situation has gotten so bad that, this December, Romania straight up canceled the results of a presidential election based on the flimsy suspicions of an intelligence agency and enormous pressure from its continental neighbors.

Now, as I understand it, the argument was that Russian disinformation had infected the Romanian elections, but I'd ask my European friends to have some perspective. You can believe it's wrong for Russia to buy social media advertisements to influence your elections. We certainly do. You can condemn it on the world stage even. But if your democracy can be destroyed with a few hundred thousand dollars of digital advertising from a foreign country, then it wasn't very strong to begin with.

Now, the good news is that I happen to think your democracies are substantially less brittle than many people apparently fear, and I really do believe that allowing our citizens to speak their mind will make them stronger still.

Which, of course, brings us back to Munich, where the organizers of this very conference have banned lawmakers representing populist parties on both the left and the right from participating in these conversations.

Now, again, we don't have to agree with everything or anything that people say, but when people represent—when political leaders represent an important constituency, it is incumbent upon us to at least participate in dialogue with them.

Now, to many of us on the other side of the Atlantic, it looks more and more like old, entrenched interests hiding behind ugly, Soviet-era words like "misinformation" and "disinformation," who simply don't like the idea that somebody with an alternative viewpoint might express a different opinion, or, God forbid, vote a different way, or, even worse, win an election.

Now, this is a security conference, and I'm sure you all came here prepared to talk about how exactly you intend to increase defense spending over the next few years in line with some new target. And that's great, because as President Trump has made abundantly clear, he believes that our European friends must play a bigger role in the future of this continent. We don't think—you hear this term, "burden sharing," but we think it's an important part of being in a shared alliance together that the Europeans step up while America focuses on areas of the world that are in great danger.

But let me also ask you, how will you even begin to think through the kinds of budgeting questions if we don't know what it is that we're defending in the first place?

I've heard a lot already in my conversations—and I've had many, many great conversations with many people gathered here in this room—I've heard a lot about what you need to defend yourselves from, and, of course, that's important. But what has seemed a little bit less clear to me and certainly, I think, to many of the citizens of Europe, is what exactly it is that you're defending yourselves for. What is the positive vision that animates this shared security compact that we all believe is so important?

And I believe deeply that there is no security if you are afraid of the voices, the opinions, and the conscience that guide your very own people.

Europe faces many challenges, but the crisis this continent faces right now, the crisis I believe we all face together, is one of our own making.

If you're running in fear of your own voters, there is nothing America can do for you. Nor, for that matter, is there anything that you can do for the American people who elected me and elected President Trump.

You need democratic mandates to accomplish anything of value in the coming years. Have we learned nothing, that thin mandates produce unstable results? But there is so much of value that can be accomplished with the kind of democratic mandate that I think will come from being more responsive to the voices of your citizens.

If you're going to enjoy competitive economies, if you're going to enjoy affordable energy and secure supply chains, then you need mandates to govern, because you have to make difficult choices to enjoy all of these things. And, of course, we know that very well in America.

You cannot win a democratic mandate by censoring your opponents or putting them in jail—whether that's the leader of the opposition, a humble Christian praying in her own home, or a journalist trying to report the news. Nor can you win one by disregarding your basic electorate on questions like who gets to be a part of our shared society.

And of all the pressings—challenges that the nations represented here face, I believe there is nothing more urgent than mass migration.

Today, almost one in five people living in this country moved here from abroad. That is, of course, an all-time high. It's a similar number, by the way, in the United States—also an all-time high.

The number of immigrants who entered the EU from non-EU countries doubled between 2021 and 2022 alone. And, of course, it's gotten much higher since.

And we know the situation, it didn't materialize in a vacuum. It's the result of a series of conscious decisions made by politicians all over the continent, and others across the world, over the span of a decade.

We saw the horrors wrought by these decisions yesterday in this very city. And, of course, I can't bring it up again without thinking about the terrible victims who had a beautiful winter day in Munich ruined. Our thoughts and prayers are with them and will remain with them. But why did this happen in the first place?

It's a terrible story, but it's one we've heard way too many times in Europe and, unfortunately, too many times in the United States as well: an asylum-seeker, often a young man in his mid-20s, already known to police, rams a car into a crowd and shatters a community.

How many times must we suffer these appalling setbacks before we change course and take our shared civilization in a new direction?

No voter on this continent went to the ballot box to open the floodgates to millions of unvetted immigrants. But you know what they did vote for? In England, they voted for Brexit. And agree or disagree, they voted for it. And more and more, all over Europe, they're voting for political leaders who promise to put an end to out-of-control migration.

Now, I happen to agree with a lot of these concerns, but you don't have to agree with me. I just think that people care about their homes. They care about their dreams. They care about their safety and their capacity to provide for themselves and their children.

And they're smart. I think this is one of the most important things I've learned in my brief time in politics. Contrary to what you might hear a couple mountains over in Davos, the citizens of all of our nations don't generally think of themselves as educated animals or as interchangeable cogs of a global economy, and it's hardly surprising that they don't want to be shuffled about or relentlessly ignored by their leaders.

And it is the business of democracy to adjudicate these big questions at the ballot box.

I believe that dismissing people, dismissing their concerns, or, worse yet, shutting down media, shutting down elections, or shutting people out of the political process protects nothing. In fact, it is the most surefire way to destroy democracy.

And speaking up and expressing opinions isn't election interference, even when people express views outside your own country, and even when those people are very influential.

And trust me, I say this with all humor, if American democracy can survive 10 years of Greta Thunberg's scolding, you guys can survive a few months of Elon Musk.

But what German democracy—what no democracy, American, German, or European—will survive is telling millions of voters that their thoughts and concerns, their aspirations, their pleas for relief are invalid or unworthy of even being considered.

Democracy rests on the sacred principle that the voice of the people matters. There is no room for firewalls. You either uphold the principle or you don't.

Europeans, the people have a voice. European leaders have a choice. And my strong belief is that we do not need to be afraid of the future.

You can embrace what your people tell you, even when it's surprising, even when you don't agree. And if you do so, you can face the future with certainty and with confidence, knowing that the nation stands behind each of you.

And that, to me, is the great magic of democracy. It's not in these stone buildings or beautiful hotels. It's not even in the great institutions that we have built together as a shared society.

To believe in democracy is to understand that each of our citizens has wisdom and has a voice. And if we refuse to listen to that voice, even our most successful fights will secure very little.

As Pope John Paul II—in my view, one of the most extraordinary champions of democracy on this continent or any other—once said, "Do not be afraid."

We shouldn't be afraid of our people, even when they express views that disagree with their leadership.

Thank you all. Good luck to all of you. God bless you.

A Rebuttal

{German Defense Minister Boris Pistorius, at gathering on international security in Munich}

Ladies and gentlemen, let me start in German. I did have a speech that I prepared for today. It was a speech which was supposed to be about security in Europe, but, to be honest, I cannot start my speech in the way that I originally intended to. I am a staunch believer in the transatlantic alliance, and I am a staunch ally and friend of America. The American dream is something that has always fascinated me and influenced me, and this is why I cannot just ignore what we heard before.

I cannot not comment on the speech we heard by the US Vice President. "We fight for your right to be against us." That is the motto, one of the mottos of the Bundeswehr, and it stands for our democracy. This democracy that was just called into question by the US Vice President, and not just the German democracy but Europe as a whole, he spoke of the annulment of democracy, and if I understood him correctly, he compares the condition of Europe with the condition that prevails in some authoritarian regimes.

Ladies and gentlemen, this is not acceptable. This is not acceptable. This is not the Europe, not the democracy where I live and where I conduct my election campaign right now, and this is not the democracy that I witness every day in our parliament. In our democracy, every opinion has a voice, and it makes it possible for parties that are partly extremist, such as the AFD, and they can campaign just as any other party.

This is democracy. And if the Vice President had the opportunity to switch on his TV set when he arrived yesterday, he would have seen one of those candidates in primetime TV. By the way, we even admit media that spread Russian propaganda, and the representatives of the federal government answer their questions. Nobody is excluded.

But democracy does not mean that a vociferous minority will automatically be right, and they cannot decide what truth is. It does not mean that anyone can say anything, and democracy must be able to defend itself against extremists that try to destroy it. I am happy to live in Europe where this democracy is defended every day against its internal and external enemies.

And therefore, I would like to explicitly contradict and oppose the impression that our democracies oppress and silence minorities. We not only know against whom we defend our countries, but also what we defend it for. It's for democracy, for freedom of opinion, for the rule of law, and the dignity of each and every one, ladies and gentlemen.

Ladies and gentlemen, but unlike the Vice President, I would also like to focus my speech on the most pressing questions of European and transatlantic security.

The last days have confirmed what many had speculated for months. The United States are pushing for a quick peace settlement between Russia and Ukraine, and they expect Europe to take the lead in securing any agreement that follows. These negotiations can be a turning point for our continent and for transatlantic relations, a historic turning point that can go into very different directions. The choices we make now will determine whether we live in peace or in crisis.

They will determine our future and the future of the next generation in Europe, but also beyond. We must ensure that Ukraine is not left alone, ladies and gentlemen, because one thing remains unchanged. There will be no lasting peace in Europe without a strong and free Ukraine. There will be no sustainable rules-based order if aggression prevails.

We must equally make sure that Russia does not emerge from this war as an even bigger threat than before. A fragile peace that only postpones the next war is not an option. Yesterday there was strong consensus among NATO Allies that imperialist powers will only respond to deterrence and strength, be it in Europe or in the Indo-Pacific. Therefore we must and we will negotiate from a position of strength.

Three things are crucial for that.

First, European and Ukrainians must play an active part in the negotiations. Only united we will be able to stand strong. Only united will we negotiate a stable and long-lasting peace.

Second, Ukraine needs to negotiate from a position of strength. Germany will therefore remain the largest supporter of Ukraine on this continent. And we will continue our engagement in the near future and beyond.

Third, the transatlantic alliance must not take anything off the table before the peace talks have even started. Discussions about Ukraine's NATO membership or territorial issues must take place at the negotiating table with careful consideration and in close coordination among Allies. At the same time, Secretary Hegseth made it very clear that the US will remain engaged in NATO and in Europe.

But the recent statements are also a strong reminder of what has been clear for many years, if we are honest. We Europeans have to contribute the lion's share to conventional deterrence and defense in Europe. We need to shape the reality we live in before it shapes us. Yesterday, in NATO, we agreed to develop a roadmap to organize the burden-shifting from the US to Europe in the years to come, and to avoid at the same time by orchestrating it that we run in capability gaps which are critical.

It is time for fewer promises now and more action. That is why my French colleague Sébastien Le Corneuil and I established the Group of Five together with the United Kingdom, Poland and Italy at the end of last year, to chart a course for a strong Europe. We will use this format to develop the roadmap in the upcoming month and discuss it with our Allies, especially with the United States. Ladies and gentlemen, in order to make European responsibility a reality, we are taking strong measures in all important areas of defense, with regards to money, material and operational readiness.

Last year, Germany committed 2% of its GDP to defense. Within just two years, we nearly doubled our investments in procurement. Other European nations have made similar successful efforts. Security guarantees the future for all of us, and for the next generation.

We have the responsibility to invest in the future. For Germany, that means further increasing our defense spending. We need substantial financial means that cannot simply be cut out of the current budget. Excluding defense spending from our national debt limit is therefore inevitable.

Security is not a short-term expenditure. It is a long-term commitment. That is why I am developing a 10-year program. We need to make defense spending more predictable.

That means achieving security next generation. At the European level, we need to act in a similar way. We must ensure that all countries can effectively strengthen their security. That should involve adapting the Maastricht Criteria to allow nations that face tight budgetary restrictions a greater flexibility to defense investments.

And it would also involve a shift towards defense in the priorities of the European Union's multi-annual financial framework, just as we heard it by Mrs von der Leyen earlier. More cash, that's the truth, must of course translate into more capabilities. It's not about money, it's about capabilities. Germany launched a defense industry strategy to create the right political, economic and regulatory framework to quickly make our defense industry more innovative, agile and resilient.

We streamlined our procurement processes and together with industry we are expanding our production capacities while pushing for a stronger European defense industrial base.

But one thing is certain. Europe needs a strong, more sovereign defense industry. We cannot afford excessive dependencies. This has never been clearer than today as we see the geopolitical landscape shifting.

Maintaining our technological advantage is crucial, particularly in areas such as artificial intelligence, space and quantum technology. These investments generate positive spillover effects across our entire research landscape and overall economy. We need more European solutions while maintaining strong cooperation with our transatlantic partners. We need both in order to increase our defense capacities as quickly and comprehensively as possible while building and maintaining a strong industrial base.

Simply put, we Europeans must develop together, build together, buy together, deploy together, even if that involves adapting and merging certain industries and setting aside national interests in some cases. This requires better coordination of who produces what to avoid duplicating efforts. We have proved that we are capable for this. The European Skysheet Initiative is an example. The same is true for the European Long-Range Strike Approach initiated by Germany and France.

And let me mention one more example, the German-Norwegian Submarine Project. Soon, German crews will be able to sail on Norwegian submarines and vice versa. This is European defense integration in action. We are inviting additional nations to join, also from across the Atlantic. This will boost NATO's naval presence from the shores of the Baltic Sea across the Atlantic all the way to the Arctic, the latter being more and more in the focus of NATO's adversaries.

Projects like these are the future of procurement. They show what we can achieve when we act together and overcome national constraints. That brings me to operational readiness. In the Russia full-scale invasion of Ukraine, we have significantly scaled up our efforts to secure NATO's eastern flank. We increased our presence in the air, on land and at sea. As of this year, 35,000 personnel stand prepared at the highest readiness levels to defend NATO's territory if needed.

In Lithuania, we are moving from a rotational to a permanent presence. Together with our Allies, we have as many as 1,400 boots on the ground today as part of the multinational battlegroup Lithuania. We are in the midst of preparing the permanent deployment of a full combat-ready brigade. We will have roughly 5,000 personnel permanently in Lithuania in the years to come. On this note, thank you very much, President Nauseda, for being such an exemplary partner in the historic endeavor.

But our commitment on the eastern flank does not and will not stop in Lithuania, also and especially after a potential peace in

Ukraine. We are well aware Russia will remain a threat. We are assuming more leadership responsibility in the multinational corps northeast to bolster deterrence and defense in the region. This is a true example of our shared commitment to security.

Ladies and gentlemen, this week has a week of decision.

Next week, it will be the German voters that will make a choice. A lot is at stake in this election. I trust that the German voters will send a strong message. Germany will remain a reliable Ally. Germany will continue to work towards a stronger and more secure Europe.

And Germany will continue to take on more responsibility and leadership in Europe. The challenges of the coming months and years will be enormous.

But so is our ability to tackle them. As long as we stand together, as long as we remain committed to our security and our values of liberal democracy, I have no doubt the future is ours to shape. Thank you.

| 15 |

Ukraine

Weeks after inauguration, President Trump proceeded to hold talks with Putin in Saudi Arabia, with conditions that may include ceding the land taken, which he subsequently defended under the excuse that Russia "fought for it" and "lost a lot of soldiers". He also called Zelenskyy a dictator and then retracted the statement days later, asking, "Did I say that?"

At the meeting between Trump, Vance, and Zelenskyy, the Ukrainian President was berated over not wearing a suit by Brian Glenn, host of "Real America's Voice" media outlet and current boyfriend of Congresswoman Marjorie Taylor Greene.

Additional Note: Before the talks, it was reported that Defense Secretary Pete Hegseth directed the U.S. Cyber Command to halt offensive operations against Russia. There was also concern, after the White House started hand-picking which news outlets had access, that Russian state media was allowed to cover the talks.

I think I have the power to end this war, and I think it's going very well. But today I heard [from Ukraine], 'Oh well, we weren't invited.' Well, you've been there for three years. You should have ended it three years – you should have never started it, you could have made a deal." -- President Trump, 18 February at Mar-a-Lago

"I told them [Ukraine] that I want the equivalent like $500 Billion worth of rare earth. And they've essentially agreed to do that so at least we don't feel stupid. Otherwise, we're stupid. I said to them we have to – 'we have to get something. We can't continue to pay this money." -- President Trump, 24 February

Remarks by President Trump and President Zelensky of Ukraine Before Bilateral Meeting

{InterContinental New York Barclay, 28 February}

Trump: Well, thank you very much, everybody. We're with the President of Ukraine, and he's made me more famous, and I've made him more famous. [Laughter] I will say he's got a great reputation. He's very, very strongly looking into all sorts of corruption and some of the problems they've had over the years. I think it's one of the primary reasons he got elected. His reputation is absolutely sterling. And it's an honor to be with you. And we spoke a couple of times, as you probably remember. And they'd like to hear every single word, and we give them every single word, and then they'll say, "Well, about today?" I think the press would like to stay in the meeting, but we have lots of witnesses, if you'd like to have it. But the country of — our country is doing phenomenally well. We are — we have the best economy we've ever had. We have the best employment numbers that we've ever had.

We have now almost 160 million people working, which is more than we've ever had. So we're doing very well in every respect. And I have a feeling that your country is going to do fantastically well. And whatever we can do. You just take care of yourself. Thank you.

Zelenskyy: Thank you very much. Thank you very much, Mr. President. Thank you very much. It's a great pleasure to me to be here, and it's better to be on TV than by phone, I think. And, Mr. President, thank you very much. And I'm not the first time to stay in New York but I know that you've never been in Ukraine.

Trump: That's right.

Zelenskyy: And your predecessor also — how do you say it in English? — didn't find time; I mean that.

Trump: Right.

Zelenskyy: So, can you give me a word that you will come to our great country?

Trump: Well, I'm going to try. And I know a lot of people — I will say this: I know a lot of people from Ukraine. They're great people. And I owned something called the Miss Universe pageants years ago, and I sold it to IMG. And when I ran for President, I thought maybe it wouldn't be the greatest thing to own the Miss Universe and Miss USA pageants. But it's a great thing. And we had a winner from Ukraine, and we've really had — we got to know the country very well in a lot of different ways. But it's a country, I think, with tremendous potential.

Zelenskyy Yes, I know it, because I'm from this country. And I want to thank you for the invitation to Washington. You invited me.

But I think — I'm sorry, but I think you forgot to tell me the date. But I think in the near future.

Trump: They'll tell you the date.

Zelenskyy: Yes, they know before us. And I want to thank you — to thank you, especially, Mr. President, to USA, to your government. Like I said, I know many people, many faces, like the Second Family, after you — my Ukrainian family, we know each other. Thank you for your support, especially now when — you know, when we have two — really, two wars in Ukraine. The first one is with corruption, you know. But we'll fight — no, we'll be winner in this fight, I'm sure. And the priority — my priority is to stop the war on Donbass and to get back our territories: Crimea, Donbass, Luhansk. Thank you for your support in this case. Thank you very much.

Trump: Well, thank you very much, Mr. President. If you remember, you lost Crimea during a different administration, not during the Trump administration.

Zelenskyy: Yeah. So you have chance to help us.

Trump: That's right. I do. But that was during the Obama administration that you lost Crimea, and I didn't think it was something that you should have. But that was done a long time ago, and I think it was handled poorly. But it's just one of those things. One of the elements that we discussed is the United States helps Ukraine, but I think that other countries should help Ukraine much more than they're doing — Germany, France, the European Union nations. They really should help you a lot more. And I think maybe, together, we'll work on that. They have to feel a little bit guilty about it because they don't do what they should be doing. You're very important to the European Union. You're very important — strategically, very important. And I think they should spend a lot more in helping Ukraine. And they know that also, and they actually tell me that, but they don't seem to produce. So I'm sure you'll talk to them, and I'll certainly be talking to them.

Zelenskyy: Thank you very much, Mr. President. And, you know, now we need — I want to tell you that we now (inaudible) the new country. And, I'm sorry, but we don't need help; we need support. Real support. And we thank — thank everybody, thank all of the European countries; they each help us. But we also want to have more — more. But I understand, so only together, America and EU — only together we can stop the war. And, you know, we are ready. We just want to tell that we are — remember that we are the biggest country in Europe, but we want to be the richest one. It's true; it's in my heart.

Trump: Well, you know, you have great people in Ukraine, and you have very talented people —

Zelenskyy: Very smart.

Trump: — in terms of manufacturing, in terms of some of the things they do. And we'll be doing — we're doing trading already, but we should be doing a lot more trading with Ukraine. But you have very talented people. They make great things. You're at the top of the line, really. So that's very important. And the other thing is I've heard you actually have — over the last fairly short period of time, you've really made some progress with Russia. I hear a lot of progress has been made. And just keep it going. It'd be nice to end that whole disaster.

Zelenskyy: First of all, I want to tell you, before — before the relations with Russia — I will prolong, just one minute — I mean, you have to know — I want world to know that now we have the new team, the new parliament, the new government. So now we (inaudible) about 74 laws, new laws, which help for our new reforms: land reform, big privatization. They did the law about concessions. Did —

we (inaudible) general for security, and we launched the Service Secretary. Is it right Service Secretary?

Aide: Yes. Anti-corruption court, as well.

Zelenskyy: An anti-corruption court. As we came, we did — we launched the anti-corruption court. It began to work on the 5th of September. It was — you know, it was — after five days, we had the new government. So, we are ready. We want to show that we — we just come. And if somebody, if you — if you want to help us, so just let's do businesses cases. We have many investment cases. We're ready.

Trump: And stop corruption in Ukraine, because that will really make you great. That will make you great personally, and it'll also be so tremendous for your nation, in terms of what you want to do and where you want to take it. Thank you very much. It's a great honor.

Zelenskyy: Thank you very much, Mr. President.

Off-Camera Question: President Zelensky, have you felt any pressure from President Trump to investigate Joe Biden and Hunter Biden?

Zelenskyy: I think you read everything. So I think you read text. I'm sorry, but I don't want to be involved to democratic, open elections — elections of USA. No, you heard that we had, I think, good phone call. It was normal. We spoke about many things. And I — so I think, and you read it, that nobody pushed — pushed me. Yes.

Trump: In other words, no pressure.

Off-Camera Question: President Trump, would — President Trump, would you like Mr. Zelensky to —

Trump: Because you know what? There was no pressure. And you know there was — and, by the way, you know there was no pressure. All you have to do it see it, what went on on the call. But you know that. But you can ask a question, and I appreciate the answer. Go ahead.

Off-Camera Question: Mr. President, would you like President Zelensky to do more on Joe Biden and investigate [inaudible]?

Trump: No. I want him to do whatever he can. This was not his fault; he wasn't there. He's just been here recently. But whatever he can do in terms of corruption, because the corruption is massive. Now, when Biden's son walks away with millions of dollars from Ukraine, and he knows nothing, and they're paying him millions of dollars, that's corruption.

When Biden's son walks out of China with $1.5 billion in a fund — and the biggest funds in the world can't get money out of China — and he's there for one quick meeting, and he flies in on Air Force Two, I think that's a horrible thing. I think it's a horrible thing. But I'm going far beyond that. I know the President, and I've read a lot about Ukraine. I've read a lot about a lot of countries. He wants to stop corruption. He was elected — I think, number one — on the basis of stopping corruption, which unfortunately has plagued Ukraine. And if he could do that, he's doing, really, the whole world a big favor. I know — and I think he's going to be successful.

Off-Camera Question: Mr. President, on Rudy Giuliani, why do you think it's appropriate for your personal attorney to get involved in government business?

Trump: Well, you'd have to ask Rudy. I will tell you —

Off-Camera Question: You mentioned it to the President here.

Trump: I will tell you this, that Rudy is looking to also find out where the phony witch hunt started, how it started. You had a Russian witch hunt that turned out to be two and half years of phony nonsense. And Rudy Giuliani is a great lawyer. He was a great mayor. He's highly respected. I've watched the passion that he's had on television over the last few days. I think it's incredible the way he's done. What he's at is he wants to find out where did this Russian witch hunt that you people really helped perpetrate — where did it start. How come it started? It was all nonsense. It was a hoax. It was a total hoax. It was a media hoax and a Democrat hoax. Where did it start? And Rudy has got every right to go and find out where that started. And other people are looking at that, too. Where did it start? The enablers — where did it all come from? It was out of thin air. And I think he's got a very strong right to do it. He's a good lawyer; he knows exactly what he's doing. And it's very important.

Off-Camera Question: Mr. President, do you believe that the emails from Hillary Clinton — do you believe that they're in Ukraine? Do you think this whole thing originated —

Trump: I think they could be. You mean the 30,000 that she deleted?

Off-Camera Question: Yes.

Trump: Yeah, I think they could very well — boy, that was a nice question. I like that question. (Laughter.) Because, frankly, I think that one of the great crimes committed is Hillary Clinton deleting 33,000 emails after Congress sends her a subpoena. Think of that. You can't even do that in a civil case; you can't get rid of evidence like that. She deleted 33,000 emails after — not before — after receiving the subpoena from the U.S. Congress. I mean, I have never heard — now, she's done far worse than that. Although, I don't know how much worse it can be. But there were many other things she did that were wrong. But that's so obvious. She gets a subpoena from the United States Congress and she deletes them. And then she said, as I remember it, that, "Oh, well, they had to do with the wedding and yoga." She does a lot of yoga, right? So they had 33,000 emails about the wedding of her daughter and yoga. I don't think so. How she got away with that one is just — but it's one of many. And it's corrupt government. Because we have corruption also, Mr. President. We have a lot of corruption in our government. And when you see what happened with Hillary Clinton, when you see what happened with Comey, and McCabe, and all of these people — we have a lot of things going on here too. Hopefully, it's going to be found out very soon. But I think that a lot of progress has been made. A lot of progress has been made.

Off-Camera Question: Will the military aid continue? Can you assure that it will continue in the future?

Trump: Well, we're working with Ukraine. And we want other countries to work with Ukraine. When I saw "work," I'm referring to money. They should put up more money. We put up a lot of money. I gave you anti-tank busters that — frankly, President Obama was sending you pillows and sheets. And I gave you anti-tank busters. And a lot of people didn't want to do that, but I did it. And I really hope that Russia — because I really believe that President Putin would like to do something. I really hope that you and President Putin get together and can solve your problem. That would be a tremendous achievement. And I know you're trying to do that.

Off-Camera Question: President Zelensky, in the phone call, you said that you would look into Joe Biden — you would ask your prosecutor to look into the matter. Have you had that conversation —

Trump: Well, I think — no, I haven't. But I think that — I think this —

Off-Camera Question: I'm asking President Zelensky.

Trump: I think that somebody, if you look at what he did, it's so bad — where his son he goes to China, he walks away with a billion and a half dollars. He goes to Ukraine and he walks away with $50,000 a month and a lot of money in addition to that. And the whole thing with the prosecutor in Ukraine. And he's on tape. This isn't like "maybe he did it, maybe he didn't." He's on tape doing this. I saw this a while ago. I looked at it and I said, "That's incredible. I've never seen anything like that." Now, either he's dumb, or he thought he was in a room full of really good friends, or maybe it's a combination of both, in his case.

Off-Camera Question: President Zelensky —

Zelenskyy: I heard your question. Thank you very much. Don't cry. I mean that we have independent country and independent general security. I can't push anyone, you know? That's it. That is the question — that is the answer. So I didn't call somebody or the new general security. I didn't ask him. I didn't push him. That's it.

Off-Camera Question: Do you feel obligated to fulfill your promises to President Trump?

Zelenskyy: Just — sorry. [As interpreted] Obligated to do what? [Speaks Ukrainian.]

Trump: You want to just —

Zelenskyy: I'm sorry. [As interpreted] Concerning the investigation, actually, I want to underscore that Ukraine is an independent country. We have a new prosecutor general in Ukraine — a highly professional man with a Western education and history to investigate any case he considers and deems appropriate. While we have many more issues to care about and to tackle, we have (inaudible), we have Maidan, we have corruption cases, as President Trump rightly mentioned about that. So we know what to do, and we know where to go and what to tackle.

Off-Camera Question: President Trump, is it appropriate to ask the Attorney General to be involved in this matter?

Trump: Go ahead.

Off-Camera Question: Did you ask House Speaker Nancy Pelosi to find a way out of impeachment yesterday?

Trump: Not at all. No. Look, she's lost her way. She's been taken over by the radical left. She may be a radical left herself, but she really has lost her way. I spoke to her about guns yesterday. She didn't even know what I was talking about. She's not interested in guns.

Off-Camera Question: Did it even come up or no?

Trump: I'll tell you what: Nancy Pelosi is not interested in guns and gun protection and gun safety. All she is thinking about is this. She's been taken over by the radical left, the whole Democrat Party. And you take a look at what's happening in the media today. The whole party is taken over by the left. And thank you very much. My poll numbers have gone up. But I don't want it to go up for this reason. When they look, and when you see what's happening, people are really angry at Democrats. They're really angry at the Democrat Party.

And things like, as an example, drug pricing — getting drugs down — things like gun safety, infrastructure, the Democrats can't talk about that because they've been taken over by a radical group of people. And Nancy Pelosi, as far as I'm concerned, unfortunately she's no longer the Speaker of the House. Thank you very much, everybody. Thank you. Thank you very much.

THE MEETING

Vance: For four years, the United States of America, we had a president who stood up at press conferences and talked tough about Vladimir Putin, and then Putin invaded Ukraine and destroyed a significant chunk of the country. The path to peace and the path to prosperity is, maybe, engaging in diplomacy. We tried the pathway of Joe Biden, of thumping our chest and pretending that the president of the United States' words mattered more than the president of the United States' actions. What makes America a good country is America engaging in diplomacy. That's what President Trump is doing.

Zelenskyy: Can I ask you?

Vance: Sure. Yeah.

Zelenskyy: OK. So he (Putin) occupied it, our parts, big parts of Ukraine, parts of east and Crimea. So he occupied it in 2014. So during a lot of years — I'm not speaking about just Biden, but those times was (Barack) Obama, then President Obama, then President Trump, then President Biden, now President Trump. And God bless, now, President Trump will stop him. But during 2014, nobody stopped him. He just occupied and took. He killed people. You know what the --"

Trump: 2015?

Zelenskyy: 2014.

Trump: Oh, 2014? I was not here.

Vance: That's exactly right.

Zelenskyy: Yes, but during 2014 'til 2022, the situation is the same, that people have been dying on the contact line. Nobody stopped him. You know that we had conversations with him, a lot of conversations, my bilateral conversation. And we signed with him, me, like, you, president, in 2019, I signed with him the deal. I signed with him, (French President Emmanuel) Macron and (former German Chancellor Angela) Merkel. We signed ceasefire. Ceasefire. All of them told me that he will never go ... But after that, he broke the ceasefire, he killed our people, and he didn't exchange prisoners. We signed the exchange of prisoners. But he didn't do it. What kind of diplomacy, JD, you are speaking about? What do you mean?

Vance: I'm talking about the kind of diplomacy that's going to end the destruction of your country. Mr. President, with respect, I think it's disrespectful for you to come into the Oval Office to try to litigate this in front of the American media. Right now, you guys are going around and forcing conscripts to the front lines because you have manpower problems. You should be thanking the president for trying to bring an end to this conflict.

Zelenskyy: Have you ever been to Ukraine that you say what problems we have?

Vance: I have been to –

Zelenskyy: Come once.

Vance: I've actually watched and seen the stories, and I know that what happens is you bring people, you bring them on a propaganda tour, Mr. President. Do you disagree that you've had problems, bringing people into your military?

Zelenskyy: We have problems –

Vance: And do you think that is respectful to come to the Oval Office of the United States of America and attack the administration that is trying to prevent the destruction of your country?

Zelenskyy: A lot of questions. Let's start from the beginning.

Vance: Sure.

Zelenskyy: First of all, during the war, everybody has problems, even you. But you have nice ocean and don't feel now. But you will feel it in the future. God bless –

Trump: You don't know that. You don't know that. Don't tell us what we're going to feel. We're trying to solve a problem. Don't tell us what we're going to feel.

Zelenskyy: I'm not telling you. I am answering on these questions.

Trump: Because you're in no position to dictate that.

Vance: That's exactly what you're doing.

Trump: You are in no position to dictate what we're going to feel. We're going to feel very good.

Zelenskyy: You will feel influenced.

Trump: We are going to feel very good and very strong.

Zelenskyy: I am telling you. You will feel influenced.

Trump: You're, right now, not in a very good position. You've allowed yourself to be in a very bad position –

Zelenskyy: From the very beginning of the war —

Trump: You're not in a good position. You don't have the cards right now. With us, you start having cards.

Zelenskyy: I'm not playing cards. I'm very serious, Mr. President. I'm very serious.

Trump: You're playing cards. You're gambling with the lives of millions of people. You're gambling with World War III.

Zelenskyy: What are you speaking about?

Trump: You're gambling with World War III. And what you're doing is very disrespectful to the country, this country that's backed you far more than a lot of people said they should have.

Vance: Have you said thank you once?

Zelenskyy: A lot of times. Even today.

Vance: No, in this entire meeting. You went to Pennsylvania and campaigned for the opposition in October.

Zelenskyy: No.

Vance: Offer some words of appreciation for the United States of America and the president who's trying to save your country.

Zelenskyy: Please. You think that if you will speak very loudly about the war, you can –

Trump: He's not speaking loudly. He's not speaking loudly. Your country is in big trouble.

Zelenskyy: Can I answer —

Trump: No, no. You've done a lot of talking. Your country is in big trouble.

Zelenskyy: I know. I know.

Trump: You're not winning. You're not winning this. You have a damn good chance of coming out OK because of us.

Zelenskyy: Mr. President, we are staying in our country, staying strong. From the very beginning of the war, we've been alone. And we are thankful. I said thanks.

Trump: If you didn't have our military equipment, this war would have been over in two weeks.

Zelenskyy: In three days. I heard it from Putin. In three days.

Trump: Maybe less. It's going to be a very hard thing to do business like this, I tell you.

Vance: Just say thank you.

Zelenskyy: I said a lot of times, thank you, to American people.

Vance: Accept that there are disagreements, and let's go litigate those disagreements rather than trying to fight it out in the American media when you're wrong. We know that you're wrong.

Trump: But you see, I think it's good for the American people to see what's going on. I think it's very important. That's why I kept this going so long. You have to be thankful.

Zelenskyy: I'm thankful.

Trump: You don't have the cards. You're buried there. People are dying. You're running low on soldiers. It would be a damn good thing, and then you tell us, 'I don't want a ceasefire. I don't want a ceasefire, I want to go, and I want this.' Look, if you can get a ceasefire right now, I tell you, you take it so the bullets stop flying and your men stop getting killed.

Zelenskyy: Of course we want to stop the war. But I said to you, with guarantees.

Trump: Are you saying you don't want a ceasefire? I want a ceasefire. Because you'll get a ceasefire faster than an agreement.

Zelenskyy: Ask our people about a ceasefire, what they think.

Trump: That wasn't with me. That was with a guy named Biden, who is not a smart person.

Zelenskyy: This is your president. It was your president.

Trump: Excuse me. That was with Obama, who gave you sheets, and I gave you Javelins. I gave you the Javelins to take out all those tanks. Obama gave you sheets. In fact, the statement is Obama gave sheets, and Trump gave Javelins. You've got to be more thankful because let me tell you, you don't have the cards. With us, you have the cards, but without us, you don't have any cards.

Vance [referring to reporter's question]: She is asking what if Russia breaks the ceasefire.

Trump: What, if anything? What if the bomb drops on your head right now? OK, what if they broke it? I don't know, they broke it with Biden because Biden, they didn't respect him. They didn't respect Obama. They respect me. Let me tell you, Putin went through a hell of a lot with me. He went through a phony witch hunt ... All I can say is this. He might have broken deals with Obama and Bush, and he might have broken them with Biden. He did, maybe. Maybe he did. I don't know what happened, but he didn't break them with me. He wants to make a deal. I don't know if you can make a deal.

The problem is I've empowered you to be a tough guy, and I don't think you'd be a tough guy without the United States. And your people are very brave. But you're either going to make a deal or we're out. And if we're out, you'll fight it out. I don't think it's going to be pretty, but you'll fight it out. But you don't have the cards. But once we sign that deal, you're in a much better position, but you're not acting at all thankful. And that's not a nice thing. I'll be honest. That's not a nice thing.

All right, I think we've seen enough. What do you think? This is going to be great television. I will say that.

PETE HEGSETH

{Opening Remarks by Secretary of Defense Pete Hegseth at Ukraine Defense Contact Group, 12 February}

Good afternoon, friends. Thank you, Secretary Healy for your leadership, both in hosting and now leading the UDCG.

This is my first Ukraine Defense Contact Group. And I'm honored to join all of you today. And I appreciate the opportunity to share President Trump's approach to the war in Ukraine.

We are at, as you said Mr. Secretary, a critical moment. As the war approaches its third anniversary, our message is clear: The bloodshed must stop. And this war must end.

President Trump has been clear with the American people – and with many of your leaders – that stopping the fighting and reaching an enduring peace is a top priority.

He intends to end this war by diplomacy and bringing both Russia and Ukraine to the table. And the U.S. Department of Defense will help achieve this goal.

We will only end this devastating war – and establish a durable peace – by coupling allied strength with a realistic assessment of the battlefield.

We want, like you, a sovereign and prosperous Ukraine. But we must start by recognizing that returning to Ukraine's pre-2014 borders is an unrealistic objective.

Chasing this illusionary goal will only prolong the war and cause more suffering.

A durable peace for Ukraine must include robust security guarantees to ensure that the war will not begin again.

This must not be Minsk 3.0.

That said, the United States does not believe that NATO membership for Ukraine is a realistic outcome of a negotiated settlement.

Instead any security guarantee must be backed by capable European and non-European troops.

If these troops are deployed as peacekeepers to Ukraine at any point, they should be deployed as part of a non-NATO mission. And they should not covered under Article 5. There also must be robust international oversight of the line of contact.

To be clear, as part of any security guarantee, there will not be U.S. troops deployed to Ukraine.

To further enable effective diplomacy and drive down energy prices that fund the Russian war machine, President Trump is unleashing American energy production and encouraging other nations to do the same. Lower energy prices coupled with more effective enforcement of energy sanctions will help bring Russia to the table.

Safeguarding European security must be an imperative for European members of NATO. As part of this Europe must provide the overwhelming share of future lethal and nonlethal aid to Ukraine.

Members of this Contact Group must meet the moment.

This means: Donating more ammunition and equipment. Leveraging comparative advantages. Expanding your defense industrial base. And importantly, leveling with your citizens about the threat facing Europe.

Part of this is speaking frankly with your people about how this threat can only be met by spending more on defense.

2% is not enough; President Trump has called for 5%, and I agree.

Increasing your commitment to your own security is a down payment for the future. A down payment as you said Mr. Secretary of peace through strength.

We're also here today to directly and unambiguously express that stark strategic realities prevent the United States of America from being primarily focused on the security of Europe.

The United States faces consequential threats to our homeland. We must – and we are – focusing on security of our own borders.

We also face a peer competitor in the Communist Chinese with the capability and intent to threaten our homeland and core national interests in the Indo-Pacific. The U.S. is prioritizing deterring war with China in the Pacific, recognizing the reality of scarcity, and making the resourcing tradeoffs to ensure deterrence does not fail.

Deterrence cannot fail, for all of our sakes.

As the United States prioritizes its attention to these threats, European allies must lead from the front.

Together, we can establish a division of labor that maximizes our comparative advantages in Europe and Pacific respectively.

In my first weeks as Secretary of Defense, under President Trump's leadership, we've seen promising signs that Europe sees this threat, understands what needs to be done, and is stepping up to the task.

For example, Sweden recently announced its largest ever assistance package. We applaud them for committing $1.2 billion in ammunition and other needed materiel.

Poland is spending 5% of GDP on defense already, which is a model for the continent.

And 14 countries are co-leading Capability Coalitions. These groups are doing great work to coordinate Europe's contributions of lethal assistance across eight key capability areas.

These are first steps. More must still be done.

We ask each of your countries to step up on fulfilling the commitments that you have made.

And we challenge your countries, and your citizens, to double down and re-commit yourselves not only to Ukraine's immediate security needs, but to Europe's long-term defense and deterrence goals.

Our transatlantic alliance has endured for decades. And we fully expect that it will be sustained for generations to come. But this won't just happen.

It will require our European allies to step into the arena and take ownership of conventional security on the continent.

The United States remains committed to the NATO alliance and to the defense partnership with Europe. Full stop.

But the United States will no longer tolerate an imbalanced relationship which encourages dependency. Rather, our relationship will prioritize empowering Europe to own responsibility for its own security.

Honesty will be our policy going forward — but only in the spirit of solidarity.

President Trump looks forward to working together, to continuing this frank discussion amongst friends, and to achieve peace through strength — together.

Thank you.

Questioning

Reporter: You focused on what Ukraine has to give up. What concessions will be demanded of Putin?

Hegseth: Hmm. I would start by saying that the arguments that have been made that somehow sitting down at the table right now is making concessions to Vladimir Putin, I just reject that outright.

Reporter: Yes, but every "peace talk" so far has been about what Ukraine has to give up — territory, NATO aspirations, sovereignty. So what exactly is Putin putting on the table?

Hegseth: Well, I don't think it's fair to say that we're just giving concessions to Putin.

Reporter: Okay, is he pulling out the Russian troops? Paying reparations? Admitting war crimes? Or is his big "compromise" that he's just taking less from Ukraine than he originally wanted?

Hegseth: Look, negotiations require both sides to make sacrifices.

Reporter: Yes, but only one side has launched a full-scale invasion. If a guy steals your house and offers to give you back half of your living room, that's not a "compromise" — that's a hostage deal.

Hegseth: I just think it's time for diplomacy.

Reporter: Diplomacy is great when both sides want peace. But when one side just wants a "pause" to recharge, that's not diplomacy — that's setting up for the next invasion.

Hegseth: So you're saying no negotiations, just endless war?

Reporter: No, I'm saying that a peace agreement where only one side makes sacrifices is not peace - that's a better saying for surrender.

Lech Wałęsa

{Open letter to Trump, 3 March}

Your Excellency Mr. President,

We watched the report of your conversation with the President of Ukraine, Volodymyr Zelensky, with fear and distaste. We find it insulting that you expect Ukraine to show respect and gratitude for the material assistance provided by the United States in its fight against Russia. Gratitude is owed to the heroic Ukrainian soldiers who shed their blood in defense of the values of the free world. They have been dying on the front lines for more than 11 years in the name of these values and the independence of their homeland, which was attacked by Putin's Russia.

We do not understand how the leader of a country that symbolizes the free world cannot recognize this.

Our alarm was also heightened by the atmosphere in the Oval Office during this conversation, which reminded us of the interrogations we endured at the hands of the Security Services and the debates in Communist courts. Prosecutors and judges, acting on behalf of the all-powerful communist political police, would explain to us that they held all the power while we held none. They demanded that we cease our activities, arguing that thousands of innocent people suffered because of us. They stripped us of our freedoms and civil rights because we refused to cooperate with the government or express gratitude for our oppression. We are shocked that President Volodymyr Zelensky was treated in the same manner.

The history of the 20th century shows that whenever the United States sought to distance itself from democratic values and its European allies, it ultimately became a threat to itself. President Woodrow

Wilson understood this when he decided in 1917 that the United States must join World War I. President Franklin Delano Roosevelt understood this when, after the attack on Pearl Harbor in December 1941, he resolved that the war to defend America must be fought not only in the Pacific but also in Europe, in alliance with the nations under attack by the Third Reich.

We remember that without President Ronald Reagan and America's financial commitment, the collapse of the Soviet empire would not have been possible. President Reagan recognized that millions of enslaved people suffered in Soviet Russia and the countries it had subjugated, including thousands of political prisoners who paid for their defense of democratic values with their freedom. His greatness lay, among other things, in his unwavering decision to call the USSR an "Empire of Evil" and to fight it decisively. We won, and today, the statue of President Ronald Reagan stands in Warsaw, facing the U.S. Embassy.

Mr. President, material aid -- military and financial -- can never be equated with the blood shed in the name of Ukraine's independence and the freedom of Europe and the entire free world. Human life is priceless; its value cannot be measured in money. Gratitude is due to those who sacrifice their blood and their freedom. This is self-evident to us, the people of Solidarity, former political prisoners of the communist regime under Soviet Russia.

We call on the United States to uphold the guarantees made alongside Great Britain in the 1994 Budapest Memorandum, which established a direct obligation to defend Ukraine's territorial integrity in exchange for its relinquishment of nuclear weapons. These guarantees are unconditional -- there is no mention of treating such assistance as an economic transaction.

Signed,

Lech Wałęsa,

former political prisoner, former President of Poland

Other Reactions

After meeting with Zelenskyy, many expressed extreme embarrassment for how he had been treated, including Republicans otherwise considered loyal to Trump. There were suggestions Ukraine be forced to have an election to depose him, but surveys in Ukraine have shown a majority support for Zelenskyy under continued martial law. Below are comments from some who currently or formerly supported Trump. Many similar sentiments have been expressed by other lawmakers and governors across the country at every level of government.

A bad day for America's foreign policy. Ukraine wants independence, free markets and rule of law. It wants to be part of the West. Russia hates us and our Western values. We should be clear that we stand for freedom. -- Don Bacon, Republican Congressman

This week started with administration officials refusing to acknowledge that Russia started the war in Ukraine. It ends with a tense, shocking conversation in the Oval Office and whispers from the White House that they may try to end all U.S. support for Ukraine. I know foreign policy is not for the faint of heart, but right now, I am sick to my stomach as the administration appears to be walking away from our allies and embracing Putin, a threat to democracy and U.S. values around the world. -- U.S. Senator Lisa Murkowski, 1 March

What we need to understand is, and what I think the president should try to do now, is to understand that part of the problem here is that he looks and sounds like an ally of Putin. -- Chris Christie, former Trump ally

---

I was nauseated, just nauseated. All my life, I have had a certain idea of about America, that we're a flawed country, but we're fundamentally a force for good in the world, that we defeated Soviet Union, we defeated fascism, we did the Marshall Plan, we did PEPFAR (President's Emergency Plan for AIDS Relief) to help people live in Africa. And we make mistakes, Iraq, Vietnam, but they're usually mistakes out of stupidity, naivete and arrogance. They're not because we're ill-intentioned. What I have seen over the last six weeks is the United States behaving vilely, vilely to our friends in Canada and Mexico, vilely to our friends in Europe. And today was the bottom of the barrel, vilely to a man who is defending Western values, at great personal risk to him and his countrymen. Donald Trump believes in one thing. He believes that might makes right. And, in that, he agrees with Vladimir Putin that they are birds of a feather. And he and Vladimir Putin together are trying to create a world that's safe for gangsters, where ruthless people can thrive. And we saw the product of that effort today in the Oval Office. And I have – I first started thinking, is it – am I feeling grief? Am I feeling shock, like I'm in a hallucination? But I just think shame, moral shame. It's a moral injury to see the country you love behave in this way. -- Republican columnist and commentator David Brooks

This week started with administration officials refusing to acknowledge that Russia started the war in Ukraine. It ends with a tense, shocking conversation in the Oval Office and whispers from the White House that they may try to end all U.S. support for Ukraine. I know foreign policy is not for the faint of heart, but right now, I am sick to my stomach as the administration appears to be walking away from our allies and embracing Putin, a threat to democracy and U.S. values around the world. -- Republicam Senator Lisa Murkowski, 1 March

Support Ukraine plenary session in Kyiv, Ukraine

{Address by President of the Republic of Finland Alexander Stubb, 24 February 2025}

Given that I'm sitting here next to you, [President Zelenskyy], this is more of a personal address than anything else. You see, I think we in Finland understand exactly what you're going through.

We have 1,340 km of border with Russia. In November 1939, Russia attacked us completely unprovoked. We have fought two existential wars against Russia. The first one was the Winter War. It lasted only 105 days and we were able to hold the line. The second one was the War of Continuation, which lasted pretty much 1,100 days.

And that's what you've been going through right now. Essentially, for me, this war is about the existence of nationhood in Ukraine, and that nationhood is based on a triangle. And that triangle is something that we thought would be respected ever since the end of World War Two, and that is independence, sovereignty and territorial integrity.

Now, in World War II, Finland had to accept a peace with Stalin. And I'm sure we're going to have to accept a peace with Putin. But the peace that we accepted had only one out of the three statehood principles. Independence.

We were the only country bordering the Soviet Union that was able to retain our true independence, but we lost our sovereignty. You know, we couldn't decide which clubs we wanted to join. We were able to join the EU only in 1995, when the Soviet Union had collapsed. And we lost 10 per cent of our territory, including the areas where my grandparents were born and where my father was born. Now, the only reason I'm saying this is that the support that you will see from the Finnish public, and I think from all around this table, is the support of identity and historical experience.

Now, my big point is that there seems to be some misunderstanding about what is going on here. Russia obviously started this war, but remember that it began its acquisition of territory and spheres of interest already in 2008 by attacking Georgia, and then in 2014 by annexing the Crimean Peninsula.

We are now here to commemorate the third anniversary of the beginning of the full-scale war. But the war has been going on for pretty much 11 years, ever since 2014. A lot of people don't understand that this is not only about Ukraine, but this is also about Europe. This is also about the United States. This is also about international law, and at the end of the day, it's about the world order.

So, if we now allow Russia to do what it wants to do, in other words, stop the existence of a Ukrainian state, then it's not only Ukraine that has lost, it's Europe that has lost, it's the West that has lost, and also the United States that has lost.

And for those who doubt this, let me say one thing very clearly. You cannot trust Putin. You cannot make a deal with Putin, because that basically means a deal also with China. I also say that for those who doubt, the only way in which Ukraine is going to fully win this war is that we continue the support that we have given you from the beginning. And I also say that if Russia gets what it wants now, trust me, it's not going to stop with Ukraine.

We know that Putin will continue because his mind is one of imperialism and spheres of interest. So self-evidently, Finland will continue to support Ukraine for as long as it takes. We're the fifth biggest donor [measured by] GDP per capita.

Let me finish off, however, by saying that I think in the past two weeks we've been sort of . . . a little bit lost.

The new American administration has come in, and we have heard conflicting messages. I believe that we need to take the initiative back. And by that, I mean to say that there needs to be something concrete on the table. So, let me propose today something that I've spoken with you about and with many around the table. It's not a peace plan, but it's a sketch of a process. And that process, in my mind, goes very simply in three phases.

The first phase is before the actual ceasefire. This is the phase when we put maximum pressure on Russia, including sanctions, including using the frozen assets, and, of course, including continuing the military support for Ukraine.

This is also the time when I think European leaders need to seriously talk about security arrangements. And of course, the lead comes from Ukraine. You have the biggest land force and most experienced land force in Europe. But there needs to be support from Europe and the backstop needs to come from the United States. All of this needs to be settled before a ceasefire is brokered, whether that's Easter or whenever, we don't know.

The second phase is the ceasefire phase, and the ceasefire basically means that there's a contact line, probably monitoring thereof. But it also means that two things are put into place.

First is a negotiation on the actual agenda and modalities of the peace process. Because there is no peace process, there is no agenda, there are no modalities. And the second one is, of course, confidence-building measures, which were mentioned here a little bit earlier. Exchange of prisoners, returning the kidnapped children, etc., etc. This is the second phase.

Then only begins the third phase, and we are far, far, far from it. And that is the actual peace process. That's when there is conversation about territory. That's when there is conversation about reconstruction, and that's when there is conversation about unraveling the sanctions.

Having said all of that – very conditional, by the way – I think we need to make clear to the Russians and everyone else that there are a few things that are completely off the table in these negotiations.

One is EU membership. It is not Russia who decides on EU membership. It is the European Union who does that. Two is NATO. It is not Russia that decides on NATO membership. It is the Alliance itself. Three is Ukrainian defence. It is not Russia that decides on what Ukraine has by its border, when, where, and how. And four: European security arrangements . . . or order. It's not Russia that decides on that. We already have a European security order and should stick to it.

So those are off the table. And let me just finish off . . . because I do think this is . . . such an important day . . . when I was watching all the colleagues on Maidan Square . . . and the rest of it. I do think this is a day when we have to honour the fallen Ukrainian heroes. I also believe that this is a day when we have to face the fact that Putin has lost this war, in the sense that we will see a European Ukraine. We will see eventually Ukraine in NATO. We've seen a unified European Union and hopefully a stronger transatlantic alliance in the long run. And on a day like this, I think it's time to pave the way for a plan for Ukrainian victory.

Slava Ukraini.

| 16 |

Gaza

The message shook the Middle East and beyond. Netanyahu was the first head of state to visit the White House during Trump's second term. He called Trump "the greatest friend of Israel in the White House" and praised him for regarding Jerusalem as its capital and moving the embassy there in his last administration.

Trump's solution is to remove Palestinians elsewhere -- insisting they don't want to be there -- and turn it into a "Middle East Riviera" under the control of the United States. He said he spoke with other leaders in the Middle East who "love the idea" but was met with rebuke from many of the nations immediately after the conference. Notably, Netanyahu avoided contradicting Trump's plan but did not give his agreement.

For context, Trump by this time had unconditionally restored all arms shipments to Israel, exited the Iran nuclear deal, and designated the Houthis as terrorists. Pulling the United States out of the United Nations Human Rights Council and having previously condemned the ICC is consistent with Trump's defense of Israel, which is accused of countless human rights violations, including genocide, and its leaders -- including Netanyahu -- have warrants for war crimes.

Press Conference with Netanyahu

{White House, 4 February 2025}

Donald Trump: Thank you, very much. That's a lot of press. Congratulations, you bring them out, you really bring them out. Today I'm delighted to welcome Israeli Prime Minister Benjamin Netanyahu, back to the White House. It's a wonderful feeling and a wonderful event. We had fantastic talks, and thank you very much, with your staff.

He's the first foreign head of state to visit during our administration. And Bibi, I want to say it's an honor to have you with us. Over the past four years, the US and the Israeli alliance has been tested more than any time in history, but the bonds of friendship and affection between the American and Israeli people have endured for generations and they are absolutely unbreakable.

They are unbreakable. I'm confident that under our leadership the cherished alliance between our two countries will soon be stronger than ever. We had a great relationship. We had great victories together four years ago, not so many victories over the past four years, however. In my first term, prime minister and I forged a tremendously successful partnership that brought peace and stability to the Middle East like it hadn't seen in decades.

Together, we defeated ISIS, we ended the disastrous Iran nuclear deal, one of the worst deals ever made, by the way, and imposed the toughest ever sanctions on the Iranian regime. We starved Hamas and Iran's other terrorist proxies, and we starved them like they had never seen before, resources and support disappeared for them.

I recognized Israel's capital, opened the American embassy in Jerusalem and got it built, by the way -- built it too just -- not only designated it but got it built at a price that nobody has seen for 40 years. We got it built. It's beautiful, all Jerusalem stone right from nearby and it was -- it's something that's very special.

And recognized Israeli sovereignty over the Golan Heights, something that they talked about for 70 years and they weren't able to get it. And I got it. And with the historic Abraham Accords, something that was really an achievement that was I think going to become more and more important because we achieved the most significant Middle East peace agreements in half a century, but the Abraham Accords in particular.

And I really believe that many countries will soon be joining this amazing peace and economic development transaction. It really is a big economic development transaction. I think we're going to have a lot of people signing up very quickly. Unfortunately for four years, nobody signed up. Nobody did anything for four years except in the negative.

Unfortunately, the weakness and incompetence of those years, those past four years, the grave damage around the globe that was done, including in the Middle East, grave damage all over the globe. The horrors of October 7th would never have happened if I were president, the Ukraine and Russia disaster would never have happened if I were president.

Over the past 16 months, Israel has endured a sustained aggressive and murderous assault on every front, but they fought back bravely. You see that and you know that. What we have witnessed is an all-out attack on the very existence of a Jewish state in the Jewish homeland. The Israelis have stood strong and united in the face of an enemy that has kidnaped, tortured, raped and slaughtered innocent men, women, children and even little babies.

I want to salute the Israeli people for meeting this trial with courage and determination and unflinching resolve. They have been strong. In our meetings today, the prime minister and I focused on the future, discussing how we can work together to ensure Hamas is eliminated and ultimately restore peace to a very troubled region.

It's been troubled, but what has happened in the last four years has not been good. I want to thank Prime Minister Netanyahu for working closely with my transition team, special envoy Steve Witkoff, who is here somewhere. Steve? Stand up, Steve, please. What a job you've done. What a good job you've done.

Proud of you, you've done a fantastic job. National Security Advisor Mike Waltz. Thank you, Mike for working so well with us. Thank you. We have in addition, Marco Rubio, who is on the phone right now, listening to every single word that we say. And he's going to be great. And Pete, congratulations. And Scott, congratulations.

I see you're here. And Karoline's been doing a great job. She's really probably talked about more than anybody here. She's done a fantastic job. And thank you very much, Karoline, we're proud of you. But we'll only be satisfied when all of these problems are solved, and we have the team to solve them. And that's going to happen and it's going to happen, I think, very quickly.

I also strongly believe that the Gaza Strip, which has been a symbol of death and destruction for so many decades and so bad for the people anywhere near it, and especially those who live there and frankly who's been really very unlucky. It's been very unlucky. It's been an unlucky place for a long time.

Being in its presence just has not been good and it should not go through a process of rebuilding and occupation by the same people that have really stood there and fought for it and lived there and died there and lived a miserable existence there. Instead, we should go to other countries of interest with humanitarian hearts, and there are many of them that want to do this and build various domains that will ultimately be occupied by the 1.8 million Palestinians living in Gaza, ending the death and destruction and frankly bad luck.

This can be paid for by neighboring countries of great wealth. It could be one, two, three, four, five, seven, eight, twelve. It could be numerous sites, or it could be one large site. But the people will be able to live in comfort and peace and we'll get -- we'll make sure something really spectacular is done.

They're going to have peace; they're not going to be shot at and killed and destroyed like this civilization of wonderful people has had to endure. The only reason the Palestinians want to go back to Gaza is they have no alternative. It's right now a demolition site. This is just a demolition site. Virtually every building is down.

They're living under fallen concrete that's very dangerous and very precarious. They instead can occupy all of a beautiful area with homes and safety and they can live out their lives in peace and harmony instead of having to go back and do it again. The US will take over the Gaza Strip and we will do a job with it too.

We'll own it and be responsible for dismantling all of the dangerous unexploded bombs and other weapons on the site, level the site and get rid of the destroyed buildings, level it out. Create an economic development that will supply unlimited numbers of jobs and housing for the people of the area. Do a real job, do something different.

Just can't go back. If you go back, it's going to end up the same way it has for 100 years. I'm hopeful that this ceasefire could be the beginning of a larger and more enduring peace that will end the bloodshed and killing once and for all. With the same goal in mind, my administration has been moving quickly to restore trust in the alliance and rebuild American strength throughout the region and we've really done that.

We're a respected nation again. A lot has happened in the last couple of weeks. We are actually a very respected nation again. I ended the last administration's de facto arms embargo on over $1 billion, in military assistance for Israel. And I'm also pleased to announce that this afternoon, the United States withdrew from the anti-Semitic UN Human Rights Council and ended all of the support for the UN Relief and Works Agency, which funneled money to Hamas, and which was very disloyal to humanity.

Today, I also took action to restore a maximum pressure policy on the Iranian regime and we will once again enforce the most aggressive possible sanctions, drive Iranian oil exports to zero and diminish the regime's capacity to fund terror throughout the region and throughout the world. We had no threat when I left office.

Iran was not able to sell oil. Nobody was buying oil because I said don't buy it. If you buy it, you're not doing any business with the United States. And Hamas was not being funded.

Hezbollah was not being funded. Nobody was being funded. There would never have been an October 7th. Two weeks ago, I once again designated the Houthis as a terrorist organization. They're trying to destroy world shipping lanes. And that's not going to happen. And over the weekend, I ordered airstrikes against senior ISIS leaders hiding in the caves of Somalia, and took them out.

Here in America, we've begun the process of deporting foreign terrorists, jihadists and Hamas sympathizers from our soil just as we have people that are extremely evil. And we're sending them out of our country. They came from jails. They came from mental institutions and insane asylums. And they were dumped into our country.

They're gang members. And we're getting them out at numbers that nobody can actually believe. And every single country is taking those people back. They said they would never take them back. And they're all taking them back. And they're taking them back very gladly. And I recently signed an executive order combating the vile wave of antisemitism that we've seen in the aftermath of the October 7th, attacks.

Together, America and Israel will renew the optimism that shines so brightly. Just four years ago, it was really a bright, beautiful light. We will restore calm and stability to the region and expand prosperity opportunity and hope to our nations and for all people of the Middle East, including the Arab and Muslim nations.

Very important. We want the Arab and Muslim nations to have peace and have tranquility and have great lives. I'd like to now invite Prime Minister Netanyahu to say a few words. And we'll take some questions afterwards. Thank you, very much.

Benjamin Netanyahu: Thank you, Mr. President. I'm honored that you invited me to be the first foreign leader to visit the White House in your second term. This is a testament to testament to your friendship and support for the Jewish state and the Jewish people. I've said this before, I'll say it again. You are the greatest friend Israel has ever had in the White House.

And that's why the people of Israel have such enormous respect for you. In your first term, you recognize Jerusalem as Israel's capital. You moved the American embassy there. You recognize Israel's sovereignty over the Golan Heights. You withdrew from the disastrous Iran nuclear deal. I remember when we spoke about it and you said this is the worst deal I've ever seen.

I'm elected. I'm walking out of it. That's exactly what you did. And I think it -- it speaks loudly for just common sense. Just looking at things and seeing them as they are. And of course, you also brokered the groundbreaking Abraham Accords in which Israel made peace with four Arab states. We did this in four months.

Nothing happened for a quarter of a century. But in four months, we were able working together under your leadership to have four historic peace accords. And now, now in the first days of your second term, you picked up right where you left off. Your leadership helped bring our hostages home. Among them, American citizens.

You freed up munitions that have been withheld from Israel, they had been withheld from Israel in the midst of a seven front war for our existence. And you just freed it. You ended unjust sanctions against law abiding Israeli citizens. You boldly confronted the scourge of antisemitism. You stopped funding, as you just said, international organizations like UNRWA that support and fund terrorists.

And today, you renewed the maximum pressure campaign against Iran. Ladies and gentlemen, all this in just two weeks. Can we imagine where we'll be in four years? I can. I know you can, Mr. President. For our part, we in Israel have been pretty busy too. Since the horrendous October 7th attack, we've been fighting our common enemies and changing the face of the Middle East.

On that infamous day, Hamas monsters savage -- savagely murdered 1200 innocent people, including more than 40 Americans. They beheaded men. They raped women. They burned babies alive. And they took 251 people hostage to the dungeons of Gaza. And after this worst attack on Jews since the Holocaust, Iran and its henchmen in the Middle East were absolutely ecstatic.

Haniyeh praised the massacre. Sinwar said that Israel was finished. Nasrallah boasted that Israel was -- here's what he said, "is feeble as a spider's web." Well, Mr. President, Haniya is gone. Sinwar is gone.

Nasrallah is gone. We've devastated Hamas. We decimated Hezbollah. We destroyed Assad's remaining armaments.

And we crippled Iran's air defenses. And in doing this, we've defeated some of America's worst enemies. We took out terrorists who were wanted for decades for shedding rivers of American blood, including the blood of 241 Marines murdered in Beirut. We accomplished all this with the indomitable spirit of our people and the boundless courage of our soldiers.

The Bible says that the people of Israel shall rise like lions. And boy, did we rise. Today, the roar of the Lion of Judah is heard loudly throughout the Middle East. Israel has never been stronger. And the Iran terror axis has never been weaker. But as we discussed, Mr. President, to secure our future and bring peace to our region, we have to finish the job.

In Gaza, Israel has three goals, destroy Hamas's military and governing capabilities, secure the release of all of our hostages and ensure that Gaza never again poses a threat to Israel. I believe, Mr. President, that your willingness to puncture conventional thinking, thinking that has failed time and time and time again, your willingness to think outside the box with fresh ideas will help us achieve all these goals.

And I've seen you do this many times. You cut to the chase. You see things others refuse to see. You say things others refuse to say. And then, after the jaws drop, people scratch their heads. And they say, you know, he's right. And this is the kind of thinking that enabled us to bring the Abraham Accords.

This is the kind of thinking that will reshape the Middle East and bring peace. We also, we also see eye to eye on Iran. That's the same Iran that tried to kill us both. They tried to kill you, Mr. President. And they tried through their proxies to kill me. We're both committed to rolling back Iran's aggression in the region and ensuring that Iran never develops a nuclear weapon.

Mr. President, ladies and gentlemen, Israel will end the war by winning the war. Israel's victory will be America's victory. We will not only win the war. Working together, we will win the peace. With your leadership, Mr. President and our partnership, I believe that we will forge a brilliant future for our region and bring our great alliance to even greater heights.

Thank you.

Donald Trump: Thank you very much, Bibi. Very nice. Thank you. And JD Vance, everybody. JD, please, vice president, stand up. He's been doing a good job. He's been working very hard on all things, but this in particular. We'll take some questions, please. Yes, ma'am, go ahead. Please. Go ahead. Yeah, go ahead.

Mr. President, can a normalization deal with Saudi Arabia be achieved without the acknowledgment of a Palestinian state? That question for you, too, Mr. Prime Minister. And Mr. President, given what you've said about Gaza, did the US send troops to help secure the security vacuum?

So, Saudi Arabia is going to be very helpful. And they have been very helpful. They want peace in the Middle East. It's very simple. Uh, we know their leader and their leaders very well. They are wonderful people. And they want peace in the Middle East. As far as Gaza is concerned, we will do what is necessary.

If it's necessary, we'll do that. We're going to take over that peace and we're going to develop it, create thousands and thousands of jobs. And it will be something that the entire Middle East can be very proud of.

But everybody feels that continuing the same process that's gone on forever over and over again and then it starts and then the killing starts, and all of the other problems start, and you end up in the same place and we don't want to see that happen. So, by the United States, with its stability and strength, owning it, especially the strength that we're developing and developed over the last fairly short period of time, I would say really since the election, I think we'll be a great keeper of something that is very, very strong, very powerful and very, very good for the area, not just for Israel, for the entire Middle East.

It's very important and we'll again have thousands of jobs. And there will be jobs for everyone, not for a specific group of people, but for everybody. OK? Please.

Benjamin Netanyahu: I think peace between Israel and Saudi Arabia is not only feasible, I think it's going to happen. I think if we had another half a year in your first term, it would have already happened.

Donald Trump: It's true. Many, many more, I agree, many more nations.

Benjamin Netanyahu: I think you can't prejudge and pre-guess how we'll achieve it. But I'm committed to achieving it and I know the president is committed to achieving it, and I think the Saudi leadership is interested to achieve it. So, we'll give it a good shot and I think we'll succeed.

Question: First of all, President Trump, did you hear from Prime Minister Netanyahu [Inaudible] guarantees that the ceasefire will go on, including Phase 2? And Prime Minister Netanyahu, for you. Why are you refusing to set up a national commission to investigate the failure of the project?

Well, I can't tell you whether or not the ceasefire will hold. We've done I think a very masterful job. We weren't helped very much by the Biden administration. I can tell you that. But we've gotten quite a few hostages out. We're going to get more out. But we're dealing with very complex people, and we are going to see whether or not it holds.

We certainly want to have more come out. They've come out damaged in many ways, damaged, very damaged people. But they're going to get better and they're going to be strong and they're going to have a good life. And we hope to get as many as possible out. Whether or not it holds, I don't know. We hope it holds.

We hope it holds.

Benjamin Netanyahu: I think that at the appropriate time, which I think will enable us to really investigate what happened, what were the causes of the failures by an independent commission that will be accepted by the majority of the people. We don't want it accepted by one half of the people and not the other. I think we should have it, and we should find out exactly what happened.

I'm insisting on it, and believe me, it will surprise a lot of people when it happens.

Donald Trump: Kelly -- Kelly, go ahead, please.

Question: Mr. President, you are outlining something that is really quite striking. You are talking about -- OK, thank you. Mr. President, Mr. Prime Minister, you are talking tonight about the United States taking over a sovereign territory. What authority would allow you to do that? Are you talking about a permanent occupation there, redevelopment?

And Mr. Prime Minister, do you see this idea as a way to expand the boundaries of Israel and to have a longer peace, even though the Israeli people know how important that land is to you and your citizens just as the space is inherited by the Palestinians as well?

I do see a long-term ownership position and I see it bringing great stability to that part of the Middle East, and maybe the entire Middle East. And everybody I've spoken to -- this was not a decision made lightly. Everybody I've spoken to loves the idea of the United States owning that piece of land, developing and creating thousands of jobs with something that will be magnificent in a really magnificent area that nobody would know.

Nobody can look because all they see is death and destruction and rubble and demolished buildings falling all over. It's just a terrible, terrible sight. I've studied it --

Donald Trump: I've studied this very closely over a lot of months, and I've seen it from every different angle. And it's a very, very dangerous place to be and it's only going to get worse. And I think this is an idea that's gotten tremendous -- and I'm talking about from the highest level of leadership, gotten tremendous praise.

And if the United States can help to bring stability and peace in the Middle East, we'll do that. Bibi?

Benjamin Netanyahu: I mentioned again tonight our three goals and the third goal is to make sure that Gaza never poses a threat to Israel again. President Trump is taking it to a much higher level. He sees a different --

Donald Trump: -- he sees a different future for that piece of land that has been the focus of so much terrorism, so much -- so many attacks against us. So, many trials and so many tribulations. He has a different idea, and I think it's worth paying attention to this. We're talking about it, he's exploring it with his people, with his staff.

I think it's something that could change history and it's worthwhile really pursuing this avenue.

Question: So, before rebuilding Gaza again and obviously [Inaudible] all the hostages, and one of them is Kevin [Inaudible], an American soldier, who is alive. How will you be sure that you will take out all the hostages and then rebuild?

Donald Trump: We're working very hard to get all the hostages. The word is all, and we are working very hard. So far, it's been moving along fairly rapidly, pretty much on schedule. I'd love to have them all out at one time, but we're taking them out and tomorrow more are being released and over the days more and then we'll go into a Phase 2. But we'd like to get all of the hostages, and if we don't, it will just make us somewhat more violent, I will tell you that, because they would have broken their word.

Mr. Witkoff and his entire group have been working 24 hours around the clock, and they want them out. And promises have been made to them, and we'll see whether or not those promises will be kept. But we want all the hostages, that's right.

Question: How much time you think it will take? Mr. President, do you support Israeli sovereignty in Judea and Samaria areas, which many believe is the biblical homeland of the Jewish people?

Donald Trump: Well, we're discussing that with many of your representatives. You're represented very well, and people do like the idea, but we haven't taken a position on it yet. But we will be -- we'll be making an announcement probably on that very specific topic over the next four weeks.

Question: Thank you so much, Mr. President. So, you just said -- OK. You just said that you think all the Palestinians should be relocated to other countries. Does that mean that you do not support the two-state solution?

Donald Trump: It doesn't mean anything about a two-state or a one-state or any other state. It means that we want to have -- we want to give people a chance at life. They have never had a chance at life because the Gaza Strip has been a hellhole for people living there. It's been horrible. Hamas has made it so bad, so bad, so dangerous, so unfair to people.

And by doing what I'm recommending that we do, it's a very strong recommendation, but it is a strong recommendation. By doing that we think we're going to bring perhaps great peace to long beyond this area. And I have to stress, this is not for Israel, this is for everybody in the Middle East -- Arabs, Muslims -- this is for everybody.

This would be where they can partake in terms of jobs and living and all of the other benefits. And I think it's very important. It just doesn't work the other way. You can't keep trying. They just -- has been going along for so many decades you can't even count. You just can't keep doing -- you have to learn from history.

You can't keep doing the same mistake over and over again. Gaza is a hellhole right now. It was before the bombing started frankly. And we're going to give people a chance to live in a beautiful community that's safe and secure. And I think you're going to see tremendous -- a tremendous outflowing of support.

I can tell you, I spoke to other leaders of countries in the Middle East and they love the idea. They say it would really bring stability and what we need is stability. Yes, sir, please. Go ahead.

Question: Thank you. Are you still committed to imposing sanctions on the ICC despite the move being stalled in the Senate? And please, a question for the prime minister as well. The president has been very clear about his desire to achieve a deal with Saudi Arabia. How do you settle this if Israel is required to renew the war against Hamas in the future?

Donald Trump: Go ahead, Bibi.

Benjamin Netanyahu: I think everybody understands that, just as the president fought and defeated al-Qaida and ISIS, that we can't leave Hamas there because Hamas will continue the battle to destroy Israel. They'll do -- you know, in this temporary ceasefire, one of their leaders comes out. You know what he says?

We're going to do October 7th, again, except we'll do it bigger. So, obviously, you can't talk about peace, uh, neither with Hamas or in the Middle East, if this, you know, toxic murderous organization is left standing any more that you could make peace in Europe after World War II, if the Nazi regime was left standing and the Nazi army was left standing.

You want a different future you've got to knock out the people who want to destroy you and destroy peace. That's what we're going to do. I think that will also bring, usher in actually, the peace with Saudi Arabia and with others. And I think there will be others too.

Question: Mr. President, I am from Afghanistan. My name is Nazira Karimi. I am an Afghan suffered woman who has high expectations from you, do we have any plan to change Afghanistan's situation? Are you able to recognize Taliban? Because I'm an Afghan journalist, Afghan suffered woman. Any comment about Afghanistan?

What's your future plan toward Afghan people, especially Afghanistan? Thank you.

Donald Trump: I have a little hard time understanding you. Where are you from?

Question: Afghanistan.

Donald Trump: Oh. [Inaudible] Actually it's a beautiful voice and a beautiful accent. The only problem is, I can't understand a word you're saying. [Laughter] But -- but I'd just say this, good luck. Live in peace. [Laughter] Go ahead, please.

Question: Thank you. Thank you. Mr. President? And Prime Minister. You said earlier today that it was tough for you to implement these sanctions on Iran.

Donald Trump: Yeah.

Question: But you did indicate that you were willing to negotiate with them. What would that look like? And are you in conversations with them? And the same for the prime minister, sir?

Donald Trump: Yeah. I hated doing it. I want Iran to be peaceful and successful. I hated doing it. I did it once before. And we brought them down to a level where they were unable to give any money. They had to survive themselves. And they had no money. They were essentially broke. And they had no money for, as I said, Hezbollah.

They had no money for Hamas. They had no money for any form of terror. The 28 -- if you call it the 28 Sites of Terror, they had no money for any of it. They had to do their own and focus on their own well-being. And I hated to do it then. And I hate it -- I hate to do it just as much now. And I say this and I say this to Iran who is listening very intently, I would love to be able to make a great deal, a deal where you can get on with your lives and you'll do wonderfully.

You'll do wonderfully. Incredible people. Industrious, beautiful, just an unbelievable group of people in Iran. And I know them well. I have many friends from Iran and many friends that are Americans from Iran. And they're very proud of Iran. But I hated to do it just so you understand. And I hope we're going to be able to do something so that it doesn't end up in a very catastrophic situation.

don't want to see that happen. I want to see -- I -- I really want to see peace. And I hope that we're able to do that. They cannot have a nuclear weapon. It's very simple. I'm not putting restrictions. I'm not -- they cannot have one thing. They cannot have a nuclear weapon. And if I think that they will have a nuclear weapon, despite what I just said, I think that's going to be very unfortunate for them.

If on the other hand, they can convince us that they won't, and I hope they can. It's very easy to do. It's actually very easy to do. I think they're going to have an unbelievable future. Yeah, please, sir.

Question: Thank you, Mr. President. You just laid out your plan for Gaza. Can you lay out your plan for Ukraine? And also --

Donald Trump: For Ukraine?

Question: For Ukraine, yes. Uh, you consider yourself a strong leader. You blame your predecessor for letting Russia to take over Ukraine. Will you demand from Putin to get out of Ukraine from sovereign territory of Ukraine?

Donald Trump: So we're dealing, right now, on the subject. I don't want to spend a lot of time because we're here for another reason. But we are having very good talks, very constructive talks on Ukraine. And we are talking to the Russians. We're talking to the Ukrainian leadership. It would have never happened, that would have never happened, it should have never happened.

I get reports every week, the number of soldiers, mostly soldiers now, the cities have been largely demolished. You talk about a -- a very sad sight to see, we talk Gaza, well, many of these cities look as bad as Gaza and worse, what's happened to them. And I want to see that end. And I want to see it end for one simple reason, the life of young people being absolutely obliterated on both sides.

You probably have 700,000 Ukrainian soldiers dead, 800,000, maybe more Russian soldiers dead. It's very flat land. And the only thing that's going to stop a bullet is a human body. In this case, usually soldiers. And the numbers are staggering when you hear the real numbers in Ukraine, what -- what the numbers are.

And this doesn't include the cities that have been demolished and all of the people that were killed. So, I want to see it stopped. We're having very good talks. And I think we're going to get it. I think something will be -- hopefully dramatically it will -- it will rise above everything. And you have to. You can't let this continue.

You can't. This is an absolute slaughter that's taking place on the beautiful farmlands of Ukraine. And we have to stop it. We can't let this continue. It's -- it's a human -- It is -- it is a human tragedy. And we're going to try very hard to stop it.

Question: Thank you very much. OK. Mr. President, what's your view about Palestinian Leader Abbas role in all the regional changes you want to do? And the question for the prime minister, what's your view on President Trump wanting to reach a deal with Iran and not a much more active military stance towards them?

Donald Trump: Go ahead, Bibi. Go ahead.

Benjamin Netanyahu: I think the president just said something that, I think, is the pivot of everything that we're talking about. He said, "Iran cannot have a nuclear weapon." And we fully agree with that. If this goal can be achieved by a maximum pressure campaign, so be it. But I think the most important thing is to focus on the goal, which the president just did. And I fully agree with.

Question: Mr. President -- President Trump --

Donald Trump: Well, I said it and he said it very well, it's -- it's a -- it's a -- it's a campaign of pressure to see if we can get something done. Uh, he doesn't want to do what some people think will automatically happen. Because they're very difficult people to deal with, as you know. But if we could solve this problem without warfare, without all of the things that you've been witnessing over the last number of years, it would be -- I think it would be a tremendous thing.

Question: Sir, do you have any plans to visit Israel? Do you have any plans to visit Israel soon?

Donald Trump: To visit where?

Question: Israel? And Gaza?

Donald Trump: Oh, well, I love -- I love Israel. I will visit there. And I'll visit Gaza. And I'll visit Saudi Arabia. And I'll visit other places all over the Middle East. The Middle East is an incredible place, so vibrant so -- so -- it's just one of the really beautiful places. And with great people. And I think a lot of bad leadership has taken place in the Middle East that has allowed this to happen.

It's just terrible. And that includes on the American side, by the way. We should have never gone in there a long time ago, spent trillions of dollars and created so much death. So it includes Americans.

But yeah, I'll be visiting a lot of different places in the Middle East. I've been invited everywhere, but I will be visiting some, yeah.

Let's go. Caitlin? Go ahead, Caitlin. Caitlin, go ahead.

Question: President Trump, just follow up on -- Just a follow up on what you were saying about the Gazans leaving Gaza going to other countries. One, where exactly are you suggesting that they should go? And two, are you saying they should return after it's rebuilt? And if not, who do you envision living there?

Donald Trump: I envision a world -- people living there, the world's people. I think you'll make that into an international, unbelievable place. I think the potential in the Gaza Strip is unbelievable. And I think the entire world, representatives from all over the world will be there and they'll --

Question: [Inaudible] Palestinians?

Donald Trump: And they'll live there. Palestinians also. Palestinians will live there, many people will live there. But they've tried the other and they've tried it for decades and decades and decades. It's not going to work it work. It didn't work. It will never work. And you have to learn from history. History has -- you know, you just can't let it keep repeating itself.

We have an opportunity to do something that could be phenomenal. And I don't want to be cute. I don't want to be a wise guy. But the Riviera of the Middle East, this could be something that could be so -- This could be so magnificent. But more importantly than that is the people that have been absolutely destroyed that live there now can live in peace in a much better situation because they are living in hell. And those people will now be able to live in peace. We'll make sure that it's done world class.

It will be wonderful for the people. Palestinians, Palestinians mostly we're talking about. And I have a feeling that despite them saying no, I have a feeling that the king in Jordan and that the general president -- but that the general in Egypt will open their hearts and will give us the kind of land that we need to get this done, and people can live in harmony and in peace.

Thank you all, very much. Thank you. Thank you very much. Thank you.

| 17 |

South Africa

The Unites States doesn't usually take a stand on the internal policies of other countries, especially if it does not directly affect America's economic interests. So why threaten to cut aid to South Africa over land redistribution? The easiest dots to connect are to Elon Musk, who was brought up in a wealthy Afrikaner family during Aparteid. (He came to America in 1995 and became an American citizen in 2001.)

The basic context is that legislation in South Africa was passed allowing some lands owned by White citizens (disproportionally under Apartheid) to be surrendered for public use. The law's basic description reads

> To provide for the expropriation of property for a public purpose or in the public interest; to regulate the procedure for the expropriation of property for a public purpose or in the public interest, including payment of compensation; to identify certain instances where the provision of nil compensation may be just and equitable for expropriation in the public interest; to repeal the Expropriation Act, 1975 (Act No. 63 of 1975); and to provide for matters connected therewith.

After Trump's public remarks and Executive Order on the subject, South Africa's President Cyril Ramaphosa told his Parliament, "We will not be bullied." The next day in his State of the Nation address, he said "We are witnessing the rise of nationalism, protectionism, the pursuit of narrow interests and the decline of common cause" in what is seen as a veiled reference to Trump.

While having suspended the whole refugee program, Trump made the exception for South Africa, offering resettlement for Afrikaners (South Africans of European descent), under the pretense of being "victims of unjust racial discrimination".

Notably, many statements made by Trump over the years regarding South African politics have been fact-checked as false, and recent remarks are being seen as parroted from the far-Right party tied to the old Apartheid regime.

Addressing Egregious Actions of The Republic of South Africa

{Executive Order, 7 February}

By the authority vested in me as President by the Constitution and the laws of the United States of America, it is hereby ordered as follows:

Section 1. Purpose. In shocking disregard of its citizens' rights, the Republic of South Africa (South Africa) recently enacted Expropriation Act 13 of 2024 (Act), to enable the government of South Africa to seize ethnic minority Afrikaners' agricultural property without compensation. This Act follows countless government policies designed to dismantle equal opportunity in employment, education, and business, and hateful rhetoric and government actions fueling disproportionate violence against racially disfavored landowners.

In addition, South Africa has taken aggressive positions towards the United States and its allies, including accusing Israel, not Hamas, of genocide in the International Court of Justice, and reinvigorating its relations with Iran to develop commercial, military, and nuclear arrangements.

The United States cannot support the government of South Africa's commission of rights violations in its country or its 'undermining United States foreign policy, which poses national security threats to our Nation, our allies, our African partners, and our interests.

Sec. 2. Policy. It is the policy of the United States that, as long as South Africa continues these unjust and immoral practices that harm our Nation:

(a) the United States shall not provide aid or assistance to South Africa; and

(b) the United States shall promote the resettlement of Afrikaner refugees escaping government-sponsored race-based discrimination, including racially discriminatory property confiscation.

Sec. 3. Assistance. (a) All executive departments and agencies (agencies), including the United States Agency for International Development, shall, to the maximum extent allowed by law, halt foreign aid or assistance delivered or provided to South Africa, and shall promptly exercise all available authorities and discretion to halt such aid or assistance.

(b) The head of each agency may permit the provision of any such foreign aid or assistance that, in the discretion of the relevant agency head, is necessary or appropriate.

Sec. 4. Refugee Resettlement and Other Humanitarian Considerations. The Secretary of State and the Secretary of Homeland Security shall take appropriate steps, consistent with law, to prioritize humanitarian relief, including admission and resettlement through the United States Refugee Admissions Program, for Afrikaners in South Africa who are victims of unjust racial discrimination. Such plan shall be submitted to the President through the Assistant to the

President and Homeland Security Advisor.

Sec. 5. General Provisions. (a) Nothing in this order shall be construed to impair or otherwise affect:

(i) the authority granted by law to an executive department or agency, or the head thereof; or

(ii) the functions of the Director of the Office of Management and Budget relating to budgetary, administrative, or legislative proposals.

(b) This order shall be implemented consistent with applicable law and subject to the availability of appropriations.

(c) This order is not intended to, and does not, create any right or benefit, substantive or procedural, enforceable at law or in equity by any party against the United States, its departments, agencies, or entities, its officers, employees, or agents, or any other person.

THE WHITE HOUSE,
February 7, 2025.

The Response

{Media Statement, 8 February 2025}

The Government of South Africa has taken note of the latest executive order issued by President Trump. It is of great concern that the foundational premise of this order lacks factual accuracy and fails to recognise South Africa's profound and painful history of colonialism and apartheid.

We are concerned by what seems to be a campaign of misinformation and propaganda aimed at misrepresenting our great nation. It is disappointing to observe that such narratives seem to have found favour among decision-makers in the United States of America.

It is ironic that the executive order makes provision for refugee status in the US for a group in South Africa that remains amongst the most economically privileged, while vulnerable people in the US from other parts of the world are being deported and denied asylum despite real hardship.

We reiterate that South Africa remains committed to finding diplomatic solutions to any misunderstandings or disputes.

ISSUED BY THE MINISTRY OF INTERNATIONAL RELATIONS AND COOPERATION
OR Tambo Building
460 Soutpansberg Road
Rietondale
Pretoria
0084

| 18 |

Education and Patriotism

Since the Civil War, there has been a battle around the teaching of American history and its influence on patriotism. The general view of the current Right is that it ought to inspire not just love of country but belief in exceptionalism. Anything taught related to race, no matter how factual and objective, is suspected of making our children "hate America" and making White people out to be the bad guys. The scapegoat term is "Critical Race Theory". CRT is a specific approach only taught in certain college classrooms, yet Right-wing media has convinced parents across the country (such as the censorship-demanding "Moms for Liberty") to protest it at PTA meetings and school boards.

The Executive Order below is the ultimate wish list for this view. This "patriotic education" will be enforced on the state level by the usual threat of funding sanctions. The battle of opinions is whether it is indoctrination to inculcate patriotism or not to do so.

Ending Radical Indoctrination in K-12 Schooling

{Executive Order, 29 January}

By the authority vested in me as President by the Constitution and the laws of the United States of America, it is hereby ordered:

Section 1. Purpose and Policy. Parents trust America's schools to provide their children with a rigorous education and to instill a patriotic admiration for our incredible Nation and the values for which we stand.

In recent years, however, parents have witnessed schools indoctrinate their children in radical, anti-American ideologies while deliberately blocking parental oversight. Such an environment operates as an echo chamber, in which students are forced to accept these ideologies without question or critical examination. In many cases, innocent children are compelled to adopt identities as either victims or oppressors solely based on their skin color and other immutable characteristics. In other instances, young men and women are made to question whether they were born in the wrong body and whether to view their parents and their reality as enemies to be blamed. These practices not only erode critical thinking but also sow division, confusion, and distrust, which undermine the very foundations of personal identity and family unity.

Imprinting anti-American, subversive, harmful, and false ideologies on our Nation's children not only violates longstanding anti-discrimination civil rights law in many cases, but usurps basic parental authority. For example, steering students toward surgical and chemical mutilation without parental consent or involvement or allowing males access to private spaces designated for females may contravene Federal laws that protect parental rights, including the Family Educational Rights and Privacy Act (FERPA) and the Protection of Pupil Rights Amendment (PPRA), and sex-based equality and opportunity, including Title IX of the Education Amendments of 1972 (Title IX). Similarly, demanding acquiescence to "White Privilege" or "unconscious bias," actually promotes racial discrimination and undermines national unity.

My Administration will enforce the law to ensure that recipients of Federal funds providing K-12 education comply with all applicable laws prohibiting discrimination in various contexts and protecting parental rights, including Title VI of the Civil Rights Act of 1964

(Title VI), 42 U.S.C. 2000d et seq.; Title IX, 20 U.S.C. 1681 et seq.; FERPA, 20 U.S.C. 1232g; and the PPRA, 20 U.S.C. 1232h.

Sec. 2. Definitions. As used herein:

(a) The definitions in the Executive Order "Defending Women from Gender Ideology Extremism and Restoring Biological Truth to the Federal Government" (January 20, 2025) shall apply to this order.

(b) "Discriminatory equity ideology" means an ideology that treats individuals as members of preferred or disfavored groups, rather than as individuals, and minimizes agency, merit, and capability in favor of immoral generalizations, including that:

(i) Members of one race, color, sex, or national origin are morally or inherently superior to members of another race, color, sex, or national origin;

(ii) An individual, by virtue of the individual's race, color, sex, or national origin, is inherently racist, sexist, or oppressive, whether consciously or unconsciously;

(iii) An individual's moral character or status as privileged, oppressing, or oppressed is primarily determined by the individual's race, color, sex, or national origin;

(iv) Members of one race, color, sex, or national origin cannot and should not attempt to treat others without respect to their race, color, sex, or national origin;

(v) An individual, by virtue of the individual's race, color, sex, or national origin, bears responsibility for, should feel guilt, anguish, or other forms of psychological distress because of, should be discriminated against, blamed, or stereotyped for, or should receive adverse treatment because of actions committed in the past by other members of the same race, color, sex, or national origin, in which the individual played no part;

(vi) An individual, by virtue of the individual's race, color, sex, or national origin, should be discriminated against or receive adverse treatment to achieve diversity, equity, or inclusion;

(vii) Virtues such as merit, excellence, hard work, fairness, neutrality, objectivity, and racial colorblindness are racist or sexist or were created by members of a particular race, color, sex, or national origin to oppress members of another race, color, sex, or national origin; or (viii) the United States is fundamentally racist, sexist, or otherwise discriminatory.

(c) "Educational service agency" (ESA) has the meaning given in 20 U.S.C. 1401(5), and the terms "elementary school," "local educational agency" (LEA), "secondary school," and "state educational agency" (SEA) have the meanings given in 34 C.F.R. 77.1(c).

(d) "Patriotic education" means a presentation of the history of America grounded in:

(i)   an accurate, honest, unifying, inspiring, and ennobling characterization of America's founding and foundational principles;

(ii)   a clear examination of how the United States has admirably grown closer to its noble principles throughout its history;

(iii) the concept that commitment to America's aspirations is beneficial and justified; and

(iv)   the concept that celebration of America's greatness and history is proper.

(e) "Social transition" means the process of adopting a "gender identity" or "gender marker" that differs from a person's sex. This process can include psychological or psychiatric counseling or treatment by a school counselor or other provider; modifying a person's name (e.g., "Jane" to "James") or pronouns (e.g., "him" to "her"); calling a child "nonbinary"; use of intimate facilities and accommodations such as bathrooms or locker rooms specifically designated for persons of the opposite sex; and participating in school athletic competitions or other extracurricular activities specifically designated for persons of the opposite sex. "Social transition" does not include chemical or surgical mutilation.

Sec. 3. Ending Indoctrination Strategy. (a) Within 90 days of the date of this order, to advise the President in formulating future policy, the Secretary of Education, the Secretary of Defense, and the Secretary of Health and Human Services, in consultation with the Attorney General, shall provide an Ending Indoctrination Strategy to the President, through the Assistant to the President for Domestic Policy, containing recommendations and a plan for:

(i) eliminating Federal funding or support for illegal and discriminatory treatment and indoctrination in K-12 schools, including based on gender ideology and discriminatory equity ideology; and

(ii) protecting parental rights, pursuant to FERPA, 20 U.S.C. 1232g, and the PPRA, 20 U.S.C. 1232h, with respect to any K-12 policies or conduct implicated by the purpose and policy of this order.

(b) The Ending Indoctrination Strategy submitted under subsection (a) of this section shall contain a summary and analysis of the following:

(i) All Federal funding sources and streams, including grants or contracts, that directly or indirectly support or subsidize the instruction, advancement, or promotion of gender ideology or discriminatory equity ideology:

(A) in K-12 curriculum, instruction, programs, or activities; or

(B) in K-12 teacher education, certification, licensing, employment, or training;

(ii) Each agency's process to prevent or rescind Federal funds, to the maximum extent consistent with applicable law, from being used by an ESA, SEA, LEA, elementary school, or secondary school to directly or indirectly support or subsidize the instruction, advancement, or promotion of gender ideology or discriminatory equity ideology in:

(A) K-12 curriculum, instruction, programs, or activities; or

(B) K-12 teacher certification, licensing, employment, or training;

(iii) Each agency's process to prevent or rescind Federal funds, to the maximum extent consistent with applicable law, from being used by an ESA, SEA, LEA, elementary school, or secondary school to directly or indirectly support or subsidize the social transition of a minor student, including through school staff or teachers or through deliberately concealing the minor's social transition from the minor's parents.

(iv) Each agency's process to prevent or rescind Federal funds, to the maximum extent consistent with applicable law, from being used by an ESA, SEA, LEA, elementary school, or secondary school to directly or indirectly support or subsidize:

(A) interference with a parent's Federal statutory right to information regarding school curriculum, records, physical examinations, surveys, and other matters under the PPRA or FERPA; or

(B) a violation of Title VI or Title IX; and

(v) A summary and analysis of all relevant agency enforcement tools to advance the policies of this order.

(c) The Attorney General shall coordinate with State attorneys general and local district attorneys in their efforts to enforce the law and file appropriate actions against K-12 teachers and school officials who violate the law by:

(i) sexually exploiting minors;

(ii) unlawfully practicing medicine by offering diagnoses and treatment without the requisite license; or

(iii) otherwise unlawfully facilitating the social transition of a minor student.

(d) The Assistant to the President for Domestic Policy shall regularly convene the heads of the agencies tasked with submitting the Ending Indoctrination Strategy under subsection (a) of this section to confer regarding their findings, areas for additional investigation, the modification or implementation of their respective recommendations, and such other policy initiatives or matters as the President may direct.

Sec. 4. Reestablishing the President's Advisory 1776 Commission and Promoting Patriotic Education. (a) The President's Advisory 1776 Commission ("1776 Commission"), which was created by Executive Order 13958 of November 2, 2020, to promote patriotic education, but was terminated by President Biden in Executive Order 13985 of January 20, 2021, is hereby reestablished. The purpose of the 1776 Commission is to promote patriotic education and advance the purposes stated in section 1 of Executive Order 13958, as well as to advise and promote the work of the White House Task Force on Celebrating America's 250th Birthday ("Task Force 250") and the United States

Semiquincentennial Commission in their efforts to provide a grand celebration worthy of the momentous occasion of the 250th anniversary of American Independence on July 4, 2026.

(b) Within 120 days of the date of this order, the Secretary of Education shall establish the 1776 Commission in the Department of Education.

(c) The 1776 Commission shall be composed of not more than 20 members, who shall be appointed by the President for a term of 2 years. The 1776 Commission shall be made up of individuals from outside the Federal Government with relevant experience or subject-matter expertise.

(d) The 1776 Commission shall have a Chair or Co-Chairs, at the President's discretion, and a Vice Chair, who shall be designated by the President from among the Commission's members. An Executive Director, designated by the Secretary of Education in consultation with the Assistant to the President for Domestic Policy, shall coordinate the work of the 1776 Commission. The Chair (or Co-Chairs) and Vice Chair shall work with the Executive Director to convene regular meetings of the 1776 Commission, determine its agenda, and direct its work, consistent with this order.

(e) The 1776 Commission shall:

(i) facilitate the development and implementation of a "Presidential 1776 Award" to recognize student knowledge of the American founding, including knowledge about the Founders, the Declaration of Independence, the Constitutional Convention, and the great soldiers and battles of the American Revolutionary War;

(ii) in coordination with the White House Office of Public Liaison, coordinate bi-weekly lectures regarding the 250th anniversary of American Independence that are grounded in patriotic education principles, which shall be broadcast to the Nation throughout calendar year 2026;

(iii) upon request, advise executive departments and agencies regarding their efforts to ensure patriotic education is appropriately provided to the public at national parks, battlefields, monuments, mu-

seums, installations, landmarks, cemeteries, and other places important to the American founding and American history, as appropriate
and consistent with applicable law;

(iv) upon request, offer advice and recommendations to, and support
the work of Task Force 250 and the United States Semiquincentennial
Commission regarding their plans to celebrate the 250th anniversary
of American Independence; and

(v) facilitate, advise upon, and promote private and civic activities
nationwide to increase public knowledge of and support patriotic education surrounding the 250th anniversary of American Independence, as appropriate and consistent with applicable law.

(f) The Department of Education shall provide funding and administrative support for the 1776 Commission, to the extent permitted by
law and subject to the availability of appropriations.

(g) Members of the 1776 Commission shall serve without compensation but, as approved by the Department of Education, shall be reim-
bursed for travel expenses, including per diem in lieu of subsistence,
as authorized by law for persons serving intermittently in the Government service (5 U.S.C. 5701-5707).

(h) Insofar as chapter 10 of title 5, United States Code (commonly
known as the Federal Advisory Committee Act), may apply to the
1776 Commission, any functions of the President under that Act, except that of reporting to the Congress, shall be performed by the Secretary of Education, in accordance with the guidelines issued by the
Administrator of General Services.

(i) The 1776 Commission shall terminate 2 years from the date of this
order, unless extended by the President.

   Sec. 5. Additional Patriotic Education Measures. (a) All relevant
agencies shall monitor compliance with section 111(b) of title I of Division J of Public Law 108-447, which provides that "[e]ach educational institution that receives Federal funds for a fiscal year shall hold
an educational program on the United States Constitution on September 17 of such year for the students served by the educational institution," including by verifying compliance with each educational

institution that receives Federal funds. All relevant agencies shall take action, as appropriate, to enhance compliance with that law.

(b) All relevant agencies shall prioritize Federal resources, consistent with applicable law, to promote patriotic education, including through the following programs:

(i) the Department of Education's American History and Civics Academies and American History and Civics Education-National Activities programs;

(ii) the Department of Defense's National Defense Education Program and Pilot Program on Enhanced Civics Education; and

(iii) the Department of State's Bureau of Educational and Cultural Affairs and Fulbright, U.S. Speaker, and International Visitor Leadership programs, as well as the American Spaces network.

Sec. 6. General Provisions. (a) Nothing in this order shall be construed to impair or otherwise affect:

(i) the authority granted by law to an executive department or agency, or the head thereof; or

(ii) the functions of the Director of the Office of Management and Budget relating to budgetary, administrative, or legislative proposals.

(b) This order shall be implemented consistent with applicable law and subject to the availability of appropriations.

(c) This order is not intended to, and does not, create any right or benefit, substantive or procedural, enforceable at law or in equity by any party against the United States, its departments, agencies, or entities, its officers, employees, or agents, or any other person.

| 19 |

The Military

The issue of transgender members of the armed forces is mentioned elsewhere in this book, but the general concern, as in late
2020, was the replacement of key figures in the military chain of command.

Late on 21 February, against precedent, President Trump fired the
chairman of the Joint Chiefs of Staff, Air Force General C.Q. Brown,
and pushed out five other admirals and generals. He also announced
his plan to remove Admiral Lisa Franchetti, the head of the U.S. Navy
and the first woman to lead a military service.

Defense Secretary Pete Hegseth later replaced the top lawyers
(Judge Advocates General) for the Army, Navy and Air Force, arguing, "Ultimately, we want lawyers who give sound constitutional
advice and don't exist to attempt to be roadblocks to anything — anything that happens in their spots."

Interview with McPherson

{24 February interview by Geoff Bennett with Rear Admiral James
McPherson (Ret.), former U.S. Undersecretary of the Army}

Bennett: For perspective, we turn now to retired Rear Admiral
James McPherson. He served as undersecretary of the Army and as
the Army's general counsel during the first Trump administration. It's

great to have you here. So let's start with President Trump's decision to fire the chairman of the Joint Chiefs, General C.Q. Brown. Brown is the first in the job since 2007 to not serve a full term, and there's the added detail that Brown, a four-star general, is being replaced with a now retired three-star general, Dan Caine, whose military service does not include any of the key assignments that were identified in law as prerequisites for the job. He will need to get a waiver. So how do you interpret this pick?

McPherson: Well, it's not surprising that he fired General Brown. That was rumored in the media many times before the inauguration and then even afterwards.

Perhaps even a greater surprise was his firing the chief of Naval operations, Admiral Franchetti, who was the first female admiral that the Navy had as its chief of naval operations. It speaks of a profound concern that perhaps the president is putting in place individuals who he can be assured would be loyal to him, and not loyal to the Constitution or loyal to the rule of law. That's the greatest concern I think many people have.

Bennett: And there's also his decision to fire the military's top lawyers, those judge advocates general known as JAGs. You had a 25-year career and the Navy, also served as its top lawyer in uniform. First, help us understand what those lawyers do in providing independent legal advice to senior military leaders.

McPherson: It's profoundly disappointing to hear the secretary of defense describe the men and women of the services; Judge Advocate General's Corps, some of the attorneys that this country has, many of whom forwent, forgo lucrative civilian careers, to serve their country. They answer their country's call. They truly are embracing a lifestyle of service. And to hear the secretary of defense describe them in a term that's not only crude, but vulgar, is just intolerable and, quite frankly, shameless.

But it also evidences a lack of understanding of what a judge advocate on the staff of a warfare commander does, what their role is. Their role is advising that warfare commander as that commander puts together an operational plan. Their role is not one of a roadblock, but one that facilitates the successful completion of a mission within the bounds of the law. They are not the ones that, if you will, say, shoot, don't shoot. They're not the ones that promulgate the rules of engagement that guide our warriors, but they advise the commander, who is the one that makes those decisions.

Bennett: Secretary Hegseth has often spoke about restoring what he calls a warrior ethos to a military that he views as having become too soft and bureaucratic. So when he says that he views the JAGs as obstacles and removing them would ostensibly remove an obstacle, what are the practical implications of that?

McPherson: Well, there's a common denominator among the three judge advocate generals of the services that he removed. They were all selected, they were all nominated by President Biden and they were confirmed by the Senate in the Biden administration. So, clearly, the commonality is, they came into office during the Biden administration, and that's why the secretary wants — wanted to get rid of them, so he could put his own people in there. What's interesting is, he directed the service secretaries to nominate names for him.

The law requires that the service secretary convene a board, and that board consists of senior officers, line officers, who will review the records of the eligible officers, that is, captains and colonels, and make a recommendation to the service secretary of the next judge advocate general. The service secretary forwards that to the White House and it's the president's decision. So it's not going to be the secretary of defense's decision. It's going to be a decision based upon, again, a recommendation that comes from a board, something also that Secretary Hegseth in his time with the FOX News interview seemed not to understand.

Bennett: And yet a president has the right to assemble a team of military leaders as he chooses. Supporters of the president have been quick to point out that Truman ousted Douglas MacArthur, Obama ousted Stanley McChrystal. Do they have a point? Or do you see something missing in their justification of President Trump's actions?

McPherson: I see something missing. And what I see missing is, they didn't take issue with any decision that the officers made. They didn't — there was no misconduct involved. They simply dismissed them because they weren't, if you will, perceived as being loyal to the president.

My fear is that they're putting people in place when that fateful day arrives and the suggestions made, as it was, in the Oval Office, should we just shoot them in the legs, my fear is that there won't be a Secretary Esper or a General Milley who says, no, Mr. President, we can't. My fear is there will be officers in the room that say, sure, we will shoot them in the legs.

Bennett: Admiral McPherson, thanks again for joining us this evening. We appreciate it.

McPherson: Thank you.

| 20 |

A Suicide

Elisa Rae Shupe was the first person in the United States to obtain legal recognition of a non-binary gender. She was also a veteran, and once challenged the use of AI as a legitimate practice for those with disabilities in an effort to obtain an otherwise rejected copyright for her book by the US Copyright Office.

One of Trump's first executive orders was to eliminate all federal policies that are supportive of transgender people.

On 27 January, Elisa Rae jumped to her death from the roof of a VA hospital building in Syracuse, NY. She was wrapped in a transgender pride flag.

On 26 February, the Pentagon announced plans to remove transgender troops from the military, as was done under Trump's first term.

The Suicide Note

Fuck You America!

I don't want your hatred.

I don't want the military decorations and medals you awarded me.

I don't want your pension money for my distinguished military service and service-connected disabilities.

I don't want your health care to treat the mental illnesses you caused.

I don't want more psychiatric ward commitments to keep me alive in a nation that I despise.

I don't want to be buried in any of your state or national cemetery's for veterans and military retirees.

I don't want to be buried anywhere on American soil.

I don't want any military honors or ceremonies to mark my death.

I don't want my ashes to be stored on American soil.

I want my ashes or remains to be spread or buried in international waters.

I don't want your flag anywhere near my body, remains, or ashes.

I don't want any members of my family other than my spouse to be on the vessel that disposes of my ashes or remains.

My death is not a surrender.

My death as a member of the third gender and transgender population does not mean you won.

It solely marks the end of our association.

You are not the land of the free.

You are not a country getting made great again.

Too much demonstrated hatred throughout your existence extinguishes any claim to previous greatness.

You are a cesspool of zealots that worship a god that does not and has not ever existed

Enjoy your new royal family and third world dictator.

I refuse to participate any further.

Have that Nazi piece of shit Elon Musk and his DOGE henchmen deduct the savings from my $93,000 of federal pensions from your bankrupt coffers.

The white man decimated and massacred the indigenous populations of the third gender on the lands now called America. It was only fitting that a white person restored it.

You cannot erase non-binary and transgender people because you give birth to more of us each day.

| 21 |

Governors Ball

The 2025 White House Governors Ball was held on Saturday, 22 February. President Donald Trump and the First Lady were in attendance, and the U.S. Army Chorus performed "Do You Hear the People Sing?" from the musical Les Misérables. The particular lyrics and their cultural context, the French Revolution, was perceived by some as a veiled political message.

> Do you hear the people sing?
> Lost in the valley of the night
> It is the music of a people who are climbing to the light
> For the wretched of the earth
> There is a flame that never dies
> Even the darkest nights will end and the sun will rise
> They will live again in freedom in the garden of the lord
> They will walk behind the ploughshare
> They will put away the sword
> The chain will be broken and all men will have their reward!
> Will you join in our crusade?
> Who will be strong and stand with me?
> Somewhere beyond the barricade is there a world you long to see?
> Do you hear the people sing?
> Say, do you hear the distant drums?
> It is the future that they bring when tomorrow comes!

One Day More!

| 22 |

The Kennedy Center

The "Social Credo" of the John F. Kennedy Center for the Performing Arts begins with the statement

As the Nation's Cultural Center, the Kennedy Center's objective is to invite art into the lives of all Americans and ensure it represents the cultural diversity of America. Our mission is to fulfill inspiration for **all**. We do this by creating a welcoming and inclusive culture where everyone belongs and benefits, and the performing arts flourish.

This seems to be no longer true. President Trump ousted Chairman David M. Rubenstein and other members, appointing his own, and then announced he had been elected unanimously as the board's chair. Trump tweeted "We're gonna make sure it's good and it's not gonna be Woke ... NO MORE DRAG SHOWS, OR OTHER ANTI-AMERICAN PROPAGANDA – ONLY THE BEST".

Press Secretary Leavitt sent notice to the Wall Street Journal:

The Kennedy Center learned the hard way that if you go woke, you will go broke. President Trump and the members of his newly-appointed board are devoted to rebuilding the Kennedy Center into a thriving and highly respected institution where all Americans, and visitors from around the world, can enjoy the arts with respect to America's great history and traditions.

According to its website as of the writing of this book, Melania Trump, First Lady of the United States was made honorary chair, and the board, all appointed by President Trump, are listed below. The board's treasurer, Shonda Rhimes, resigned.

- Brian D. Ballard, lobbyist and founder of lobbying firm Ballard Partners
- Dana Blumberg, wife of New England Patriots owner Robert Kraft
- Pamela Bondi, attorney general
- Mary Helen Bowers, professional fitness coach
- Hannah F. Buchan, former hedge-fund manager and campaign fundraiser
- Robert A. Castellani, entrepreneur and philanthropist
- Elaine Chao, United States secretary of transportation (2017 to 2021), resigned after January 6th.
- Pamella Roland DeVos, fashion designer
- Patricia Duggan, Trump megadonor
- John Falconetti
- Emilia May Fanjul, wife of sugar magnate and Trump megadonor Pepe Fanjul
- Jennifer Fischer
- Lynette Friess

- Sergio Gorr, White House director of presidential personnel
- Pamela Gross, former White House adviser to the first lady
- Lee Greenwood, Nashville singer-songwriter
- Kate Adamson Haselwood
- Laura Ingraham, Fox News presenter
- Michele Kessler, wife of Howard Kessler, instrumental in developing affinity credit cards
- Dana Kraft (Blumberg), wife of billionaire owner and CEO of Kraft Group
- Mindy Levine, wife of New York Yankees president Randy Levine
- Lynda Lomangino, wife of Florida recycling and waste management mogul who co-founded the super-PAC Right for America dedicated to reelecting Trump
- Allison Lutnick, wife of commerce secretary nominee Howard Lutnick
- Douglas Manchester, businessman and philanthropist
- Catherine B. Reynolds, philanthropist, businesswoman, CEO of The Catherine B. Reynolds Foundation
- Denise Saul
- Dan Scavino, White House deputy chief of staff for national security
- Cheri Summerall, mother of Susie Wiles
- Usha Vance, lawyer, wife of Vice-President JD Vance
- Susie Wiles, White House chief of staff
- Andrea Wynn
- Paolo Zampolli, businessman, Ambassador (Permanent Mission of Dominica to the United Nations)

A long list of performers and productions have canceled their shows and events, including Grammy and Pulitzer Prize winner Rhiannon Giddens, and the production of "Hamilton".

On 13 February, actress Issa Rae announced on Instagram she is canceling "An Evening With Issa Rae", slated for March, writing

Unfortunately, due to what I believe to be an infringement on the values of an institution that has faithfully celebrated artists of all backgrounds through all mediums, I've decided to cancel my appearance at this venue.

Adam Weiner of the band Low Cut Connie canceled his appearance, stating

Upon learning that this institution that has run nonpartisan for 54 years is now chaired by President Trump himself and his regime, I decided I will not perform there," he wrote on social media, adding that friends and fans were going to be "directly negatively affected by this administration's policies and messaging.

Singer and songwriter Ben Folds, advisor to the National Symphony Orchestra, resigned.

Hamilton Statement

Political disagreement and debate are vital expressions of democracy. These basic concepts of freedom are at the very heart of Hamilton. However, some institutions are sacred and should be protected from politics. The Kennedy Center is one such institution.

The Kennedy Center was founded over 50 years ago with a sincere bipartisan spirit. Indeed, it was founded during the administration of President Dwight Eisenhower, named after President John F. Kennedy, and opened in 1971 under the administration of Richard M. Nixon. The Kennedy Center was meant to be for all Americans, a place where we could all come together in celebration of the arts. Politics have never affected the presentation of thousands of shows and the display of extraordinary visual arts.

However, in recent weeks we have sadly seen decades of Kennedy Center neutrality be destroyed. The recent purge by the Trump Administration of both professional staff and performing arts events at or originally produced by the Kennedy Center flies in the face of everything this national cultural center represents. This spirit of non-partisanship ended on February 7, 2025, with the firing of Kennedy Center President Deborah Rutter, the Chairman of the Board David Rubenstein, numerous other Kennedy Center board members, and the cancellation of important programming. These actions bring a new spirit of partisanship to the national treasure that is the Kennedy Center.

Given these recent actions, our show simply cannot, in good conscience, participate and be a part of this new culture that is being imposed on the Kennedy Center. Therefore, we have cancelled the third engagement of Hamilton at the Kennedy Center, originally scheduled for March 3-April 26, 2026.

Hamilton was proudly performed at the Kennedy Center in 2018 during the first Trump administration. We are not acting against his administration, but against the partisan policies of the Kennedy Center as a result of his recent takeover.

Our cancellation is also a business decision. Hamilton is a large and global production, and it would simply be financially and personally devastating to the hundreds of employees of Hamilton if the new leadership of the Kennedy Center suddenly cancelled or re-negotiated our engagement. The actions of the new Chairman of the Board in recent weeks demonstrate that contracts and previous agreements simply cannot be trusted. This is sad, because basic integrity and the rule of law have long been great American principles that help serve as a foundation for our Nation.

I have personally loved the Kennedy Center since touring it as a seventh grader in 1977 along with the Lincoln Memorial and the Jefferson Memorial. I watched the first Kennedy Center Honors in 1978.

Regardless of the political climate, I have always felt at home at The Kennedy Center, and I am grateful for every person who has spent the last 50 years making it a beacon of nonpartisanship and celebration. But we cannot presently support an institution that has been forced by external forces to betray its mission as a national cultural center that fosters the free expression of art in The United States of America.

Richard Grenell, President of the Center, responded:

Let's be clear on the facts. Seller and Lin Manuel first went to the New York Times before they came to the Kennedy Center with their announcement that they can't be in the same room with Republicans. This is a publicity stunt that will backfire. The Arts are for everyone - not just for the people who Lin likes and agrees with. The American people need to know that Lin Manuel is intolerant of people who don't agree with him politically. It's clear he and Sellers don't want Republicans going to their shows. Americans see you, Lin.

| 23 |

Message from Illinois

One of the most outstanding and defiant critics of the Trump administration is JB Pritzker, Governor of Illinois.

The following remarks were from a statement made 19 February and published as "Remarks as Prepared for Delivery". The bulk of it relates to state business, and so only portions that refers to federal and national issues is presented here.

State of the State and Budget Address

...

I believe strongly that we must continue our firm commitment to building up the rainy day fund, new funding for public schools, investing in economic growth and jobs and improving much needed services to working families and to the most vulnerable. These are things that we cannot compromise on, particularly when we face the uncertainty of the federal government's haphazard, ready fire, aim tactics toward everyday Americans. I know it's in fashion at the federal level right now to just indiscriminately slash school funding, healthcare coverage, support for farmers and veterans services. They say they're doing it to eliminate inefficiencies, but only an idiot would think that we should eliminate emergency response in a natural disaster, education and health care for disabled children, gang crime investigations, clean air and water programs, monitoring of nursing home abuse, nuclear reactor regulation and cancer research. Here in Illinois, ten years ago, we saw the consequences of a rampant ideological gutting of government. It genuinely harmed people. Our citizens hated it. Trust me, I won an entire election in part on just how much they hated it.

So while this budget makes sacrifices, it preserves Illinois' progress toward delivering what children and families need most, we ought to be focused on making life more affordable for everyday Illinoisans with the new tariffs that are already put in place by President Trump and the ones that he has proposed, the cost of everyday goods like tomatoes and beef and beer is likely to rise again. It's confounding that when this happens. It seems like large corporations just hike up prices to drive up profits, while everyday people get stuck with the bill. It's not right, and we ought to call out the federal government and the companies on it.

We can do something about it at the state level. Last year, we lowered taxes on parents when we enacted the child tax credit and permanently eliminated the state grocery tax together, saving Illinois ins more than half a billion dollars per year. This year, we're going to need to do even more to address high prices and counteract Trump's tariffs that will raise taxes on working families at the top of the list. We need to lower health care costs. One of the great ironies of our modern age is that breakthroughs in research are producing medications that can treat and even cure long standing chronic diseases, but the high cost of these drugs are making them unaffordable for people who need them the most. What's causing that well, patients, healthcare providers and independent pharmacists will all tell you that pharmacy benefit managers or PBM's are driving up prices.

...

Nursing, advanced manufacturing, early childhood education and beyond. I mean, with lower tuition rates and greater presence across the state, especially in rural areas, community colleges provide the flexibility and the affordability that students need. This is a consumer driven, student centered proposal that will help fill the needs of regional employers in high need sectors and create a pathway to stable quality jobs for more Illinoisans. This is my seventh state of the state address, and I've come before you to present a budget in good years and in bad in years of crisis and years of relative stability, there's a whole industry of back seat belly acres in this state and around the country who make a profession out of rhetorically tearing down Illinois and suggesting that if we would just enact one of their magic bean fixes, that we would never face another difficult budget year. But there's one thing that I've learned as governor. There are no magic bean fixes, and each year there's some difficulty that requires us to work hard to overcome it. This year, the surfacing difficulty is Donald Trump's and Elon Musk's plan to steal Illinois' tax dollars and deny our citizens the protection and the services that they need. I want to offer you a few examples. 20 million Americans, 700,000 of them here in Illinois will lose health care coverage if congressional Republicans are successful in their effort to cut the Affordable Care Act and rural hospitals across Illinois will be shuttered. The Trump administration cut off funding for food safety inspectors for nearly a month, impacting more than 70 meat and poultry facilities in Illinois. Without these inspectors, the supply chain collapses. Prices go through the roof, from farmers to truckers to meat packers to retailers, jobs will be lost. Meals on Wheels, programs which home deliver 12 million meals per year to 100,000 seniors and people with disabilities in Illinois are on the federal chopping block. This is real. The new administration and the Republican Congress and Elon Musk intend to take these programs away for all the Illinoisians watching at home. Let me be clear, this is going to affect your daily lives. Our state budget can't make up for the damage that is done to people across our state. If they succeed, there are people, some in my own party, who think that if you just give Donald Trump everything that he wants, he'll make an exception, and he'll spare you some of the harm. I'll ignore the moral abdication of that position for just a second to say almost none of these people have had the experience with the president that I do. I once swallowed my pride to offer him what he values most public praise on the Sunday news shows in return for ventilators and N-95 masks during the worst of the pandemic, we made a deal, and it turns out his promises were as broken as the BiPAP machines he sent us instead of ventilators going along to get along does not work. Just ask the Trump fearing red state governors.

You can boo all you want. Until your constituents lose these services, those Trump states, red state governors are dealing with the same cuts that we are and I won't be fooled twice. Last week, our federal courts returned a verdict, rightfully condemning the once unchecked power of a former speaker of this house. Now if you applauded that decision like I did, then I expect you to defend and applaud those same federal courts as they checked this president in his quest for unrestrained power.

I've been reflecting these last four weeks on two important parts of my life, my work, helping to build the Illinois Holocaust Museum, and the two times that I've had the privilege of reciting the oath of office for Illinois Governor. As some of you know, Skokie, Illinois once had one of the largest populations of Holocaust survivors anywhere in the world. In 1978, Nazis decided that they wanted to march there. The leaders of that march knew that the images of swastika clad young men goose stepping down a peaceful suburban street would terrorize the local Jewish population, so many of whom had never recovered from their time in German concentration camps. The prospect of that march sparked a legal fight that went all the way to the Supreme Court. It was a Jewish lawyer from the ACLU who argued the case for the Nazis, contending that even the most hateful of speech was protected under the First Amendment. As an American and as a Jew, I find it difficult to resolve my feelings around that Supreme Court case, but I am grateful that the prospect of Nazis marching in their streets spurred the survivors and other Skokie residents to act. They joined together to form the Holocaust Memorial Foundation and build the first Illinois Holocaust Museum in a storefront in 1981- a small but important forerunner, the one I helped to build 30 years later. Here, I do not invoke the specter of Nazis lightly, but I know the history intimately, and have spent more time than probably anyone in this room with people who survived the Holocaust. Here's what I've learned. The root that tears apart your house's foundation begins as a seed, a seed of distrust and hate and blame. The seed that grew into a dictatorship in Europe a lifetime ago didn't arrive overnight. It started with everyday Germans mad about inflation and looking for someone to blame. I'm watching with a foreboding dread what is happening in our country right now, a president who watches a plane go down in the Potomac and suggests without facts or findings, that a diversity hire is responsible for the crash, or the Missouri Attorney General, who just sued Starbucks, arguing that consumers pay higher prices for their coffee because the baristas are too female and non-white. The authoritarian playbook is laid bare here they point to a group of people who don't look like you and tell you to blame them for your problems. I just have one question, what comes next after we've discriminated against, deported or disparaged all the immigrants and the gay and lesbian and transgender people, the developmentally disabled, the women and the minorities, once we've ostracized our neighbors and betrayed our friends after that, when the problems we started with are still there staring us in the face, what comes next? All the atrocities of human history lurk in the answer to that question, and if we don't want to repeat history, then for God's sake, in this moment, we better be strong enough to learn from it.

I swore the following oath on Abraham Lincoln's Bible. I do solemnly swear That I will support the Constitution of the United States and the Constitution of the State of Illinois, and that I will faithfully discharge the duties of the office of Governor according to the best of my ability. My oath is to the Constitution of our state and of our country. We don't have kings in America, and I don't intend to bend the knee.

I'm not speaking up in service to my ambitions, but in deference to my obligations. If you think I'm overreacting and sounding the alarm too soon, consider this, it took the Nazis one month, three weeks, two days, eight hours and 40 minutes to dismantle a constitutional republic. And all I'm saying is that when the five-alarm fire starts to burn, every good person better be ready to man a post with a bucket of water. Or if you want to stop it from raging out of control, those Illinois Nazis did end up holding their march in 1978 just not in Skokie. After all the blowback from the case, they decided to march in Chicago. Instead, only 20 of them showed up, but 2,000 people came to counter protest. The Chicago Tribune reported that day that the rally sputtered to an unspectacular end after 10 minutes, it was Illinoisians who smothered those embers before they could burn into a flame. Tyranny requires your fear and your silence and your compliance. Democracy requires your courage. So gather your justice and humanity Illinois, and do not let the tragic spirit of despair overcome us when our country needs us the most. Thank you.

| 24 |

Regency and the Judiciary

I think what the American people need to understand that hasn't been covered well by mass media is that our government is in the process of experiencing a hostile takeover. And it's not just by business elites in general but by a faction of business elites who have a very specific political program, that is, as you said, years in the making. It didn't come out of Musk's head. It didn't come out of nowhere, but it has been developed over decades and it calls itself the New Monarchy, the New Monarchism. And neo-reactionist belief systems militate against democracy. What they want is to replace democracy as we've known it with corporate monarchy in which CEOs are our rulers. And that's really what we saw at the inauguration -- that front Row in which you pointed out those corporate CEOs were placed in front of cabinet members, that is to signify this new nobility that's going to rule over us. -- Professor Brooke Harrington, 25 February

At the heart of these 40 days, we find the question of a President's power. It is outlined in the Constitution, but over the last 240 years, the prerogatives and limitations of the President and the Executive Branch, now a massive bureaucracy, have been challenged, decided upon, and reinterpreted again and again. Both sides fear the disagreement between presidential actions and the judiciary's restraint may cause a constitutional crisis. What Americans don't agree on is who will be responsible — the President or the courts.

Political scientists aren't quiet on this. The Bright Line Watch February 2025 survey, titled "Accelerated transgressions in the second Trump presidency", lays out public perception in detail. Brendan Nyhan of Dartmouth has much to say, with statements such as "The president is openly violating the law and Constitution on a daily basis" and "Trump is using the classic elected authoritarian playbook", even comparing Trump's actions to those of Hungary's Viktor Orban pursuing autocracy. Nyhan is one of over 800 political scientists that signed a letter warning that Trump is threatening both the rule of law and constitutional checks and balances.

Meanwhile, Representative Claudia Tenney proposed making Trump's birthday a national holiday, coinciding with Flag Day, being June 14th. Congressman Joe Wilson proposed a $250 bill with Trump's image on it, and the BlueSky group Republican Voters Against Trump called out "It's a cult" while others called such things "bootlicking". At present, there are only a handful of public spaces named after him:

- Donald J. Trump State Park, in New York state, located on land donated by Trump in 2006
- Trump Drive in Kalispell, Montana
- President Donald J. Trump Highway, a section of U.S. Route 287 in Oklahoma
- The Donald J. Trump Justice Complex in Lyon County, Nevada
- President Donald J. Trump Avenue, in Hialeah, Florida, renamed from Palm Avenue

A square, station, and (illegal) settlement are being planned in Israel with his name. The last of these, "Trump Heights", is named in honor of him recognizing (against international law) the Golan Heights as part of Israel.

On 25 February, Trump showed off new hats, saying "Trump Was Right About Everything", a slogan recently touted by MAGA politicians and pundits. This expression was attacked by critics due to its similarity with authoritarian slogans, particularity Mussolini's "Il Duce ha sempre ragione" (The Leader is always right).

Judicial Actions

Over 80 court cases have challenged and contested Trump's Orders and actions. Here is a small sample:

- DC Judge Loren AliKhan issued a preliminary injunction indefinitely blocking the freezing of federal grants and loans.
- DC Judge Amir Ali ordered the Trump administration to pay foreign aid-related money owed to government contractors and nonprofit groups as part of the legal battle over USAID and State Department freezes.
- Judge Jamal Whitehead in Seattle issued a preliminary injunction on halting the suspending of refugee admissions and funding, saying that Trump's actions "amount to an effective nullification of congressional will in establishing the nation's refugee admissions program", and "The president has substantial discretion ... to suspend refugee admissions. But that authority is not limitless".

On the other side of the coin, Trump is suing Chicago and the State of Illinois for sanctuary city practices, including not sharing information with federal agencies. Trump also placed the State of Maine under investigation after Governor Janet Mills told Trump, "See you in court", regarding noncompliance of his Order regarding transgender athletes.

The sum of all these Executive Orders, actions, responses, and threats had led many to the conclusion that Trump is establishing, or even has already established a rule that is no longer consistent with our Constitutional Republic.

Statement from Governor Kathy Hochul on Congestion Pricing

{On 19 February, the White House tweeted "CONGESTION PRICING IS DEAD. Manhattan, and all of New York, is SAVED. LONG LIVE THE KING! –President Donald J. Trump" with a mock-up of TIME Magazine featuring the president with a crown. New York Governor Kathy Hochul responded that day.}

Public transit is the lifeblood of New York City and critical to our economic future — as a New York, like President Trump, knows very well.

Since this first-in-the-nation program took effect last month, congestion has dropped dramatically and commuters are getting to work faster than ever. Broadway shows are selling out and foot traffic to local businesses is spiking. School buses are getting kids to class on time, and yellow cab trips increased by 10 percent. Transit ridership is up, drivers are having a better experience, and support for this program is growing every day.

We are in a nation of laws, not ruled by a king. The MTA has initiated legal proceedings in the Southern District of New York to preserve this critical program. We'll see you in court.

Ensuring Accountability for All Agencies

{Executive Order, 18 February}

By the authority vested in me as President by the Constitution and the laws of the United States of America, it is hereby ordered:

Section 1. Policy and Purpose. The Constitution vests all executive power in the President and charges him with faithfully executing the laws. Since it would be impossible for the President to single-handedly perform all the executive business of the Federal Government, the Constitution also provides for subordinate officers to assist the President in his executive duties. In the exercise of their often-considerable authority, these executive branch officials remain subject to the President's ongoing supervision and control. The President in turn is regularly elected by and accountable to the American people. This is one of the structural safeguards, along with the separation of powers between the executive and legislative branches, regular elections for the Congress, and an independent judiciary whose judges are appointed by the President by and with the advice and consent of the Senate, by which the Framers created a Government accountable to the American people.

However, previous administrations have allowed so-called "independent regulatory agencies" to operate with minimal Presidential supervision. These regulatory agencies currently exercise substantial executive authority without sufficient accountability to the President, and through him, to the American people. Moreover, these regulatory agencies have been permitted to promulgate significant regulations without review by the President.

These practices undermine such regulatory agencies' accountability to the American people and prevent a unified and coherent execution of Federal law. For the Federal Government to be truly accountable to the American people, officials who wield vast executive power must be supervised and controlled by the people's elected President.

Therefore, in order to improve the administration of the executive branch and to increase regulatory officials' accountability to the American people, it shall be the policy of the executive branch to ensure Presidential supervision and control of the entire executive branch. Moreover, all executive departments and agencies, including so-called independent agencies, shall submit for review all proposed and final significant regulatory actions to the Office of Information and Regulatory Affairs (OIRA) within the Executive Office of the President before publication in the *Federal Register*.

Sec. 2. Definitions. For the purposes of this order:

(a) The term "employees" shall have the meaning given that term in section 2105 of title 5, United States Code.

(b) The term "independent regulatory agency" shall have the meaning given that term in section 3502(5) of title 44, United States Code. This order shall not apply to the Board of Governors of the Federal Reserve System or to the Federal Open Market Committee in its conduct of monetary policy. This order shall apply to the Board of Governors of the Federal Reserve System only in connection with its conduct and authorities directly related to its supervision and regulation of financial institutions.

(c) The term "independent regulatory agency chairman" shall mean, with regard to a multi-member independent regulatory agency, the chairman of such agency, and shall mean, with regard to a single-headed independent regulatory agency, such agency's chairman, director, or other presiding officer.

(d) The term "head" of an independent regulatory agency shall mean those appointed to supervise independent regulatory agencies and in whom the agencies' authorities are generally vested, encompassing the chairman, director, or other presiding officer, and, as applicable, other members, commissioners, or similar such officials with responsibility for supervising such agencies.

Sec. 3. OIRA Review of Agency Regulations. (a) Section 3(b) of Executive Order 12866 of September 30, 1993 ("Regulatory Planning and Review"), as amended, is hereby amended to read as follows:

"(b) "Agency," unless otherwise indicated, means any authority of the United States that is an "agency" under 44 U.S.C. 3502(1), and shall also include the Federal Election Commission. This order shall not apply to the Board of Governors of the Federal Reserve System or to the Federal Open Market Committee in its conduct of monetary policy. This order shall apply to the Board of Governors of the Federal Reserve System only in connection with its conduct and authorities directly related to its supervision and regulation of financial institutions.".

(b) The Director of the Office of Management and Budget (OMB) shall provide guidance on implementation of this order to the heads of executive departments and agencies newly submitting regulatory actions under section 3(b) of Executive Order 12866. Agency submissions by independent regulatory agencies under such section shall commence within the earlier of 60 days from the date of this order, or completion of such implementation guidance.

Sec. 4. Performance Standards and Management Objectives. The Director of OMB shall establish performance standards and management objectives for independent agency heads, as appropriate and consistent with applicable law, and report periodically to the President on their performance and efficiency in attaining such standards and objectives.

Sec. 5. Apportionments for Independent Regulatory Agencies. The Director of OMB shall, on an ongoing basis:

(a) review independent regulatory agencies' obligations for consistency with the President's policies and priorities; and

(b) consult with independent regulatory agency chairmen and adjust such agencies' apportionments by activity, function, project, or object, as necessary and appropriate, to advance the President's policies and priorities. Such adjustments to apportionments may prohibit independent regulatory agencies from expending appropriations on particular activities, functions, projects, or objects, so long as such restrictions are consistent with law.

Sec. 6. Additional Consultation with the Executive Office of the President. (a) Subject to subsection (b), independent regulatory agency chairmen shall regularly consult with and coordinate policies and priorities with the directors of OMB, the White House Domestic Policy Council, and the White House National Economic Council.

(b) The heads of independent regulatory agencies shall establish a position of White House Liaison in their respective agencies. Such position shall be in grade 15 of the General Schedule and shall be placed in Schedule C of the excepted service.

(c) Independent regulatory agency chairmen shall submit agency strategic plans developed pursuant to the Government Performance and Results Act of 1993 to the Director of OMB for clearance prior to finalization.

Sec. 7. Rules of Conduct Guiding Federal Employees' Interpretation of the Law. The President and the Attorney General, subject to the President's supervision and control, shall provide authoritative interpretations of law for the executive branch. The President and the Attorney General's opinions on questions of law are controlling on all employees in the conduct of their official duties. No employee of the executive branch acting in their official capacity may advance an interpretation of the law as the position of the United States that contravenes the President or the Attorney General's opinion on a matter of law, including but not limited to the issuance of regulations, guidance, and positions advanced in litigation, unless authorized to do so by the President or in writing by the Attorney General.

Sec. 8. General Provisions. (a) If any provision of this order, or the application of any provision to any person or circumstance, is held to be invalid, the remainder of this order and the application of its provisions to any other persons or circumstances shall not be affected thereby.

(b) Nothing in this order shall be construed to impair or otherwise affect:

(i)   the authority granted by law to an executive department, agency, or the head thereof; or

(ii) the functions of the Director of the Office of Management and Budget relating to budgetary, administrative, or legislative proposals.

(c) This order shall be implemented consistent with applicable law and subject to the availability of appropriations.

(d) This order is not intended to, and does not, create any right or benefit, substantive or procedural, enforceable at law or in equity by any party against the United States, its departments, agencies, or entities, its officers, employees, or agents, or any other person.

Accelerated transgressions in the second Trump presidency

{Excerpts from the Bright Line Watch February 2025 survey. The full text is available on BrightLineWatch.Org, and includes many other analyses and forecasts of interest.}

Assessments of democratic performance

- Assessments of the overall performance of American democracy on a 0–100 scale have fallen to the lowest levels observed since we began tracking this measure in 2017: 53 among the public and 55 among experts.
- Out of 30 principles of democratic performance, the percentage of experts who say the US mostly or fully meets the standard plummeted by more than 30 percentage points on six principles and declined by 10–20 points on eleven others.
- Republican ratings of U.S. democracy increased slightly (59 on our 0–100 scale), but even Trump's co-partisans perceive significant declines since November 2024 in the extent to which legal investigations of public officials are free from political influence, campaign donations influence public policy, and the patriotism of political adversaries is respected.

Threats to democracy

- Among Republicans, a majority (55%) of those whose allegiance is primarily to Trump rather than to the GOP say "Having a strong leader who does not have to bother with Congress" is a good way of governing the country.

- Political science experts regard the pardoning of January 6 offenders and firings of executive branch officials as the gravest threats to American democracy in the first weeks of the Trump administration, followed closely by the roles and influence of Elon Musk and his Department of Government Efficiency.

- Experts rated Kash Patel being confirmed as FBI director and the White House revoking media credentials for journalists as events that were highly likely to occur and threatening to democracy — with 63% assessing the threat as extraordinary.

- Large majorities of Republicans approve of Trump administration actions that are rated by experts as threatening to democracy, whereas even larger majorities of Democrats disapprove.

Forecasts of future threats to democracy

- The set of events that experts identified as most likely to occur which pose the greatest threat to democracy include the confirmation of Patel as FBI director (now official) and the Trump administration revoking the media credentials of journalists covering the White House.

- After adjusting for a bias toward pessimism, forecasts of negative future events for democracy correspond closely between political science experts and forecasters on the Metaculus prediction platform.

Support for aggression and violence

- Democrats are more supportive of aggressive action – including violence – against corporate CEOs in the name of economic justice than are Republicans. They are also more supportive of aggressive action against CEOs than against Republicans.

- Younger Democrats are more willing than older Democrats to endorse violence against CEOs or in the name of economic justice.
- Members of both parties are similarly supportive of aggressive action against members or leaders of the other party; support for property crimes or threats and harassment online is higher than support for physical violence.

Threats to democracy

{The following recent events, including Biden's pardons, are listed in the order experts determined threat levels, starting with the highest estimation. The top half had more than half the respondents consider the act an "extraordinary or serious threat", 95% for the January 6th pardons. The last four were surveyed to have been considered more beneficial than detrimental.}

- Donald Trump pardons nearly all individuals charged in connection with the Jan. 6 Capitol attack, including violent offenders.
- Donald Trump fires at least twelve inspectors general without the 30-day notice to Congress required by the Inspector General Act.
- The Trump administration fires Department of Justice officials who worked on criminal investigations of Trump's actions as president.
- Donald Trump and Secretary of State Marco Rubio moving to shut down the US Agency for International Development (USAID).
- Elon Musk serves as a close adviser to President Trump and the Department of Government Efficiency.

- Tech CEOs donate millions to Trump inauguration and take actions intended to curry favor with the new administration.
- DOGE employees obtain access to federal personnel and payment systems.
- Donald Trump issues an executive order seeking to deny citizenship to people born in the U.S. whose parents are not lawful permanent residents.
- Donald Trump dismissing members of the Equal Employment Opportunity Commission and National Labor Relations Board before the expiration of their terms.
- The White House budget office orders a pause to all grants and loans disbursed by the federal government.
- The Trump administration withdraws security protections for high-profile figures, such as Dr. Anthony Fauci, Gen. Mark Milley, and John Bolton, who have publicly clashed with Trump and face credible threats to their safety.
- The Senate confirms Pete Hegseth as Trump's defense secretary.
- Donald Trump launches a cryptocurrency memecoin that is initially valued at billions of dollars.
- Meta replaces its third-party fact-checking program with a "Community Notes" system in the United States.
- Donald Trump orders the construction of a facility for holding as many as 30,000 migrants at the naval base in Guantanamo Bay, Cuba.
- Meta relaxes its content moderation guidelines in the United States.
- Donald Trump declares a national emergency at the U.S.-Mexico border, citing threats from cartels, criminal gangs, and other illicit activities.
- Joe Biden grants a "full and unconditional" pardon of his son Hunter Biden, absolving him of existing federal charges and shielding him from future prosecution for federal crimes.

- Donald Trump revokes Joe Biden's executive order on addressing risks from artificial intelligence (AI).
- Joe Biden grants a preemptive pardon to five members of his family besides Hunter Biden, shielding them from future prosecution for federal crimes.
- Donald Trump delays enforcement of the so-called TikTok ban after taking office.
- Donald Trump seeks to use the Alien Enemies Act to deport foreign gang members.
- Joe Biden grants a preemptive pardon to Dr. Anthony Fauci, retired Gen. Mark Milley, and members of the House of Representatives committee that investigated the Jan. 6, 2021 attack on the Capitol, shielding them from future prosecution for federal crimes.
- Joe Biden states that the Equal Rights Amendment to the U.S. Constitution should be considered legally part of the Constitution.
- Ex-US Senator Bob Menendez (Democrat — New Jersey) sentenced to 11 years in federal prison for accepting bribes from foreign governments

Sotomayor Interview

{On 11 February 2025, Knight Foundation CEO Maribel Pérez Wadsworth interviewed U.S. Supreme Court Justice Sonia Sotomayor in front of students at the Padrón Campus of Dade College in Miami. A full transcript is not available at this time, but the following excepts have been reported.}

We adults have messed up the world for you. If you're relying on the adults to fix it, it ain't gonna happen.

Laws are made by whom? By people. So who changes laws? People. They don't get changed by being a bystander in life and letting things you don't like roll over you.

People who you disagree with are not bad people, they have different ideas.

Good people do bad things. Good colleagues sometimes have silly thoughts, but it doesn't make them bad or silly.

Before you make choices about the direction anything should be going in this country, actually study it, and don't trust that any one news source is giving you the whole picture.

Court decisions stand whether one particular person chooses to abide by them or not ... It doesn't change the foundation that it's still a court order that someone will respect at some point.

We must be cognizant that every time we upset precedent, we upset people's expectations and the stability of law ... It rocks the boat in a way that makes people uneasy about whether they're protected or not protected by the law.

We're gonna lose our democracy [without information literacy].

| 25 |

Resignations

There have been many resignations in anticipation of the new administration, and others in the course of events. Those who resigned or chose to retire since inauguration include:

- David Lebryk, the highest-ranking Treasury Department career official, over Musk's access to sensitive information
- Jim Jones, the director of the Food and Drug Administration's food division, over "indiscriminate cuts"
- Michelle King, the top official at the Social Security Administration, over DOGE access to sensitive information
- Steven Reilly, a lead engineer at the Technology Transformation Services arm of the General Services Administration, over DOGE access to sensitive information
- Seven federal prosecutors, over acting Deputy Attorney General Emil Bove ordereing them to drop criminal corruption charges against New York City Mayor Eric Adams (including Danielle Sassoon, see below)
- Bradley Weinsheimer, a senior ethics official in the Justice Deaprtment, over being reassigned to working on Sanctuary Cities
- Denise Cheung, the head of the criminal division in the U.S. Attorney's Office in Washington, D.C., over being directed to investigate Biden without cause or evidence

- Over 20 DOGE civil service employees, over being asked to "dismantle critical public services" in violation of their Constitutional oath

Mitch McConnell, Senator

{It is notable here that although he voted to acquit the impeachment for inciting insurrection, he publicly stated Trump was "practically and morally responsible".}

I've never liked calling too much attention to today's date, February 20th. But I figured my birthday would be as good a day as any to share with our colleagues a decision I made last year about how I'll approach the 119th Congress.

During my time in the Senate, I've only really answered to two constituencies — the Republican conference and the people of Kentucky.

Over the years, that first group trusted me to coordinate campaigns, to count votes, to steer committees, to take the majority, and on nine occasions, to lead our conference. Serving as Republican Leader was a rare — and, yes, rather specific — childhood dream. And just about a year ago, I thanked my colleagues for their confidence, which allowed me to fulfill it. To the distinguished members of this body I've had the privilege to lead, I remain deeply grateful.

Today, however, it's appropriate for me to speak about an even deeper allegiance and an even longer-standing gratitude. Seven times, my fellow Kentuckians have sent me to the Senate. Every day in between I've been humbled by the trust they've placed in me to do their business here. Representing our Commonwealth has been the honor of a lifetime.

I will not seek this honor an eighth time. My current term in the Senate will be my last.

I've been a student of history my entire life. I can't remember the last time I didn't have a stack of biographies or political memoirs on my nightstand. And I know well how tempting it can be to read history with a sense of determinism: Assuming that, somehow, notorious failures were inevitable ... that crowning triumphs were predestined. And in either case, that lives and careers followed orderly paths. This, of course, isn't how things work. And I've never had to look further than my own life to recognize it.

I've never lost sight of the fact that, without my mother's devoted care, a childhood encounter with polio could have turned out a lot worse. That, unless my father had taken a job in the Bluegrass State, my interest in politics might have run its course somewhere else entirely. That, if it weren't for an eleventh-hour, outside-the-box idea on the campaign trail, my Senate career might've been over before it began. Or that, if not for the people of Kentucky time and again agreeing that leadership delivers and electing to send me back here, it would have been someone else from somewhere else taking that seat at the table where I've had the chance to work ... and strategize and fight and win.

I grew up reading about the greatness of Henry Clay. But there were times when the prospect of etching my name into his desk in this chamber felt like more of a long-shot than making it in the Major Leagues.

I got a front-row seat to the greatness of Senator John Sherman Cooper of Kentucky as a summer intern in his office. But at so many moments in my early career, the idea of following in his footsteps here felt more distant than the moon.

So the only appropriate thing to take away today, apart from a healthy dose of pride, is my immense gratitude — for the opportunity to take part in the consequential business of the Senate and the nation.

Gratitude to the people I represent: Kentucky's families and farmers and miners and servicemembers and small business owners. Gratitude to loyal friends, dedicated volunteers, and talented staff who have helped me serve them better. Gratitude to this institution that has repaid my devotion so generously over the years, and to so many colleagues who have become dear friends.

Gratitude to my family for their support and particularly to my ultimate teammate and confidante for the past 32 years: Elaine's leadership and wise counsel, in their own right, have made her the most seasoned Cabinet official in modern history. On top of all that, her devotion to me — and to Kentucky — is much more than I deserve.

When I arrived in this chamber, I wasn't coming with a Governor's statewide executive experience or a House member's appreciation for Washington dynamics. I knew my hometown of Louisville, and I had spent the previous few years working hard to learn what mattered to folks across the rest of the Commonwealth. And yet, within weeks of swearing the oath, I was here on this floor talking with colleagues from other far-flung corners of the country, discussing solutions to a farm income crisis and infrastructure challenges that affected our different states in similar ways.

I learned quickly that delivering for Kentucky meant finding the ways the Commonwealth's challenges were tied to national debates: Seeing to it that major agriculture legislation remembered Kentucky farmers, including when they needed extraordinary assistance, like the tobacco buyout ... making sure that nationwide steps on transportation infrastructure included resources for modernizing the Brent Spence Bridge, which supports billions of dollars in economic activity in Kentucky and the surrounding region every day ... and, with the trust of the local community, finishing a task first assigned by President Reagan: the safe destruction of America's legacy chemical weapons at Blue Grass Army Depot. Efforts like these have spanned the length of my Senate career. And I've been humbled by each and every opportunity to help Kentucky punch above its weight.

Of course, the Senate has to grapple with foundational questions that reach even more broadly across American life...and even further into posterity. We're trusted, on behalf of the American people, to participate in the appointment of the federal judiciary ... to be the final check on the assembly of power in courts, beyond the reach of representative politics ... and to ensure that the men and women who preside over them profess authentic devotion to the rule of law above all else.

When members of this body ignore, discount, or pervert this fundamental duty, they do so not just at the peril of the Senate, but the entire nation. The weight of our power to advise and consent has never been lost on me. And I've been honored to perform my role in confirming judges who understand theirs.

On this floor, there is no place to hide from the obligations of Article One, the Senate's unique relationship with Article Three or our role in equipping the powers of Article Two.

Here, every debate over agriculture or infrastructure or education or taxes is downstream of the obligations of national security. Every question of policy here at home is contingent on our duty to provide for the common defense.

One of the first times I spoke at length on this floor as a freshman, I was compelled to join the debate over strengthening the deterrence of America's nuclear triad. Whether to expand the U.S. military's hard-target nuclear capability was an interesting question to pose to someone whose most recent job had been running a county government. But there, of course, was the founders' brilliance at work: The hopes and dreams of every American are tied up in our ability to protect and defend the nation and its interests. Every family traveling abroad, and every worker and small business owner whose livelihood depends on foreign trade — they depend in turn on the credibility of America's commitments to friends and the strength of her threats to enemies.

In turn, the safety and success of the men and women who volunteer to serve this great nation in uniform depend on the work we do here to ensure that enemies think twice before challenging them and never face a fair fight.

Thanks to Ronald Reagan's determination, the work of strengthening American hard power was well underway when I arrived in the

Senate. But since then, we've allowed that power to atrophy. And today, a dangerous world threatens to outpace the work of rebuilding it.

So, lest any of our colleagues still doubt my intentions for the remainder of my term: I have some unfinished business to attend to.

In our work, most of us in this body develop an appreciation for the Senate itself – its written rules, its collegial norms, even its pace of play. And yet so often, I've watched colleagues depart, venting their frustration at the confines of the institution or mourning what they perceive to be the decline of its norms.

Regardless of the political storms that may wash over this chamber during the time I have remaining, I assure our colleagues that I will depart with great hope for the endurance of the Senate as an institution.

There are any number of reasons for pessimism. But the strength of the Senate is not one of them. This chamber is still the haven where the political minority can require a debate. It is still the crucible in which jurists are tested for their fidelity to upholding the Constitution and laws as they were written. The Senate is still equipped for work of great consequence, and, to the disappointment of my critics, I'm still here on the job.

Danielle Sassoon

February 12, 2025

BY EMAIL
The Honorable Pamela Jo Bondi
Attorney General of the United States
U.S. Department of Justice
950 Pennsylvania Avenue NW
Washington, D.C. 20530
Re:United States v. Eric Adams, 24 Cr. 556 (DEH)

Dear Attorney General Bondi:

On February 10, 2025, I received a memorandum from acting Deputy Attorney General Emil Bove, directing me to dismiss the indictment against Mayor Eric Adams without prejudice, subject to certain conditions, which would require leave of court. I do not repeat here the evidence against Adams that proves beyond a reasonable doubt that he committed federal crimes; Mr. Bove rightly has never called into question that the case team conducted this investigation with integrity and that the charges against Adams are serious and supported by fact and law. Mr. Bove's memo, however, which directs me to dismiss an indictment returned by a duly constituted grand jury for reasons having nothing to do with the strength of the case, raises serious concerns that render the contemplated dismissal inconsistent with my ability and duty to prosecute federal crimes without fear or favor and to advance good-faith arguments before the courts.

When I took my oath of office three weeks ago, I vowed to well and faithfully discharge the duties of the office on which I was about to enter. In carrying out that responsibility, I am guided by, among other things, the Principles of Federal Prosecution set forth in the Justice Manual and your recent memoranda instructing attorneys for the Department of Justice to make only good-faith arguments and not to use the criminal enforcement authority of the United States to achieve political objectives or other improper aims. I am also guided by the values that have defined my over ten years of public service. You and I have yet to meet, let alone discuss this case. But as you may know, I clerked for the Honorable J. Harvie Wilkinson III on the U.S. Court of Appeals for the Fourth Circuit, and for Justice Antonin Scalia on the U.S. Supreme Court. Both men instilled in me a sense of duty to contribute to the public good and uphold the rule of law, and a commitment to reasoned and thorough analysis. I have always considered it my obligation to pursue justice impartially, without favor to the wealthy or those who occupy important public office, or harsher treatment for the less powerful.

I therefore deem it necessary to the faithful discharge of my duties to raise the concerns expressed in this letter with you and to request an opportunity to meet to discuss them further. I cannot fulfill my obligations, effectively lead my office in carrying out the Department's priorities, or credibly represent the Government before the courts, if I seek to dismiss the Adams case on this record.

A. The Government Does Not Have a Valid Basis To Seek Dismissal

Mr. Bove's memorandum identifies two grounds for the contemplated dismissal. I cannot advance either argument in good faith. As you know, the Government "may, with leave of court, dismiss an indictment" under Federal Rule of Criminal Procedure 48(a). "The principal object of the 'leave of court' requirement is apparently to protect a defendant against prosecutorial harassment, e.g., charging, dismissing, and recharging, when the Government moves to dismiss an indictment over the defendant's objection." Rinaldi v. United States, 434 U.S. 22, 30 n.15 (1977). "But the Rule has also been held to permit the court to deny a Government dismissal motion to which the defendant has consented if the motion is prompted by considerations clearly contrary to the public interest." Id., see also JM § 9-2.050 (reflecting Department's position that a "court may decline leave to dismiss if the manifest public interest requires it"). The reasons advanced by Mr. Bove for dismissing the indictment are not ones I can in good faith defend as in the public interest and as consistent with the principles of impartiality and fairness that guide my decision making.

First, Mr. Bove proposes dismissing the charges against Adams in return for his assistance in enforcing the federal immigration laws, analogizing to the prisoner exchange in which the United States freed notorious Russian arms dealer Victor Bout in return for an American prisoner in Russia. Such an exchange with Adams violates commonsense beliefs in the equal administration of justice, the Justice Manual, and the Rules of Professional Conduct. The "commitment to the rule of law is nowhere more profoundly manifest" than in criminal justice. Cheney v. United States Dist. Ct., 542 U.S. 367, 384 (2004) (alterations and citation omitted). Impartial enforcement of the law is the bedrock of federal prosecutions. See Robert H. Jackson, The Federal Prosecutor, 24 J. Am. Jud. Soc'y 18 (1940). As the Justice Manual has long recognized, "the rule of law depends upon the evenhanded administration of justice. The legal judgments of the Department of Justice must be impartial and insulated from political influence." JM § 1-8.100. But Adams has argued in substance—and Mr. Bove appears prepared to concede—that Adams should receive leniency for federal crimes solely because he occupies an important public position and can use that position to assist in the Administration's policy priorities.

Federal prosecutors may not consider a potential defendant's "political associations, activities, or beliefs." Id. § 9-27.260; see also Wayte v. United States, 470 U.S. 598, 608 (1985) (politically motivated prosecutions violate the Constitution). If a criminal prosecution cannot be used to punish political activity, it likewise cannot be used to induce or coerce such activity. Threatening criminal prosecution even to gain an advantage in civil litigation is considered misconduct for an attorney. See, e.g., D.C. Bar Ethics Opinion 339; ABA Criminal Justice Standard 3-1.6 ("A prosecutor should not use other improper considerations, such as partisan or political or personal considerations, in exercising prosecutorial discretion."). In your words, "the Department of Justice will not tolerate abuses of the criminal justice process, coercive behavior, or other forms of misconduct." Dismissal of the indictment for no other reason than to influence Adams's mayoral decision-making would be all three. The memo suggests that the issue is merely removing an obstacle to Adams's ability to assist with federal immigration enforcement, but that does not bear scrutiny. It does not grapple with the differential treatment Adams would receive compared to other elected officials, much less other criminal defendants. And it is unclear why Adams would be better able to aid in immigration enforcement when the threat of future conviction is due to the possibility of reinstatement of the indictment followed by conviction at trial, rather than merely the possibility of conviction at trial. On this point, the possibility of trial before or after the election cannot be relevant, because Adams has selected the timing of his trial.

Rather than be rewarded, Adams's advocacy should be called out for what it is: an improper offer of immigration enforcement assistance in exchange for a dismissal of his case. Although Mr. Bove disclaimed any intention to exchange leniency in this case for Adams's assistance in enforcing federal law,[1] that is the nature of the bargain laid bare in Mr. Bove's memo. That is especially so given Mr. Bove's comparison to the Bout prisoner exchange, which was quite expressly a quid pro quo, but one carried out by the White House, and not the prosecutors in charge of Bout's case.

The comparison to the Bout exchange is particularly alarming. That prisoner swap was an exchange of official acts between separate sovereigns (the United States and Russia), neither of which had any claim that the other should obey its laws. By contrast, Adams is an American citizen, and a local elected official, who is seeking a personal benefit—immunity from federal laws to which he is undoubtedly subject—in exchange for an act—enforcement of federal law—he has no right to refuse. Moreover, the Bout exchange was a widely criticized sacrifice of a valid American interest (the punishment of an infamous arms dealer) which Russia was able to extract only through a patently selective prosecution of a famous American athlete.[2] It is difficult to imagine that the Department wishes to emulate that episode by granting Adams leverage over it akin to Russia's influence in international affairs. It is a breathtaking and dangerous precedent to reward Adams's opportunistic and shifting commitments on immigration and other policy matters with dismissal of a criminal indictment. Nor will a court likely find that such an improper exchange is consistent with the public interest. See United States v. N.V. Nederlandsche Combinatie Voor Chemische Industrie ("Nederlandsche Combinatie"), 428 F. Supp. 114, 116-17 (S.D.N.Y. 1977) (denying Government's motion to dismiss where Government had agreed to dismiss charges against certain defendants in exchange for guilty pleas by others); cf. In re United States, 345 F.3d 450, 453 (7th Cir. 2003) (describing a prosecutor's acceptance of a bribe as a clear example of a dismissal that should not be granted as contrary to the public interest). Second, Mr. Bove states that dismissal is warranted because of the conduct of this office's former U.S. Attorney, Damian Williams, which, according to Mr. Bove's memo, constituted weaponization of government as defined by the relevant orders of the President and the Department. The generalized concerns expressed by Mr. Bove are not a basis to dismiss an indictment returned by a duly constituted grand jury, at least where, as here, the Government has no doubt in its evidence or the integrity of its investigation.

As Mr. Bove's memo acknowledges, and as he stated in our meeting of January 31, 2025, the Department has no concerns about the conduct or integrity of the line prosecutors who investigated and charged this case, and it does not question the merits of the case itself. Still, it bears emphasis that I have only known the line prosecutors on this case to act with integrity and in the pursuit of justice, and nothing I have learned since becoming U.S. Attorney has demonstrated otherwise. If anything, I have learned that Mr. Williams's role in the investigation and oversight of this case was even more minimal than I had assumed. The investigation began before Mr. Williams took office, he did not manage the day-to-day investigation, and the charges in this case were recommended or approved by four experienced career prosecutors, the Chiefs of the SDNY Public Corruption Unit, and career prosecutors at the Public Integrity Section of the Justice Department. Mr. Williams's decision to ratify their recommendations does not taint the charging decision. And notably, Adams has not brought a vindictive or selective prosecution motion, nor would one be successful. See United States v. Stewart, 590 F.3d 93, 121-23 (2d Cir. 2009); cf. United States v. Biden, 728 F. Supp. 3d 1054, 1092 (C.D. Cal. 2024) (rejecting argument that political public statements disturb the "'presumption of regularity' that attaches to prosecutorial decisions").

Regarding the timing of the indictment, the decision to charge in September 2024—nine months before the June 2025 Democratic

Mayoral Primary and more than a year before the November 2025 Mayoral Election—complied in every respect with longstanding Department policy regarding election year sensitivities and the applicable Justice Manual provisions. The Justice Manual requires that when investigative steps and charges involving a public official could be seen as affecting an election the prosecuting office must consult with the Public Integrity Section, and, if directed to do so, the Office of the Deputy Attorney General or Attorney General. See JM §§ 9-85.210, 9-85.500. As you are aware, this office followed this requirement. Further, the Justice Department's concurrence was unquestionably consistent with the established policies of the Public Integrity Section. See, e.g., Public Integrity Section, Federal Prosecution of Election Offenses 85 (2017) (pre-election action may be appropriate where "it is possible to both complete an investigation and file criminal charges against an offender prior to the period immediately before an election"). The Department of Justice correctly concluded that bringing charges nine months before a primary election was entirely appropriate.

The timing of the charges in this case is also consistent with charging timelines of other cases involving elected officials, both in this District and elsewhere. See, e.g., United States v. Robert Menendez, 23 Cr. 490 (SHS) (S.D.N.Y.) (indictment in September 2023); United States v. Duncan Hunter, 18 Cr. 3677 (S.D. Cal.) (indictment in August 2018). I am not aware of any instance in which the Department has concluded that an indictment brought this far in advance of an election is improper because it may be pending during an electoral cycle, let alone that a validly returned and factually supported indictment should be dismissed on this basis. When first setting the trial date, the District Court and the parties agreed on the importance of completing the trial before the upcoming mayoral election—including before the Democratic primary in which Adams is a candidate—so that the voters would know how the case resolved before casting their votes. (See Dkt. 31 at 38-44). Adams has decided that he would prefer the trial to take place before rather than after the June

2025 primary, notwithstanding the burden trial preparation would place on his ability to govern the City or campaign for re-election. But that is his choice, and the District Court has made clear that Adams is free to seek a continuance. (See Dkt. 113 at 18 n.6). The parties therefore cannot argue with candor that dismissing serious charges before an election, but holding open the possibility that those charges could be reinstated if Adams were re-elected, would now be other than "clearly contrary to the manifest public interest." United States v. Blaszczak, 56 F.4th 230, 238-39 (2d Cir. 2022) (internal quotation marks omitted).

Mr. Bove's memo also refers to recent public actions by Mr. Williams. It is not my role to defend Mr. Williams's motives or conduct. Given the appropriate chronology of this investigation and the strength of the case, Mr. Williams's conduct since leaving government service cannot justify dismissal here. With respect to pretrial publicity, the District Court has already determined that Mr. Williams's statements have not prejudiced the jury pool. The District Court has also repeatedly explained that there is no evidence that any leaks to the media came from the prosecution team—although there is evidence media leaks came from the defense team—and no basis for any relief. (See Dkt. 103 at 3-6; Dkt. 49 at 4-21). Mr. Williams's recent op-ed, the Court concluded, generally talks about bribery in New York State, and so is not a comment on the case. (Dkt. 103 at 6 n.5). Mr. Williams's website does not even reference Adams except in the news articles linked there. (See Dkt. 99 at 3). And it is well settled that the U.S. Attorneys in this and other districts regularly conduct post-arrest press conferences. See United States v. Avenatti, 433 F. Supp. 3d 552, 567-69 (S.D.N.Y. 2020) (describing the practice); see also, e.g., "New Jersey U.S. Attorney's Office press conference on violent crime," YouTube, https://www.youtube.com/watch?v=oAEDHQCE91A (announcing criminal charges against 42 defendants). In short, because there is in fact nothing about this prosecution that meaningfully differs from other cases that generate substantial pretrial publicity, a court is likely to view the weaponization rationale as pretextual.

Moreover, dismissing the case will amplify, rather than abate, concerns about weaponization of the Department. Despite Mr. Bove's observation that the directive to dismiss the case has been reached without assessing the strength of the evidence against Adams, Adams has already seized on the memo to publicly assert that he is innocent and that the accusations against him were unsupported by the evidence and based only on "fanfare and sensational claims." Confidence in the Department would best be restored by means well short of a dismissal. As you know, our office is prepared to seek a superseding indictment from a new grand jury under my leadership. We have proposed a superseding indictment that would add an obstruction conspiracy count based on evidence that Adams destroyed and instructed others to destroy evidence and provide false information to the FBI, and that would add further factual allegations regarding his participation in a fraudulent straw donor scheme.

That is more than enough to address any perception of impropriety created by Mr. Williams's personal conduct. The Bove memo acknowledges as much, leaving open the possibility of refiling charges after the November 2025 New York City Mayoral Election. Nor is conditioning the dismissal on the incoming U.S. Attorney's ability to re-assess the charges consistent with either the weaponization rationale or the law concerning motions under Rule 48(a). To the contrary, keeping Adams under the threat of prosecution while the Government determines its next steps is a recognized reason for the denial of a Rule 48(a) motion. See United States v. Poindexter, 719 F. Supp. 6, 11-12 (D.D.C. 1989) (allowing Government to "to keep open the option of trying [certain] counts" would effectively keep the defendant "under public obloquy for an indefinite period of time until the government decided that, somehow, for some reason, the time had become more propitious for proceeding with a trial").

B. Adams's Consent Will Not Aid the Department's Arguments

Mr. Bove specifies that Adams must consent in writing to dismissal without prejudice. To be sure, in the typical case, the defendant's consent makes it significantly more likely for courts to grant motions to dismiss under Rule 48(a). See United States v. Welborn, 849 F.2d 980, 983 (5th Cir. 1988) ("If the motion is uncontested, the court should ordinarily presume that the prosecutor is acting in good faith and dismiss the indictment without prejudice."). But Adams's consent—which was negotiated without my office's awareness or participation—would not guarantee a successful motion, given the basic flaws in the stated rationales for dismissal. See Nederlandsche Combinatie, 428 F. Supp. at 116-17 (declining to "rubber stamp" dismissal because although defendant did not appear to object, "the court is vested with the responsibility of protecting the interests of the public on whose behalf the criminal action is brought"). Seeking leave of court to dismiss a properly returned indictment based on Mr. Bove's stated rationales is also likely to backfire by inviting skepticism and scrutiny from the court that will ultimately hinder the Department of Justice's interests. In particular, the court is unlikely to acquiesce in using the criminal process to control the behavior of a political figure.

A brief review of the relevant law demonstrates this point. Although the judiciary "[r]arely will . . . overrule the Executive Branch's exercise of these prosecutorial decisions," Blaszczak, 56 F.4th at 238, courts, including the Second Circuit, will nonetheless inquire as to whether dismissal would be clearly contrary to the public interest. See, e.g., id. at 238-42 (extended discussion of contrary to public interest standard and cases applying it); see also JM § 9-2.050 (requiring "a written motion for leave to dismiss . . . explaining fully the reason for the request" to dismiss for cases of public interest as well as for cases involving bribery). At least one court in our district has rejected a dismissal under Rule 48(a) as contrary to the public interest, regardless of the defendant's consent. See Nederlandsche Combinatie, 428 F. Supp. at 116-17 ("After reviewing the entire record, the court has determined that a dismissal of the indictment against Mr. Massaut is not in the public interest. Therefore, the government's motion to dismiss as to Mr. Massaut must be and is denied."). The assigned District Judge, the Honorable Dale E. Ho, appears likely to conduct a searching inquiry in this case. Notably, Judge Ho stressed transparency during this case, specifically explaining his strict requirements for non-public filings at the initial conference. (See Dkt. 31 at 48-49). And a rigorous inquiry here would be consistent with precedent and practice in this and other districts.

Nor is there any realistic possibility that Adams's consent will prevent a lengthy judicial inquiry that is detrimental to the Department's reputation, regardless of outcome. In that regard, although the Flynn case may come to mind as a comparator, it is distinct in one important way. In that case, the Government moved to dismiss an indictment with the defendant's consent and faced resistance from a skeptical district judge. But in Flynn, the Government sought dismissal with prejudice because it had become convinced that there was insufficient evidence that General Flynn had committed any crime. That ultimately made the Government's rationale defensible, because "[i]nsufficient evidence is a quintessential justification for dismissing charges." In re Flynn, 961 F.3d 1215, 1221 (D.C. Cir.), reh'g en banc granted, order vacated, No. 20-5143, 2020 WL 4355389 (D.C. Cir. July 30, 2020), and on reh'g en banc, 973 F.3d 74 (D.C. Cir. 2020). Here no one in the Department has expressed any doubts as to Adams's guilt, and even in Flynn, the President ultimately chose to cut off the extended and embarrassing litigation over dismissal by granting a pardon.

C. I Cannot in Good Faith Request the Contemplated Dismissal

Because the law does not support a dismissal, and because I am confident that Adams has committed the crimes with which he is charged, I cannot agree to seek a dismissal driven by improper considerations. As Justice Robert Jackson explained, "the prosecutor at his best is one of the most beneficent forces in our society, when he acts from malice or other base motives, he is one of the worst." The

Federal Prosecutor, 24 J. Am. Jud. Soc'y 18 ("This authority has been granted by people who really wanted the right thing done—wanted crime eliminated—but also wanted the best in our American traditions preserved."). I understand my duty as a prosecutor to mean enforcing the law impartially, and that includes prosecuting a validly returned indictment regardless whether its dismissal would be politically advantageous, to the defendant or to those who appointed me. A federal prosecutor "is the representative not of an ordinary party to a controversy, but of a sovereignty whose obligation to govern impartially is as compelling as its obligation to govern at all." Berger v. United States, 295 U.S. 78, 88 (1935).

For the reasons explained above, I do not believe there are reasonable arguments in support of a Rule 48(a) motion to dismiss a case that is well supported by the evidence and the law. I understand that Mr. Bove disagrees, and I am mindful of your recent order reiterating prosecutors' duty to make good-faith arguments in support of the Executive Branch's positions. See Feb. 5, 2025 Mem. "General Policy Regarding Zealous Advocacy on Behalf of the United States." But because I do not see any good-faith basis for the proposed position, I cannot make such arguments consistent with my duty of candor. N.Y.R.P.C. 3.3; id. cmt. 2 ("A lawyer acting as an advocate in an adjudicative proceeding has an obligation to present the client's case with persuasive force. Performance of that duty while maintaining confidences of the client, however, is qualified by the advocate's duty of candor to the tribunal.").

In particular, the rationale given by Mr. Bove—an exchange between a criminal defendant and the Department of Justice akin to the Bout exchange with Russia—is, as explained above, a bargain that a prosecutor should not make. Moreover, dismissing without prejudice and with the express option of again indicting Adams in the future creates obvious ethical problems, by implicitly threatening future prosecution if Adams's cooperation with enforcing the immigration laws proves unsatisfactory to the Department. See In re Christoff, 690 N.E.2d 1135 (Ind. 1997) (disciplining prosecutor for threatening to renew a dormant criminal investigation against a potential candidate for public office in order to dissuade the candidate from running); Bruce A. Green & Rebecca Roiphe, Who Should Police Politicization of the DOJ?, 35 Notre Dame J.L. Ethics & Pub. Pol'y 671, 681 (2021) (noting that the Arizona Supreme Court disbarred the elected chief prosecutor of Maricopa County, Arizona, and his deputy, in part, for misusing their power to advance the chief prosecutor's partisan political interests). Finally, given the highly generalized accusations of weaponization, weighed against the strength of the evidence against Adams, a court will likely question whether that basis is pretextual. See, e.g., United States v. Greater Blouse, Skirt & Neckwear Contractors, 228 F. Supp. 483, 487 (S.D.N.Y. 1964) (courts "should be satisfied that the reasons advanced for the proposed dismissal are substantial and the real grounds upon which the application is based").

I remain baffled by the rushed and superficial process by which this decision was reached, in seeming collaboration with Adams's counsel and without my direct input on the ultimate stated rationales for dismissal. Mr. Bove admonished me to be mindful of my obligation to zealously defend the interests of the United States and to advance good-faith arguments on behalf of the Administration. I hope you share my view that soliciting and considering the concerns of the U.S. Attorney overseeing the case serves rather than hinders that goal, and that we can find time to meet.

In the event you are unwilling to meet or to reconsider the directive in light of the problems raised by Mr. Bove's memo, I am prepared to offer my resignation. It has been, and continues to be, my honor to serve as a prosecutor in the Southern District of New York.

Very truly yours,

DANIELLE R. SASSOON
United States Attorney
Southern District of New York

| 26 |

Resistance

There have been continuous protests across the country, starting with the People's March in January. By February, the "50501" movement hit all state capitals and other cities, its name referring to "50 protests, 50 states, one day" protesting Trump, Musk, and Project 2025. The "Day of Action" on February 17 was named "Not My Presidents Day". The "Day Without Immigrants" protest and boycott took place on 3 February. Other events went under such names as "Economic Blackout" and "Stand Up for Science 2025". Vigils were held, including one in the District of Columbia, by Catholic Cardinal Robert McElroy, the recently elected Archbishop of Washington.

There have also been protests against the far-Right and fascism in other countries that included opposition to Trump (and even Musk). On the day of Trump's inauguration, protests were held in London, Brussels, Mexico City, Tijuana, Panama City, and Manila. The "Tell Trump to Toque Off" movement gathered in front of the U.S. embassy in Ottawa and U.S. consulates across Canada on 15 February. A 'Canada First' rally was held to condemn Trump's comments about becoming the 51st state. Perhaps the most reported incidents are Canadians booing the American National Anthem at sporting events, with apologists stressing that their ire is against the government of the United States and not its people.

Trump attended Super Bowl LIX, which beforehand decided to remove the "END RACISM" message from the field. He left during the half-time show by Kendrick Lamar, which featured a racial justice message and was performed exclusively by People of Color. Lyrics included the lines "The revolution 'bout to be televised; You picked the right time, but the wrong guy".

Congressmen facing constituents at home has been rough, being booed and shouted down at town halls across the country. After weeks of this, Representative Richard Hudson, chair of the National Republican Congressional Committee, now advises Republicans to not hold more town halls, claiming that "in-person town halls are no longer effective because Democrat activists are threatening democracy by disrupting the actual communication at town halls".

Some legislators are taking an opposite stand. At a chamber luncheon in Ohio, Republican U.S. Representative Troy Balderson said executive orders are "getting out of control". Still supporting Trump, he asserts only Congress can do certain things, adding by example that "Congress has to decide whether or not the Department of Education goes away. Not the president, not Elon Musk. Congress decides."

The Hispanic caucus -- generally favorable to Trump -- gave warning against passing a budget bill that aligns with Trump's plans for cuts.

Vance and his family were pushed out of a ski resort by pro-Ukraine protesters.

Flags are flying upside-down. This has been common in recent years by anyone whose choice lost the election, but it seems to be more common. A large upside-down flag was even draped at Yosemite, as well as smaller ones in Acadia, Maine.

It has not all been without effect. Trump has rolled back many actions due to public outcry, from no longer threatening the jobs of Park Service workers, to removing those sent to Guantanamo (after a lawsuit by the ACLU), to restoring funding for 9/11 health programs.

A Pardon Refused

Pamela Hemphill, called the "MAGA granny" by social media users, pleaded guilty and was sentenced to 60 days in prison for her participation in January 6th. She refused her pardon, saying people are trying to "rewrite history and I don't want to be part of that".

> Accepting a pardon would only insult the Capitol police officers, rule of law and, of course, our nation. I pleaded guilty because I was guilty, and accepting a pardon also would serve to contribute to their gaslighting and false narrative. We were wrong that day, we broke the law -- there should be no pardons. -- Pamela Hemphill interview with the BBC

Chris Kluwe at City Council Meeting

{Ex-NFL punter Chris Kluwe was arrested protesting the city's decision to display a plaque that features the words "Magical, Alluring, Galvanizing, Adventurous". He was subsequently fired from his high school coaching position.}

Unfortunately, it is clear this council does not listen, so instead, I'm going to take my time to say what MAGA has stood for these past three weeks. MAGA stands for trying to erase trans people from existence. MAGA stands for resegregation and racism.

Since his inauguration nearly a month ago, Mr. Trump has signed multiple executive orders targeting transgender people, most recently one banning transgender athletes from women's sports. One order asserts the federal government recognizes only two sexes — male and female — and that "these sexes are not changeable and are grounded in fundamental and incontrovertible reality," and another aims to restrict transgender people from serving in the military.

MAGA stands for firing air traffic controllers while planes are crashing. MAGA stands for firing the people overseeing our nuclear arsenal. MAGA stands for firing military veterans and those serving them at the VA, including canceling research on veteran suicide. MAGA stands for cutting funds to education, including for disabled children.

The Trump administration has moved aggressively to fire federal employees in various agencies, including at the Departments of Veterans Affairs and Education and the Consumer Financial Protection Bureau, the Federal Aviation Administration and the U.S. Forest Service.

MAGA is profoundly corrupt, unmistakably anti-democracy, and, most importantly, MAGA is explicitly a Nazi movement. You may have replaced a swastika with a red hat, but that is what it is.

I will now engage in the time-honored American tradition of peaceful civil disobedience.

Marc Elias Letter to Elon Musk

{On Valentine's Day, Musk tweeted, "You and Marc Elias are undermining civilization. Did you guys suffer childhood trauma or something? This seems like a generational trauma transfer issue." This response was published on 20 February by Elias.}

Mr. Musk,

You recently criticized me and another prominent lawyer fighting for the rule of law and democracy in the United States. I am used to being attacked for my work, particularly on the platform you own and dominate.

I used to be a regular on Twitter, where I amassed over 900,000 followers — all organic except for the right-wing bots who seemed to grow in number. Like many others, I stopped regularly posting on the site because, under your stewardship, it became a hellscape of hate and misinformation.

I also used to buy your cars — first a Model X and then a Model S — back when you spoke optimistically about solving the climate crisis. My family no longer owns any of your cars and never will.

But this is not the reason I am writing. You don't know me. You have no idea whether I have suffered trauma and if I have, how it has manifested. And it's none of your business.

However, I will address your last point about generational trauma. I am Jewish, though many on your site simply call me "a jew." Honestly, it's often worse than that, but I'm sure you get the point. There was a time when Twitter would remove antisemitic posts, but under your leadership, tolerating the world's oldest hatred now seems to be a permissible part of your "free speech" agenda.

Like many Jewish families, mine came to America because of trauma. They were fleeing persecution in the Pale of Settlement — the only area in the Russian Empire where Jews were legally allowed to reside. Even there, life was difficult — often traumatic. My family, like others, lived in a shtetl and was poor. Worse, pogroms were common — violent riots in which Jews were beaten, killed and expelled from their villages.

By the time my family fled, life in the Pale had become all but impossible for Jews. Tsar Nicholas II's government spread anti-Jewish propaganda that encouraged Russians to attack and steal from Jews in their communities. My great-grandfather was fortunate to leave when he did. Those who stayed faced even worse circumstances when Hitler's army later invaded.

That is the generational trauma I carry. The trauma of being treated as "other" by countrymen you once thought were your friends. The trauma of being scapegoated by authoritarian leaders. The trauma of fleeing while millions of others were systematically murdered. The trauma of watching powerful men treat it all as a joke — or worse.

As an immigrant yourself, you can no doubt sympathize with what it means to leave behind your country, extended family, friends and neighbors to come to the United States. Of course, you probably had more than 86 rubles in your pocket. You probably didn't ride for nine days in the bottom of a ship or have your surname changed by immigration officials. Here is the ship manifest showing that my family did. Aron, age three, was my grandfather.

As new immigrants, life wasn't easy. My family lived in cramped housing without hot water. They worked menial jobs — the kind immigrants still perform today.

Some may look down on those immigrants — the ones without fancy degrees — but my family was proud to work and grateful that the United States took them in. They found support within their Jewish community and a political home in the Democratic Party.

I became a lawyer to give back to the country that gave my family a chance. I specialize in representing Democratic campaigns because I believe in the party. I litigate voting rights cases because the right to vote is the bedrock of our democracy. I speak out about free and fair elections because they are under threat.

Now let me address the real crux of your post.

You are very rich and very powerful. You have thrown in with Donald Trump. Whether it is because you think you can control him or because you share his authoritarian vision, I do not know. I do not care.

Together, you and he are dismantling our government, undermining the rule of law and harming the most vulnerable in our society. I am just a lawyer. I do not have your wealth or your platform. I do not control the vast power of the federal government, nor do I have millions of adherents at my disposal to harass and intimidate my opponents. I may even carry generational trauma.

But you need to know this about me. I am the great-grandson of a man who led his family out of the shtetl to a strange land in search of a better life. I am the grandson of the three-year-old boy on that journey. As you know, my English name is Marc, but my Hebrew name is Elhanan (אֶלְחָנָן) — after the great warrior in David's army who slew a powerful giant.

I will use every tool at my disposal to protect this country from Trump. I will litigate to defend voting rights until there are no cases left to bring. I will speak out against authoritarianism until my last breath.

I will not back down. I will not bow or scrape. I will never obey.

Defiantly,

Marc Elias

Bernie Sanders

{Transcript of message sent out 31 January}

Thanks very much for joining me. We are living in a dangerous and unprecedented moment in American history and I'm getting a lot of calls from people who are not only upset about what's happening, but are wondering how we best go forward. Well, let me tell you. we've got to be smart, we've got to be organized and we've got to fight back. This is not a time for wallowing in despair and hiding under the covers. The stakes are just too high. We're not just fighting for ourselves. We're fighting for our kids, for future generations, We're fighting for the future of this planet.

The first two weeks of this presidency Donald Trump defied the Constitution by ending birthright citizenship, fired government watchdogs, allowed drilling along our coastlines pardoned violent insurrectionists, suspended all foreign aid and tried to cut off virtually all federal funding.

So, how so we go forward.?

First, to be effective, we've got to understand what is in fact is happening around us right now. Second, we need a short term strategy. What we do tomorrow and the next day and the day after that. Third, we need a long term strategy. How do we build a movement that gains political power?

Here is, in my view, a brief overview as to what is happening under Trump.

Most importantly, the move toward oligarchy in our country, government run by the rich and the powerful is proceeding rapidly. And it's not being done secretly. A little a week ago Donald Trump was inaugurated for his second term, standing right behind him were the three richest men in the world: Elon Musk, Jeff Bezos and Mark Zuckerberg, men who have become over $200 billion dollars richer since Trump was elected and who now are worth almost a trillion dollars more money than the bottom half of American society--170 million people. But it's not just oligarchy that we should worry about. This country under Trump is moving rapidly toward authoritarianism.

Just a few examples: in violation of the constitution and federal law, Trump attempted the other day to suspend all federal grants and loans. That means he blocked money for Medicaid, Head Start, food stamps, homeless veterans etc., etc.,

Tens of millions of Americans, some of the most vulnerable people in our country were impacted by that decision. Fortunately, Americans all across the country stood up in outrage and said , no, no. And with the help of the courts, much, but not all of that freeze in funding was rescinded. You may have noticed that Trump is intimidating the media. With lawsuits against ABC, CBS, Meta, and the Des Moines Register. If Trump does not like what media reports, he is threatening them with lawsuits, undermining the first amendment. That is a direct movement toward authoritarianism.

Now that is a very broad overview of where we are today. In terms of short term strategy, we've got to mobilize as strongly as we can against Trump's dangerous proposals. And let me just say this, importantly, yes, the Republicans control the House and the Senage but do not forget their majorities are small.

In the House a body of 435 members they have a 4 vote majority. That is a razor thin margin and their legislation can be defeated. There are an number of Republicans out there who won in Democratic districts by small margins. So let me tell you, these guys do respond to phone calls and emails. So if there's a piece of legislation you disagree with, get on the phone and call the Capitol switchboard at 202-224-2131.

And what is some of that legislation that we should be concerned about?

Republicans right now are working toward on what is called the budget reconciliation bill. The most important element which would be a massive tax break for the wealthy to be paid for by large cuts in Medicaid and other programs that working families and low income people desperately need. At a time of unprecedented income and wealth inequality, when so many of our people are struggling to put food on the table we must not savage programs for working families to provide huge tax breaks for billionaires.

We must vigorously oppose Trump's efforts at mass deportation. Yes, we must strengthen our borders, yes, we should deport people who have been convicted of serious crimes. But no, no we cannot destroy families who have lived and worked in this country peacefully for decades. Not only is Trumps mass deportation program immoral, it will have a severely negative impact on our economy.

As all of you know, we are seeing extreme weather disturbances and devastation in our country and all over the world related to climate change. Think about LA. Think about North Carolina. We must vigorously oppose this absurd drill baby drill doctrine which will only make an incredibly dangerous climate situation even worse.

And those are just a few of the issues that are coming down the pipe. But we cannot just play defense. We have got to be on the offense. Please never forget that the agenda that we are fighting for is widely supported widely supported by working families all across this country and we must continue to fight for that agenda. The American people do not want cuts to Medicaid and the privatization of Medicare. They understand that health care is a human right not a privilege. We must continue the struggle for Medicare for all so that every American has the health care that he or she needs. That is not a radical idea. That is what Americans want. Federal minimum wage of $7.25 an hour is a starvation wage. We must raise that minimum wage to a living wage at least $17 an hour. If you work forty hours a week in America, you should not be living in poverty.

All over this country we have a major housing crisis. And it's not just 800,000 who are homeless. It is millions of working of working families who are spending 40, 50, 60% of their limited incomes on housing. Instead of spending almost a trillion dollars a year on a wasteful and bloated Pentagon budget we have got to build millions of units of low income and affordable housing. And when we do that, we put large numbers of people to work at good paying union jobs. I could go on and on, but let me conclude by saying this:

The United States is the wealthiest nation in the history of the world. If we stand together and oppose right wing efforts to divide us up by our race, by our religion, our sexual orientation, or where we were born, if we stand together there is nothing that we cannot accomplish.

Bottom line, let us go forward and fight for a government and an economy that works for all, not just a few.

We simply do not have the luxury of moaning and groaning. We have got to stand up and fight back. We can do it. Lets go forward together.

Thank you very much.

Other Warnings and Commentary

All members of Congress swore allegiance to the Constitution. They didn't ask just Democrats to defend America against all enemies. The house is on fire, y'all. I'll do everything I can to extinguish that flame, but I am begging my Republican colleagues to remember their oath. -- Gwen Moore, U.S. Representative, 11 February

A coup is underway against Americans as professors of human rights and dignities, and against Americans as citizens of a Democratic Republic. each hour this goes unrecognized makes the success of the coup more likely. -- Timothy Snyder, historian specializing in the Soviet Union and the Holocaust

The Alt-US Park Service

This online resistance effort, may or may not be run by those associated with the National Park Service. It started on 27 January 2017 "as a response to restrictions placed on the official National Park Service social media accounts". Its social media channels provide constant updates about what is going on in the government, particularly government workers. The admins of the social media channels, and some commenters, occasionally claim inside information, or things not being reported in the media.

Their Facebook page describes them as "The official 'Resistance' team of U.S. National Park Service" whose mission is "to stand up for the National Park Service to help protect and preserve the environment for present and future generations".

An iconic painting by Robert Bissell was posted, becoming a commonly shared meme. Letters say "RESIST" and feature bears lifting a tree into place like the flag at Iwo Kima.

A website using the group's name encourages volunteering, speaking out, donating to causes, and sharing ecological research. The website linked to their social media accounts has a message for President Trump and visitors as of the writing of this book:

> You've previously shut down our social media use and eroded environmental protections, but you can't silence our collective voice. "Our Parks" is our stand to safeguard our environment and prevent four more years of destruction. Join us to protect our national parks for future generations. Sign our pledge now. Your vote is your voice.

Anonymous

Known to most as a group of hackers, it is an amorphous, worldwide, uncentralized quasi-movement of independent, unconnected individuals. Members of the group may form a rough consensus around some issues. In the case of American politics, ominous videos are promulgated with conflicting messages. Some vow to take down Trump, and in fact took credit for having doxxed his social security number, phone number, and other detials. (Despite this information being available online without hacking, the White House vowed those responsible will be brought to justice.) Other Anonymous videos support Musk's purported efforts to clean out waste, and by extension, the Deep State.

Unlike Anonymous's Project Chanology in 2008 -- the first worldwide protest ever organized online -- there isn't much presence at protests, ordinarily marked by people wearing Guy Fawkes masks.

Truth or Godwin

Various philosophers, activists, and others, including experts on political extremism, have labeled Trump a fascist or leading us to fascism. Some used the term in earnest as early as 2015 when he called for a Muslim ban, while others didn't use the term until January 6th, 2021. In 2016, JD Vance wrote he feared Trump could be "America's Hitler", and former Trump staff members John F. Kelly and Mark Milley have described Trump as a fascist. Regardless of previous or current affiliations or allegiances, the list goes on, so much that there is an entire article on Wikipedia on the subject.

The problem, of course, is that anyone can use the label in political rhetoric, and have done so. It's become a crying wolf issue. Right-wing propaganda even reframes fascism as 'Cultural Marxism', i.e. Wokeism, the near-opposite of how the term is used in political science. Of course, any ideology, Left or Right, can be weaponized, but I suspect future historians will see these times in a light where the danger is more from the Conservative rather than Liberal side. Perhaps not ironically given history, fear of "radical Liberal ideology" is what drove millions to the far-Right.

Whoever is right or wrong, this has escalated the stakes, but surprisingly not the rhetoric. Some may believe it was Biden and a Liberal-run Deep State that arranged the assassination attempts in 2024, even though the shooter in Pennsylvania was determined to be ultra-conservative (and was tracking the tours of both Trump and Biden for targets of opportunity). And yet there was no storming of the Capitol in 2025, or even efforts to overturn the election. Biden extended all the expected courtesies of transition that were denied to him by Trump.

The resistance seems to not be of the "fight fire with fire" variety, at least at this point. The question for the future will be if doing so would have made a difference for the better or worse. These are the sorts of discussions happening on the streets (or screens).

Centers for Disease Control and Prevention, Alternatives

Given the order to not disclose pandemic information without the President's authorization, and having left the WHO, many have turned elsewhere for data on outbreaks. Some of their site's data has been removed, such as AIDS statistics, but was then restored, possibly due to court orders requiring DOGE to restore all government websites to their previous condition. Alternative sources of information being suggested on social media are the AMA and the site Physicians for a Healthy Democracy (https://www.physiciansforahealthydemocracy.org/).

In addition to widespread avian flu, the major cause of spiked egg prices, we now have the first U.S. measles death since 2015, with outbreaks in several places around the country. Surprisingly, RFK, Jr. is encouraging vaccinations, something contrary to his prior advocacy against them. However, the administration has ordered the CDC to indefinitely postpone a public meeting of its vaccine advisory panel. Upcoming months will undoubtedly justify or assuage fears.

| 27 |

English

One of the last acts in this first forty days of his second Presidency was to declare English the official language of the United States. This leaves the United Kingdom, Australia, Costa Rica, and Eritrea as nations without a formally designated language. Sources have previously described the primary languages of the United States as English and Spanish.

About one-fifth of Americans currently speak a language at home other than English. Historically, the main reason for Spanish-Speaking Americans is that most of the land West of the Louisiana purchase was previously part of Mexico. Also, the United States current has a territorial claim over the self-governing Commonwealth of Puerto Rico.

{Author's Note: In my home town of Buffalo, New York, a medium-sized city, over 90 languages are spoken at home as of the writing of this book, with about 17% of residents speaking some other primary language. The seven most common languages spoken by those learning English are Spanish, Arabic, Karen (a Southeast Asian language), Somali, Burmese, Swahili, and Bengali.}

Designating English as the Official Language of The United States

{Executive Oder, 1 March 2025}

By the authority vested in me as President by the Constitution and the laws of the United States of America, it is hereby ordered:

Section 1. Purpose and Policy. From the founding of our Republic, English has been used as our national language. Our Nation's historic governing documents, including the Declaration of Independence and the Constitution, have all been written in English. It is therefore long past time that English is declared as the official language of the United States. A nationally designated language is at the core of a unified and cohesive society, and the United States is strengthened by a citizenry that can freely exchange ideas in one shared language.

In welcoming new Americans, a policy of encouraging the learning and adoption of our national language will make the United States a shared home and empower new citizens to achieve the American dream. Speaking English not only opens doors economically, but it helps newcomers engage in their communities, participate in national traditions, and give back to our society. This order recognizes and celebrates the long tradition of multilingual American citizens who have learned English and passed it to their children for generations to come.

To promote unity, cultivate a shared American culture for all citizens, ensure consistency in government operations, and create a pathway to civic engagement, it is in America's best interest for the Federal Government to designate one — and only one — official language. Establishing English as the official language will not only streamline communication but also reinforce shared national values, and create a more cohesive and efficient society.

Accordingly, this order designates English as the official language of the United States.

Sec. 2. Definitions. For purposes of this order:
(a) "Agency" has the meaning given to it in section 3502 of title 44,

United States Code, except that such term does not include the Executive Office of the President or any components thereof.

(b) "Agency Head" means the highest-ranking official of an agency, such as the Secretary, Administrator, Chairman, or Director, unless otherwise specified in this order.

Sec. 3. Designating an Official Language for the United States. (a) English is the official language of the United States.

(b) Executive Order 13166 of August 11, 2000 (Improving Access to Services for Persons with Limited English Proficiency), is hereby revoked; nothing in this order, however, requires or directs any change in the services provided by any agency. Agency heads should make decisions as they deem necessary to fulfill their respective agencies' mission and efficiently provide Government services to the American people. Agency heads are not required to amend, remove, or otherwise stop production of documents, products, or other services prepared or offered in languages other than English.

(c) The Attorney General shall rescind any policy guidance documents issued pursuant to Executive Order 13166 and provide updated guidance, consistent with applicable law.

Sec. 4. General Provisions. (a) Nothing in this order shall be construed to impair or otherwise affect:

(i)   the authority granted by law to an executive department or agency, or the head thereof; or

(ii) the functions of the Director of the Office of Management and Budget relating to budgetary, administrative, or legislative proposals.

(b) This order shall be implemented consistent with applicable law and subject to the availability of appropriations.

(c) This order is not intended to, and does not, create any right or benefit, substantive or procedural, enforceable at law or in equity by any party against the United States, its departments, agencies, or entities, its officers, employees, or agents, or any other person.

THE WHITE HOUSE,
March 1, 2025.

White House Fact Sheet

DESIGNATING ENGLISH AS THE OFFICIAL LANGUAGE: Today, President Donald J. Trump signed an Executive Order designating English as the official language of the United States.

- The Order rescinds a Clinton-era mandate that required agencies and recipients of federal funding to provide extensive language assistance to non-English speakers.
- This designation specifically allows agencies to keep current policies and provide documents and services in other languages, but encourages new Americans to adopt a national language that opens doors to greater opportunities.
- Agencies will have flexibility to decide how and when to offer services in languages other than English to best serve the American people and fulfill their agency mission.

UNIFYING THE AMERICAN PEOPLE: It is long past time English is recognized as the official language of the United States.

- Since our nation's founding, English has been the language of our nation, with historic documents like the Declaration of Independence and the Constitution written in English.
- A national language strengthens the fabric of our society, empowering citizens old and new.
- While over 350 languages are spoken in the United States, English remains the most widely used across the country.

- Roughly 180 countries have an official language – the United States is one of the few nations in the world to have no official language designated.
- More than 30 states and five U.S. territories have already embraced English as the official language.
- Establishing English as the official language promotes unity, establishes efficiency in government operations, and creates a pathway for civic engagement.
- This Order celebrates multilingual Americans who have learned English and passed it down, while empowering immigrants to achieve the American Dream through a common language.

PROMISES KEPT: President Trump has long championed the idea that English should be the official language of the United States.

- With this Executive Order, President Trump affirms that a common language fosters national cohesion, helps newcomers engage in communities and traditions, and enriches our shared culture.

| 28 |

State of the Union

Now a few days after the 40-day mark, we close with the President's Address to Congress. One journalist suggested it was the first time that no one from the opposing party stood at any point during a State of the Union speech. Dozens of delegates walked out over the course of the speech, many wielding placards saying "Save Medicaid" and "Elon Steals". A paper sign held by New Mexico Representative Melanie Stansbury, reading "This is not normal", was ripped from her hands and thrown away by Republican Representative Lance Gooden of Texas. Stansbury later explained her sign as "an SOS to the world".

To the amusement by some viewers, the cameraman panned to Elon Musk in the balcony when the President said, "the days of rule by unelected bureaucrats are over".

One social media commenter described it as his usual campaigning but with the verb tenses changed. There already has been extensive fact-checking done, the results consistent with Donald Trump's notorious liberality with facts and figures. There was some laughter during his listing claims of government waste -- from both sides of the aisle, but for different reasons. Perhaps the funniest comment -- laughed at by those on -- was Trump's claim that $8 million was spent "for making mice transgender", which is now understood to refer to money spent on transgenic mice for medical research.

The Address

{4 March 2025}

Thank you. Thank you very much. Thank you very much. It's a great honor. Thank you very much, Speaker Johnson, Vice President Vance, the First Lady of the United States.

Members of the United States Congress, thank you very much. And to my fellow citizens, America is back.

Six weeks ago, I stood beneath the dome of this Capitol and proclaimed the dawn of the golden Age of America. From that moment on, it has been nothing but swift and unrelenting action to usher in the greatest and most successful era in the history of our country. We have accomplished more in 43 days than most administrations accomplished in four years or eight years. And we are just getting started.

I return to this chamber tonight to report that America's momentum is back. Our spirit is back, our pride is back, our confidence is back. And the American dream is surging bigger and better than ever before.

It's never been anything like it. The presidential election of November 5 was a mandate like has not been seen in many decades. We won all seven swing states, giving us an electoral college victory of 312 votes. We won the popular vote by big numbers and won counties in our country.

[Boos, then chants of "USA!"]

And won counties in our country 2,700 [more booing] to 525. But a map that reads almost completely red for Republican.

Now, for the first time in modern history, more Americans believe that our country is headed in the right direction than the wrong direction. In fact, it's an astonishing record, 27-point-swing, the most ever.

Likewise, small business optimism saw its single largest one-month gain ever recorded. A 41-point jump.

Representative Al Green: [shouting, stands and shakes his cane] Mr President, you don't have a mandate!

House Speaker Mike Johnson: Our members are directed to uphold and maintain decorum in the House, and to cease any further disruptions - that's your warning. Members are engaging in willful and continuing breach of decorum, and the chair is prepared to direct the Sergeant at Arms to restore order to the joint session.

Mr. Green, take your seat. Take your seat, sir. [inaudible shouting]

House Speaker Mike Johnson: Take your seat. [Shouting] Finding that members continue to engage in willful and concerted disruption of proper decorum. The chair now directs the Sergeant at Arms to restore order. [Applause] Remove this gentleman from the chamber. [Green is removed]

Members are directed to uphold and maintain decorum in the House. Mr. President, you continue.

Thank you. Over the past six weeks, I have signed nearly 100 executive orders and taken more than 400 executive actions, a record to restore common sense, safety, optimism and wealth all across our wonderful land. The people elected me to do the job and I'm doing it. In fact, it has been stated by many that the first month of our presidency, it's our presidency, is the most successful in the history of our nation.

By many. And what makes it even more impressive is that. You know who number two is, George Washington. How about that. How about it? I don't know about that list, but. But we'll take it. Within hours of taking the oath of office, I declared a national emergency on

our southern border, and I deployed the U.S. military and border patrol to repel the invasion of our country. And what a job they've done.

As a result, illegal border crossings last month were by far the
lowest ever recorded ever. They heard my words and they chose not
to come much easier that way. In comparison, under Joe Biden, the
worst president in American history. There were hundreds of thousands of illegal crossings a month, and virtually.

All of them, including murderers, drug dealers, gang members and
people from mental institutions and insane asylums were released
into our country. Who would want to do that? This is my fifth such
speech to Congress, and once again, I look at the Democrats in front
of me and I realize there is absolutely nothing I can say to make them
happy, or to make them stand or smile or applaud. Nothing I can
do. I could find a cure to the most devastating disease, a disease that
would wipe out entire nations, or announce the answers to the greatest economy in history, or the stoppage of crime to the lowest levels
ever recorded. And these people sitting right here will not clap, will
not stand, and certainly will not cheer for these astronomical achievements. They won't do it no matter what.

Five. Five times I've been up here, it's very. Sad and it just
shouldn't be this way. So Democrats sitting before me. For just this
one night, why not join us in celebrating so many incredible wins for
America? For the good of our nation? Let's work together and let's
truly make America great again.

Every day my administration is fighting to deliver the change
America needs to bring a future that America deserves, and we're doing it. This is a time for big dreams and bold action. Upon taking office, I imposed an immediate freeze on all federal hiring, a freeze on
all new federal regulations, and a freeze on all foreign aid.

I terminated the ridiculous green new scam. I withdrew from the
unfair Paris Climate accord, which was costing us trillions of dollars
that other countries were not paying. I withdrew from the corrupt
World Health Organization. And I also. Withdrew from the anti-
American UN Human Rights Council. We ended all of Biden's envi-

ronmental restrictions that were making our country far less safe and totally unaffordable. And importantly, we ended the last administration's insane electric vehicle mandate. Saving our auto workers and companies from economic destruction.

To unshackle our economy. I have directed that for every one new regulation, 10 old regulations must be eliminated, just like I did in my very successful first day. And in that first term, we set records on ending unnecessary rules and regulations like no other president had done before. We ordered all federal workers to return to the office. They will either show up for work in person or be removed from their job.

And we ended weaponized government where, as an example, a sitting president is allowed to viciously prosecute his political opponent like me. How did that work out? [crowd shouting] Not too good, not too good.

And I have stopped all government censorship and brought back free speech in America. It's back. And two days ago, I signed an order making English the official language of the United States of America. I renamed the Gulf of Mexico, the Gulf of America. And likewise, I renamed, for a great president, William McKinley. Mount McKinley again. Beautiful Alaska.

We've ended the tyranny of so-called diversity, equity and inclusion policies all across the entire federal government and indeed the private sector and our military. And our country will be woke no longer.

We believe that whether you are a doctor, an accountant, a lawyer or an air traffic controller, you should be hired and promoted based on skill and competence, not race or gender. Very important. You should be hired based on merit.

And the Supreme Court, in a brave and very powerful decision, has allowed us to do so. Thank you. Thank you very much. Thank you.

We have removed the poison of critical race theory from our public schools, and I signed an order making it the official policy of the

United States government that there are only two genders, male and female. I also signed an executive order to ban men from playing in women's sports.

Three years ago, Peyton McNabb was an all-star high school athlete, one of the best preparing for a future in college sports. But when her girls volleyball match was invaded by a male. He smashed the ball so hard in Peyton's face, causing a traumatic brain injury, partially paralyzing her right side and ending her athletic career. It was a shot like she's never seen before. She's never seen anything like it. Peyton is here tonight in the gallery, and Peyton, from now on, schools will kick the men off the girls team or they will lose all federal funding. And if you really want to see numbers, just take a look at what happened in the women's boxing, weightlifting, track and field, swimming or cycling where a male recently finished a long-distance race. Five hours and 14 minutes ahead of a woman for a new record by five hours, broke the record by five hours.

It's demeaning for women and it's very bad for our country. We're not going to put up with it any longer. What I've just described is only a small fraction of the commonsense revolution that is now, because of us sweeping the entire world. Common sense has become a common theme, and we will never go back, never, ever going to let that happen.

Joe Biden especially let the price of eggs get out of control. The egg price is out of control, and we're working hard to get it back down. Secretary, do a good job on that. You inherited a total mess from the previous administration. Do a good job.

A major focus of our fight to defeat inflation is rapidly reducing the cost of energy. The previous administration cut the number of new oil and gas leases by 95%, slowed pipeline construction to a halt, and closed more than 100 power plants. We are opening up many of those power plants right now. And frankly, we have never seen anything like it.

That's why on my first day in office, I declared a national energy emergency. As you've heard me say many times. We have more liquid gold under our feet than any nation on earth and by far. And now I fully authorize the most talented team ever assembled to go and get it. It's called drill, baby, drill.

My administration is also working on a gigantic natural gas pipeline in Alaska, among the largest in the world, where Japan, South Korea, and other nations want to be our partner with investments of trillions of dollars each has never been anything like that one. It will be truly spectacular. It's all set to go. The permitting is gotten, and later this week, I will also take historic action to dramatically expand production of critical minerals and rare earths here in the USA.

To further combat inflation. We will not only be reducing the cost of energy, but will be ending the flagrant waste of taxpayer dollars. And to that end, I have created the brand new Department of Government Efficiency -- DOGE. Perhaps you've heard of it.

They have, which is headed by Elon Musk, who is in the gallery tonight. Thank you, Elon. He's working very hard. He didn't need this. He didn't need this. Thank you very much. We appreciate it. Everybody here even this side appreciates it I believe. They just don't want to admit that.

Just listen to some of the appalling waste. We have already identified $22 billion. From HHS to provide free housing and cars for illegal aliens, $45 million for diversity, equity and inclusion scholarships in Burma. $40 million to improve the social and economic inclusion of sedentary migrants. Nobody knows what that is. $8 million to. Promote LGBTQ I plus in the African nation of Lesotho, which nobody has ever heard of. $60 million for indigenous peoples and Afro-Colombian empowerment in Central America. $60 million. $8 million for making mice transgender.

This is real. $32 million for a left-wing propaganda operation in Moldova. $10 million for male circumcision in Mozambique. $20 million for the Arab Sesame Street in the Middle East. It's a program, $20 million for a program $1.9 billion to recently created Decarbonization of Homes Committee headed up. And we know she's involved. Just at the last moment, the money was passed over by a woman named Stacey Abrams. Have you ever heard of her. [boos] A $3.5 million consulting contract for lavish fish monitoring, $1.5 million for voter confidence in Liberia. $14 million for social cohesion in Mali.

$59 million. For illegal alien hotel rooms in New York City. He's a real estate developer. He's done very well. $250,000 to increase vegan local climate action innovation in Zambia, $42 million for social and behavior change in Uganda. $14 million for improving public procurement in Serbia. $47 million for improving learning outcomes in Asia. Asia is doing very well with learning. You know what we're doing should use it ourselves. Now, $101 million for DEI contracts at the Department of Education. The most ever paid. Nothing even like it.

Under the Trump administration. All of these scams and there are far worse. But I didn't think it was appropriate to talk about them. They're so bad. Many more have been found out and exposed and swiftly terminated by a group of very intelligent, mostly young people headed up by Elon, and we appreciate it. We found hundreds of billions of dollars of fraud. And we've taken back the money and reduced our debt to fight inflation and other things. Taken back a lot of that money. We got it just in time. This is just the beginning.

The Government Accountability Office, a federal government office, has estimated annual fraud of over $500 billion in our nation, and we are working very hard to stop it. We're going to we're also identifying shocking levels of incompetence and probable fraud in the Social Security program for our seniors, and that our seniors and people that we love rely on. Believe it or not, government databases list 4.7 million Social Security members from people. aged 100 to 109 years old. [Boos, "that's false"] It lists 3.6 million people from ages 110 to 119. I don't know any of them. I know some people that are rather elderly, but not quite that elderly.

3.47 million people from ages 120 to 129, 3.9 million people from ages 130 to 139. 3.5 million people from ages 140 to 140, ma'am. And money is being paid to many of them. And we're searching right now. In fact, Pam, Good luck. Good luck. You're going to find it. But a lot of money is paid out to people because it just keeps getting paid and paid and nobody does. And it really hurts Social Security and hurts our country. 1.3 million people from ages. 150 to 159 and over 130,000 people according to the Social Security databases, are age over. 160 years old. We have a healthier country than I thought, Bobby. [applause] Including to finish 1039 people between the ages of 220 and 229, one person between the age of 240 and 249 and one person is listed at 360 years of age. More than 100 years, more than 100 years older than our country.

But we're going to find out where that money's going, and it's not going to be pretty. By slashing all of the fraud, waste and theft we can find, we will defeat inflation, bring down mortgage rates, lower car payments and grocery prices, protect our seniors, and put more money in the pockets of American families. And today, interest rates took a beautiful drop. Big, beautiful drop. It's about time.

And in the near future, I want to do what has not been done in 24 years balance the federal budget we're going to balance. With that goal in mind. We have developed in great detail what we are calling the gold card. Which goes on sale very, very soon. For $5 million. We will allow the most successful job creating people from all over the world to buy a path to U.S. citizenship.

It's like the green card, but better and more sophisticated. And these people will have to pay tax in our country. They won't have to pay tax from where they came, the money that they've made, you wouldn't want to do that. But they have to pay tax, create jobs. They'll also be taking people out of colleges and paying for them so that we can keep them in our country, instead of having them before being forced out.

Number one at the top school as an example, being forced out and not allowed to stay and create tremendous numbers of jobs and great success for a company out there. So while we take out the criminals, killers, traffickers and child predators who are allowed to enter our country under the open border policy of these people, the Democrats, the Biden administration, the open border. insane policies that you've allowed to destroy our country.

We will now bring in. Brilliant, hard working, job creating people. They're going to pay a. Lot of money. and we're going to reduce our debt with that money. Americans have given us a mandate for bold and profound change. For nearly 100 years, the federal bureaucracy has grown until it has crushed our freedoms, ballooned our deficits, and held back America's potential in every possible way.

The nation founded by pioneers. And risk takers, now drowns under millions. And. Millions of pages of. Regulations and debt. Approvals that should take ten days to get. Instead, take ten years, 15 years, and even 20 years before you rejected it.

Meanwhile, we have hundreds of thousands of federal workers who have not been showing up to work. My administration will reclaim power from this unaccountable bureaucracy, and we will restore true democracy to America again.

And any federal bureaucrat who resists this change will be removed from office immediately. Because we are draining the swamp. It's very simple. And the days of rule by unelected bureaucrats are over.

And the next phase of our plan to deliver the greatest economy in history is for this Congress to pass tax cuts for everybody. They're in there. They're waiting for you to vote. And I'm sure that the people on my right. I don't mean the Republican right, but my right right here. I'm sure you're going to vote for those tax cuts, because otherwise I don't believe the people will ever vote you into office.

So I'm doing a big favor by telling you that. But I know this group is going to be voting for the tax cuts.

Thank you. It's a very, very big part of our plan. We had tremendous success in our first term with it, a very big part of our plan. We're seeking permanent income tax cuts all across the board and to get urgently needed relief to Americans hit especially hard by inflation. I'm calling for no tax on tips, no tax on overtime and no tax on Social Security benefits for our great seniors.

And I also want to make interest payments on car loans tax deductible, but only if the car is made in America. And by the way, we're going to have growth in the auto industry like nobody's ever seen. Plants are opening up all over the place. Deals are being made, never seen. That's a combination of the election win and tariffs. It's a beautiful word isn't it. That along with our other policies, will allow our auto industry to absolutely boom, it's going to boom. Spoke to the majors today. All three, the top people and they're so excited.

In fact, already numerous car companies have announced that they will be building massive automobile plants in America. with Honda just announcing a new plant in Indiana. One of the largest anywhere in the world. And this has taken place since our great victory on November 5th, a date which will hopefully go down as one of the most important in the history of our country.

In addition, as part of our tax cuts, we want to cut taxes on domestic production and all manufacturing. And just as we did before, we will. provide 100% expensing. It will be retroactive to January 20th, 2025. And it was one of the main reasons why our tax cuts were so successful in our first term, giving us the most successful economy in the history of our country. First term, we had a great first term.

If you don't make your product in America, however, under the Trump administration, you will pay a tariff. And in some cases a rather large one. Other countries have used tariffs against us for decades, and now it's our turn to start using them against those other countries. On average, the European Union, China, Brazil, India, Mexico and Canada, have you heard of them? And countless other nations charge us tremendously higher tariffs than we charge them. It's very unfair. India charges US auto tariffs higher than 100%.

China's average tariff on our products is twice what we charge them. And South Korea's average tariff is four times higher. Think of that four times higher. And we give so much help militarily and in so many other ways to South Korea. But that's what happens. This is happening by friend and foe. This system is not fair to the United

States and never was. And so on April 2nd, I wanted to make it April 1st.

But I didn't -- want to be accused of April Fool's Day. That's what that's not. Just one day was, of course, that's a lot of money, but we're going to do it in April. I'm a very superstitious person. April 2nd, Reciprocal tariffs kick in. and whatever they tariff us, other countries we will tariff them. That's reciprocal -- back and forth whatever they tax us we will tax them.

If they do non-monetary tariffs to keep us out of their market. Then we will do non-monetary barriers to keep them out of our market. There's a lot of that too. They don't even allow us in their market. We will take in trillions and trillions of dollars that create jobs like we have never seen before.

I did it with China and I did it with others, and the Biden administration couldn't do anything about it because there was so much money. They couldn't do anything about it.

We have been ripped off for decades by nearly every country on Earth, and we will not let that happen any longer. Much has been said over the last three months about Mexico and Canada, but we have very large deficits with both of them.

But even more importantly, they've allowed fentanyl to come into our country at levels never seen before, killing hundreds of thousands of our citizens and many very young, beautiful people destroying families. Nobody's ever seen anything like it. They are, in effect, receiving subsidies of hundreds of billions of dollars. We pay subsidies to Canada and to Mexico of hundreds of billions of dollars. And the United States will not be doing that any longer. We're not going to do it any longer.

Thanks to our America First policies we're putting into place. We have. had $1.7 trillion of new investment in America in just the past few weeks. The combination of the election and our economic policies that people of SoftBank, one of the most brilliant anywhere in the world, announced a $200 billion investment: open AI and Oracle, Larry Ellison announced $500 billion investment, which they wouldn't have done if Kamala had won.

Apple announced $500 billion investment. Tim Cook called me. He said, I cannot spend it fast enough. It's going to be much higher than that, I believe. They'll be building their plants here instead of in China. And just yesterday, Taiwan Semiconductor, the biggest in the world, most powerful in the world has a tremendous amount -- 97% of the market announced a $165 billion investment to build the most powerful chips on Earth right here in the USA.

And we're not giving them any money. Your Chips Act is a horrible, horrible thing. We give hundreds of billions of dollars. And it doesn't mean a thing. They take our money and they don't spend it all that meant to them. We're giving them no money. All that was important to them was they didn't want to pay the tariff. So they came in that building. And many other companies are coming.

We don't have to give them money. We just want to protect our businesses and our people, and they will come because they won't have to pay tariffs if they build in America. So it's very amazing. You should get rid of the Chip Act. And whatever's left over. Mr. Speaker, you should use it to reduce debt or any other reason you want to.

Our new trade policy will also be great for the American farmer. I love the farmer. Who will now be selling into our home market, the USA, because nobody is going to be able to compete with you. Because there's goods that come in from other companies, countries and companies. They're really, really in a bad position in so many different ways. They're uninspected. They may be very dirty and disgusting, and they come in and they pour in and they hurt our American farmers. The tariffs will go on agricultural product coming into America and our farmers starting on April 2nd.

It may be a little bit of an adjustment period. We had that before when I made the deal with China. $50 billion in purchases, and I said, just bear with me. And they did. They did. Probably have to bear with me again, and this will be even better. That was great. The problem with it was that Biden didn't enforce it. He didn't enforce it — $50 billion of purchases. And we were doing great. But Biden did not enforce it, and it hurt our farmers. But our farmers are going to have a field day right now. So to our farmers, have a lot of fun. I love you, too. I love you, too.

They're all going to happen. And I have also impose a 25% tariff on foreign aluminum, copper, lumber and steel. Because if we don't have, as an example, steel. and lots of other things, we don't have a military and frankly won't have we just won't have a country very long. Here today is a proud American steelworker, fantastic person from Decatur, Alabama, Jeff Dennard. Has been working at the same steel plant for 27 years. At a job that has allowed him to serve as the captain of his local volunteer fire department, raise seven children with his beautiful wife, Nicole, and over the years provide a loving home for more than 40 foster children. So great, Jeff. Thank you, Jeff. Thank you, Jeff.

Stories like Jeff's remind us that tariffs are not just about protecting American jobs. They're about protecting the soul of our country. Tariffs are about making America rich again and making America great again. And it's happening. And it will happen rather quickly. There'll be a little disturbance. But we're okay with that. It won't be much. No. You know until [gestures].

And look, And look where Biden took us to. Very low. The lowest we've ever been. Jeff, I want to thank you very much. And I also want to recognize another person who has devoted herself to foster care community. She worked so hard on it, a very loving person. Our magnificent first lady of the United States. Melania's work has yielded incredible results, helping prepare our nation's future leaders as they enter the workforce.

Our first lady is joined by two impressive young women. Very impressive. Hailey Ferguson, who benefited from the First Ladies Fostering the Future initiative and is poised to complete her education, become a teacher, and Elliston Berry, who became a victim of an illicit Deepfake image produced by a peer. With Elliston's help, the Senate just passed the Take It Down Act, and this is so important.

Thank you very much, John. John Thune thank you, stand up, John. Thank you John. Thank you all very much. Thank you. And thank you to John Thune and the Senate. Great job to criminalize the publication of such images online. Just terrible, terrible thing. And once it passes the House, I look forward to signing that bill into law. Thank you. And I'm going to use that bill for myself, too, if you don't mind. There's nobody gets treated worse than I do online. Nobody. That's great. Thank you very much to the Senate. Thank you.

But if we truly care about protecting Americans children, no step is more crucial than securing America's borders. Over the past four years, 21 million people poured into the United States. Many of them were murderers, human traffickers, gang members and other criminals from the streets of dangerous cities all throughout the world because of Joe Biden's insane and very dangerous open border policies. They are now strongly embedded in our country, but. We are getting them out and getting them out fast.

And I want to thank Tom Homan and Christie. And I want to thank you and Paul of Border Patrol. I want to thank you. What a job they've all done. Everybody Border Patrol, ICE or law enforcement in general is incredible. We have to take care of our law enforcement.

Last year, a brilliant 22-year-old nursing student named Laken Riley, the best in her class, admired by everybody, went out for a jog on the campus of the University of Georgia. That morning, Laken was viciously attacked, assaulted, beaten, brutalized, and horrifically murdered. Laken was stolen from us by a savage illegal alien gang member. Who was arrested while trespassing across Biden's open southern border and then set loose into the United States under the heartless policies of that failed administration. It was indeed a failed administration. He had then been arrested. and released in a Democrat run sanctuary city, a disaster before ending the. life of this beautiful young angel. With us this evening are Laken's beloved mother, Alison, and her sister Lauren.

Last year, I told Laken's grieving parents that we would ensure their daughter would not have died in vain. That's why the very first bill I signed into law as your 47th president mandates the detention of all dangerous criminal aliens who threaten public safety. It's a very strong, powerful act. It's called the Laken Riley Act. So, Allison and Lauren, America will never, ever forget our beautiful Laken Hope Riley.

Thank you very much. Since taking office, my administration has launched the most sweeping border and immigration crackdown in American history. And we quickly achieved the lowest numbers of illegal border crossers ever recorded. Thank you. The media and our friends in the Democrat Party kept saying we needed new legislation. We must have legislation to secure the border. But it turned out that all we really needed was a new president. Thank you.

Joe Biden didn't just open our borders, he flew illegal aliens over them to overwhelm our schools, hospitals and communities throughout the country. Entire towns like Aurora, Colorado, and Springfield, Ohio, buckled under the weight of the migrant occupation and corruption like nobody's ever seen before. Beautiful towns destroyed. Now, just as I promised in my inaugural address, we are achieving the great liberation of America.

But there still is much work to be done. Here tonight is a woman. I have gotten to know. Alexis Nungaray from Houston. Wonderful woman last June. Alexis' 12-year-old daughter. Her precious Jocelyn walked to a nearby convenience store. She was kidnaped, tied up, assaulted for two hours under a bridge and horrifically murdered. Arrested and charged with this heinous crime are two illegal alien monsters from Venezuela, released into America by the last administration through their ridiculous open border. The death of this beautiful 12-year-old girl, and the agony of her mother and family touched our entire nation greatly.

Alexis, I promised that we would always remember your daughter, your magnificent daughter. And earlier tonight I signed an order keeping my word to you. One thing I have learned about Jocelyn is that she loved animals so much. She loved nature. Across Galveston Bay, from where Jocelyn lived in Houston, you will find a magnificent

National Wildlife Refuge, a pristine peaceful, 34,000-acre sanctuary for all of God's creatures on the edge of the Gulf of America. Alexis, moments ago, I formally renamed that refuge in loving memory of your beautiful daughter, Jocelyn.

So, Mr. Vice President, if you would. May I have the order? Thank you very much. All three savages charged with Jocelyn and Laken's murderers were members of the Venezuelan prison gang, the toughest gang, they say, in, the world known as [Tren de Aragua]. Two weeks ago, I officially designated this gang, along with Ms13 and the bloodthirsty Mexican drug cartels, as foreign terrorist organizations. They are now officially in the same category as ISIS, and that's not good for them. Countless thousands of these terrorists were welcomed into the U.S. by the Biden administration. But now every last one will be rounded up and forcibly removed from our country. Or if they're too dangerous, put in jail, standing trial in this country because we don't want them to come back ever.

With us this evening is a warrior on the frontlines of that battle. Border patrol agent Roberto Ortiz, great guy. In January, Roberto and another agent were patrolling by the Rio Grande near an area known as Cartel Island. Doesn't sound too nice to me when heavily armed gunmen started shooting at them. Roberto saw that his partner was totally exposed at great danger.

And he leapt into action, returning fire and providing crucial seconds for his fellow agent to seek safe safety. Just and just barely. I have some of the prints of that event and it was not good. Agent Ortiz, we salute you for your great courage and, for your line of fire that you took and for the bravery that you showed. We honor you, and we will always honor you. Thank you, Roberto, very much. Thank you, Roberto.

And I actually got to know him on my many calls to the border. He's a great, great gentleman. The territory to the immediate south of our border is now dominated entirely by criminal cartels. That murder, rape, torture and exercise total control. They have total control over a whole nation posing a grave threat to our national security.

The cartels are waging war in America, and it's time for America to wage war on the cartels, which we are doing.

Five nights ago, Mexican authorities, because of our tariff policies being imposed on them. Think of this, handed over to us 29 of the biggest cartel leaders in their country. That has never happened before. They want to make us happy, first time ever. But we need Mexico and Canada to do much more than they've done. And they have to stop the fentanyl and drugs pouring into the USA. They're going to stop it. I have sent Congress a detailed funding request, laying out exactly how we will eliminate these threats to protect our homeland and complete the largest deportation operation in American history, larger even than the current record holder, President Dwight Eisenhower.

A moderate man, but someone who believe very strongly in borders. Americans expect Congress to send me this funding without delay so I can sign it into law. So, Mr. Speaker, John Thune, both of you, I hope you're going to be able to do that. Mr. speaker. Thank you, Mr. Leader. Thank you. Thank you very much. And let's get it to me. I'll sign it so fast you won't even believe it.

And as we reclaim our sovereignty, we must also bring back law and order to our cities and towns. In recent years, our justice system has been turned upside down by radical left lunatics. Many jurisdictions virtually seized enforcing the law against dangerous repeat offenders while weaponizing law enforcement against political opponents. Like me. My administration has acted swiftly and decisively to restore fair, equal, and impartial justice under the constitutional rule of law, starting at the FBI and the DOJ. Pam, Good luck. Kash. Wherever you may be. Good luck. Good luck, Pam Bondi. Good luck. So important. Better do a great job, Kash. Thank you, thank you. Kash.

They've already started very strong. They're going to do a fantastic job. You're going to be very proud of them. We're also once again giving our police officers the support, protection and respect they show dearly deserved. They have to get it they have such a hard, dangerous job, but we're going to make it less dangerous. The problem is the bad guys don't respect the law, but they're starting to respect it and they soon will respect it.

This also includes our great fire departments throughout the country. Our firemen and women are unbelievable people and we'll never forget them. And besides that, they voted for me in record numbers so I have no chance.

One year ago this month, 31-year-old New York. Police officer Jonathan Diller, unbelievably wonderful person and a. great officer was gunned down at a traffic stop on Long Island. I went to his funeral. The vicious criminal charged with his murder had 21 prior arrests. And they were rough arrests. So he was a real bad one. The thug in the seat next to him had. 14 prior arrests. And went by the name of killer. He was killer. He killed other people. They say a lot of them.

I attended Officer Tiller's service, and when I met his wife and one year old son, Ryan, it was very inspirational, actually. His widow's name is Stephanie and she is here tonight. Stephanie. Thank you very much, Stephanie. Thank you very. Stephanie. We're going to make sure that Ryan knows his dad was a true hero, New York's finest. And we're going to get these cold-blooded killers and repeat offenders off our streets. So we're going to do it fast. Gotta to stop it.

And get out with 28 arrests, they push people into subway trains. They hit people over the head, back of the head with baseball bats. We got to get them out of here. I have already signed an executive order requiring a mandatory death penalty for anyone who murders a police officer.

And tonight, I'm asking Congress to pass that policy into permanent law. I'm also asking for a new crime bill getting tougher on repeat offenders while enhancing protections for America's police officers so they can do their jobs without fear of their lives being totally destroyed. They don't want to be killed. We're not going to let them be killed.

Joining us in the gallery tonight is a young man who truly loves our police. His name is D.J. Daniel. He is 13 years old. And he has always dreamed of becoming a police officer himself. But in 2018, D.J.

was diagnosed with brain cancer. The doctors gave him five months at most to live. That was more than six years ago. Since that time, D.J. and his dad have been on a quest to make his dream come true. And D.J. has been sworn in as an honorary law enforcement officer.

Actually, a number of times piece the police love him, the police departments love him. And tonight, D.J., we're going to do you the biggest honor of them all. I am asking our new Secret Service Director, Sean Curran, to officially make you an agent of the United States Secret Service. Thank you. D.J.

D.J.'s doctors believe his cancer likely came from a chemical he was exposed to when he was younger. Since 1975, rates of child cancer have increased. by more than 40%. Reversing this trend is one of the top priorities for our new Presidential Commission to Make America Healthy Again. Chaired by our new Secretary of Health and Human Services, Robert F. Kennedy Jr. By with name Kennedy, you would have thought everybody over here would have been cheering. How quickly they forget.

Our goal is to get toxins out of our environment, poisons out of our food supply. and keep our children healthy and strong. As an example, not long ago and you can't even believe these numbers, 1 in 10,000 children had autism, 1 in 10,000. and now it's 1 in 36. There's something wrong, 136, think of that. So we're going to find out what it is. And there's nobody better than Bobby.

And all of the people that are working with you. You have the best to figure out. What is going on. Okay, Bobby. Good luck. It's a very important job. Thank you. Okay. Thank you.

My administration is also working to protect our children from toxic ideologies in our schools. A few years ago, January Littlejohn and her husband discovered that their daughter's school had secretly socially transitioned their 13-year-old little girl. Teachers and administrators conspired to deceive. January and her husband, while encouraging her daughter to use a new name and pronouns. they them pronouns actually or without telling January. Who is here tonight and is now a courageous advocate against this form of child abuse. January. Thank you. Thank you, thank you very much. Thank you.

Stories like this are. Why, shortly after taking office, I signed an executive order banning public schools from indoctrinating our children with transgender ideology. All right. I also signed an order to cut off all taxpayer funding to any institution that engages in the sexual mutilation of our youth.

And we feel so much better for it, don't we? Don't we feel better? Our service.

Members won't be activists and ideologues. They will be fighters and warriors. They will fight for our country. And, Pete. Congratulations. Secretary of defense, today and he's not big into the woke movement, I can tell you. I know him well. I am pleased to report that in January, the U.S. Army had its single best recruiting month in 15 years. And that all armed services are having among the best recruiting results ever in the history of our services. What a difference. And, you know, it was just a few months ago where the results were exactly the opposite. We couldn't recruit anywhere. We couldn't recruit.

Now we're having the best results, just about that we've ever had. What a tremendous turnaround. It's really a beautiful thing to see people love our country again. It's very simple. They love our country and they love being in our military again. So it's a great thing. And thank you very much. Great job. Thank you.

We're joined tonight by a young man, Jason Hartley. Who knows the weight of that call of duty. Jason's father, grandfather and great grandfather all wore the uniform. Jason tragically lost his dad, who was also a Los Angeles County sheriff's deputy, when he was just a boy. And now he wants to carry on the family legacy of service. Jason is a senior in high school, A six letter varsity athlete, a really good athlete, they say. A brilliant student with a 4.46. That's good GPA. And his greatest dream is to attend the US. Military Academy at West Point. And Ja--Jason, that's a very big deal getting in, That's a hard one to get into. But I'm pleased to inform you that your application has been accepted. You will soon be joining the third cadet. Thank you. Jason. You're going to be on the long, great line, Jason.

AS commander in Chief. My focus is on building the most powerful military of the future as a first step. I'm asking Congress to fund a state of the art Golden Dome Missile defense shield to protect our homeland. All made in the USA.

And Ronald Reagan wanted to do it long ago, but the technology just wasn't there. Not even close. But now we have the technology. It's incredible actually. And other places that they have it. Israel has it. Other places have it. And the United States should have it too, right? Kim. Right. They should have it too. So I want to thank you, but it's a very, very important. This is a very dangerous world. We should have it. We want to be protected, and we're going to protect our citizens like never before. To boost our defense industrial base, we are also going to resurrect the American shipbuilding industry including commercial shipbuilding and military shipbuilding.

And for that purpose, I am announcing tonight that we will create a new office of shipbuilding in The White House and offer special tax incentives to bring this industry home to America, where it belongs. We used to make so many ships. We don't make them anymore very much. But we're going to. Make them very fast very soon. It will have a huge impact to further enhance our national security.

My administration will be Reclaiming the Panama Canal. And we've already started doing it. Just today, a large American company announced they are buying both ports around the Panama Canal and lots of other things having to do with the Panama Canal and a couple of other canals. The Panama Canal was built by Americans for Americans, not for others. But others could use it. But it was built at tremendous cost of American blood and treasure. 38,000 workers died building the Panama Canal. They died of malaria. They died of snakebites and mosquitoes. Not a nice place to work. They paid them very highly to go there. Knowing there was a 25% chance that they would die. The most expensive project also that was ever built in our country's history.

If you bring It up to modern day costs, it was given away by the Carter administration for $1. But that agreement has been violated very severely. We didn't give it to China. We gave it to Panama, and we're taking it back. Now we have Marco Rubio in charge. Good luck. Marco. Now we know who to blame. If anything goes wrong. Now, Marco has been amazing and he's going to do a great job. Think of it. He got 100 votes. You know, he was approved with. Actually 99, but the 100th was this gentleman. And I feel very certain. So let's assume he got 100 votes. And I'm either very, very happy about that or I'm very concerned about it. But he's already proven I mean, he's a great gentleman. He's respected by everybody. And we appreciate you voting for Marco. He's going to do a fantastic job. Thank you. Thank you. He's doing a great job. Great, great.

And I also have a message tonight for the incredible people of Greenland. We strongly support your right to determine your own future. And if you choose, we welcome you into he United States of America. We need Greenland for national security and even international security. And we're working with everybody involved to try and get it. But we need it really for international world security. And I think we're going to get it. One way or the other. We're going to get it. We will keep you safe. We will make you rich. And together, we will take Greenland to heights like you have never thought possible before. It's a very small population, but very, very large piece of land and very, very important for military security.

America is once again standing strong against the forces of radical Islamic terrorism. Three and a half years ago, ISIS terrorists killed 13 American service members. and countless others. In the Abbey Gate bombing during the disastrous and incompetent withdrawal from Afghanistan. Not that they were withdrawing, it was the way they withdrew. Perhaps the most embarrassing moment in the history of our country.

Tonight, I am pleased to announce that we have just apprehended the top terrorist responsible for that atrocity. And he is right now on his way here to face the swift sword of American justice. And I want to thank, especially the government of Pakistan for helping arrest this monster. This was a very momentous day for those 13 families who I actually got to know very well, most of them whose children were murdered and the many people that were so badly, over 42 people so badly injured on that fateful day in Afghanistan. What a horrible day. Such incompetence was shown that when Putin saw what happened, I guess he said, well, maybe this is my chance. That's how bad it was. Should have never happened. Grossly incompetent people.

I spoke to many of the parents and loved ones and they're all in our hearts tonight. I spoke to him on the phone. We had a big call. Every one of them called. And everybody was on the line and they did nothing but cry with happiness. They were very happy. As happy as you can be under those circumstances. Their child, brother, sister, son, daughter was. killed for no reason whatsoever in the Middle East. We're bringing back our hostages from Gaza. In my first term, we achieved one of the most groundbreaking peace agreements in generations, the Abraham Accords.

And now we're going to build on that foundation to create. A more peaceful and prosperous future for the entire region. A lot of things are happening in the Middle East. People have been talking about that so much lately, with everything going on with Ukraine and Russia. But a lot of things are happening in the Middle East's rough neighborhood, actually.

I'm also working tirelessly to end the savage conflict in Ukraine. Millions of Ukrainians and Russians have been needlessly killed or wounded in this horrific and brutal conflict with no end in sight. The United States has sent hundreds of billions of dollars to support Ukraine's defense with no security. With no energy. Do you want to keep it going for another five years? Yeah, yeah, you would say Pocahontas says yes. 2000 people have been killed every single week, more than that, they're Russian young people, they're Ukrainian young people. They're not Americans. But I want it to stop.

Meanwhile, Europe has sadly spent more money buying Russian oil and gas than they have spent on defending Ukraine by far. Think of that. They've spent more buying Russian oil and gas than they have defending, and we've spent perhaps $350 billion like taking candy from a baby. That's what happened. And they've spent $100 billion. What a difference it is. And we have. An ocean separating us. And they don't. But we're getting along very well with them and lots of good things are happening. Biden has authorized more money in this fight. than Europe has spent by billions and billions of dollars. It's hard to believe that they wouldn't have stopped it and said at some point, come on, let's equalize. You got to be equal to us. That didn't happen.

Earlier today, I received an important letter from President Zelensky of Ukraine. The letter reads, Ukraine is ready to come to the negotiating table as soon as possible to bring lasting peace closer. Nobody wants peace more than the Ukrainians, he said. My team and I stand ready to work under President Trump's strong leadership to get a peace that lasts. We do really value how much America has done to help Ukraine maintain its sovereignty and independence. Regarding the agreement on. Minerals and Security, Ukraine is ready to sign it at any time that is convenient for you.

I appreciate that he sent this letter, just got it a little while ago. Simultaneously, we've had serious discussions with Russia and have received strong signals that they are ready for peace. Wouldn't that be beautiful? Wouldn't that be beautiful? Wouldn't that be beautiful? It's time to stop this madness. It's time to halt the killing. It's time to end this senseless war. If you want to end wars, you have to talk to both sides.

Nearly four years ago, amid rising tensions, a history teacher named Mark Fogel was detained in Russia and sentenced to 14 years in a penal colony. Rough stuff, the previous administration barely lifted a finger to help him. They knew he was innocent. But they had no idea where to begin. But last summer, I promised his 95-year-old mother, Malphine that we would bring her boy safely back home. After 22 days in office. I did just that. And they are here tonight. To

Mark and his great mom. We are delighted to have you safe and sound and with us.

As fate would have it, Mark. Fogel was born in a small rural town in Butler, Pennsylvania. Have you heard of it? Where his mother has lived for the past 78 years? I just happened to. Go there last July 13th for a rally. That was not pleasant. And that is where I met his beautiful mom right. Before I walked onto that stage. And I told her I would not forget what she said about her son, and I never did that. I never forgot. Less than ten minutes later, at that same rally. Gunfire rang out and a sick and deranged assassin unloaded eight bullets from his sniper's perch into a crowd of many thousands of people. My life was saved by a fraction of an inch. But some were not so lucky.

Corey Comparator was a firefighter, a veteran, a Christian, a husband, a devoted father, and above all, a protector. When the sound of gunshots pierced the air, it was a horrible sound. Corey knew. instantly what it was and what to do. He threw himself on top of his wife and daughters. And shielded them from the bullets with his own body. Corey was hit really hard. You know the story. From there. He sacrificed his life to save theirs. Two others very fine people were also seriously hit. but thankfully, with the help of two great country doctors, we thought they were gone and they were saved. So those doctors had great talent. We're joined by Corey's wife, Helen, who was his high school sweetheart. And their two beloved daughters Allison and Kaylee. Thank you. To Helen and Allison and Kaylee - Corey is looking down on his three beautiful ladies right now. And he is cheering you on. He loves you. He is cheering you on. Corey was taken from us much too soon, but his destiny was to leave us all with a shining example of the selfless devotion of a true. American patriot. It was love like Corey's that built our country and its love like Corey's. That is going to make our country more majestic than ever before.

I believe that my life was saved. That day and Butler for a very good reason. I was saved by God to make America great again, I believe that. Thank you. Thank you. Thank you very much. From the patriots of Lexington and Concord to the heroes of. Gettysburg and

Normandy. From the warriors who crossed the Delaware, to the trail-blazers who climbed the Rockies, and from. The legends who soared at Kitty Hawk. To the astronauts who touched the moon.

Americans have always been the people who defied all odds, Transcended all dangers made the most extraordinary sacrifices, and did whatever it took. to defend our children, our country and our freedom. And as we have seen in this chamber tonight, that same strength, faith, love and spirit is still alive and thriving in the hearts of the American people, despite the best efforts of those who would try to censor us, silence us, break us, destroy us. Americans are today a proud, free, sovereign and independent nation that will always be free, and we will fight for it till death. We will never let anything happen. To our beloved country because we are a country of doers, dreamers, fighters and survivors. Our ancestors crossed a vast ocean, strode into the unknown wilderness and carved their fortunes from the rock and soil of a perilous and very dangerous frontier. They chased our destiny across a boundless continent. They built the rail-roads, laid the highways, and graced the world with American Marvels like the Empire State Building, the mighty Hoover Dam, and the towering Golden Gate Bridge. They lit the world with electricity, broke free of the force of gravity, fired up the engines of American industry, vanquished the communist fascists and Marxists all over the world, and gave us countless modern wonders. Sculpted out of iron, glass, and steel.

We stand on the shoulders of these pioneers who won and built the modern age. These workers who poured their sweat into the sky-lines of our cities, these warriors who shed their blood on fields of battle, who gave everything they had. For our rights and for our freedom. Now it is our time to take up the righteous cause of American liberty, and it is our turn to take America's destiny into our own hands. And begin the most thrilling days in the history of our country. This will be our greatest era. With God's help, over the next four years, we are going to lead this nation even higher, and we are going to forge the freest most advanced, most dynamic and most dominant civilization ever. To exist on the face of this Earth. We are going to create the highest quality of life, build the safest and wealthiest and healthiest and most vital communities anywhere in the world.

We are going to conquer the vast frontiers of science, and we are going to lead humanity into space and plant the American flag on the planet Mars, and even far beyond. And through it all, we are going to rediscover. The unstoppable power of the American spirit and we are going to renew unlimited promise of the American dream.

Every single day. We will stand up and we will fight, fight, fight for the country our citizens believe in and for the country people deserve. My fellow Americans, get ready. for an incredible future, because the golden age of America has only just begun. It will be like nothing that has ever. been seen before. Thank you. God bless you and God bless America.

Democratic Response

{U.S. Senator Elissa Slotkin, following the State of the Union address by President Donald Trump}

Hi everyone. I'm Elissa Slotkin. I'm honored to have the opportunity to speak tonight. It's late — so I promise to be a lot shorter than what you just watched.

I won't take it personally if you've never heard of me. I'm the new senator from the great state of Michigan, where I grew up. I've been in public service my entire life, because I happened to be in New York City on 9/11 when the twin towers came down. Before the smoke cleared, I knew I wanted a life in national security.

I was recruited by the CIA and did three tours in Iraq, alongside the military. In between, I worked at the White House under President Bush and President Obama, two very different leaders who both believed that America is exceptional.

You can find that same sense of patriotism here in Wyandotte, Michigan, where I am tonight. It's a working-class town just south of Detroit. President Trump and I both won here in November. It might not seem like it, but plenty of places like this still exist all across the United States – places where people believe that if you work hard, and play by the rules, you should do well and your kids do better.

It reminds me of how I grew up. My dad was a lifelong Republican, my mom a lifelong Democrat. But it was never a big deal. Because we had shared values that were bigger than any one party.

We just went through another fraught election season. Americans made it clear that prices are too high and that government needs to be more responsive to their needs. America wants change. But there is a responsible way to make change, and a reckless way. And, we can make that change without forgetting who we are as a country, and as a democracy.

So that's what I'm going to lay out tonight.

Because whether you're in Wyandotte or Wichita, most Americans share three core beliefs: That the Middle Class is the engine of our country. That strong national security protects us from harm. And that our democracy, no matter how messy, is unparalleled and worth fighting for.

Let's start with the economy.

Michigan literally invented the Middle Class: the revolutionary idea that you could work at an auto plant and afford the car you were building. That's the American Dream. And in order to expand and protect the Middle Class, we have to do a few, basic things:

We need to bring down the price of things we spend the most money on: Groceries. Housing. Healthcare. Your car.

We need to make more things in America with good-paying, union jobs — and bring our supply chains back home from places like China.

We need to give American businesses the certainty they need to invest and create the jobs of the future.

And we need a tax system that's fair for people who don't happen to make a billion dollars.

Look, President Trump talked a big game on the economy, but it's always important to read the fine print. So: do his plans actually help Americans get ahead?

Not even close.

President Trump is trying to deliver an unprecedented giveaway to his billionaire friends. He's on the hunt to find trillions of dollars to pass along to the wealthiest in America. And to do that, he's going to make you pay in every part of your life.

Grocery and home prices are going up, not down — and he hasn't laid out a credible plan to deal with either.

His tariffs on allies like Canada will raise prices on energy, lumber, cars — and start a trade war that will hurt manufacturing and farmers.

Your premiums and prescriptions will cost more because the math on his proposals doesn't work without going after your health care.

Meanwhile, for those keeping score, the national debt is going up, not down. And if he's not careful, he could walk us right into a recession.

And one more thing: In order to pay for his plan, he could very well come after your retirement – the Social Security, Medicare, and VA benefits you worked your whole life to earn. The President claims he won't, but Elon Musk just called Social Security "the biggest Ponzi scheme of all time."

While we're on the subject of Elon Musk, is there anyone in America who is comfortable with him and his gang of 20-year-olds using their own computer servers to poke through your tax returns, your health information, and your bank accounts? No oversight. No protections against cyberattack. No guardrails on what they do with your private data.

We need more efficient government. You want to cut waste, I'll help you do it. But change doesn't need to be chaotic or make us less safe.

The mindless firing of people who work to protect our nuclear weapons, keep our planes from crashing, and conduct the research that finds the cure for cancer — only to re-hire them two days later? No CEO in America could do that without being summarily fired.

OK, so we've talked about our economic security. How about national security?

Let's start with the border. As someone who spent my whole career protecting our homeland, every country deserves to know who and what is coming across its border. Period. Democrats and Republicans should all be for that.

But securing the border without actually fixing our broken immigration system is dealing with the symptom not the disease. America is a nation of immigrants. We need a functional system, keyed to the needs of our economy, that allows vetted people to come and work here legally. So I look forward to the President's plan on that.

Because here's the thing: Today's world is deeply interconnected. Migration, cyber-threats, AI, environmental destruction, terrorism — one nation cannot face these issues alone. We need friends in all corners — and our safety depends on it.

President Trump loves to promise "peace through strength." That's actually a line he stole from Ronald Reagan. But let me tell you, after the spectacle that just took place in the Oval Office last week, Reagan must be rolling over in his grave. We all want an end to the war in Ukraine, but Reagan understood that true strength required America to combine our military and economic might with moral clarity.

And that scene in the Oval Office wasn't just a bad episode of reality TV. It summed up Trump's whole approach to the world. He believes in cozying up to dictators like Vladimir Putin and kicking our friends, like Canada, in the teeth. He sees American leadership as merely a series of real estate transactions.

As a Cold War kid, I'm thankful it was Reagan and not Trump in office in the 1980s. Trump would have lost us the Cold War.

Donald Trump's actions suggest that, in his heart, he doesn't believe we are an exceptional nation. He clearly doesn't think we should lead the world.

Look, America's not perfect. But I stand with most Americans who believe we are still exceptional. Unparalleled. And I would rather have American leadership over Chinese or Russian leadership any day of the week.

Because for generations, America has offered something better.

Our security and our prosperity, yes. But our democracy, our very system of government, has been the aspiration of the world. And right now, it's at risk.

It's at risk when a president decides he can pick and choose what rules he wants to follow, when he ignores court orders or the Constitution itself, or when elected leaders stand idly by and just let it happen.

But it's also at risk when the President pits Americans against each other, when he demonizes those who are different, and tells certain people they shouldn't be included.

Because America is not just a patch of land between two oceans. We are more than that. Generations have fought and died to secure the fundamental rights that define us. Those rights and the fight for them make us who we are.

We are a nation of strivers. Risk-takers. Innovators. And we are never satisfied.

That is America's superpower.

And look, I've lived and worked in many countries. I've seen democracies flicker out. I've seen what life is like when a government is rigged. You can't open a business without paying off a corrupt official. You can't criticize the guys in charge without getting a knock at the door in the middle of the night.

So as much as we need to make our government more responsive to our lives today, don't for one moment fool yourself that democracy isn't precious and worth saving.

But how do we actually do that? I know a lot of you have been asking that question.

First, don't tune out. It's easy to be exhausted, but America needs you now more than ever. If previous generations had not fought for democracy, where would we be today?

Second, hold your elected officials, including me, accountable. Watch how they're voting. Go to town halls and demand they take action. That's as American as apple pie.

Three, organize. Pick just one issue you're passionate about — and engage. And doom scrolling doesn't count. Join a group that cares about your issue, and act. And if you can't find one, start one.

Some of the most important movements in our history have come from the bottom up.

In closing, we all know that our country is going through something right now. We're not sure what the next day is going to hold, let alone the next decade.

But this isn't the first time we've experienced significant and tumultuous change as a country. I'm a student of history, and we've gone through periods of political instability before. And ultimately, we've chosen to keep changing this country for the better.

But every single time, we've only gotten through those moments because of two things: Engaged citizens and principled leaders.

Engaged citizens who do a little bit more than they're used to doing to fight for the things they care about. And principled leaders who are ready to receive the ball and do something about it.

So thank you tonight for caring about your country. Just by watching, you qualify as engaged citizens. And I promise that I, and my fellow Democrats, will do everything in our power to be the principled leaders that you deserve.

Goodnight everyone.

Republican Response

{Given by Congressman Juan Ciscomani of Arizona}

Buenas noches. Soy Juan Ciscomani, Congresista del 6to distrito en Arizona. Es un honor poderme dirigir a ustedes desde el Capitolio de los Estados Unidos como el primer emigrante de México elegido para el Congreso Federal del estado de Arizona. Hace apenas unas semanas tomé juramento para mi puesto. Y les puedo decir que ya me he dado cuenta que Washington necesita una nueva perspectiva.

Yo emigré a Estados Unidos con mis padres cuando era niño en busca de una mejor vida, de una nueva oportunidad: llegamos para luchar por el sueño americano. Un sueño que mi esposa Laura y yo hemos tenido la oportunidad de vivir. Y queremos que nuestros 6 hijos, al igual que cada estadounidense, tengan aún mejores oportunidades de alcanzar sus sueños.

La primera vez que juré ante la Constitución fue el día que me hice ciudadano de los Estados Unidos. La segunda vez que juré ante la Constitución fue el día que me hice miembro del congreso de los Estados Unidos. Estoy agradecido por las oportunidades que nuestro gran país le ha dado a mi familia y a millones de familias en busca del sueño americano.

Y hoy estamos en un punto crítico en la historia de nuestra nación. Ahora, más que nunca, necesitamos luchar agresivamente por los valores que han hecho posible el sueño americano para tantos. Pero como podemos ver, el presidente Biden y su administración continúan impulsando políticas que lastiman a nuestras familias. Los resultados hablan por sí mismos:

- El costo de vivienda está fuera de control.
- La leche y el pan siguen subiendo de precio y ahora comprar huevos parece un lujo.
- La gasolina aún sigue cara, lo cual afecta el costo de todo lo que consumimos

- Es casi imposible comprar casa por el costo, y las tasas de interés tan altas
- Y la crisis de drogas - como el fentanilo - continúa robando miles de vidas y destruyendo familias. La sobredosis de fentanilo es la causa más alta de muertes entre jóvenes en mi condado, sobrepasando a los accidentes automovilísticos. Pero lamentablemente, esto está sucediendo a través del país entero. Es una crisis y continúa empeorando.

El Presidente Biden nos quiere decir que todo va de maravilla. Pero porque no nos sentimos de maravilla? El sueño americano parece inalcanzable y lamentablemente, el presidente sigue sin ejercer liderazgo al no presentar ningún remedio viable. No ha tenido soluciones y claramente aun no las tiene. Pero los republicanos de la Cámara de Representantes ya hemos comenzado a ofrecer una dirección diferente, una dirección que enfrenta directamente los temas más importantes para las familias de nuestro país. Bajo el liderazgo del presidente de la cámara de representantes Kevin McCarthy, hemos hecho un "Compromiso con Estados Unidos", un compromiso con cada uno de ustedes, que da prioridad a una economía fuerte; a una nación segura; a un futuro basado en la libertad; y a un gobierno que rinda cuentas.

Necesitamos:

- Proteger y fortalecer el futuro de Seguro Social y Medicare. El cortar estos programas no es una opción.
- Combatir la inflación y reducir el costo de vida al frenar el gasto desmedido del gobierno que sube los precios de productos de consumo diario.
- Aumentar la seguridad fronteriza, invertir en infraestructuras y tecnología para evitar los cruces ilegales de tráfico de drogas y la explotación del tráfico humano.
- Asegurar que todos los estudiantes puedan tener éxito y dar una voz a los padres de familia

- Defender la seguridad nacional al apoyar a nuestras tropas al invertir en un ejército eficiente y eficaz. Y a nuestros veteranos con sus necesidades de salud y económicas.
- Tomar con seriedad la amenaza que China presenta a nuestra seguridad, libertad y prosperidad.
- Restaurar nuestra independencia energética y reducir el precio de la gasolina y la electricidad
- Reducir el crimen y proteger la seguridad pública.
- Hacer el costo de consultas médicas más transparente y fácil de comprender para todos.

Necesitamos un gobierno que rinde cuentas a sus ciudadanos. No uno con líderes que siempre tengan excusas y se enfoquen más en criticar al otro partido que en buscar soluciones reales. Podemos hacer mejor. Debemos hacer mejor. Así es cómo vamos a proteger el sueño americano para nuestros hijos.

Como les compartí, crecí en Tucson, Arizona, donde mi papá trabajó como conductor de autobús de la ciudad para darnos a mis hermanas y a mí una oportunidad al sueño americano. De esa manera mostró a sus hijos el valor del trabajo y nos enseñó amor y respeto hacia nuestro país. Y nos demostró que con determinación y trabajo duro, no hay límites en esta gran nación. Mi mamá ha sido el pilar de fe en nuestra familia. Siempre orando y recordándonos que con fe, todo es posible.

Si hablas con mi papá hoy, él te dirá: "¿En qué otro lugar del mundo podemos tener nuestra historia? Llegamos a este país sin nada. Aprendimos inglés, nos sumergimos en la cultura, alcanzamos la ciudadanía, conduzco un autobús la mayoría de mi vida, y mi hijo ahora es miembro del Congreso de los Estados Unidos."

¿Dónde más pudiéramos tener nuestra historia?

La respuesta es sencilla: en ninguna otra parte del mundo. Esto sucede aquí en los Estados Unidos - el país de la oportunidad.

Y como mi historia hay muchas! Existen millones de ejemplos de personas, migrantes o no, que han tenido la oportunidad de crear su propia historia de éxito en diversas áreas.

Por eso es importante seguir luchando por nuestro país y mis colegas republicanos y yo estamoscomprometidos a proteger y fortalecer el sueño americano para todos. Como republicanos, creemos en un gobierno que trabaje para la gente y que rinda cuentas, creemos en la responsabilidad fiscal y en el poder del esfuerzo humano. Creemos en la libertad individual y en el excepcionalismo americano.

El sueño americano no se trata solo de éxito financiero. Se trata de ser libre de alcanzar nuestra felicidad. Y es por eso que el sueño americano es un sueño en el que creo firmemente.

Es un sueño que estoy viviendo.

Es un sueño que nos une a todos.

Es un sueño que está vivo.

Y es un sueño que vale la pena defender y que unidos podemos hacer realidad.

Pongamos a un lado las divisiones y enfoquémonos en los resultados, así podremos mantener este sueño vivo para las próximas generaciones.

El futuro de nuestra unión es fuerte. Porque nuestra gente es fuerte. Podemos sobrepasar cualquier obstáculo. Nuestros mejores días aún están por delante.

Gracias. Que Dios los bendiga.

Y que Dios SIEMPRE bendiga a los Estados Unidos de América.

Buenas noches.

AFTERWORD

I fully reveal my bias now. I have tried to give an honest and accurate space to the documents and statements that have made up these last forty days, and posting criticisms and reactions to them as a contextual part of this small slice of history. But no writer, however objective in intention, is without a conscience. There is always room to see behind the curtain of a page. We don't check our souls at the coat closet in exchange for an ISBN ticket. So here it is, for those who want to know:

On the last day of February 2025, Air Force One carried President Donald Trump back to Florida, along with the boxes that were seized by the FBI early in the Biden administration. So many of the acts and statements of the last forty days seem like the fulfillment of a "revenge tour" that so many of Trump's admirers hoped for. Revoking Biden's access to briefings -- as had been done to him -- was to be expected, regardless of the reasons given. So many political adversaries were fired, replaced, and relieved of their security details, arguably in need them in the first place over so much inflammatory, conspiratorial, partisan rhetoric against them. In fact, openly-voiced promises of political retribution were the reason Anthony Fauci and the members of the J6 committee were pardoned. Those who cried weaponized lawfare are to be expected to attempt it themselves, as evidenced by previous and current actions to stack the deck, whereas so many of the judges and lawyers who tried and convicted Trump were Republicans — some appointed by him.

Those who attempted to stop the transition of power by force in 2021 weren't pardoned before he left office, but have been now, something JD Vance said would never happen. The J6 Choir may even sing at the Kennedy Center. For most Americans, this is just so surreal.

Like in 2020, every days seems to bring something you must look at closely to see if it isn't from a site like The Onion or the Babylon Bee. The term "satire singularity" comes to mind, where satire is indistinguishable from real news. Pics of Elon Musk with a chainsaw (at CPAC) are paired with pictures of Macho Man in the 2006 movie "Idiocracy", a title that seems to come up more often when Trump is in office.

Even after saying there was not a connection, nearly every Executive Order plays some Project 2025 tune, even in terminology. Every potshot that can be taken against Biden is taken, occasionally extending the blame to Obama. It didn't matter that his deal with Canada he so harshly criticized turned out to be the deal he made himself years earlier. It was never about facts or reality. Those who often cast the spell of "Facts don't care about your feelings" are now countered with "Every attack is a confession".

The Democrat Party (DNC), of course, is doing little. It's like they've given up. Maybe they know they share in the responsibility of someone like Trump (and those who use him) coming to power. After all, it was a lackluster or even defiant absence of Harris voters that determined the outcome, not some statistically nonexistent "overwhelming majority" MAGA fans insist give credence to the notion Trump was given a mandate by The People. This two-horse race to the bottom, and increasingly extreme pendularity between Left and Right, is for another time to ponder. What matters now is how the public responds to things as they happen. And ANYTHING could happen now that so many norms have been broken and safeguards removed.

Those who are all for this "owning the libs" agenda in every respect may not care. An alarming number of people said they would prefer a Trump dictatorship to a Biden Presidency. But the world cares. Our (former) allies care. Our enemies care, though not in a good way. Political scientists, journalists, and pretty much anyone else who have been labeled by Trump and company as not to be trusted, are using words like "fascist coup".

Frankly, we Americans don't know what the word means. If we did, we'd kick ourselves, because we always had a streak of it in us. In many ways, Nazi Germany was modeled after American policies of native genocide and Jim Crow apartheid. If it weren't for Pearl Harbor, we might have sided with the Third Reich. Our memories are too short to recall that there were beer parties around the nation when Hitler rolled into Paris. And the first thing we did when we declared war was to round up over a hundred thousand citizens of Japanese descent and put them in camps. And few are aware of REX 86, a program that reads like a crackpot conspiracy but is public record now.

It is my opinion -- and that of many others across the political spectrum -- that we have lost control of our nation. Many tolerate it because they are still conditioning themselves with the same media channels that radicalized so many of us leading up to January 6th, the nature of which is distorted into total denial and unreality. We don't know what help will come from without or within. The most some will do is share the #FOFO hashtag as bad things happen to Trump voters. But many agree with the meme that says, "If you ever wondered what you would do in 1930s Nazi Germany, you're doing it now". Mind you, 1933 didn't seem so bad. But the signs were there where it would lead, and may lead again. As 1944 ended with Germany against the world, Trump is already being touted by people across the globe as the greatest threat to world peace.

Some of my friends are voicing rhetorical explanations for every failure of gaffe, borrowed from the usual suspect media channels. Others are horrified, seeing a pattern that justifies a surge in passports and other contingent plans. One acquaintance posted a meme reading "REPORT ILLEGAL ALIENS - in your neighborhood - at schools - at work - at church - at restaurants - There is nowhere to hide!" while others I know probably were among those who spammed the number, reporting Elon Musk and Melania Trump.

Most, but not all, of the Trump and "Let's Go Brandon!" flags were taken down after the election. For many, I suspect him winning was more important symbolically than actually supporting him. Countless people are expressing regrets online, mostly those whose policies affected their livelihoods. Especially those who lost government jobs, incredulous about not being protected by anti-DEI mandates. A pastor I know likened Biden to Hitler during his first State of the Union because of red lighting in the background. He missed the wording that MAGA extremists -- and not everyday Republicans -- were a danger to America, something difficult to argue after January 6th without a heavy dose of conspiracies. His feed was filled with "please pray for our country". He is strangely silent now.

I myself will continue to call and write and educate. Maybe I'll keep a copy of Hannah Arendt's "Origins of Totalitarianism" in my pocket. Maybe I will "aim to misbehave" and in the words of Joe Lewis, get into some "good trouble". Maybe I will write books from my personal "Dagobah" about everyday ways people can make better a world that seems unjust and out of our control. In fact, I intend to do exactly that, regardless of what happens.

I really hope that I and so many others are overreacting. I will be happy to feel foolish about it in four years. Even if I disagree with so many policies and actions, maybe those who blankly keep repeating "everything is going to be great, just wait and see" aren't wholly unjustified.

The reader of the future will have to answer this question.

APPENDIX: LIST OF EXECUTIVE ORDERS

Since President Truman, no president has come close to a thousand Executive Orders, or even an average of more than a hundred per year in office. Obama made 276 total, a bit less than Clinton and George W. Bush. Trump had 220 in his first term, more than Biden (162), who was accused of ruling by decree when he undid many of Trump's first term Orders.

In his first 40 days of office, President Trump signed 80 Executive Orders. He revoked over 65 of President Biden's Executive Orders and memos in his second Order alone, repeatedly labeling many of them as "harmful". His Orders routinely use terms like "radical" when referring to any non-conservative view or policy targeted.

20 January

EO 14147: Ending the Weaponization of the Federal Government
Signed: January 20, 2025
Published: January 28, 2025

EO 14148: Initial Rescissions of Harmful Executive Orders and Actions
Signed: January 20, 2025
Published: January 28, 2025
Revokes: EO 13985, January 20, 2021; EO 13986, January 20, 2021; EO 13987, January 20, 2021; EO 13988, January 20, 2021; EO 13989, Janu-

ary 20, 2021; EO 13990, January 20, 2021; EO 13992, January 20, 2021; EO 13993, January 20, 2021; EO 13995, January 21, 2021; EO 13996, January 21, 2021; EO 13997, January 21, 2021; EO 13999, January 21, 2021; EO 14000, January 21, 2021; EO 14002, January 22, 2021; EO 14003, January 22, 2021; EO 14004, January 25, 2021; EO 14006, January 26, 2021; EO 14007, January 27, 2021; EO 14008, January 27, 2021; EO 14009, January 28, 2021; EO 14010, February 2, 2021; EO 14011, February 2, 2021; EO 14012, February 2, 2021; EO 14013, February 4, 2021; EO 14015, February 14, 2021; EO 14018, February 24, 2021; EO 14019, March 7, 2021; EO 14020, March 8, 2021; EO 14021, March 8, 2021; EO 14022, April 1, 2021; EO 14023, April 9, 2021; EO 14027, May 7, 2021; EO 14029, May 14, 2021; EO 14030, May 20, 2021; EO 14031, May 28, 2021; EO 14035, June 25, 2021; EO 14037, August 5, 2021; EO 14044; EO 14045, September 13, 2021; EO 14049, October 11, 2021; EO 14050, October 19, 2021; EO 14052, November 15, 2021; EO 14055, November 18, 2021; EO 14057, December 8, 2021; EO 14060, December 15, 2021; EO 14069, March 15, 2022; EO 14070, April 5, 2022; EO 14074, May 25, 2022; EO 14075, June 15, 2022; EO 14082, September 12, 2022; EO 14084, September 30, 2022; EO 14087, October 14, 2022; EO 14089, December 13, 2022; EO 14091, February 16, 2023; Memo. of March 13, 2023; EO 14094, April 6, 2023; EO 14096, April 21, 2023; EO 14099, May 9, 2023; EO 14110, October 30, 2023; EO 14115, February 1, 2024; EO 14124, July 17, 2024; EO 14134, January 3, 2025; EO 14135, January 3, 2025; EO 14136, January 3, 2025; EO 14137, January 3, 2025; EO 14138, January 3, 2025; EO 14139, January 3, 2025; Memo. of January 3, 2025; Memo. of January 3, 2025; Memo. of January 3, 2025; Memo. of January 3, 2025; Memo. of January 3, 2025; Memo. of January 3, 2025; Memo. of January 6, 2025; Memo. of January 6, 2025; Memo. of January 14, 2025; Memo. of January 14, 2025; EO 14143, January 16, 2025

See: EO 14183, January 27, 2025

EO 14149: Restoring Freedom of Speech and Ending Federal Censorship

Signed: January 20, 2025
Published: January 28, 2025

EO 14150: America First Policy Directive to the Secretary of State
Signed: January 20, 2025
Published: January 29, 2025
See: EO 13985, January 20, 2021

EO 14151: Ending Radical and Wasteful Government DEI Programs and Preferencing
Signed: January 20, 2025
Published: January 29, 2025

EO 14152: Holding Former Government Officials Accountable for Election Interference and Improper Disclosure of Sensitive Governmental Information
Signed: January 20, 2025
Published: January 29, 2025

EO 14153: Unleashing Alaska's Extraordinary Resource Potential
Signed: January 20, 2025
Published: January 29, 2025

EO 14154: Unleashing American Energy
Signed: January 20, 2025
Published: January 29, 2025
Revokes: EO 11991, May 24, 1977; EO 13990, January 20, 2021; EO 13992, January 20, 2021; EO 14008, January 27, 2021; EO 14007, January 27, 2021; EO 14013, February 4, 2021; EO 14027, May 7, 2021; EO 14030, May 20, 2021; EO 14037, August 5, 2021; EO 14057, December 8, 2021; EO 14072, April 22, 2022; EO 14082, September 12, 2022; EO 14096, April 21, 2023
See: Memo. of January 27, 2021

EO 14155: Withdrawing the United States From the World Health Organization
Signed: January 20, 2025
Published: January 29, 2025
Revokes: EO 13987, January 20, 2021

EO 14156: Declaring a National Energy Emergency
Signed: January 20, 2025
Published: January 29, 2025
See: EO 14193, February 1, 2025

EO 14157: Designating Cartels and Other Organizations as Foreign Terrorist Organizations and Specially Designated Global Terrorists
Signed: January 20, 2025
Published: January 29, 2025
Amends: EO 13224, September 23, 2001
See: EO 14193, February 1, 2025; EO 14195, February 1, 2025

EO 14158: Establishing and Implementing the President's "Department of Government Efficiency"
Signed: January 20, 2025
Published: January 29, 2025
See: EO 14210, February 11, 2025; EO 14219, February 19, 2025

EO 14159: Protecting the American People Against Invasion
Signed: January 20, 2025Published: January 29, 2025
Revokes: EO 13993, January 20, 2021; EO 14010, February 2, 2021; EO 14011, February 2, 2021; EO 14012, February 2, 2021

EO 14160: Protecting the Meaning and Value of American Citizenship
Signed: January 20, 2025
Published: January 29, 2025

EO 14161: Protecting the United States From Foreign Terrorists and Other National Security and Public Safety Threats
Signed: January 20, 2025
Published: January 30, 2025

EO 14162: Putting America First in International Environmental Agreements
Signed: January 20, 2025
Published: January 30, 2025

EO 14163: Realigning the United States Refugee Admissions Program
Signed: January 20, 2025
Published: January 30, 2025
Revokes: EO 14013, February 4, 2021

EO 14164: Restoring the Death Penalty and Protecting Public Safety
Signed: January 20, 2025
Published: January 30, 2025

EO 14165: Securing Our Borders
Signed: January 20, 2025
Published: January 30, 2025

EO 14166: Application of Protecting Americans From Foreign Adversary Controlled Applications Act to TikTok
Signed: January 20, 2025
Published: January 30, 2025

EO 14167: Clarifying the Military's Role in Protecting the Territorial Integrity of the United States
Signed: January 20, 2025
Published: January 30, 2025

EO 14168: Defending Women From Gender Ideology Extremism and Restoring Biological Truth to the Federal Government
Signed: January 20, 2025
Published: January 30, 2025
Rescinds: EO 13988, January 20, 2021; EO 14004, January 25, 2021; EO 14021, March 8, 2021; EO 14075, June 15, 2022
See: EO 14183, January 27, 2025; EO 14185, January 27, 2025; EO 14201, February 5, 2025

EO 14169: Reevaluating and Realigning United States Foreign Aid
Signed: January 20, 2025
Published: January 30, 2025

EO 14170: Reforming the Federal Hiring Process and Restoring Merit to Government Service
Signed: January 20, 2025
Published: January 30, 2025
See: EO 14210, February 11, 2025

EO 14171: Restoring Accountability to Policy-Influencing Positions Within the Federal Workforce
Signed: January 20, 2025
Published: January 31, 2025
Reinstates: EO 13957, October 21, 2020
Revokes: EO 14003, January 22, 2021

EO 14172: Restoring Names That Honor American Greatness
Signed: January 20, 2025
Published: January 31, 2025

21 January

EO 14173: Ending Illegal Discrimination and Restoring Merit-Based Opportunity

Signed: January 21, 2025
Published: January 31, 2025
Revokes: EO 11246, September 24, 1965; EO 12898, February 11, 1994; EO 13583, August 18, 2011; EO 13672, July 21, 2014; Memo. of October 5, 2016

EO 14174: Revocation of Certain Executive Orders

Signed: January 21, 2025
Published: January 31, 2025

22 January

EO 14175: Designation of Ansar Allah as a Foreign Terrorist Organization

Signed: January 22, 2025
Published: January 31, 2025

23 January

EO 14176: Declassification of Records Concerning the Assassinations of President John F. Kennedy, Senator Robert F. Kennedy, and the Reverend Dr. Martin Luther King, Jr.

Signed: January 23, 2025
Published: January 31, 2025

EO 14177: President's Council of Advisors on Science and Technology
Signed: January 23, 2025
Published: January 31, 2025
See: EO 12968, August 2, 1995; EO 14009, September 29, 2023
Revokes: EO 14007, January 27, 2021

EO 14178: Strengthening American Leadership in Digital Financial Technology
Signed: January 23, 2025
Published: January 31, 2025
Revokes: EO 14067, March 9, 2022

EO 14179: Removing Barriers to American Leadership in Artificial Intelligence
Signed: January 23, 2025
Published: January 31, 2025

24 January

EO 14180: Council To Assess the Federal Emergency Management Agency
Signed: January 24, 2025
Published: January 31, 2025

EO 14181: Emergency Measures To Provide Water Resources in California and Improve Disaster Response in Certain Areas
Signed: January 24, 2025
Published: January 31, 2025

EO 14182: Enforcing the Hyde Amendment
Signed: January 24, 2025

Published: January 31, 2025
Revokes: EO 14076, July 8, 2022; EO 14079, August 3, 2022

27 January

EO 14184: Reinstating Service Members Discharged Under the Military's COVID-19 Vaccination Mandate
Signed: January 27, 2025
Published: February 3, 2025

EO 14183: Prioritizing Military Excellence and Readiness
Signed: January 27, 2025
Published: February 3, 2025
See: EO 14148, January 20, 2025; EO 14168, January 20, 2025
Revokes: EO 14004, January 25, 2021

EO 14185: Restoring America's Fighting Force
Signed: January 27, 2025
Published: February 3, 2025
See: EO 13950, September 22, 2020; EO 14168, January 20, 2025

EO 14186: The Iron Dome for America
Signed: January 27, 2025
Published: February 3, 2025

28 January

EO 14187: Protecting Children From Chemical and Surgical Mutilation
Signed: January 28, 2025
Published: February 3, 2025

29 January

EO 14188: Additional Measures To Combat Anti-Semitism
Signed: January 29, 2025
Published: February 3, 2025
See: EO 13899, December 11, 2019

EO 14189: Celebrating America's 250th Birthday
Signed: January 29, 2025
Published: February 3, 2025
See: EO 14029, May 14, 2021
Reinstates: EO 13933, June 26, 2020; EO 13934, July 3, 2020; EO 13978, January 18, 2021

EO 14190: Ending Radical Indoctrination in K-12 Schooling
Signed: January 29, 2025
Published: February 3, 2025
See: EO 13958, November 2, 2020; EO 13985, January 20, 2021

EO 14191: Expanding Educational Freedom and Opportunity for Families
Signed: January 29, 2025
Published: February 3, 2025

31 January

EO 14192: Unleashing Prosperity Through Deregulation
Signed: January 31, 2025
Published: February 6, 2025
See: EO 12866, September 30, 1993

1 February

EO 14193: Imposing Duties To Address the Flow of Illicit Drugs Across Our Northern Border
Signed: February 1, 2025
Published: February 7, 2025
See: Proc. 10886, January 20, 2025; EO 14156, January 20, 2025; EO 14157, January 20, 2025; Memo. of January 20, 2025; EO 14197, February 3, 2025

EO 14194: Imposing Duties To Address the Situation at Our Southern Border
Signed: February 1, 2025
Published: February 7, 2025
See: Proc. 10886, January 20, 2025; EO 14198, February 3, 2025

EO 14195: Imposing Duties To Address the Synthetic Opioid Supply Chain in the People's Republic of China
Signed: February 1, 2025
Published: February 7, 2025
See: Proc. 10886, January 20, 2025; EO 14157, January 20, 2025; Memo. of January 20, 2025; EO 14200, February 5, 2025

3 February

EO 14196: A Plan for Establishing a United States Sovereign Wealth Fund
Signed: February 3, 2025
Published: February 10, 2025

EO 14197: Progress on the Situation at Our Northern Border
Signed: February 3, 2025

Published: February 10, 2025
See: EO 14193, February 1, 2025

EO 14198: Progress on the Situation at Our Southern Border
Signed: February 3, 2025
Published: February 10, 2025
See: EO 14194, February 1, 2025

4 February

EO 14199: Withdrawing the United States From and Ending Funding to Certain United Nations Organizations and Reviewing United States Support to All International Organizations
Signed: February 4, 2025
Published: February 10, 2025

5 February

EO 14200: Amendment to Duties Addressing the Synthetic Opioid Supply Chain in the People's Republic of China
Signed: February 5, 2025
Published: February 11, 2025
See: EO 14195, February 1, 2025

EO 14201: Keeping Men Out of Women's Sports
Signed: February 5, 2025
Published: February 11, 2025
See: EO 14168, January 20, 2025

6 February

EO 14202: Eradicating Anti-Christian Bias
Signed: February 6, 2025
Published: February 12, 2025

EO 14203: Imposing Sanctions on the International Criminal Court
Signed: February 6, 2025
Published: February 12, 2025
See: Proc. 8693, July 24, 2011

7 February

EO 14204: Addressing Egregious Actions of the Republic of South Africa
Signed: February 7, 2025
Published: February 12, 2025

EO 14205: Establishment of the White House Faith Office
Signed: February 7, 2025
Published: February 12, 2025
See: EO 13198, January 29, 2001; EO 13280, December 12, 2002; EO 13342, June 1, 2004; EO 13397, March 7, 2006; EO 13559, November 17, 2010
Amends: EO 13279, December 12, 2002; EO 13280, December 12, 2002; EO 13342, June 1, 2004; EO 13397, March 7, 2006

EO 14206: Protecting Second Amendment Rights
Signed: February 7, 2025
Published: February 12, 2025

10 February

EO 14207: Eliminating the Federal Executive Institute
Signed: February 10, 2025
Published: February 14, 2025

EO 14208: Ending Procurement and Forced Use of Paper Straws
Signed: February 10, 2025
Published: February 14, 2025

EO 14209: Pausing Foreign Corrupt Practices Act Enforcement To Further American Economic and National Security
Signed: February 10, 2025
Published: February 14, 2025

11 February

EO 14210: Implementing the President's "Department of Government Efficiency" Workforce Optimization Initiative
Signed: February 11, 2025
Published: February 14, 2025
See: EO 14158, January 20, 2025; EO 14170, January 20, 2025; Presidential Memorandum, January 20, 2025

12 February

EO 14211: One Voice for America's Foreign Relations
Signed: February 12, 2025
Published: February 18, 2025

13 February

EO 14212: Establishing the President's Make America Healthy Again Commission
Signed: February 13, 2025
Published: February 19, 2025

14 February

EO 14213: Establishing the National Energy Dominance Council
Signed: February 14, 2025
Published: February 20, 2025

EO 14214: Keeping Education Accessible and Ending COVID-19 Vaccine Mandates in Schools
Signed: February 14, 2025
Published: February 20, 2025

18 February

EO 14215: Ensuring Accountability for All Agencies
Signed: February 18, 2025
Published: February 24, 2025
Amends: EO 12866, September 30, 1993

EO 14216: Expanding Access to In Vitro Fertilization
Signed: February 18, 2025
Published: February 24, 2025

19 February

EO 14217: Commencing the Reduction of the Federal Bureaucracy
Signed: February 19, 2025
Published: February 25, 2025
Revokes: Memo. of November 13, 1961; EO 13318, November 21, 2003
Amends: EO 13562, December 27, 2010

EO 14218: Ending Taxpayer Subsidization of Open Borders
Signed: February 19, 2025
Published: February 25, 2025

EO 14219: Ensuring Lawful Governance and Implementing the President's "Department of Government Efficiency" Deregulatory Initiative
Signed: February 19, 2025
Published: February 25, 2025
See: EO 12866, September 30, 1993; EO 13422, January 18, 2007; EO 14158, January 20, 2025

25 February

EO 14220: Addressing the Threat to National Security From Imports of Copper
Signed: February 25, 2025
Published: February 28, 2025

EO 14221: Making America Healthy Again by Empowering Patients With Clear, Accurate, and Actionable Healthcare Pricing Information

Signed: February 25, 2025
Published: February 28, 2025

ACKNOWLEDGEMENTS

This was a one-man project. But no man is an island, at least not one of any stature or sanity. I did not enjoy my Political Science studies in college, and felt the need to unlearn nearly all of the economics involved when I entered the (real?) business world. The negative attitude toward that milieu was quenched out by my Father, Jerome W. Stuczynski, who proved that 'business ethics' didn't have to be an oxymoron. The debt to him can never be paid.

But my education did serve me well. I owe gratitude for Dr. Biacco for my skills in journalism. Going back a bit more, I would thank Mr. John Mumm for teaching critical thinking skills in Freshman English at St. Mary's High School in Lancaster, NY. (I suspect such a brazen attempt at such things was responsible for his short tenure.) Overhanging all other mental endeavors is Philosophy, for which I owe my personal mentor, Professor Robert Nielsen, and Business Ethics and Logic professor Dr. John Abbarno, a debt as great as the proposed pension for Socrates.

In my college years I had met, through my sister Sharon who was schooling at SUNY Fredonia, Mike Mitchell, who once ran for mayor of the City of Dunkirk. He challenged some of my unexamined notions of society and politics, and I regret losing touch before his passing.

Too numerous to remember let alone mention, I would thank all those who I have engaged in dialectic. I appreciate all civility, patience, and respect I have ever received, especially from those with whom I do not agree. I particularity respect V. September McCrady, with whom I have had many spirited debates and have agreed to disagree many times, and sometimes think she may have been right in some of those instances after all. Her getting involved in politics for all the right reasons would get my vote, even if I may not join her party. My Lodge Brother, Ed Draves, is someone else who would always have my vote. Inspired by Jimmy Carter, he got elected as a School Board Trustee for the Orchard Park Central School District, and I watched him brave insults and return only kindness and civility. If only we all had such gentility and integrity ...

I thank all of these, but in a very special way I thank my daughter, Christina Stock. She stood up to make a difference in the community and beyond since 2020, publicly encouraging her neighbors toward civic involvement and education. I could not be prouder.

I thank the main contributor to ConsiderReconsider.Com over the years, Dr. Barry Fagin, columnist for the Colorado Springs Gazette and professor in the Department of Computer Science at the United States Air Force Academy. His thoughtful writing is an inspiration. I also shout out to Jeremy Gloff and my dear friend Rob Hubbard for their insightful words. And I would be most remiss if I omitted Jim Shanor, who brought me in to become co-moderator of the Global Citizenship forum on Linkedin. I miss him.

I thank my guests on my Contemplation in Action podcast. David Newman, whom I talk politics with all too often, and helped support his campaign for being on the board of the Town of Wales. Also my mentor in beekeeping, I am happy to call him my friend. And I value my time with John Schunak, whose lunches over the years have provided hours of meaningful discussion of life and politics. His questions and positions have helped me clarify my own views.

Lastly, but most certainly not least, I thank my wife, not just because she went through the pains of transcribing a speech of Steve Bannon ("diesel therapy?") and others, but for putting up with me talking way too much about the subject matter. Then again, she did appreciate me talking about it as a book project rather than a daily, real-life, society-wide Kobayashi Maru. Win or lose, there is no one else I would rather be with in life.

About the Author

Ken Stuczynski is a researcher and writer on myriad topics, including science and religion, culture and politics, business and economics, as well as spiritual and esoteric subjects. He received his B.A. in Philosophy from D'Youville College (now University), with a concentration in Ethics and a minor in Psychology. He is also a Freemason and Interfaith minister.

His usual vocation is ownership of a Web Development company, Kentropolis Internet, but is transitioning to authoring and publishing as owner of Amorphous Publishing Guild. Most of his essays, editorials, and reporting over the last 25 years can be found on his intellectual blog, ConsiderResonsider.Com

Politically, Ken's views have evolved and changed over the years, with a major awakening moment in 2020, when he wrote and published "Some White Guy's Book". He has canvassed and campaigned for Republican, Democrat, and Independent candidates, and is a strong proponent of third-party voting and fundamental improvements in the democratic process to break the two-party paradigm that, as he believes, led us to a race to the bottom. Despite his passion for some issues, he believes critical reasoning and civility are the most necessary foundations for any educated and useful public debate.

Ken lives in Buffalo, New York, with his wife and pets, all of whom seem to have tolerated well his bouts of research and doomscrolling that led to this book.

To learn more about the author,
follow, or subscribe to his newsletter
and receive updates on future publications, visit

KenVille.Net

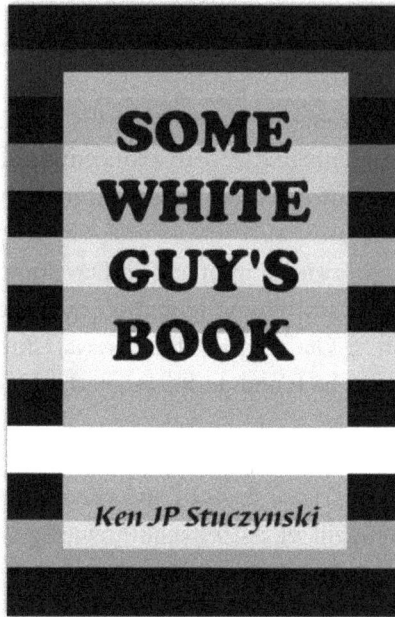

SOME
WHITE
GUY'S
BOOK

Ken JP Stuczynski

ALSO BY THE AUTHOR

With unique life experiences and unconventional thinking, a self-acknowledged "White guy" tackles race and ethnicity in America, covering disparate ways we view history, society, and ourselves. Candidly explore different sides of issues, such as White guilt, cancel culture, Southern pride, religious intolerance, political correctness, and what roles White people and People of Color can play in building a common future. Discover how prejudices intersect poverty, crime, the justice system, religion, and patriotism. Includes first-hand experience and research of the George Floyd protests, contrasted with the Civil Rights Movement of the 1960s. Available worldwide in softcover and eBook.

www.ingramcontent.com/pod-product-compliance
Lightning Source LLC
Chambersburg PA
CBHW050226270326
41914CB00003BA/587